Public Acceptability of Congestion Charging in China

Qiyang Liu

Public Acceptability of Congestion Charging in China

palgrave
macmillan

Qiyang Liu
School of Urban Planning and Design
Peking University
Shenzhen, China

ISBN 978-981-19-0235-2 ISBN 978-981-19-0236-9 (eBook)
https://doi.org/10.1007/978-981-19-0236-9

This Palgrave Macmillan imprint is published by the registered company Springer Nature Singapore Pte Ltd.
The registered company address is: 152 Beach Road, #21-01/04 Gateway East, Singapore 189721, Singapore

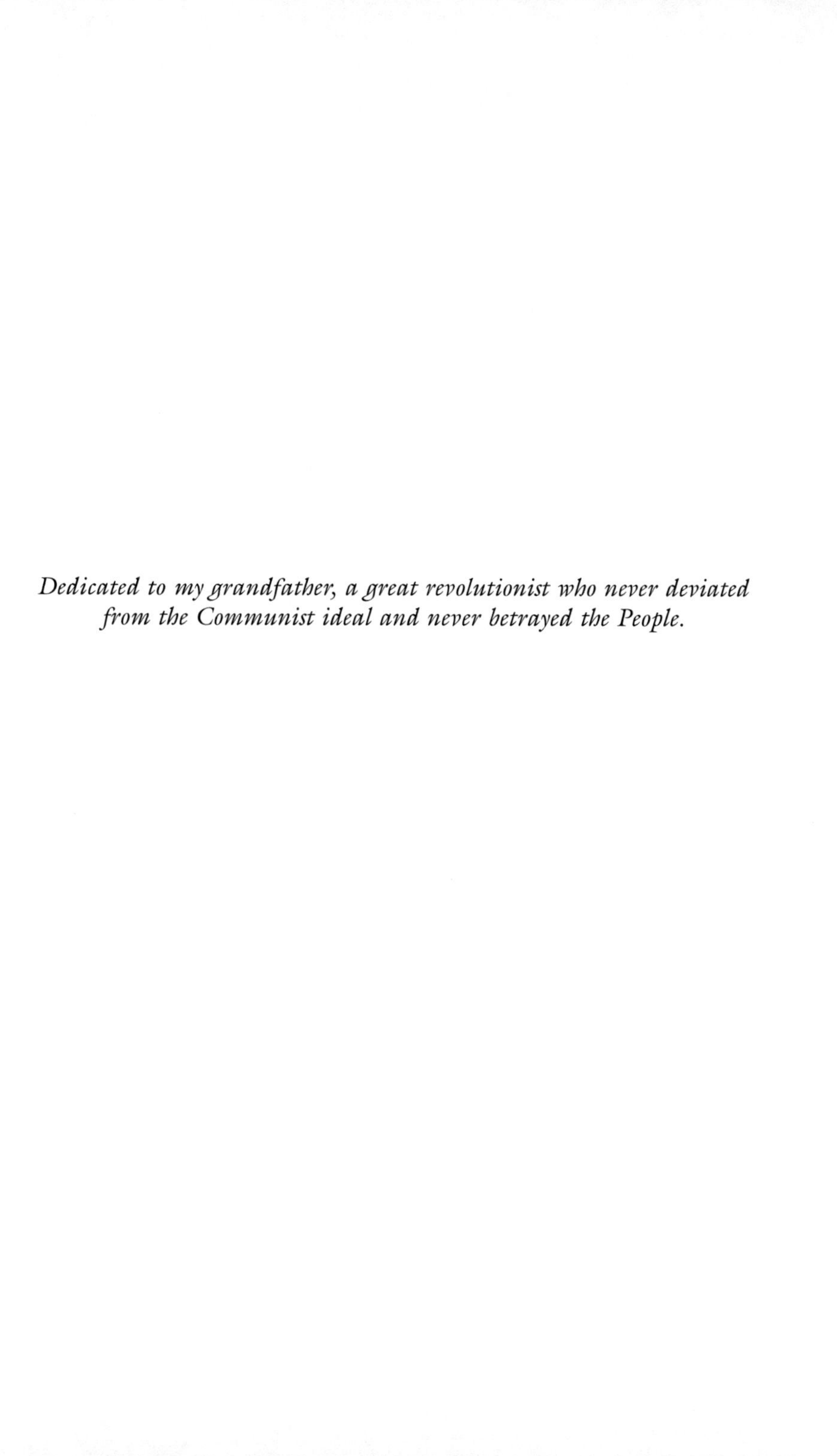

Dedicated to my grandfather, a great revolutionist who never deviated from the Communist ideal and never betrayed the People.

Preface

The purpose of this book is to explore the public acceptability of congestion charging in the Chinese context and to discuss whether Western notions of public acceptability are transferrable to a different context. I am fascinated by Chinese politics, probably because it is always shrouded in mist. A transport policy, which is usually not perceived as a politically sensitive topic, can be a mirror of a much wider Chinese society and politics, which can be exceptionally difficult for outsiders to observe, by focusing on many other sensitive policies.

This book should be of interest to the Chinese cadres who are theoretically responsible for "serving the People". It should also be of interest to researchers studying the public acceptability of congestion charging, transport policies in the Chinese context, policy transfer and policymaking in authoritarian regimes.

I would like to express my sincere gratitude to my supervisors, Professor Karen Lucas and Professor Greg Marsden, for their support throughout my Ph.D. I didn't realise how lucky I was to have both of them as my supervisors until I finished my Ph.D. Their critical reading resulted in useful feedback that enriched this book, and discussions with them were challenging, productive and enjoyable. With their guidance, I have developed an inextinguishable passion for knowledge, methods to seek knowledge, and the humbleness of recognising the limitations of my knowledge. Most importantly, I have learned the moral standards an academic should hold.

I would also like to thank my parents. Their support from the first days of studying in the UK to the capstone of my Ph.D. has been unquestioning and essential. What this book owes to them I believe is the critical thinking I inherited from my mom and the scrupulous way of doing things from my dad.

I would like to thank my wife, Yan Ma, who read the work, discussed various interesting issues, and helped with my daily life. I met her in the first week after I arrived in Leeds. My life in the UK would be much more tedious without her. The burden of doing this Ph.D. was lessened substantially by her support. She is looking forward to a day when I can be less dissatisfied with Chinese civic society.

I would like to extend my gratitude to colleagues in ITS, University of Leeds: Prof. Samantha Jamson, Dr. Jeremy Shires, Dr. Ann Jopson, Prof. Anthony May, Prof. Jillian Anable, Prof. Zia Wadud, Dr. Thiago Guimarães, Dr. Jeroen Bastiaanssen, and Dr. Zihao An. I am also grateful to Prof. Noreen McDonald, Prof. Steve Ison, Dr. Todd Litman, Prof. Karl-Henrik Robèrt, Prof. Göran Broman, Prof. Antonio Negri, Prof. Fredric Jameson, Prof. Domenico Losurdo, and Prof. Zygmunt Bauman, for their generous comments and critiques. Thanks for all the discussions which helped to shape this research.

Shenzhen, China
December 2021

Qiyang Liu

Contents

List of Figures

List of Tables

CHAPTER 1

Introduction

1.1 Overview of the Study

The rationale for this research was to explore the notion of public acceptability in the Chinese context through particular policy responses to a hypothetical congestion charge in Beijing. The overarching aim of the research was to understand the public acceptability of congestion charging in the Chinese context. This research adds to the knowledge base on the public acceptability of road pricing schemes by investigating this issue in an authoritarian state.

The public acceptability of road pricing schemes is not new in the literature. This issue has been extensively discussed since the '90s in democracies in which lay citizens can exercise their power by voting against a proposed scheme. However, this issue has rarely been investigated in other polities, and even more problematic is the fact that a few Chinese scholars have recently started to apply Western context-based frameworks uncritically to examine public acceptability issues in the Chinese context (Li et al., 2019; Sun et al., 2016; Wang et al., 2019). Given the differences in culture and political system between China and the West, it is highly questionable whether these Western context-based key determinants and frameworks for assessing public acceptability can be applied to the Chinese context. Such direct applications may distort our understanding of the problem and mislead policymaking.

Q. Liu, *Public Acceptability of Congestion Charging in China*,
https://doi.org/10.1007/978-981-19-0236-9_1

To make sense of the relationship, it is important to place the research within the wider philosophical and cultural context of the studied site. However, since none of the previous researchers even attempted to do so, in this book, I take the responsibility of exploring the philosophical, cultural and social underpinnings of public acceptability in a typical authoritarian state, China (Sect. 2.3).

I adopted a mixed-methods approach in this research. Qualitative methods are necessary to understand the complex public acceptability issue and to generate a framework for assessing it in the Chinese context, which can be verified by using quantitative methods. Firstly, semi-structured interviews with twelve key stakeholders were undertaken to explore policymakers' understanding of public acceptability and their motivations for considering it. Secondly, nine focus groups were conducted to identify key determinants of public acceptability in the Chinese context. Qualitative approaches helped to reveal to what extent the Western notions of public acceptability are transferrable to the Chinese context and to propose a framework for analysing public acceptability in China. Thirdly, an attitude survey was conducted to explore the extent to which acceptability constructs matter. A final sample of 1,104 valid responses was obtained and then analysed using structural equation modelling (SEM).

My thesis is that (a) there are multiple barriers for Chinese policymakers (cadres, simplified Chinese: 干部; pinyin: *ganbu*[1]) to considering public acceptability, but very few factors urging them to think about it. Since the notion of "an acceptable policy" is interpreted as a policy that is tolerable for the majority of people, the motivation for considering public acceptability in the Chinese context is to avoid mass incidents instead of convincing voters of the benefits they can get from the implementation of the policy (see Chapters 4 and 5). (b) Most determinants of public acceptability of congestion charging identified in the Western context cannot easily be used to understand and investigate public acceptability in the Chinese context: some are inappropriate to investigate public acceptability in the Chinese context, including personal freedom, privacy

[1] Cadre, originally a French word, has been adopted by communists. It means "the best of us" or "dedicated" in the Communist official discourse. The meaning of the term may differ between the Mao era and the post-Mao era, but basically, cadres are expected to be party loyalists, self-sacrificial, and hardworking. In general, this can be seen as the Chinese term for officials at all levels.

concerns, revenue allocation, and transparency; and some have to be interpreted in different ways, including information, perceived effectiveness, and perceived equity (see Chapter 5). (c) Trust in government and trust towards experts played a dominant role in gaining public support for congestion charging, obedience to authority and conformity to social norms have significant impacts on public acceptability in the Chinese context, and some key determinants identified in the literature did not significantly influence public acceptability in this context, such as information and perceived effectiveness of previous policies and congestion charging (see Chapter 6).

1.2 Historical Context for the Research

After the death of Chairman Mao and the downfall of the Gang of Four (simplified Chinese: 四人帮)[2] in the late 1970s, policies of "Reform and Opening Up" were implemented in Mainland China, bringing about a revolution, including reform of both the political and economic structure and corresponding changes in many areas. Since no one could be in such an impregnable political position as Mao, power started to decentralise. Consequently, a market-based economic management system was introduced into a country whose people, for 30 years, had been practically brainwashed into regarding the market as "evil capitalism" (simplified Chinese: 万恶的资本主义) (e.g., Vogel, 2011). The profound changes the economic reform made have had far-reaching effects. Over 3 decades of rapid economic growth, one of the most remarkable results of the reform, has had a profound effect not only on China, but also on the entire world. With the fast-developing economy, people's quality of life has improved significantly.

Before the national reform, as the socialist planned economy suggested and practised, only very basic goods were guaranteed for citizens to support the rapid development of heavy and military industry. The term *quality of life* did not even appear in public common parlance (e.g., Naughton, 2007). The most visible change after the national reform

[2] A political faction composed of four Chinese Communist Party officials (Jiang Qing, Zhang Chunqiao, Yao Wenyuan and Wang Hongwen) who controlled the power organs of the CCP in the later period of the Cultural Revolution. They fell from power one month after Mao's death. Their downfall is usually regarded as the end of a turbulent era in China.

was the improvement in material wealth. Individual vehicle ownership and use, for example, as one of the symbols of wealth and social status, has gradually become a pervasive phenomenon in ordinary Chinese households (Feng & Li, 2013).

Consequently, by the early 1990s, transport-related problems, such as congestion and air pollution, had become, and remain, among the most irreconcilable problems in every city in China (e.g., Mackett, 1999). On the one hand, traffic congestion is well recognised. The government has made a determined effort on infrastructure construction (e.g., Yu et al., 2012a, b), as well as implementing policies to alleviate traffic congestion, such as the nationwide Smooth Traffic Project, which was launched in February 2000 (People's Daily, 2000). On the other hand, transport-related air pollution attracted little public attention before 2013. Most citizens discussed air pollution issues from a bystander's perspective, considering it an issue for vulnerable groups or people from areas with particular concentrations of heavy industry. In January 2013, 30 provinces were shrouded by smog on four occasions, reducing visibility to a few hundred metres. Since the reporter Chai Jing's film *Under the Dome* swept across Mainland China in 2013 (Hatton, 2015; Powers, 2016), there has been animated discussion on air pollution in which various sections of society participated, especially lay citizens (e.g., Jiang, 2015; Wong, 2013).

However, the Chinese Government's efforts at mitigating smog have not been effective. The Beijing Emergency Management Committee issued its highest air pollution alert and made an announcement at 18:00 on December 7, 2015, suggesting that all primary schools, junior high schools and high schools be closed for 3 days and that companies and organisations adopted flexible working time. This was the first time the authority had issued a red alert (The Guardian, 2015). As a counter-measure to mitigate these harmful circumstances, a license plate ban policy (odd–even alternate days), which was adopted in the central urban area in 2008, was extended to the metropolitan area. Up to August 2015, the number of motor vehicles in Beijing exceeded 5.57 million (Beijing Municipal Environmental Protection Bureau, 2015). A number of researchers indicated that the prime source of PM 2.5, one of the major pollutants, considered as the major cause of smog in Chinese cities, is vehicle exhaust (e.g., Sun et al., 2006). To solve the problem, Beijing's Municipal Commission of Transport intimated that a pilot congestion charge would be studied as one part of the congestion control action plan in 2016, aiming at improving the urban street network, encouraging green travel, and reducing traffic congestion.

A wide variety of policy measures have already been introduced to achieve a sustainable transport system, specifically aimed at reducing car travel and encouraging more sustainable modes of transport (Pan, 2011). To reduce car use, an end-number license plate policy, which limits the days vehicles can be operated, has been implemented in Beijing, Chengdu and some other cities since 2014 (Wang et al., 2014). A license plate lottery has been implemented to reduce the growth in car ownership in Beijing. It requires individual purchasers to wait for the monthly license plate lottery to have their passenger cars registered. Similarly, a car license auction policy has been adopted in cities such as Shanghai and Guangzhou. Bus Rapid Transit (BRT) and public bicycle projects have also been introduced in many big cities (e.g., Zeng, 2012).

Both the government and external experts have announced that transport-related problems have been perceptibly alleviated by these measures (e.g., Beijing Municipal Commission of Transport, 2011). Meanwhile, public dissatisfaction with these policies has been widely reported (e.g., Beijing News, 2011; China News Service, 2015; Sohu, 2013). Public resistance to these policies was regarded as one of the main reasons for their relatively low effectiveness (e.g., Yardley, 2006). Although there is only a small handful of examples of Chinese citizens directly opposing policies introduced by the government, people react in more roundabout ways, such as taking a *collective stroll* (simplified Chinese: 散步; pinyin: *sanbu*)[3] (e.g., Franceschini & Negro, 2014; Zhu, 2017). In the transport field, for example, many Shanghai residents registered vehicles in other cities, which was regarded as one of the main reasons why the effectiveness of the new plate quota policy was exaggerated (e.g., Chen & Zhao, 2013; Wang, 2010). These kinds of restrictive measures are at the more radical end of transport policy, and because they are not yet having the necessary impacts, further restrictive policies could become necessary. However, given the restrictions and signs of noncompliance or gaming of the system, public acceptability needs to be explored.

In terms of Schade and Schlag's (2000) definition, acceptability refers to the "(affirmative) attitude towards a specific object". Because of the

[3] A pervasive form of protest in contemporary China, first taken by Xiamen citizens as a reaction to the PX project.

high costs they incur and the travel mode change they require, travel demand management strategies might be unacceptable (Jakobsson et al., 2000). Many previous studies in Western countries illustrated the importance of public acceptability (e.g., Jaensirisak et al., 2005; Jakobsson et al., 2000). Jones (1998) considered the design of acceptable schemes as one of the principal barriers to implementing economic disincentives such as pricing for using road space. However, public acceptability of transport policies has not been sufficiently studied in China. This could be due to the lack of public engagement in the policymaking process.

Apart from the differences in political systems between China and the West, cultural differences may also play a role. De Jong (2012) looked at Chinese values when thinking about policy development in the transport field. However, de Jong's analysis was limited by its oversimplification of philosophical factors and the exclusion of many other cultural and political factors. In this book, I seek to fill these gaps by developing context-sensitive understandings of public acceptability. I do so by taking the potential Beijing congestion charge as a case study through which to develop and test a new framework.

1.3 Research Focus and Scope

There has been a long history of Chinese public policy that has been announced as "serving the people" by the authority and external experts, but which usually activated public opposition and sometimes feelings of animosity (e.g., Cai, 2010; Li & Li, 2010; Steinhardt, 2015; Tong & Lei, 2013a, b). This schism clearly manifests a lack of concern about public acceptability in the Chinese policymaking arena. This research, therefore, explores the rationale for considering the public acceptability of proposed schemes and how public attitudes towards the proposed scheme are formed. It is timely and important to conduct this research at this time, as contemporary protests in China have increasingly gained the attention of academics and policymakers. Most importantly, and in common with much of the social science research, this study can contribute to improving public policy outcomes by systematically exploring barriers to generating active public support in the Chinese context, which involves examining the transferability of Western concepts and policies to a different context.

As discussed, to explore public attitudes and responses to the introduction of a congestion charging policy, it is important to understand the philosophical, cultural and political underpinnings of public acceptability in the Chinese context. However, public acceptability has rarely been examined in the Chinese context compared to the large body of empirical work examining determinants of public acceptability in the Western context. Although some fragmentary culture-specific factors have been considered (Sun et al., 2016), the selection of these factors was subjective, and it was never explained. Moreover, the results cannot be interpreted by directly applying Western context-based frameworks. Therefore, there is a need to explore these complexities further.

Figure 1.1 shows the research focus and scope of the study. Congestion charging has been considered as a measure to alleviate traffic congestion and smog in big Chinese cities after implementing various restrictive policies to control car ownership and use. To implement congestion charging in Chinese cities, the public acceptability of the policy needs to be investigated.

In particular, within the current research, attention has been drawn to policymakers' intentions and motivations to consider public opinions in the policymaking. Since most congestion charging policies have been implemented in democracies, the underlying reasons for considering public acceptability in the Chinese context have to be explored prior to further investigation into the determinants of public acceptability. However, as China observers have repeatedly pointed out, policymaking

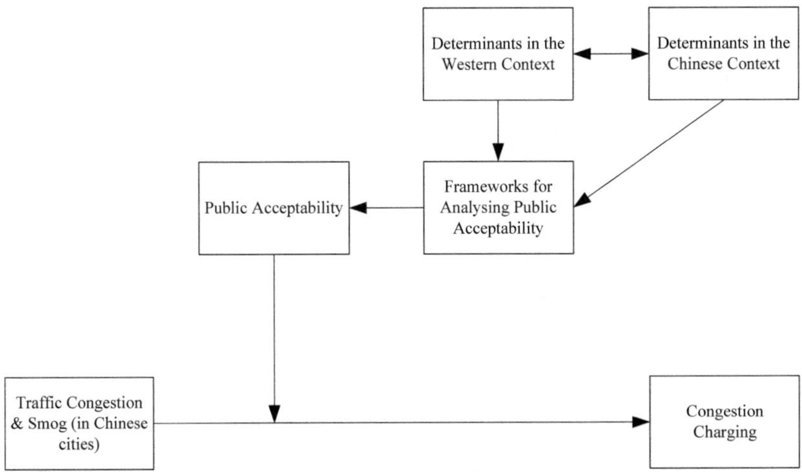

Fig. 1.1 Research Focus and Scope

is generally mist-shrouded (e.g., Feng et al., 2016; Lee & Shen, 2009; Lieberthal & Oksenberg, 1990; Lu, 2018). Therefore, this thesis takes an abductive approach to explore and interpret policymakers' ideas about public opinions.

Frameworks for assessing public acceptability and its determinants in the Western context need to be reviewed thereafter. This research then focuses on exploring which factors may affect public opinion, what policy outcomes were deemed unacceptable and how citizens would accept or oppose the introduction of a congestion charging policy. I began with a focus group discussion to explore factors that may potentially influence public acceptability, and then applied SEM to analyse the relationships among the different aspects of public acceptability.

Ultimately, the research adds to existing investigations into the public acceptability of transport policy, in addition to contributing new insights to the knowledge base surrounding policy transfer and diffusion by arguing the role contextual factors play in public acceptability in this case.

1.4 Research Questions

To meet the aim, three research questions were formulated to explore public acceptability in the Chinese context from both a policymakers' perspective and citizens' attitudes and responses towards a wide set of issues relating to the introduction of congestion charging policy. This allows an exploration of why public acceptability is still an issue for an authoritarian regime like the PRC, what policy outcomes were perceived as problematic, and to what extent wider cultural, political and social issues may influence citizens' attitudes towards congestion charging. The research questions investigate whether Western context-based concepts, frameworks and determinants of public acceptability are transferable to the Chinese context.

Public acceptability matters because of its impact on the effectiveness of government intervention and consideration for election in a democracy (e.g., Bristow et al., 2010; Diepeveen et al., 2013). However, it is still questionable whether public acceptability matters in a one-party state. Even if it matters, it may play a different role given the authoritarian nature of China's political system. Thus, the first research question is:

RQ1: Do Chinese Policymakers Consider Public Acceptability, and Why?

In particular, this research explored (a) who the policymakers are, (b) their motivations to consider (or not) the public acceptability of a proposed scheme, (c) how policymakers understood public acceptability and put it into practice and (d) how policymakers perceived public acceptance of previous transport policies and, if relevant, other policies. This research question is answered by stakeholder interviews (Sect. 3.3.1).

Due to the differences in culture and political system between China and the West, it is important to know if Western context-based frameworks can be used to investigate public acceptability in the Chinese context. The following two research questions explored the nature of the issue in the Chinese context and explored the factors that influence public acceptability in the Chinese context.

RQ2: To What Extent Are Western Notions of Public Acceptability Transferrable to the Chinese Context?

Addressing Research Question 2 included (a) interpreting the notions of "to accept" and "acceptability" in the Chinese context, and the relationship between acceptance and acceptability, (b) identifying the potential determinants of public acceptability that are in line with the literature, (c) exploring culture-specific factors that may potentially influence public acceptability in the Chinese context, (d) exploring the interactions between these determinants and (e) discussing the reasons why some determinants in the Western context are not applicable to the Chinese context. Focus group discussions contributed to answering this research question. This work helped me to evaluate the expectations from the literature review critically.

RQ3: What Factors Are Public Acceptability of Congestion Charging Influenced by in the Chinese Context?

The aim of this question was to examine the relationship between public acceptability and its key determinants in the Chinese context empirically, informed by the findings of RQ1 and RQ2. The attitude survey data enabled exploration of the roles these factors played in the public acceptability of congestion charging. These data further enabled a discussion of the appropriateness of Western frameworks for assessing public acceptability in the Chinese context.

1.5 Outline of the Thesis

Chapter 2 presents the literature review. It contains three main bodies of literature: (a) frameworks for assessing public acceptability in the West and determinants that have been considered, (b) public acceptability studies in the Chinese context and (c) culture-specific factors that might influence public acceptability in the Chinese context and the rationale to consider these factors. It sets out the research questions in light of identified gaps in the literature.

Chapter 3 first gives a general introduction to the research design and methodology, followed by concise introductions of different methods used in each step of the study. Section 3.3 introduces the stakeholder interviews and the abductive research strategy, Sect. 3.4 introduces focus group discussions, and Sect. 3.5 describes the quantitative survey and the SEM. Ethical considerations are presented in Sect. 3.6.

Chapter 4 presents the results from stakeholder interviews that answer the first research question—whether and why public acceptability is an issue in the Chinese context. It illustrates the interpretation of policymakers' concerns about public and political acceptability and then discusses whether public acceptability matters in the same way in the Chinese context.

Chapter 5 presents the results from focus group discussions held with nine groups. The focus group exercise was necessary both to expand on some of the issues identified in the small sample of interviews and to test the meaning, validity and use of different constructs from the literature relating to public acceptability in the Chinese context. This answered Research Questions 2 and 3, and it enabled the design of a questionnaire survey.

Chapter 6 presents the results of the questionnaire, including descriptive results and the results of the SEM. This chapter explored the extent to which determinants of acceptability matter, the strength and directionality of those relationships, and how distinct they are from frameworks established in the literature.

Chapter 7 proposes a framework for public acceptability in the Chinese context by combining findings from both the qualitative exploration and the quantitative survey. This framework is compared with Western context-based frameworks to discuss the appropriateness of Western frameworks for assessing public acceptability in the Chinese context.

Chapter 8 draws the conclusions, including main findings for each research question, limitations of the research and implications for the Beijing congestion charge and future research.

References

Beijing Municipal Commission of Transport. (2011). *The comprehensive congestion-alleviation measures are effective*. [Online]. https://archive.is/20120729143830/http://www.bjjtw.gov.cn/gzdt/ywsds/201105/t20110523_36570.htm#selection-391.0-391.8. Accessed 27 July 2019 (in Chinese).

Beijing Municipal Environmental Protection Bureau. (2015). *Guo I old vehicles, banned to enter the city center from next year*. [Online]. http://www.bjepb.gov.cn/bjepb/323265/397983/424801/index.html. Accessed 27 July 2019 (in Chinese).

Bristow, A. L., Wardman, M., Zanni, A. M., & Chintakayala, P. K. (2010). Public acceptability of personal carbon trading and carbon tax. *Ecological Economics, 69*(9), 1824–1837.

Cai, Y. (2010). *Collective resistance in China: Why popular protests succeed or fail*. Stanford University Press.

Chen, X., & Zhao, J. (2013a). Bidding to drive: Car license auction policy in Shanghai and its public acceptance. *Transport Policy, 27*, 39–52.

China News Service. (2015). *Beijing plan to pilot congestion charge, citizens: Not reasonable*. [Online]. http://news.sohu.com/20151205/n429872590.shtml. Accessed 27 July 2019 (in Chinese).

De Jong, M. (2012). The pros and cons of Confucian values in transport infrastructure development in China. *Policy and Society, 31*(1), 13–24.

Diepeveen, S., Ling, T., Suhrcke, M., Roland, M., & Marteau, T. M. (2013). Public acceptability of government intervention to change health-related behaviours: A systematic review and narrative synthesis. *BMC Public Health, 13*(1), 756.

Feng, S., & Li, Q. (2013). *Car ownership control in Chinese mega cities: Shanghai, Beijing and Guangzhou*. Journeys (LTA Academy Singapore).

Feng, W., Gu, B., & Cai, Y. (2016). The end of China's one-child policy. *Studies in Family Planning, 47*(1), 83–86.

Franceschini, I., & Negro, G. (2014). The 'Jasmine Revolution' in China: The limits of the cyber-utopia. *Postcolonial Studies, 17*(1), 23–35.

Hatton, C. (2015). *Under the Dome: The smog film taking China by storm*. BBC China Blog. BBC.

Jaensirisak, S., Wardman, M., & May, A. D. (2005). Explaining variations in public acceptability of road pricing schemes. *Journal of Transport Economics and Policy, 39*(2), 127–153.

Jakobsson, C., Fujii, S., & Gärling, T. (2000). Determinants of private car users' acceptance of road pricing. *Transport Policy, 7*(2), 153–158.

Jiang, S. (2015). *5 things to know about China's 'Inconvenient Truth'*. http://edition.cnn.com/2015/03/02/asia/china-smog-documentary/. Accessed 27 July 2019.

Jones, P. (1998). Urban road pricing: Public acceptability and barriers to implementation. In K. J. Button & E. T. Verhoef (Eds.), *Road pricing, traffic congestion and the environment*. Edward Elgar Publishing.

Lee, C. K., & Shen, Y. (2009). China: The paradox and possibility of a public sociology of labor. *Work and Occupations, 36*(2), 110–125.

Li, W., & Li, Y. (2010). An analysis on social and cultural background of the resistance for China's education reform and academic pressure. *International Education Studies, 3*(3), 211–215.

Li, X., Shaw, J. W., Liu, D., & Yuan, Y. (2019). Acceptability of Beijing congestion charging from a business perspective. *Transportation, 46*(3), 753–776.

Lieberthal, K., & Oksenberg, M. (1990). *Policy making in China: Leaders, structures, and processes*. Princeton University Press.

Lu, N. (2018). *The dynamics of foreign-policy decisionmaking in China*. Routledge.

Mackett, R. (1999). Towards the solution of urban transport problems in China. *Journal of Environmental Sciences, 11*(3), 334–338.

Naughton, B. (2007). *The Chinese economy: Transitions and growth*. MIT Press.

Pan, H. (2011). *Implementing sustainable urban travel policies in China*. International Transport Forum. [Online]. http://www.internationaltransportforum.org/jtrc/DiscussionPapers/DP201112.pdf. Accessed 27 July 2019.

People's Daily. (2000). *Chinese government supports smooth traffic project*. [Online]. http://en.people.cn/english/200003/11/eng20000311C106.html. Accessed 27 July 2019 (in Chinese)

Powers, D. S. (2016). 'Under the Dome' on Chinese air pollution, a documentary by Chai Jing. *Journal of Public Health Policy, 37*(1), 98–106.

Schade, J., & Schlag, B. (2000). *Acceptability of urban transport pricing*. Valtion Taloudellinen Tutkimus.

Sohu. *A Chinese-style trouble: Difficult to get a license plate, more difficult than giving birth to a child*. [Online]. https://news.sohu.com/s2013/5599/s367867944/. Accessed 27 July, 2019 (in Chinese).

Steinhardt, H. C. (2015). From blind spot to media spotlight: Propaganda policy, media activism and the emergence of protest events in the Chinese public sphere. *Asian Studies Review, 39*(1), 119–137.

Sun, X., Feng, S., & Lu, J. (2016). Psychological factors influencing the public acceptability of congestion pricing in China. *Transportation Research Part F: Traffic Psychology and Behaviour, 41*, 104–112.

Sun, Y., Zhuang, G., Tang, A., Wang, Y., & An, Z. (2006). Chemical characteristics of PM2. 5 and PM10 in haze-fog episodes in Beijing. *Environmental Science & Technology, 40*(10), 3148–3155.

The Beijing News. (2011). *Polls show that almost eighty percent of people think congestion alleviation measures are ineffective*. http://auto.people.com.cn/GB/1049/15213780.html. Accessed 27 July 2019 (in Chinese).

The Guardian. (2015). *Beijing issues first pollution red alert as smog engulfs capital*. [Online]. http://www.theguardian.com/environment/2015/dec/07/beijing-pollution-red-alert-smog-engulfs-capital. Accessed 27 July 2019.

Tong, Y., & Lei, S. (2013a). *Social protest in contemporary China, 2003–2010: Transitional pains and regime legitimacy*. Routledge.

Tong, Y., & Lei, S. (2013b). War of position and microblogging in China. *Journal of Contemporary China, 22*(80), 292–311.

Vogel, E. F. (2011). *Deng Xiaoping and the transformation of China*. Belknap Press of Harvard University Press.

Wang, R. (2010). Shaping urban transport policies in China: Will copying foreign policies work? *Transport Policy, 17*(3), 147–152.

Wang, Y., Wang, Y., Xie, L., & Zhou, H. (2019). Impact of perceived uncertainty on public acceptability of congestion charging: An empirical study in China. *Sustainability, 11*(1), 129.

Wang, L., Xu, J., & Qin, P. (2014). Will a driving restriction policy reduce car trips?—The case study of Beijing, China. *Transportation Research Part A: Policy and Practice, 67*, 279–290.

Wong, H. (2013). *2013 will be remembered as the year that deadly, suffocating smog consumed China*. [Online]. http://qz.com/159105/2013-will-be-remembered-as-the-year-that-deadly-suffocating-smog-consumed-china/. Accessed 27 July 2019.

Yardley, J. (2006). *First comes the car, then the $10,000 license plate*. [Online]. http://www.nytimes.com/2006/07/05/world/asia/05china.html?_r=1&. Accessed 27 July 2019.

Yu, N., De Jong, M., Storm, S., & Mi, J. (2012a). The growth impact of transport infrastructure investment: A regional analysis for China (1978–2008). *Policy and Society, 31*(1), 25–38.

Yu, N., De Jong, M., Storm, S., & Mi, J. (2012b). Transport infrastructure, spatial clusters and regional economic growth in China. *Transport Reviews, 32*(1), 3–28.

Zeng, H. (2012). *China transportation briefing: Booming public bikes*. [Online]. http://thecityfix.com/blog/china-transportation-briefing-booming-public-bikes/. Accessed 27 July 2019.

Zhu, Z. (2017). Backfired government action and the spillover effect of contention: A case study of the anti-PX protests in Maoming China. *Journal of Contemporary China, 26*(106), 521–535.

CHAPTER 2

Observations from the Literature

Three bodies of literature were reviewed to formulate a rationale for this study and to explore the issue of public acceptability in general. Section 2.1 presents a systematic review of literature on the public acceptability of transport policies in the Western context. Section 2.2 introduces relevant studies in the Chinese context. Section 2.3 takes a wider look at the Chinese context to explore other context-specific determinants of public acceptability in China.

2.1 Public Acceptability in the Western Context

Changes in travel behaviour and the adaption of particular lifestyles, influencing individuals' perceived quality of life, may be unavoidable (Miola, 2008). Accordingly, many Western scholars concluded that this approach requires taking into account public acceptability. Schade and Schlag (2003) declared that in a democratic society, the introduction of societal, political and technological innovations must come via the democratic process. With specific reference to congestion charging, Gray and Begg (2001) stated that:

> The likelihood of large-scale, city wide charging being delivered successfully depends as much on local authorities winning "hearts and minds" (of key stakeholders, the media and, ultimately, the public), as it does on

Q. Liu, *Public Acceptability of Congestion Charging in China*, https://doi.org/10.1007/978-981-19-0236-9_2

> producing an integrated transport strategy or overcoming any technical difficulties. (p. 5)

The term *accept* is defined as "to take willingly something that is offered; to say 'yes' to an offer, invitation, etc." or "to receive something as suitable or good enough" (p. 5). To avoid the inaccuracy of terms like *behavioural acceptance* and *attitudinal acceptance*, Schade and Schlag (2000, p. 5) introduced acceptability as "the affirmative attitude towards a specific object like road pricing". In this study, acceptability refers to the attitudes towards a hypothetical situation where the policy has not yet been introduced, whereas acceptance is considered as a behavioural reaction towards an implemented policy.

Previous studies on public acceptability are mostly based on three main themes: (a) pricing measures, such as congestion charges (de Groot & Steg, 2006; Schuitema et al., 2010); (b) altering travel modes, such as investment in public transport and cycling infrastructure (Eriksson et al., 2008) and (c) new technologies, such as fuel and vehicle technologies (Jensen et al., 2013). Among these, pricing measures, normally considered as push measures, involve a charge for some service or resource that has traditionally been free for the public with the specific aim of reducing traffic congestion. Since individual interests are inevitably affected by these measures, there is an intense focus on public acceptability in the literature. The provision of alternatives to car-based transport is often described as offering pull measures. Such measures are often used in conjunction with pricing to increase the acceptability of pricing measures (Kottenhoff & Freij, 2009) or as a comparison to pricing measures (Eriksson et al., 2008). Various evidence has demonstrated that pull measures are generally more acceptable than push measures (de Groot & Schuitema, 2012; Eriksson et al., 2008; Joireman et al., 2001) because push measures are considered more coercive and restrictive (Jakobsson et al., 2000; Steg et al., 2006). Since a pull measure will be more acceptable regardless of the social norm towards the policy and the behavioural costs (de Groot & Schuitema, 2012), the acceptability of pull measures has been given much less priority in research. Research on the public acceptability of new technologies focuses on new vehicles and alternative fuels achievable in the long term, such as fuel cell vehicles. Public acceptability is being considered as a key theme in the literature on electric vehicles due to the different nature of the charging arrangements and alternative pricing structures (Morton et al., 2011). Savvanidou et al.

(2010) investigated the acceptability of biofuels in Northern Greece. They stated that public acceptability could be increased by linking biofuels with farm employment opportunities, thus identifying social and economic benefits. There is a wide range of acceptability issues concerning sustainable transport in the Western context; however, it is impracticable to go through them all. Since it is a relatively more imperative issue for pricing measures, the focus of this section is on the public acceptability of road pricing.

Schlag and Teubel (1997) analysed the public acceptability of different kinds of transport pricing measures based on many previous studies and research projects. They sketched a structure of acceptability issues and identified five major issues of public acceptability of pricing measures: (a) whether people have access to information that influences their perceptions, attitudes and personal norms; (b) whether people believe the measure could be effective; (c) individual claims such as privacy concerns; (d) how revenues are used and (e) equity issues.

2.1.1 Five Major Issues of Public Acceptability

2.1.1.1 Information

Some have suggested that to accept a scheme, people have to be aware of background information, information about the aims of policies and details about the implementation of the measure (Gärling & Schuitema, 2007; Tertoolen et al., 1998; Verplanken et al., 1997). Also, details of congestion charging schemes can significantly influence public acceptability (e.g., Clee, 2007; Litman, 2012) because the complexity of the scheme can directly influence how people perceive its effectiveness (e.g., Bonsall & Lythgoe, 2009; Rye et al., 2008).

2.1.1.2 Perceived Effectiveness and Efficiency

Effectiveness refers to the extent to which the measure can reach its predetermined goal, while efficiency is about a comparison between the cost–benefit relationships of several possible measures (Schade & Schlag, 2000). As roads are historically free of charge for the public, there must be convincing reasons for a charge for road use or parking to avoid emotional resistance. It is clear that to acquire public support, a pricing scheme needs to be perceived as an effective measure to achieve the targeted goals (e.g., Jaensirisak et al., 2005; Rienstra et al., 1999; Viegas, 2001).

2.1.1.3 *Individual Claims*

Individual claims include two main aspects: (a) car dependence and (b) privacy concern. The public acceptability of pricing measures is greatly influenced by the extent of car dependence because it leads to a decline in choices of travel modes (Cullinane & Cullinane, 2003; Litman, 1999; Newman & Kenworthy, 1999). However, not only instrumental motivations but also symbolic and affective motivations substantially influence car dependence (Steg, 2005). These motivations may be among the reasons why the public is resistant to pricing measures that aim at reducing car use.

Privacy concerns include the protection of private data and the right to free choice. Since extensive travel behaviour data has to be collected for electronic road pricing, people fear the abuse of their personal data. The impacts of privacy concern on public acceptability remain controversial—some regarded it as one of the major reasons why successful demonstration projects may result in limited implementation (Borins, 1988; Hau, 1990), whereas Link and Polak (2003) showed that neither policymakers nor citizens considered privacy issues a major barrier to introducing road pricing schemes.

2.1.1.4 *Revenue Allocation*

Revenue reallocation and transparency is another key determinant of public acceptability in the literature (e.g., Eliasson & Mattsson, 2006; Farrell & Saleh, 2005; Hensher & Puckett, 2007; Santos & Shaffer, 2004; Schuitema & Steg, 2008; Thorpe et al., 2000). Schlag and Teubel (1997) presumed that the public acceptability of pricing measures is lower than other restrictive schemes such as access controls because other push measures do not generate revenue, and therefore there is a need to reallocate it. Since people habitually associate pricing measures with another form of taxation, the public acceptability of pricing schemes depends on unequivocally proclaiming how the payers can benefit from the revenue.

2.1.1.5 *Equity*

Equity refers to giving as much consideration to one group of people as is given to other groups based on the principles of even-handed dealing (e.g., Kim et al., 2013; Raux & Souche, 2004). Transport equity mainly concerned the fairness in access to road infrastructure in a large amount of literature (e.g., Bröcker et al., 2010; Giuliano, 1994; Litman, 2002). In the case of pricing policies, it is also about the distribution of costs and benefits (Schlag & Teubel, 1997; Viegas, 2001). Interpersonal and interregional equities are also included in the public acceptability of road pricing schemes.

2.1.2 Problem Perceptions, Awareness of Solutions, and Trust Issues

2.1.2.1 Problem Perceptions

All these five issues depend on the understanding of problems (e.g., Oehry, 2010) and the awareness of possible solutions to alleviate these problems (e.g., Bird & Morris, 2006; Stokes & Taylor, 1995; Taylor & Brook, 1998). However, problem perception and awareness may just be a prerequisite for solving the complex acceptability issue.

2.1.2.2 Awareness of Solutions

The awareness of possible solutions to transport problems is also a sine qua non, and sometimes a barrier to acquiring public support for pricing schemes. For instance, Bird and Vigor (2006) found that although the public recognised congestion as a major problem, British people prefer improving public transport to road pricing because they regard road pricing as an unfair policy for low-income individuals and those who live in rural areas. Thus, the authorities must promulgate the effectiveness of pricing measures and provide convincing reasons for integrating public transport improvement and pricing measures rather than merely optimising public transport.

2.1.2.3 Trust in Government

Roughly three-quarters of residents in Edinburgh voted against a road pricing scheme, which had been on the agenda for almost a decade, in 2005. The failure of the Edinburgh road user charging scheme was ascribed to the unattractiveness of the solution, especially to public transport users who were unconvinced about a road pricing-induced improvement in public transport (Gaunt et al., 2007). A lack of trust in government was deemed the underlying cause of this failure. Similarly, McQuaid and Grieco (2005) put forward several reasons related to trust issues. For instance, suspicions were aroused because implementing such schemes always reminds people of previous unsuccessful revenue-earning schemes. Saunders (2005) found it uncertain whether people voted against the general congestion charging concept, the particular proposed scheme or the council for wider reasons. He regarded the opposition to the scheme as a synthesis of all the three factors, which suggests that trust in government in general may influence the public acceptability of the proposed congestion charging scheme.

2.1.3 *Social and Personal Norms*

2.1.3.1 Social Norms

The conceptual framework proposed by Schlag and Teubel (1997) provides a practical tool for understanding and analysing public acceptability. However, in this framework, the construct *social norms* is only regarded as factors shaping aims that the public wants to reach. All the main elements are indirectly influenced by social norms and attitudes through the construct *public awareness of options and their evaluation*. Due to the lack of direct connections between social norms and the five major elements, acceptability is a rational choice that maximises one's utility.

Social impact on public acceptability has been highlighted in many studies. The concept *social norm* is derived from the theory of planned behaviour (Ajzen, 1991). It suggested predicting individuals' behaviour by examining the intention to exhibit this behaviour, which is influenced by the attitude towards the behaviour, the subjective norm and perceived behavioural control. Subjective norm refers to the perceived social norm, which, in detail, means "the respondent's assumption about whether their closest (family, friends) would think that they should accept the strategy". Schade and Schlag (2000) found that social pressure is positively connected with the acceptability of transport pricing measures and that social norm has the most predictive power given the level of information, perceived effectiveness and general personal outcome expectations. Considering that most people are inclined to endeavour to be consonant with others' behaviour (Festinger, 1962), Schade and Schlag assumed that a respective alignment of personal attitudes is likely to happen if social norms are altered from resistance to an acceptance to pricing measures.

The social pressure towards individuals was further emphasised in their later research (Schade & Schlag, 2003). Social pressure from acquaintances such as family members, relatives and friends motivates people to conform with others' behaviour, significantly influencing personal opinions, feelings and behavioural intentions. Thus, Schade and Schlag (2003) assumed that the public acceptability of pricing schemes could be improved if social norms are changed in a favourable way towards road pricing.

Concisely, the more positive the perceived social norm is in regard to a proposed pricing scheme, the stronger an individual's willingness to accept the strategy should be (Kitamura et al., 1999). However, the term social norms in this research is very case-specific, and it refers to "the respondent's assumption about whether his significant other would think that he should accept the strategy" (Schade & Schlag, 2003).

Social norms are conceived as exogenous variables constraining individuals' behaviour in the social science literature; for instance, sociologists focused on how social norms motivate people to act (e.g., Coleman, 1994; Hechter & Opp, 2001) and legalists advocated social norms as efficient alternatives to legal rules (e.g., Ellickson, 2009; Posner, 2009). It is likely that the public acceptability of congestion charging is influenced by a wider set of social norms, which have not yet been sufficiently explored in the transport field.

This study expands social norms for the scheme to a wider set of norms, including three dimensions: (a) acceptance as a norm of obedience to authority, (b) acceptance as a result of social conformity and (c) acceptance as a norm of following the Party.

a. Firstly, it is necessary to consider the norm of accepting something proposed by the government in the Chinese context. This is about how people perceive something as acceptable and how people will respond if they disagree about the policy. Such social norms may directly influence people's definition of what is acceptable, and hence they may lead to a misunderstanding of the acceptability of a transport policy if the Western notion of acceptability is used. For instance, there is evidence that Western motorists are more likely to accept charges if they believe the government has already decided to implement the charge (Schade & Baum, 2007). However, in the Chinese context, it is highly likely that lay citizens will always obey the authorities and accept whatever the authorities offer. Therefore, it is worth considering the norm of obedience to authority in this study. It is explained in detail in Sect. 2.3.1.3.
b. The extent to which people sense social pressure from others and the way they react to the pressure is important. Since the influence of social norms is considered a result of people's desire for social integration and consonance (Bicchieri, 2005), the degree of constraints

that social pressure imposes on an individual should also be considered. It is important to see the sphere of social norms' influence against a general cultural background in which social conformity plays a more significant role than in an individualist culture. This is argued in Sect. 2.3.2.1.

c. To what extent are social norms influenced by political factors? Börjesson et al. (2012) analysed the successful experience of implementing a congestion charge in Stockholm and indicated that with all political parties' support for the charges, the acceptance was improved. Political factors could be more explicitly reflected in the framework rather than mentioned in revenue allocation and equity issues. For example, trust in government was a determining factor in acceptability issues (Gaunt et al., 2007; Kim et al., 2013). A social norm of trusting in government may, perhaps, increase the acceptability. If political factors are potentially important explicators of acceptability, then it is necessary to consider the role of political ideology as an influence, as the two cannot be thought of separately (e.g., Gastil et al., 2008; Shook & Fazio, 2009). The definition of ideology varies, but it concerns a normative vision that is believed to be the absolute truth by a nation, a government or its people (e.g. Eagleton, 1991; James & Steger, 2010). Political ideologies focus on how society should be organised. Thus, the political ideologies of the public could be an underlying factor determining whether a policy is regarded as acceptable. Political ideology may be less important when comparing public acceptability between Western democracies because notions of conservatism, socialism and liberalism exist across different places, although to varying degrees. However, when considering using a Western context-based framework to understand acceptability in the Chinese context, the ideological differences do need to be considered. There are several important issues that have not been well studied in Western context-based literature. Considering the differences between Chinese and Western polity, three questions may need to be answered to analyse the impact of political ideology. Firstly, in what direction does the ideology influence people's anticipation of a transport policy? Secondly, what type of relationship is there between the public and government? Finally, to what extent does the ideological gap between the public and the government influence the acceptability of transport policies? These are expanded in Sect. 2.3.3.

2.1.3.2 Personal Norms

Personal norm was a reason to follow, which is independent of an individual's expectation of others' compliance (Bicchieri, 2010). Those who strictly follow personal norms are believed to be more resistant to social influence; hence, they may sometimes act in conflict with social norms. In the case of congestion charging, public acceptability was correlated with one's pro-environmental attitudes (Eliasson & Jonsson, 2011; Eriksson et al., 2006, 2008).

2.1.4 Summary

This section has presented a review of public acceptability literature in the Western context that has identified and tested key determinants of public acceptability. Previous research has suggested that the public acceptability of congestion charging depends on problem perception, information, the perceived effectiveness of the scheme, individual freedom, revenue allocation, perceived equity, social and personal norms, and trust in government. However, these findings are all based on a Western, democratic, individualistic cultural and political context. This explores the extent to which the concept of acceptability and its determinants is transferrable to a different context. The next section reviews relevant research in the Chinese context and identifies gaps in the research.

2.2 Previous Studies in the Chinese Context

This section reviews the literature on the public acceptance of transport policies in the Chinese context. This section will identify gaps in the literature—most of the previous studies focused on exploring the public acceptance of implemented policies using Western context-based frameworks. This may lead to misunderstandings of public attitudes towards a proposed scheme in the Chinese context.

2.2.1 Research on Public Acceptance and Acceptability

Previous studies on transport policies in the Chinese context focus on three themes: (a) investment in transport infrastructures (e.g., Hong et al., 2011; Hou & Li, 2011; Li et al., 2016; Loo, 1999; Sun & Cui, 2018; Yu et al., 2012a, 2016), (b) encouraging travel behaviour change by improving sustainable travel modes such as public transport and cycling (e.g., Cervero & Day, 2008; Cherry & Cervero, 2007; Cherry et al., 2016; Feng et al., 2017; Gan & Ye, 2018; Geng et al., 2016; Liu & Ceder, 2015; Tang & Lo, 2008; Zhang et al., 2015) and (c) fiscal measures such as fuel taxes, a vehicle quota system and a license plate ban (e.g., Chen & Zhao, 2013; Feng & Ma, 2010; Hao et al., 2011; Liu et al., 2018; Nie, 2017; van Vuuren et al., 2003; Xiao et al., 2017; Yang et al., 2017; Zhang et al., 2018; Zhou et al., 2010). Most previous studies on Chinese transport demand management policies revolved around the environmental and economic impact (He et al., 2005; He & Qiu, 2016; Kenworthy & Hu, 2002; Pucher et al., 2007). Some research has focused on the effectiveness of policies. For example, Feng et al. (2012) performed a time series analysis of the auction market and deduced that continuously releasing more plates to control the plate price would have short-term effects. However, there are quite limited studies from the public's perspective.

Public acceptability has been considered in research on the effectiveness of car ownership controlling policies in the past decade (Chen & Zhang, 2012; Chen & Zhao, 2013; Hao, et al., 2011; Sun et al., 2016).

To the best of my knowledge, public acceptance of transport policies in the Chinese context was first investigated by Chen and Zhao. They examined the preference variation in the public acceptability of car license auction policy. The results indicated that the most significant distinction in public acceptability lies between local plate car owners, non-car owners and those who registered their plates in neighbouring cities. Further, they found that local car owners' acceptance of the policy significantly increased as they had invested in and become beneficiaries of the policy. Chen and Zhao argued that the high public acceptance of the policy could not be seen as citizens' support for the policy but an increasing number of people being in the license owner's club.

Drawing lessons from the theoretical model of acceptance of road pricing proposed by Jakobsson et al. (2000), Chen and Zhao (2013) conducted the first study that systematically investigated public acceptance of car license auction policy in Shanghai. Nonetheless, they attempted to add some special variables to the generic theoretical model to investigate the public acceptance issues in the Chinese context more effectively, including equity issues (government vehicles, comparison to other cities, transparency), the implementation process (information provision, bidding process), and unintended consequences (speculation, non-local licenses). These variables covered almost all the five major issues of public acceptability suggested by Schlag and Teubel (1997). Revenue allocation was not directly reflected in this framework, but this could be related to transparency and trust in government.

Although the complex framework included a variety of determinants and seemingly provided a comprehensive understanding of the public acceptability issues in the Chinese context, the selection of Chinese context-based variables was not reasonably explained. Most of the culture-specific determinants were reflected as equity issues, but this notion of perceived equity, as well as its distinctions from that in the Western context, were not clarified. Furthermore, some issues such as comparisons to other cities and non-local licenses have appreciable particularities that are not widely generalisable beyond the specific region. Although it is insightful that people expect others to have a higher acceptance of the policy, it can hardly be conceptualised as a determinant of public acceptability. In short, the framework added some culture-specific factors into Western context-based frameworks, but these factors were picked without a grounded understanding of the Chinese context.

Chen et al. (2008) surveyed people's perceptions of traffic congestion and attitudes towards several policy options in Shanghai, including the restriction of new vehicle license, an increase in the parking charge in the city centre, road pricing, construction of park and ride facilities for driving travellers, expansions of roads, improvements in the walking and cycling infrastructures, pedestrian zones, and improvements in public transport. The results demonstrated that almost all options that require self-sacrifices are unlikely to be acceptable, especially congestion charging. Instead, citizens prefer policies enforcing public service.

The public acceptability of congestion charging in the Chinese context was first investigated by Sun et al. (2016). The results revealed two main differences from the Western context: (a) the relationship between perceived effectiveness and acceptability was nonsignificant and (b) sociodemographic variables were not significantly related to acceptability. It is bizarre that the authors almost directly applied Schlag and Teubel's (1997) framework but deleted some very important factors, such as trust in government.[1]

[1] It is highly likely that the authors knew the importance of considering this; however, this is fully understandable, because asking this kind of question in China is politically sensitive, and it is unclear what questions should be asked to investigate this factor in the Chinese context.

2.2.2 *Research Gaps*

The aforementioned evidence shows that most of the researchers attempted to analyse Chinese transport policies by using Western context-based frameworks. Although they all tried to add some culture-specific contents into the Western framework (or sometimes delete them), researchers in the transport field have not, to date, systematically reviewed the Chinese context and analysed its possible impact on public acceptability of transport policies. This is problematic because it is unknown whether other factors should be considered in the Chinese context, as would be suggested for example by the work that highlighted the role of government cars. It could also be problematic because constructs that might be labelled the same, such as trust in government, might mean very different things in the Chinese context. There is therefore a risk that in developing a body of research and looking at international comparability, there is a false sense of compatibility.

Researchers have been increasingly aware of this problem. For instance, Wang (2010) analysed the special context of Chinese cities and its influence on the local applicability of foreign policies. Wang argued that a congestion charge may not be as beneficial as it in foreign cities because of the land use structure, the large proportion of government vehicles, and a rapid motorisation trend. Moreover, some case-specific factors acted as barriers to implementing policies transferred from other countries. For instance, the effectiveness of Shanghai's car license auction policy was considered overstated because many Shanghai residents managed to avoid license plate fees by registering their vehicles in neighbourhood cities. The results suggested that institutional and structural differences between Chinese and foreign cities must be considered. Thus, contextual factors significantly influence the applicability of transport policies, including high population density, rapid growth in income and motorisation, the rapid urbanisation process and structural change, a powerful government, institutional settings (urban–rural dichotomy), and the history of urban development. However, researchers have only focused on the impact of macroscopic factors on the effectiveness of policies whilst omitting the role of the public.

A few scholars have discussed cultural factors and their relationship to transport. De Jong (2012), for example, concluded that Confucian values had impacted transport infrastructure development (see also de Jong et al., 2010; Mu et al., 2011; Yu et al., 2012a). With a special focus on

Confucianist values (see Sect. 2.3.1.2), they argued that many important elements of Confucianism have positively influenced China's development, such as the role of family, collectivism and the role of Confucianist moral domestication; nevertheless, these traditions bring problems, such as a lack of understanding of the rule of law, institutional abuses and the collective nature of public facilities.

However, Confucianism is not the only philosophical body influencing China. Separating Confucianism from the other schools of thoughts, however, may cause a disastrous misunderstanding of the Chinese context, especially the interrelationship between Confucianism, Legalism and Taoism. In addition, de Jong (2012) did not consider its correlation with Chinese Socialism. This can be problematic because the institutional structure in contemporary China was formed in Mao's era and has been gradually reformed during the post-Mao era: the impact of traditional Confucian values on the public's attitudes towards policies must be placed into this social context to gain a reasonable understanding.

2.3 Exploring Potential Determinants of Acceptability in the Chinese Context

Cultural differences in acceptability issues are significant. For instance, de Groot and Steg (2006) examined the effect of transport pricing policies that were intended to reduce car use on individuals' quality of life and public acceptability. They showed by a univariate analysis that the acceptability judgements differed among five countries: respondents from the Netherlands and Sweden were less optimistic about transport pricing than Italians and Czechs. This implies that cultural factors may have an influence on public acceptability. Cultural differences were also presented by Schmöcker et al. (2012), who found that determinants of public acceptability, including social problem awareness, self-problem awareness and personal problem awareness, were much higher in the UK than in Japan.

To explore culture-specific determinants that may influence the public acceptability of congestion charging in the Chinese context, Sect. 2.3 presents a review of traditional Chinese philosophical schools, culture and the political system in contemporary China. Marsden and Stead (2011) suggested that transport and other public policies have much in common in their influences on policy transfer. Thus, the literature on the public acceptability of, and attitudes towards other public policies is also reviewed since there is limited research on public acceptability of transport policies in the Chinese context.

2.3.1 Philosophical Underpinnings

In the prolonged course of its development, China has formed unique historical and cultural traditions. These traditions influence not only Chinese policymaking, but also the way Chinese people experience, sense, perceive and think. To get an insight into the public acceptability issue in the Chinese context, it is necessary to base the argument on a philosophical perspective. This section is organised as follows: (a) a comparison between Chinese and Western philosophies; (b) a brief description of four major Chinese philosophical currents: Confucianism (儒家), Taoism (道家), Legalism (法家) and Mahayana Buddhism (汉传佛教); and (3) discussions of the potential impacts of philosophical factors on the public acceptability of congestion charging in China.

2.3.1.1 Comparison Between Chinese and Western Philosophies

In the history of the Chinese civilisation, the term *philosophy* (simplified Chinese: 哲学; pinyin: *zhexue*) did not exist until the beginning of twentieth century. To compare Chinese schools of thought with the Western philosophies, some Chinese newspapers took the appellation from a Japanese philosopher's translation *zhexue* (Chen, 2012). There remains discussion about whether it is appropriate to name Chinese schools of thought as philosophy (e.g., Defoort, 2001; Hegel & Brown, 2006). Despite this contention, it is evidently clear that Chinese and Western philosophies are distinct from each other in at least two essential ways.

The most significant difference between Chinese and Western thought is the understanding and use of the term *conception*. Western philosophical schools base their discussions on a clear theoretical or empirical analysis of a particular concept. However, Chinese schools of thought tend to use extremely vague concepts without proposing well-explained definitions or conceptions. Furthermore, Chinese schools of thought neglect the delimitation of discussion, which makes their conclusions generalisable but ambiguous. Thus, logical thinking and related fields such as philosophy and science have not been developed based on that thinking pattern (cf. Chan, 2008; Russell, 2013).

The other important divergence is the purpose of Western philosophies and Chinese schools of thought. Although there is no universally accepted answer for the purpose of philosophy, Western philosophers focus on understanding and explaining the world from different perspectives. There is no clear evidence showing a close relationship between

Western philosophers and the ruling classes. However, instead of developing a theory to seek the truth, the purpose (or at least one of the major purposes) of Chinese schools of thought is specifically to propose administrative strategies for the ruling classes. In other words, Chinese schools of thought are more likely to be guidelines of practice rather than theories to explain the world.

These two major differences are the basis for understanding how philosophical factors might influence the public acceptability of road pricing.

2.3.1.2 A Brief Description of Four Major Chinese Philosophical Schools

Confucianism

At least four major philosophical bodies are influencing present-day Chinese society. Confucianism is intended to be the official value, and it has been vigorously publicised and supported by the ruling classes for nearly 2,000 years. It is not only the most influential school of thought, but it has also become a crucial part of the Chinese value system. Moreover, after the re-illustration of the Confucian classics in the Song Dynasty, Neo-Confucianism strongly influenced Japanese, Korean and Vietnamese culture (van Ess et al., 2005). Although influenced by Taoism and Mahayana Buddhism, Neo-Confucianism attempted to eliminate the superstitious and mystical elements, to frame a secular and rationalist form of Confucianism (Huang, 1999). Thus, ethical thoughts were reinforced to permeate various classes of society. Although the emphasis has shifted in the modern development of the theory, the core of Confucianism is constant. On the one hand, Confucianism is strongly related to politics. Political authority is regarded as the fundamental requirement for the stability of society (e.g., Pye & Pye, 2009). Consequently, Confucianism is regarded as one of the bases of authoritarianism in east Asian countries (e.g., Fukuyama, 1995). On the other hand, ethically, it emphasises the importance of self-cultivation. The central theme is benevolence, which refers to harmonious relations between people (e.g., Legge, 2009).

These two aspects were integrated by one of the most important concepts, *Nei Sheng Wai Wang* (内圣外王), convincing people to be perfect through self-cultivation and to propel society forward to a great harmony through enlightenment and practice. This concept leads to the worship of rulers with high moral character. Meanwhile, many Confucians considered themselves assistants and consultants of the rulers. As a result, they used moralisation to create and maintain moral order, which ensured that all members of society were given a stable moral recognition and a moral orientation for the social status (Englehart, 2000; Wright, 1960).

Confucianism takes ethics as its core concept, sustained by a comprehensive ethical system. The family culture plays a primary role in this system, which is constituted by four categories of concepts: *Zhong* (忠), *Xiao* (孝), *Ren* (仁), and *Yi* (义) (Lee, 1998). *Xiao*, regulating the relationships between family members, advocates humbleness and obedience to elder family members. *Zhong*, which generalises *Xiao* to political life, requires absolute loyalty to the emperor.[2] *Yi* is a horizontal expansion of the term *Xiao*. It generalises the relationship within the family to a larger range of friends. As the reaction to *Xiao*, the term *Ren* suggests that authoritative family members are kind and merciful to younger family members (Yao, 2000). The decisive characteristic of this system is the differential mode of association (Fei et al., 1992); its influence is discussed in Sect. 2.3.2.1.

Taoism

Unlike the strong desire for participation in political affairs that Confucianists publicised, the connotation of Taoism is similar to naturalism. The term *Tao* (道) means way or principle. The founder of Taoism, Laozi, proposed the term *Tao* as the nature of the universe, within which laws and forces operate in the world (Laozi et al., 2007). This theory is acknowledged and inherited by all the Taoist schools, and it is considered the core of Taoism. Consequently, Taoism draws close attention to exploring the nature of the world (e.g., Chuang-tzu & Palmer, 2006). Taoism focuses on contemplating and observing the way of change, which it considers the nature of being. Needham et al. (1963; Needham, 1981) considered Taoism the source of intuitive scientific philosophy; further, he thought Taoism was the source of the most attractive factors of Chinese people's personality.

[2] The meaning of *Zhong* has changed over time. Before China's adoption of Legalism in the Qin Dynasty, Zhong merely regulated the vassal–lord relationship. This relationship was very much like the long-established custom in Europe "the vassal of my vassal is not my vassal". The pre-Qin notion of *Zhong* can be best exemplified by stories of pre-Qin assassins (see, for example, Sima, 2011), such as Zhuan Zhu (鱄诸), Yao Li (要離) and Yu Rang (豫讓). The notion has been utilised by Legalist thinkers as a theoretical foundation for absolute loyalty or obedience to the emperor.

Taoist propriety and ethics may vary depending on the particular school, but they tend to emphasise action through non-action, naturalness, simplicity and spontaneity (Weber & Gerth, 1953). Unlike the Confucianist claims that the change of the world is deliberate, Taoism believes the representational world is the incarnation of the spontaneous and unintentional *Tao*. A thought of renouncing the world emanated from Taoism, rooted in Chinese people's minds, especially intellectuals. On the one hand, Taoism is the dominant component of idealism in Chinese people's mind since many intellectuals intend to be unworldly when they participate in political affairs. On the other hand, it is a consolation for people who suffer political frustration (Kuang-Chien, 1971; Yip, 2004).

The political impact of Taoism is not as significant as Confucianism and Legalism (see Sect. 2.3.1.3). However, its influence on intellectual élites' daily life, such as art, music and poetry, is incalculable.

Originating from philosophical Taoism, religious Taoism developed the term *Tao* into a faith. It renounces the naturalism for which philosophical Taoism advocates and deifies ancient Taoist sages as gods, which is precisely what Laozi and Zhuangzi rejected. Religious Taoism draws its cosmological foundation from Yin Yang (阴阳) and Five Phases (五行), which originated from the school of Naturalists rather than from philosophical Taoism (Robinet, 1997). Robinet (1997) identified the components of religious Taoism as (a) philosophical Taoism, (b) techniques for achieving ecstasy, (c) practices for achieving longevity and immortality and (d) exorcism. The components in the emergence of religious Taoism show that this religion is more a combination of prehistoric folk religions and alchemy influenced by Confucianism and Buddhism than a heritage of philosophical Taoism.

Confucianism and Taoism are both competitive and complementary. Together, they form the Chinese humanist structure and sustain the super-stability of Chinese society (Low, 2011; Suen et al., 2007).

Legalism

Another prominent school of thought is Legalism, notwithstanding that its development has stagnated since the Han Dynasty. Progressively formed in the long-term administrative practice by socio-political reformers (e.g., Rickett & Guan, 2001), it formed the guiding principles for the first emperor, Qin Shi Huang, and his imperial administration system (Fu, 1996). However, the term *Legalism* was not proposed until

Sima Tan's book *The Essential Implications of the Six Houses of Thought* (论六家要旨) in the Western Han Dynasty, which is about 200 years after most of the so-called Legalist sages in the Warring States period (Sima & Sima, 1959). In this book, Sima clustered a group of thinkers and reformers such as Han Fei, Guan Zhong and Shang Yang as Legalists. Interestingly, most of the representatives of Legalism were trained by Confucianist thinkers. Qian Mu considered that rather than the etiquette on which Mencius focused, Legalist reformers such as Wu Qi engaged in political activities, flourishing Confucius's thought (Xiong, 1938). According to the *Records of the Grand Historian* (史记; Sima, 2011), the culminating figure of Legalism, Han Fei, synthesised the methodologies from his predecessors and epitomised the thought of the school. He conclude that *Fa* (法; law, standard, regulation), *Shu* (术; tactics, strategy, procedure), and *Shi* (势; situational advantage, power, authority) are all indispensable and should be coordinated. Han Fei's idea was nourished by a Confucianist, Xunzi, who believed that human nature is evil. Thus, mandatory measures are necessary to compel people to renounce evil. Meanwhile, influenced by the founder of Taoism, Laozi, he interpreted the *Tao Te Ching* (道德经) as a political text. He asserted that ideal rulers do not directly interfere in politics, but make laws that act like an inevitable force of nature; thus, the public will not resist (Han & Watson, 1964). As Han Fei was considered the most eminent Legalist philosopher and the integrator of the Legalist ideology, there are clear interactions between Legalism and Confucianism and Taoism.

Although it is hard to find direct connections between so-called Legalist philosophers, their ideas shared some common features. Legalist thinkers rejected Confucianists' espousal of a regime based on the personal magnetism of the aristocrats because their private interests undermine their sovereignty. Han Fei indicated that officials are accustomed to abusing their position and seeking favours from foreign powers. Thus, he urged the ruler to control those officials strictly through the *Fa*, preventing officials from exceeding their authority and punishing them if they intended to deceive the ruler.

In the long imperial period, the official ideology relatively remained Legalist practice concealed with Confucian rhetoric, commonly described as *Wai Ru Nei Fa* (simplified Chinese: 外儒内法; outside Confucianist, inside Legalist)—the ruling class generalised Confucianism (Mahayana Buddhism was also taken as an external face of the imperial system after the Tang Dynasty) to maintain social stability while the government continued to be run by Legalism (Goldin, 2011; Lyon, 2008). There is evidence that Legalism also played an indispensable role in Chairman Mao's concept of governing (e.g., Leng, 1977).

Mahayana Buddhism

Mahayana Buddhism is a Chinese version of Buddhism that is influenced by Taoism and Confucianism. Although its influence on political systems is very limited, Buddhism's influence on the public is considerable (Needham et al., 1963). On the one hand, as a foreign religion, the spread of Buddhism among the Chinese benefited from the adoption of traditional Chinese values. On the other hand, Buddhism has the ideological content and concrete practices to penetrate through to ordinary people and to complement the weaknesses of Confucianism and Taoism. The ultimate concern of Buddhist doctrine is the agony of life. Buddhists state that life and death is the sea of bitterness; hence, the only way to extricate yourself from this predicament is to face life and death squarely. How people face their death before departing the world has been a conundrum since ancient times, but neither Confucianism nor Taoism discusses this theme. Therefore, Buddhism remedies the flaw in traditional Chinese schools of thought, satisfying the people's spiritual need.

However, the disengagement doctrine conflicts with the core will and detailed content of Confucianism and Taoism, which is rooted in Chinese people's minds. Buddhism concerns spirit more than flesh, the afterlife more than present life, and a world of deities more than a world of secularity, emphasising the misery of being in the world and the happiness of obtaining nirvana. Thus, during the spreading process, Buddhism has gradually been Sinicised[3] through its compatibility with Confucianism and Taoism. This process, unavoidably, focused on the secularisation and functionalization of primordial Buddhist doctrines.

In the historical process, these four schools of thought have all been self-sufficient and self-contained, but also interactive. All these philosophical currents emphasise establishing moral norms to maintain the stability of society by the inculcation of shame and the complementary threat of ostracism (Benedict, 1967). Compared to the Western guilt culture, this widely accepted shame culture suggests the far-reaching significance of

[3] Sinicisation is a process whereby non-Chinese societies come under the influence of Chinese culture, particularly Han Chinese culture, language, societal norms and ethnic identity.

social norms in east Asian countries (Wong & Tsai, 2007). However, an insurmountable gap between the dominant and the dominated is also created and perpetuated by these thoughts, leading to people's periodic hostility towards the ruling classes.

2.3.1.3 Potential Impacts of Chinese Schools of Thought

This section discusses how Chinese schools of thoughts may potentially influence public acceptability in the Chinese context.

To Accept or Endure?

What the public considers acceptable should come to the fore in this research because it is evident that the notion of acceptability has to be interpreted in a different way in the Chinese context.

Chinese philosophers and schools of thoughts flourished during the Spring and Autumn period and the Warring States period.[4] There was a great cultural and intellectual expansion in China, and is generally considered the Golden Age of Chinese philosophy (e.g., Graham, 1989). It was the era when the system of ancient rules of etiquette and ethics were well developed and performed, but it was also the age of property disintegration. Consequently, feudal lords were eager to expand their territories and consolidate their ruling positions (e.g., Loewe & Shaughnessy, 1999). Thus, almost all the ancient Chinese thinkers dedicated themselves as counsellors (mostly political advisors, although some of them could also be military [e.g., Sun Tzu, 2011] or economic counsellors).

The term *to accept* is explained in English as *to make a favourable response to an offer*, which could be regarded as an initiative act to approve or consent to a proposed scheme with favour. However, to accept means something different in the Chinese language. Ancient Chinese society was characterised by rigid hierarchy and savage political oppression (e.g., Flad, 2011; Pines, 2012). Instead of accepting an option, it is more accurate to describe the reaction as *to obey* or *to endure*.

[4] The Spring and Autumn period was from approximately 771 to 476 BC. Its name derives from a chronicle of the state of Lu, the Spring and Autumn Annals. During this period, dukes and marquesses obtained de facto regional autonomy, defying the authority of *Tianzi* (天子, son of god) and waging wars amongst themselves. The Partition of Jin (三家分晋), the most powerful state, is commonly considered as the end of the Spring and Autumn period and the beginning of the Warring States period (475 BC to 221 BC) in which the most far-reaching institutional reform in Chinese history took place.

To maintain the stability of society, the public was under pressure to follow a series of social norms. These social norms were not restricted to a particular period of time. Originating from different schools of thought, their pressures have gradually become rooted in Chinese people's minds during more than 2,000 years of incessant adaption and cultivation.

Confucius's way of maintaining social stability depends on promulgating the sense of hierarchy and the willingness to sustain the rigid social hierarchy (Jacobs et al., 1995; Kutcher, 2000; Zhang et al., 2005). An obsession with the immense hierarchical system gave people a clear social identity and more importantly, discouraged them from jeopardising their social identities. Then a social norm of worshipping the authority was formed to drive the public to conform blindly to the social norms the ruling classes required. Thus, dominated by such social norms, in most cases obedience to authority was the proper way to act for the public, who were at a low level in the hierarchical system (e.g., Kelman & Hamilton, 1989).

This form of social norm is further enhanced by both philosophical and religious Taoism. Taoist philosophers believe that people can representatively change the actual existence of an object by metaphysically changing its name (Chuang-tzu, & Palmer, 2006; Laozi et al., 2007). Since everything is decided by subjective sensations, Chinese people are enthusiastic about acquiring spiritual victories (Lu, 1990). Many inherent weaknesses identified by Chinese thinkers during the New Cultural Movement are derived from Taoism, such as a detached life perspective, willingness to be a fence rider, and a bystander attitude (e.g., Lin, 2013). These characteristics, on the one hand, make people indifferent to others; on the other hand, they keep Chinese people from showing dissatisfaction with authority. Thus, acceptance is always a superficial demonstration of endurance in the Chinese context.

In most cases, if personal interests are not seriously violated, it is more accurate to describe Chinese people's behaviour as to obey than to accept a transport policy. That is, to act according to what they have been asked or ordered to do by an authority, or to behave according to an instruction. Although people may have to sacrifice their personal interests because of a transport policy, especially a pricing scheme, under the influence of such a social norm, they may incline to endure, to continue or carry on, despite obstacles or hardships, and to tolerate or put up with something unpleasant.

Legal Consciousness

As discussed in Sect. 2.3.1.1, due to the advisory tradition, Chinese philosophers did not attempt to build theories to explain the world but to offer effective measures to rule the state. In other words, the ultimate purpose of Chinese schools of thought is to ensure the functioning of the state apparatus. Consequently, individual rights are sometimes unavoidably considered expendable. Generally speaking, this utilitarian tradition has caused a lack of a sense of justice in the Chinese context.

The concept of natural law, which comprises inherent rights conferred by the nature (see Corbett, 2009; Hayek, [1960] 2014; Hobbes, [1651] 2006; Locke, [1690] 1978), is at least one of the most important foundations of Western jurisprudence (Clinton, 1997; Finnis, 2011). However, there has never been such a concept in traditional Chinese intellectual history. The Chinese interpretation of the laws is very much in line with the Western concept of positive laws, which refers to laws adopted by certain authorities for "the safety of citizens, the preservation of states, and the tranquillity and happiness of human life" (Dyck, 2004). Since the legislative and executive system in contemporary Mainland China is complex and perplexing for the public, it is hard for the public to distinguish between what a government is going to achieve and a set of standards that society must follow (Gustafsson et al., 2008; Sutter, 2012). Thus, policies are not distinct from laws in the Chinese context. In this regard, the way the public interprets a policy and the perceived relationship between policies and laws are different from those in the West.

Legal consciousness refers to the empowerment of individuals regarding issues involving the law. It helps us to understand how significant people think the law is in relation to their daily life (e.g., Merry, 1990). Although people might not be familiar with the details and minutiae of the law, they make sense of their experience by relying on legal categories and concepts (Silbey, 1998). However, a lack of legal consciousness is identified as one of the shared characteristics of Chinese people in the literature on various academic disciplines (Erie, 2012; Gallagher, 2006; O'Brien & Li, 2004; Wong, 2003). This is, to some extent, because legal consciousness is incompatible with traditional Chinese schools of thoughts.

To maintain the hierarchical system and to promulgate monarchism, Confucianists after the Han dynasty advocated blind loyalty towards the supreme ruler (e.g., Frederickson, 2002). Specifically, they suggested unconditional obedience without resistance, supervision or criticism as the behavioural norm of public–authority relations, monarch–subject relations, and all forms of superior–subordinate relations (e.g., Park & Chesla, 2007; Park et al., 2005). Moreover, Confucianism does not give a definition of objective justice, which is regarded as an inherent component of the law (d'Amato, 2011). For instance, in the famous story about Bo Yi and Shu Qi, Confucius rhapsodised their practice of showing loyalty to a tyrant and their support of the old hierarchical system (Legge, 2009). He eulogised them for their personal judgement and practice of *Yi*; however, he turned his back on objective justice.

Since Confucianism was taken as the appearance of the imperial system while Legalism was the actual strategic guideline for the emperor, Legalist views of the legal system could be more influential in shaping Chinese people's legal consciousness. Based on safeguarding the monarchical power, Legalist theory provides a series of methods to strengthen the army and enrich the state, aiming to serve the supreme ruler. The most significant characteristic is that Legalist thinkers affirmed the absolute power of the supreme ruler. They believed that interpersonal relationships result from contradictions between personal interests. Thus, the supreme ruler needs to have unchallengeable supremacy and absolute power to rule his subjects (Han & Watson, 1964; Shang, 2017; Sima, 2011). Consequently, law was regarded as a tool for the supreme ruler to dominate the public and officials. In other words, this seemingly obvious rule of law theory is an external face of a rule of man core. Therefore, the traditional Chinese absolute monarchic system derived from Legalist theory is a predominant barrier to legal consciousness in the Chinese public.

A lack of legal consciousness may lead to a lack of awareness of rights (Abrego, 2011). As they do not consider their rights and responsibilities, it is unlikely that Chinese citizens balance cost and benefit in the same way as Western people do—one must bear the cost but should never expect the benefits. This is the epitome of the traditional Chinese relationship between the ruler and the ruled.

The Relationship Between the Ruler and the Ruled

This section focuses on the Legalist ideas of the relationship between the ruler and the ruled because this idea has been practised throughout the history of Chinese civilisation. The following three representative quotes from one of the most important Legalist classics *The Book of Lord Shang* (

商君书; Duyvendak, 1928) introduce the Legalist idea of the state-people relationship.

> A weak people means a strong state and a strong state means a weak people. Therefore, a country, which has the right way, is concerned with weakening the people. If they are simple they become strong,[5] and if they are licentious they become weak. Being weak, they are law-abiding; being licentious, they let their ambition go too far; being weak, they are serviceable, but if they let their ambition go too far, they will become strong. Therefore is it said: "To remove the strong by means of a strong people brings weakness; to remove the strong by means of a weak people brings strength."[6] (p. 153)

This indicates the Legalist interpretation of the state–people relationship, which is an antagonistic relationship in which a good ruler should deprive and oppress the people (the ruled) to make the country strong. Lord Shang further proposed his principles for weakening the people, aiming at compelling the people to depend on the state.

> If the people live in humiliation, they value rank; if they are weak, they honour office; and if they are poor, they prize rewards. If the people are governed by means of punishments, they enjoy service, and if the people are made to fight by means of rewards, they scorn death.[7] (p. 154)

He then explained his principles for policymaking:

> If the government takes such measures as the people hate, the people are made weak,[8] and if it takes such measures as the people like, the people are made strong. But a weak people means a strong state, and a strong people

[5] As a military power, or for the state/the ruler.

[6] The original text: 民弱國彊,民彊國弱,故有道之國,務在弱民.樸則彊,淫則弱,弱則軌,淫則越志;弱則有用,越志則彊.故曰:以彊去弱者弱,以弱去彊者彊. This means that to control the people more effectively, the ruler should use weak people (shameless, lazy, greedy, etc.) to control strong people (upright, honest, brave, etc.), because only in that way will strong people be terminated so that only weak people are left. Therefore, the ruler does not need to be afraid of the people.

[7] The original text: 民辱則貴爵,弱則尊官,貧則重賞.以刑治民則樂用,以賞戰民則輕死.

[8] Weak and strong here should not be interpreted as physically strong or weak; weakness is about whether people can be independent individuals without depending on the state. Legalist philosophers focus on making a state militarily powerful.

> means a weak state. If the government takes such measures as the people like, they are made strong, and if strong people are made even stronger, the army becomes doubly weak; but if the government takes such measures as the people hate, they are made weak, and if weak people are made even weaker, the army becomes doubly strong. Therefore, by strengthening the people, one becomes doubly weak, and perishes; by weakening the people, one becomes doubly strong and attains supremacy.[9] (p. 155)

Although such principles have been partly practised by different autocratic rulers in different cultural contexts, so far as I know, Lord Shang is the only one who blatantly advocated such an extreme state–people relationship and probably the first one who systematically proposed a series of policies to deprive and oppress the people. However, this is not merely a theory. Lord Shang's idea was unreservedly practised by the Qin Kingdom, and it helped Qin rulers to conquer all the other six kingdoms, unifying China for the first time (Chang, 2007; Lewis, 2009). After the short reign of the Qin Dynasty, the tradition of *outside Confucianism inside Legalism* progressively formed (Fu, 1993; Zhao, 2015). Under the Confucianist veneer of benevolence and righteousness, Lord Shang's ideas never perished. The vast majority of emperors, who are highly praised nowadays, were practitioners of Legalism and Lord Shang's theory, such as Han Wudi, Sui Wendi, Tang Taizong, Wu Zhao,[10] Song Taizu,[11] Yuan Shizu, Ming Taizu and Qing Shengzu (see Fan, 2016; Guo & Guo, 2008; Heng, 1999; Hsiao, 1976). Also, Legalist ideas, including the aforementioned theory of Lord Shang, significantly influenced modern East Asia, such as Japanese militarism from the Meiji Restoration to the end of World War II, and it remains an influence in contemporary China (see Holcombe, 2011; Pines, 2014).

The Legalist idea of the state–people relationship may influence the public acceptability of congestion charging in various ways. Firstly, it further explains why the Chinese term acceptability has to be interpreted as the extent to which the public is willing to obey the authority, instead of the Western interpretation, the quality of being able to be agreed to or approved of. Secondly, due to more than 2,000 years of practice of such

[9] The original text: 政作民之所樂,民彊;民彊而彊之,兵重弱.政作民之所惡,民弱;民弱而弱之,兵重彊.故以彊重弱,削;弱重彊,王.

[10] The only empress in Chinese history.

[11] Titles ending with "zu" indicate the founders of dynasties.

a theory, the public may greatly depend on the state/elites/the supreme ruler. Therefore, it is unlikely that the assumption of economic man will still hold. Thirdly, the perception of revenue allocation may be distinct from the West because of this state–people relationship. In democracies, public acceptability is influenced by revenue allocation from which lay citizens can get benefits. However, in the Chinese context, whatever benefits the public gets from the government should be deemed as infinite imperial graciousness, which can only be awarded but can never be required.

Equity

This monarch-based ideology unavoidably leads to an unequal society. The higher the class people belong to, the more priority and the less responsibility they have. As the hierarchical tradition is rooted in Chinese people's mind, inevitably, equity issues were not a major concern for either the ruling classes or their advisory thinkers throughout history.

It seems that Legalist philosophers attempt to apply equal laws to all criminal offenders, no matter what social class they belong to. Han Fei expounded this view (Han & Watson, 1964):

> The law does not favour the noble, as an ink line does not yield to the crooked wood. Wherever the law applies, the wise cannot evade, nor can the brave defy. Punishment applies to a minister, as rewards apply to a common man.

However, as previously discussed, the Legalist notion of the law has never been the law that concerns social justice, but a tool to enslave the people, including nobles. Moreover, there are also clues in ancient legal documents from the Qin Dynasty that represented the idea of Legalism as refuting the existence of the concept of equality in Legalist theory. The law tried to ensure that the severity of penalty would be commensurate with the seriousness of the crime. However, there were still many unequal laws in the Qin legal system so that nobles and officials were favoured, providing them multiple ways to mitigate penalties (Dutton, 1992; Lewis, 2009; Liu, 1998; Yates, 1995). Legalist philosophers had raised no objections to these rules. In addition, some of these rules were probably related to Legalist philosophies such as collective punishment. Legalist viewpoints on nobles are based on the belief that nobles and ministers are more likely to shake the foundation of the monarchical system (see Han & Watson,

1964). In other words, the appearance of equality in Legalist philosophers' statements was not based on a notion of justice, but it was designed to consolidate the monarchical regime.

Han Fei's view on three types of basic social relations shows that Legalist thinkers despised equality. This is reflected in the concept of *San Gang* (三纲), translated as the three cardinal guides (ruler guides subject, father guides son and husband guides wife). *San Gang* and *Wu Chang* (五常), translated as the five constant virtues (benevolence, righteousness, propriety, wisdom and fidelity), has had a great influence on Chinese history. This concept, usually regarded as the Confucianist ethical code, is considered the cultural foundation of Chinese people by its supporters; meanwhile, it is severely criticised by its opponents as a spiritual shackle that has manacled the Chinese people for thousands of years (Chow, 2013; Schwarcz, 1986; see also Cheung & Liu, 2004; Mok & Wong, 2013; Schneider, 2003; Su & Littlefield, 2001). However, the essence of *San Gang* did not originate from Confucianism, but from a Legalist kernel overlaid by a Confucianist shell (Yu, 2003). Thus, what Legalist philosophers proposed is just a more callous tool to maintain the social stratification than the Confucianist proposal.

Notwithstanding Confucianist and Legalist philosophers' enthusiasm for maintaining the hierarchical system, the concept of equality is an important component of Taoism and Mahayana Buddhism.

The equality of all living creatures is a religious philosophy and the foundation of the faith of Mahayana Buddhism. Buddhism also suggests that people should treat all things and creatures equally with Buddhist enlightenment (e.g., Fromm et al., 1970). Although Buddhism does not concentrate on institutional improvement, this concept would improve the equality of social institutions. Buddhism claims that all beings have Buddha nature (Yamamoto, 1974), illustrating that the difference between the Buddha and other beings is their consciousness (e.g., Liu, 1982). Thus, people were invigorated by this hypothesis, which suggested that all beings have the chance to become Buddha (Brown, 1991; Hookham, 1991). However, Buddhist ideas of equality lost their original meaning after Buddhism was introduced into China because of the formidable oppression of feudal ethical codes. In fact, the concept of equality is limited to *Vimuttimagga* (the path of freedom, a Buddhist concept of non-self) in the Chinese version of Buddhism.

The Taoist concept of equality can be summarised in two ways: equality between people and harmonious relationships between humans and nature. Taoist philosophers believed that physiological differences do not result in inequalities in human nature (Chuang-tzu & Palmer, 2006). *The Book of Chuang Tzu* narrates many stories about those who are handicapped in body but perfect in spirit, metaphorically illustrating that differences in innate ability should not influence equality between people. Moreover, in contrast with Confucianism, Taoist philosophers praised gender equality (which is also ignored by other Chinese philosophical currents). Laozi considered that all things in the universe are a unity of Yin and Yang (Laozi et al., 2007). Both male and female have talents, but in different domains. Thus, he suggested that male and female are equal because their advantages are complementary. Taoist philosophers also suggested that society should be equal, again; in opposition to Confucianism, they suggested that the old *Li* (礼, propriety) should be abolished due to its maintenance of the hierarchical system (Loewe, 1993; Major, 1993). They proposed a series of conceptions for an ideal society; for instance, Laozi considered there should not be rulers but administrators of society, who would guide but not interfere in social life (Laozi et al., 2007; Seidel, 1969).

Although the thought realm and spirit state of Taoist philosophers are exceedingly high concerning equality issues, the Taoist concepts of equality are operationally flawed. These thinkers emphasised the importance of equality in society, but they did not recommend any practical way to achieve an equal society. Therefore, the envisaged future Laozi and Chuang-tzu delineated is more likely to be a political utopia. Moreover, their concept of equality in the economy inclines to egalitarianism. This philosophical tradition brings about resentment in society when the economy grows since income disparities will unavoidably accompany the economic growth. Consequently, it may significantly influence the public acceptability of a pricing scheme. This issue is discussed in Sect. 2.3.2.

The anarchist society they imagined seems to be politically equitable, but it lacks a realistic foundation. Taoist philosophers advocated that the unequal social order should be broken, but the ideal social orders they proposed are impractical. Hence, Taoist concepts of equity were rare in practice, but nonetheless, they imperceptibly influenced the public view of equity.

If Confucianism was the founder of the idea that some groups of people are inferior to other groups, literally *Zun Bei* (尊卑), then Taoism is the destroyer of such an idea. When Confucian thoughts compel people to obey an unequal scheme, Taoist thought always offers a surreptitious intention to decline the scheme. However, because of the egalitarian tendency of Taoism, the public is used to venting discontent with the scheme. This could be a barrier to evaluating the actual acceptability of a scheme. A rational choice of whether a proposed scheme is acceptable or not should be based on rational ideas about equality. However, egalitarian thought leads the public to an emotional expression and a fierce confrontation between the winners and the losers. Moreover, the Taoist concept of equity contains a strong anti-authority awareness (Chang, 1963; Kirkland, 2004). Nevertheless, since it is an esoteric theory, only a small number of intellectual élites are familiar with philosophical Taoism, and its influence is rather limited.

Furthermore, due to the interconnectedness of Chinese schools of thoughts, the Taoist concept of equity has altered during its development. Many Taoist philosophers after the Han Dynasty had a Confucianist background, which significantly influenced their understanding of equity (Sailey, 1978). Some Taoist philosophers attempted to synthesise other schools of thoughts, for instance the book *Huainanzi* (simplified Chinese: 淮南子) consists of a collection of essays blending Taoist, Confucianist, Legalist, Mohist, Naturalist and Agronomist concepts (see Loewe, 1994). However, the purpose of this text, unlike the pre-Qin Taoism, was to admonish Emperor Wu of the Han Dynasty to decentralise his power and to moderate the unification of the nation. In other words, some Taoist thinkers after the Han Dynasty also became deeply involved in politics, as Confucianist and Legalist thinkers did, thereby shifting their ground to consider equity issues.

Thus, (a) social equity or justice has never been a major concern in Chinese philosophical traditions and (b) the interpretation of equity in the Chinese context should be egalitarianism.

2.3.2 Cultural and Historical Influences

The term *culture* is a broad concept that has been given numerous interpretations and definitions by different scholars. Tylor (2010) defined culture as "that complex whole which includes knowledge, belief, art, morals, law, custom and any other capabilities and habits acquired by man as a member of society". Anthropologists considered culture as both a social and historical phenomenon (Holloway, 1969; James, 2014; Kroeber & Kluckhohn, 1952). As an outcome of human creativity and an accumulation of the history of human society, it condenses into and dissociates from substance (Kroeber & Kluckhohn, 1952; see also Triandis, 1994; Williams, 1983). It is a sublimation of perceptual experience and knowledge on the objective world, and it turns into a generally recognised inheritable ideology for human beings to communicate with each other (Cole & Scribner, 1974).

According to the Cambridge English Dictionary, culture refers to "the way of life, especially the general customs and beliefs, of a particular group of people at a particular time". Compared to the definition in English, the term culture is a generalised concept in the Chinese context, basically consistent with the anthropologists' definition. However, since Chinese people tend to put everything into the domain of Chinese culture, the concept itself becomes elusive. Thus, to analyse the impact of cultural factors on public acceptability of transport policies, we focus on thinking patterns and behavioural traditions that have taken shape in different historical stages of the Chinese people and their potential influences over the acceptability of transport policy.

The influence of philosophical tradition is indubitably significant to the intellectual élite. However, it is unlikely that the public is directly influenced by these schools of thoughts, whose theories are obscure, particularly when the literacy rate is low (Lee, 2000). The real influence of ancient philosophers' thoughts is asserted through the formation of a culture. In the process of forming the traditional culture, some of the thoughts were propagated and have finally become powerful social norms (Confucianism, Legalism), some have faded from public memory (for instance Mohism, Logicians) and some still influence the public via a different appearance, but the new appearance has long departed from its original idea (Taoism) (see Cohen, 1991; Wu & Xiao, 2001).

Forty values in Chinese traditional culture were identified by a survey of Chinese values (Chinese Culture Connection, 1987). In addition, Fan (2000) added 31 more core values that were considered equally important. I next discuss some key aspects that might influence the public acceptability of transport policies.

2.3.2.1 *Integration and Social Stabilisation*

Most of the traditional values have been established as consequences of the ruling classes' need to maintain social stability, such as tolerance for others, harmonious relationships with others, solidarity with others, non-competitiveness and contentedness with one's position in life (Chinese

Culture Connection, 1987). Apparently, these traditional values originated from Chinese schools of thoughts, but their influence on the public is independent of philosophical currents, and it has spontaneously deepened during the historical process. In addition, these traditional values imperceptibly enhance the impact of social norms.

Since social norms lead behaviour in a certain situation as "mental representations of appropriate behaviour" (Aarts & Dijksterhuis, 2003), their impacts largely depend on how people think of other people's opinions. In the Chinese context, people are educated to keep harmonious relationships with others and to try to avoid confrontation as much as possible (Kirkbride et al., 1991). It is interesting to explore the role social norms play in public acceptability. On the one hand, Chinese people might be more likely to conform to social norms; hence, social norms may be more important in the Chinese context; on the other hand, since people are used to getting along, what they express outwardly may not be what they feel inwardly; hence, social norms may considerably influence their behaviour but be less influential on attitudes.

2.3.2.2 Egalitarianism

The notion of equity has varied between the ruling classes and peasants (Berthoff, 1982; Muller et al., 1989). The divergence of the notions of equity reflects different ideas of wealth distribution between different social classes. The ideas of wealth distribution in traditional Chinese society could generally be classified as social class-based wealth distribution (for example, the Confucianist idea of wealth distribution) and egalitarian wealth distribution (for example, the Taoist idea of wealth distribution). The most far-reaching aphorism about equality is Confucius's theory of *Bu Huan Gua Er Huan Bu Jun* (simplified Chinese: 不患寡而患不均), translated as do not worry about poverty, but rather about the uneven distribution of wealth (Legge, 2009; see also Chu & Gardner, 1990). Confucius emphasised eradicating absolute poverty through the *courtesy of Qi* and abolishing relative poverty through Confucianist ethics. Not only did he focus on instrumental aspects of business ethics, but he also correlated moral cultivation with distributive justice (e.g., Ip, 2009a, 2009b). It is easy to see that Confucius wanted *to abolish* relative poverty, which inclines to egalitarianism. However, as we discussed before, the Confucian concept of equality is advocated to protect the interests of upper classes and to maintain a relatively stable social order. Thus, the nature of the Confucianist concept of equality throws a few sops to the public to protect the interests and priorities of the ruling classes. Besides Confucianism, the concept of equality proposed by other thinkers could be regarded as a differential distribution of wealth, income and land based on political power or influence (see Feng & Bodde, 1983; Moore, 1967).

However, it is more important to look at the public view of the concept of equity in this study. History shows that a multitude of ordinary people considered an absolutely equal distribution of wealth as the ideal distribution model for the society (e.g., Riskin et al., 2001; Vermeer, 2004). There is a clear evolutionary process for the egalitarian concept of the Chinese public. At first, peasants' desire was confined to an equal distribution of wealth since they believed the fundamental cause of inequality was the land system. Then they appealed against unequal political rights. In the later period of ancient China, this egalitarian tradition expanded to an institutional level. It evolved into peasants' opposition to landowners, their land system and autocracy (Rawski & Li, 1992; Wilkinson, 2000; Zhao, 1986). There are many examples from peasant revolts in Chinese history that egalitarianism has always been the most powerful slogan to call out public support for uprisings (e.g., Christiansen & Rai, 2014; Little, 1989). Unlike the ruling class and the scholar-bureaucrat class, who based their understanding of equity on a Confucian theory, peasant revolts in China were always tinged with elements of religion and mysticism, especially religious Taoism (e.g., Ping, 2001). With these religious interpretations, the egalitarian concept was further strengthened, rising from a pragmatic expectation of acquiring proper wealth and political rights to a spiritual sustenance of a utopian society.

Due to the limitation of the peasantry and egalitarianism itself, it could not be supported or recognised by other social classes in society. The egalitarian concept could not even be carried through to the end in peasant revolts; it became a mere formality of smallholders' utopias (Wilkinson, 2000; see also Xu, 2003). Thus, the impact of egalitarianism is not reflected in achievements in social practice, but it had a far-reaching influence on people's thoughts, and it was an inner protest against exploitation and oppression. People may not usually feel that they are oppressed, but when they perceive something as inequitable, they inevitably generalise the hostile emotion into a wider range of government behaviour.

Although it was unrealistic to avoid exploitation, the antagonism towards landlordism and the request for their own land derived from peasants' egalitarian ideology was more than just a fantasy. When people put their egalitarian ideology into practice, it always brings about extensive armed insurrections (Lindley, 1866; Lorge, 2006). However, although egalitarianism could be a lethal weapon to undermine the regime base of feudal dynasties, it has never established a practical administrative system. Those who held the slogan of egalitarianism very often joined the privileged classes after they won a partial victory (e.g., Reilly, 2004; Spence, 1996). In other words, peasants' egalitarianism might be good for destroying an unequal system, but it is also dangerous because it rarely persists.

Perhaps the best example of egalitarian thoughts in the New China was the Great Leap Forward (simplified Chinese: 大跃进; see Bachman, 2006; MacFarquhar & Mao, 1989). This was an economic and social campaign led by Mao, aiming to transform the country rapidly from a traditional agricultural society to a socialist society through industrialisation (Yang, 2008). It ended in catastrophe and caused the Great Chinese Famine between 1959 and 1962, leaving an estimated 18 million to 46 million victims (Dikötter, 2010; Kung & Lin, 2003; Ó Gráda, 2011; Yang, 2008, 2012). Although Mao had criticised egalitarianism before, it is evident that the idea of the Great Leap Forward was significantly influenced by egalitarian thought (Bian, 2002). In 1958, it was decided that people's communes, which had governmental, political and economic functions, would be the new form of fundamental organisation throughout rural China (Zweig, 1983). In the communes, everything originally owned by individuals or households, such as private animals, stored grains and items in the private kitchen, was contributed to the commune. Everything was shared by members in the commune. The egalitarian distribution of wealth severely discouraged enthusiasm for production and finally resulted in a nationwide economic recession (Chen & Zhou, 2007). Mao was compelled to self-criticise in the Seven Thousand Cadres Conference (simplified Chinese: 七千人大会) in 1962, and he was marginalised within the party (Fu, 2015). At that time, he started to draw a mental sketch of the Cultural Revolution (Clark, 2008; MacFarquhar, 1997). However, contrary to an egalitarian distribution at the grassroots level, special treatment of and domineering behaviour from cadres was also a common phenomenon. All rural resources were controlled and managed by the communes; all productive activities were also assigned by commune cadres (Domes, 1982; Zhang et al., 2004). Moreover, some modest party leaders such as Liu Shaoqi implemented a series of allowances for cadres during the Great Chinese Famine (Dittmer, 1974). This greatly exacerbated the public dissatisfaction with cadres when millions of people were suffering starvation. Thus, egalitarian thought precipitated an unavoidable conflict between cadres and peasants, and finally it became an essential factor that supported and aggravated the Cultural Revolution (Barnouin & Yu, 1993; Lieberthal, 1995; MacFarquhar, 1997). The egalitarianism that formed the spiritual foundation of the Great Leap Forward, was a stratified, economic egalitarianism. However, the egalitarian thoughts reflected in the Cultural Revolution were generalised to political egalitarianism to some extent (Lee, 1980; Jin, 1999).

It is noticeable that egalitarian thought is always used as a powerful tool to instigate rebellions, but it soon becomes an encumbrance to achieving the intended goals. In other words, egalitarian thought is always destructive of social and economic stability. Since the implementation of Reform and Open policy, there has been a period of social and economic transition (Howell, 1993; Luo, 2004; Wu, 2010; see also Hellman, 1998). The striking gap between the rich and the poor (Cheng et al., 2002) undoubtedly arouses egalitarian thoughts in the public. Thus, the influence of egalitarian thought should not be ignored.

Egalitarianism may influence public acceptability of proposed policies in the following ways (see also Liu, 2022; Liu et al., 2019; Liu et al., 2020; Liu et al., 2021a, b):

- A call for egalitarian revenue allocation. When people get the feeling that a particular group of people suffers less from the proposed scheme, discontent is unavoidable.
- A feeling of being oppressed. The discontented mood can diffuse quickly across the public because no one is happy with being charged without any expected benefits. Thus, members of a variety of social strata feel oppressed to some extent. Due to Chinese egalitarianism, the winners from the policy may not deem themselves as winners, but the losers will recognise that they are losers without the slightest hesitation.
- Conflict between winners and losers. Due to Chinese egalitarianism, lay-citizens will not easily be convinced that they are winners from the policy. Moreover, the government, which will be considered as the biggest winner, will ineluctably become a common target of public criticism.

2.3.3 Summary

This section has briefly introduced Chinese traditional schools of thoughts, cultural values, and history. These bodies of literature comprehensively explicate the Chinese context and explore culture-specific factors that are potentially important for the public acceptability of congestion charging. There are at least four issues that to consider in research on public acceptability in the Chinese context. Firstly, due to the traditional state–people relations and China's political system, public acceptability may play a different role in policymaking, which should be properly understood prior to investigating the determinants of public acceptability. Secondly, because of a long tradition of Confucian–Legalist cultivation, a norm of obedience to authority is rooted within Chinese people, who conform to traditional standards of behaviours that the ruling classes require. Thirdly, attitudes towards the government in general may significantly influence the acceptability of the proposed scheme—those who believe the government has every right to do whatever it wants, as obedient subjects of an emperor, can never find the words of the government unacceptable. Fourthly, the Chinese interpretation of equity has a pronounced egalitarian tendency, which may lead to an expectation of egalitarian distribution of resources. Consequently, antipathy between different groups may be exacerbated because of a policy that favours some groups of people, such as congestion charging. Lastly, rural–urban migrants and other *hukou*-related inequity issues are worth consideration since migrants might be the biggest losers from the policy.

References

Aarts, H., & Dijksterhuis, A. (2003). The silence of the library: Environment, situational norm, and social behavior. *Journal of Personality and Social Psychology, 84*(1), 18.

Abrego, L. J. (2011). Legal consciousness of undocumented Latinos: Fear and stigma as barriers to claims-making for first- and 1.5-generation immigrants. *Law & Society Review, 45*(2), 337–370.

Ajzen, I. (1991). The theory of planned behavior. *Organizational Behavior and Human Decision Processes, 50*(2), 179–211.

Bachman, D. (2006). *Bureaucracy, economy, and leadership in China: The institutional origins of the Great Leap Forward*. Cambridge University Press.

Barnouin, B., & Yu, C. (1993). *Ten years of turbulence: The Chinese cultural revolution*. Routledge.

Benedict, R. (1967). *The chrysanthemum and the sword: Patterns of Japanese culture*. Houghton Mifflin Harcourt.

Berthoff, R. (1982). Peasants and artisans, puritans and republicans: Personal liberty and communal equality in American history. *The Journal of American History, 69*(3), 579–598.

Bian, Y. (2002). Chinese social stratification and social mobility. *Annual Review of Sociology*, 91–116.

Bicchieri, C. (2005). *The grammar of society: The nature and dynamics of social norms*. Cambridge University Press.

Bicchieri, C. (2010). Norms, preferences, and conditional behavior. *Politics, Philosophy & Economics, 9*(3), 297–313.

Bird, J., & Morris, J. (2006). *Steering through change: Winning the debate on road pricing*. Institute for Public Policy Research.

Bird, J., & Vigor, A. (2006). *Charging forward-a review of public attitudes towards road pricing in the UK*.

Bonsall, P., & Lythgoe, B. (2009). Factors affecting the amount of effort expended in responding to questions in behavioural choice experiments. *Journal of Choice Modelling, 2*(2), 216–236.

Borins, S. F. (1988). Electronic road pricing: An idea whose time may never come. *Transportation Research Part A: General, 22*(1), 37–44.

Börjesson, M., Eliasson, J., Hugosson, M. B., & Brundell-Freij, K. (2012). The Stockholm congestion charges—5 years on. Effects, acceptability and lessons learnt. *Transport Policy, 20*, 1–12.

Bröcker, J., Korzhenevych, A., & Schürmann, C. (2010). Assessing spatial equity and efficiency impacts of transport infrastructure projects. *Transportation Research Part B: Methodological, 44*(7), 795–811.

Brown, B. E. (1991). *The Buddha nature: A study of the Tathāgatagarbha and Ālayavijñāna* (Vol. 11). Motilal Banarsidass Publ.

Cervero, R., & Day, J. (2008). Suburbanization and transit-oriented development in China. *Transport Policy, 15*(5), 315–323.

Chan, W. T. (2008). *A Source Book in Chinese Philosophy*. Princeton University Press.

Chang, C. (1963). Creativity and Taoism: A study of Chinese philosophy, art, and poetry. *Philosophy East and West, 13*(1), 74–77.

Chang, C. S. (2007). *The Rise of the Chinese Empire: Nation, state, & imperialism in early China, ca. 1600 BC–AD 8*. University of Michigan Press.

Chen, H., Pu, X., Xiangzhao, F., & Fen, L. (2008). Public attitudes towards policy instruments for congestion mitigation in Shanghai. *Chinese Journal of Population Resources and Environment, 6*(3), 40–47.

Chen, X. (2000). Growing up in a collectivist culture: Socialization and socioemotional development in Chinese children. In A. L. Comunian & U. P. Gielen

(Eds.), *International perspectives on human development* (pp. 331–353). Pabst Science.

Chen, X., & Zhang, H. (2012, January). Evaluate the effects of car ownership policies in Chinese megacities: A contrastive study of Beijing and Shanghai. In *91st Annual Meeting. Transportation Research Board Conference* (pp. 22–26).

Chen, X., & Zhao, J. (2013). Bidding to drive: Car license auction policy in Shanghai and its public acceptance. *Transport Policy, 27*, 39–52.

Chen, Y., & Zhou, L. A. (2007). The long-term health and economic consequences of the 1959–1961 famine in China. *Journal of Health Economics, 26*(4), 659–681.

Cheng, F., Zhang, X., & Shenggen, F. (2002). Emergence of urban poverty and inequality in China: Evidence from household survey. *China Economic Review, 13*(4), 430–443.

Cherry, C., & Cervero, R. (2007). Use characteristics and mode choice behavior of electric bike users in China. *Transport Policy, 14*(3), 247–257.

Cherry, C. R., Yang, H., Jones, L. R., & He, M. (2016). Dynamics of electric bike ownership and use in Kunming, China. *Transport Policy, 45*, 127–135.

Cheung, M., & Liu, M. (2004). The self-concept of Chinese women and the indigenization of social work in China. *International Social Work, 47*(1), 109–127.

Chow, T. T. (2013). *May Fourth Movement*. Harvard University Press.

Christiansen, F., & Rai, S. M. (2014). *Chinese politics and society: An introduction*. Routledge.

Chu, H., & Gardner, D. K. (1990). *Learning to Be a Sage: Selections from the "Conversations of Master Chu," Arranged Topically*. University of California Press.

Chuang-tzu, & Palmer, M. (2006). *The Book of Chuang Tzu*. Penguin UK.

Clark, P. (2008). *The Chinese cultural revolution: A history*. Cambridge University Press.

Clee, A. (2007). *Driving away the traffic: What lessons can New York learn from London and Stockholm's experiences with congestion charging*. Tufts University.

Clinton, R. L. (1997). *God and man in the law: The foundations of Anglo-American constitutionalism*. University Press of Kansas.

Cohen, M. L. (1991). Being Chinese: The peripheralization of traditional identity. *Daedalus*, 113–134.

Cole, M., & Scribner, S. (1974). *Culture & thought: A psychological introduction*. Wiley.

Coleman, J. S. (1994). *Foundations of social theory*. Harvard University Press.

Corbett, R. (2009). The question of natural law in Aristotle. *History of Political Thought, 30*(2), 229–250.

Cullinane, S., & Cullinane, K. (2003). Car dependence in a public transport dominated city: Evidence from Hong Kong. *Transportation Research Part D: Transport and Environment, 8*(2), 129–138.

D'Amato, A. (2011). *On the connection between law and justice* (Faculty Working Papers No. 2). http://scholarlycommons.law.northwestern.edu/facultyworkingpapers/2

De Groot, J., & Schuitema, G. (2012). How to make the unpopular popular? Policy characteristics, social norms and the acceptability of environmental policies. *Environmental Science & Policy, 19*, 100–107.

De Groot, J., & Steg, L. (2006). Impact of transport pricing on quality of life, acceptability, and intentions to reduce car use: An exploratory study in five European countries. *Journal of Transport Geography, 14*(6), 463–470.

De Jong, M. (2012). The pros and cons of Confucian values in transport infrastructure development in China. *Policy and Society, 31*(1), 13–24.

De Jong, M., Mu, R., Stead, D., Ma, Y., & Xi, B. (2010). Introducing public–private partnerships for metropolitan subways in China: What is the evidence? *Journal of Transport Geography, 18*(2), 301–313.

Defoort, C. (2001). Is there such a thing as Chinese philosophy? Arguments of an implicit debate. *Philosophy East and West*, 393–413.

Dikötter, F. (2010). *Mao's great famine: The history of China's most devastating catastrophe, 1958–1962.* Bloomsbury Publishing USA.

Dittmer, L. (1974). *Liu Shao-Chi and the Chinese cultural revolution: The politics of mass criticism* (No. 10). University of California Press.

Domes, J. (1982). New Policies in the Communes: Notes on Rural Societal Structures in China, 1976–1981. *The Journal of Asian Studies, 41*(02), 253–267.

Dutton, M. R. (1992). *Policing and punishment in China: From patriarchy to "the people"* (Vol. 141). Cambridge University Press.

Duyvendak, J. J. L. (1928). *The Book of Lord Shang*. Probsthain.

Dyck, A. R. (2004). *A commentary on Cicero.* University of Michigan Press.

Eagleton, T. (1991). *Ideology: An introduction* (Vol. 9). Verso.

Eliasson, J., & Jonsson, L. (2011). The unexpected "yes": Explanatory factors behind the positive attitudes to congestion charges in Stockholm. *Transport Policy, 18*(4), 636–647.

Eliasson, J., & Mattsson, L. G. (2006). Equity effects of congestion pricing: Quantitative methodology and a case study for Stockholm. *Transportation Research Part A: Policy and Practice, 40*(7), 602–620.

Ellickson, R. C. (2009). *Order without law: How neighbors settle disputes.* Harvard University Press.

Englehart, N. A. (2000). Rights and culture in the Asian values argument: The rise and fall of Confucian ethics in Singapore. *Human Rights Quarterly, 22*(2), 548–568.

Erie, M. S. (2012). Property rights, legal consciousness and the new media in China: The hard case of the 'toughest nail-house in history.' *China Information, 26*(1), 35–59.

Eriksson, L., Garvill, J., & Nordlund, A. M. (2006). Acceptability of travel demand management measures: The importance of problem awareness, personal norm, freedom, and fairness. *Journal of Environmental Psychology, 26*(1), 15–26.

Eriksson, L., Garvill, J., & Nordlund, A. M. (2008). Acceptability of single and combined transport policy measures: The importance of environmental and policy specific beliefs. *Transportation Research Part A: Policy and Practice, 42*(8), 1117–1128.

Fan, C. S. (2016). *Culture, institution, and development in China: The economics of national character*. Routledge.

Fan, Y. (2000). A classification of Chinese culture. *Cross Cultural Management: An International Journal, 7*(2), 3–10.

Farrell, S., & Saleh, W. (2005). Road-user charging and the modelling of revenue allocation. *Transport Policy, 12*(5), 431–442.

Fei, X., Hamilton, G. G., & Wang, Z. (1992). *From the soil, the foundations of Chinese society: A translation of Fei Xiaotong's Xiangtu Zhongguo, with an introduction and epilogue*. University of California Press.

Feng, S., & Ma, Z. (2010). *Performance analysis on private vehicle plate auction in Shanghai*. 6th Advanced Forum on Transportation of China (AFTC 2010).

Feng, S. W., Li, Q., & Xu, D. (2012). *The Private Car License Plate Auction in Shanghai: Macro-Effectiveness and Micro-Mechanisms*[C]. COTA International Conference of Transportation Professionals, Beijing.

Feng, J., Dijst, M., Wissink, B., & Prillwitz, J. (2017). Changing travel behaviour in urban China: Evidence from Nanjing 2008–2011. *Transport Policy, 53*, 1–10.

Feng, Y., & Bodde, D. (1983). *A history of Chinese philosophy* (Vol. 1). Princeton University Press.

Festinger, L. (1962). *A theory of cognitive dissonance* (Vol. 2). Stanford University Press.

Finnis, J. (2011). *Natural law and natural rights*. Oxford University Press.

Flad, R. K. (2011). *Salt production and social hierarchy in ancient China: An archaeological investigation of specialization in China's Three Gorges*. Cambridge University Press.

Frederickson, H. G. (2002). Confucius and the moral basis of bureaucracy. *Administration & Society, 33*(6), 610–628.

Fromm, E., Suzuki, D. T., & De Martino, R. (1970). *Zen Buddhism and psychoanalysis*. Harpercollins.

Fu, Z. (1996). *China's legalists: The earliest totalitarians and their art of ruling*. ME Sharpe.

Fu, Q. (2015). From the founding to the ruling party: The identity crisis of Mao Zedong and the Communist Party of China. *Fudan Journal of the Humanities and Social Sciences, 8*(3), 447–469.

Fu, Z. (1993). *Autocratic tradition and Chinese politics*. Cambridge University Press.

Fukuyama, F. (1995). Confucianism and democracy. *Journal of Democracy, 6*(2), 20–33.

Gallagher, M. E. (2006). Mobilizing the law in China: "Informed disenchantment" and the development of legal consciousness. *Law & Society Review, 40*(4), 783–816.

Gan, H., & Ye, X. (2018). Will commute drivers switch to park-and-ride under the influence of multimodal traveler information? A stated preference investigation. *Transportation Research Part F: Traffic Psychology and Behaviour, 56*, 354–361.

Gärling, T., & Schuitema, G. (2007). Travel demand management targeting reduced private car use: Effectiveness, public acceptability and political feasibility. *Journal of Social Issues, 63*(1), 139–153.

Gastil, J., Black, L., & Moscovitz, K. (2008). Ideology, attitude change, and deliberation in small face-to-face groups. *Political Communication, 25*(1), 23–46.

Gaunt, M., Rye, T., & Allen, S. (2007). Public acceptability of road user charging: The case of Edinburgh and the 2005 referendum. *Transport Reviews, 27*(1), 85–102.

Geng, J., Long, R., & Chen, H. (2016). Impact of information intervention on travel mode choice of urban residents with different goal frames: A controlled trial in Xuzhou, China. *Transportation Research Part A: Policy and Practice, 91*, 134–147.

Giuliano, G. (1994). Equity and fairness considerations of congestion pricing. *Transportation Research Board Special Report*, 242.

Goldin, P. R. (2011). Persistent Misconceptions about Chinese "Legalism." *Journal of Chinese Philosophy, 38*(1), 88–104.

Graham, A. C. (1989). *Disputes ofthe Tao: Philosophical arguments in ancient china*. Open Court.

Gray, D., & Begg, D. (2001). *Delivering congestion charging in the UK: What is required for its successful introduction?* Robert Gordon University.

Guo, S., & Guo, B. (Eds.). (2008). *China in search of a harmonious society*. Lexington Books.

Gustafsson, B. A., Shi, L., & Sicular, T. (Eds.). (2008). *Inequality and public policy in China*. Cambridge University Press.

Han, F., & Watson, B. (1964). *Han Fei Tzu*. Columbia University Press.

Hao, H., Wang, H., & Ouyang, M. (2011). Comparison of policies on vehicle ownership and use between Beijing and Shanghai and their impacts on fuel consumption by passenger vehicles. *Energy Policy, 39*(2), 1016–1021.

Hau, T. D. (1990). Electronic road pricing: Developments in Hong Kong 1983–1989. *Journal of Transport Economics and Policy, 24*(2), 203–214.

Hayek, F. A. (1960 [2014]). *The constitution of liberty*. Routledge.

He, K., Huo, H., Zhang, Q., He, D. (2005). Oil consumption and CO_2 emissions in China's road transport: Current status, future trends, and policy implications. *Energy Policy, 33*(12), 1499–1507.

He, L. Y., & Qiu, L. Y. (2016). Transport demand, harmful emissions, environment and health co-benefits in China. *Energy Policy, 97*, 267–275.

Hechter, M., & Opp, K. D. (Eds.). (2001). *Social norms*. Russell Sage Foundation.

Hegel, G. W. F., & Brown, R. F. (2006). *Lectures on the history of philosophy: Greek philosophy* (Vol. 1). Oxford University Press.

Hellman, J. S. (1998). Winners take all: The politics of partial reform in post communist transitions. *World Politics, 50*(02), 203–234.

Heng, C. K. (1999). *Cities of aristocrats and bureaucrats: The development of medieval Chinese cityscapes*. University of Hawaii Press.

Hensher, D. A., & Puckett, S. M. (2007). Congestion and variable user charging as an effective travel demand management instrument. *Transportation Research Part A: Policy and Practice, 41*(7), 615–626.

Hobbes, T. (1651 [2006]). *Leviathan*. A&C Black.

Holcombe, C. (2011). *A history of East Asia: From the origins of civilization to the twenty-first century*. Cambridge University Press.

Holloway Jr, R. L. (1969). Culture: A human domain. *Current Anthropology*, 395–412.

Hong, J., Chu, Z., & Wang, Q. (2011). Transport infrastructure and regional economic growth: Evidence from China. *Transportation, 38*(5), 737–752.

Hookham, S. K. (1991). *The Buddha within: Tathagatagarbha doctrine according to the Shentong interpretation of the Ratnagotravibhaga* (No. 104). SUNY Press.

Hou, Q., & Li, S. M. (2011). Transport infrastructure development and changing spatial accessibility in the Greater Pearl River Delta, China, 1990–2020. *Journal of Transport Geography, 19*(6), 1350–1360.

Howell, J. (1993). *China opens its doors: The politics of economic transition*. Harvester Wheatsheaf.

Hsiao, K. C. (1976). Legalism and autocracy in traditional China. *Chinese Studies in History, 10*(1–2), 125–143.

Huang, S. C. (1999). *Essentials of neo-Confucianism: Eight major philosophers of the Song and Ming periods*. Greenwood Publishing Group.

Ip, P. K. (2009). Is Confucianism good for business ethics in China? *Journal of Business Ethics, 88*(3), 463–476.

Ip, P. K. (2009). The challenge of developing a business ethics in China. *Journal of Business Ethics, 88*(1), 211–224.

Jacobs, L., Guopei, G., & Herbig, P. (1995). Confucian roots in China: A force for today's business. *Management Decision, 33*(10), 29–34.

Jaensirisak, S., Wardman, M., & May, A. D. (2005). Explaining variations in public acceptability of road pricing schemes. *Journal of Transport Economics and Policy, 39*(2), 127–153.

Jakobsson, C., Fujii, S., & Gärling, T. (2000). Determinants of private car users' acceptance of road pricing. *Transport Policy, 7*(2), 153–158.

James, P. (2014). *Urban sustainability in theory and practice: Circles of sustainability*. Routledge.

James, P., & Steger, M. (2010). *Globalization and culture, Vol. 4: Ideologies of globalism*. Sage.

Jensen, A. F., Cherchi, E., & Mabit, S. L. (2013). On the stability of preferences and attitudes before and after experiencing an electric vehicle. *Transportation Research Part D: Transport and Environment, 25*, 24–32.

Jin, Q. (1999). *The culture of power: The Lin Biao incident in the Cultural Revolution*. Stanford University Press.

Joireman, J. A., Lasane, T. P., Bennett, J., Richards, D., & Solaimani, S. (2001). Integrating social value orientation and the consideration of future consequences within the extended norm activation model of proenvironmental behaviour. *British Journal of Social Psychology, 40*(1), 133–155.

Kelman, H. C., & Hamilton, V. L. (1989). *Crimes of obedience: Toward a social psychology of authority and responsibility*. Yale University Press.

Kenworthy, J., & Hu, G. (2002). Transport and urban form in Chinese cities: an international comparative and policy perspective with implications for sustainable urban transport in China. *disP-The Planning Review, 38*(151), 4–14.

Kim, J., Schmöcker, J. D., Fujii, S., & Noland, R. B. (2013). Attitudes towards road pricing and environmental taxation among US and UK students. *Transportation Research Part A: Policy and Practice, 48*, 50–62.

Kirkbride, P. S., Tang, S. F., & Westwood, R. I. (1991). Chinese conflict preferences and negotiating behaviour: Cultural and psychological influences. *Organization Studies, 12*(3), 365–386.

Kirkland, R. (2004). *Taoism: The enduring tradition*. Routledge.

Kitamura, R., Nakayama, S., & Yamamoto, T. (1999). Self-reinforcing motorization: Can travel demand management take us out of the social trap? *Transport Policy, 6*(3), 135–145.

Kottenhoff, K., & Freij, K. B. (2009). The role of public transport for feasibility and acceptability of congestion charging—The case of Stockholm. *Transportation Research Part A: Policy and Practice, 43*(3), 297–305.

Kroeber, A. L., & Kluckhohn, C. (1952). *Culture: A critical review of concepts and definitions*. Harvard University.

Kuang-Chien, C. (1971). ON THE AMPHIBIAN NATURE OF THOUGHT. *Chinese Studies in Philosophy, 2*(4), 264–267.

Kung, J. K. S., & Lin, J. Y. (2003). The causes of China's Great Leap Famine, 1959–1961*. *Economic Development and Cultural Change, 52*(1), 51–73.

Kutcher, N. (2000). The fifth relationship: Dangerous friendships in the Confucian context. *The American Historical Review, 105*(5), 1615–1629.

Laozi, Roig, J. V., & Little, S. (2007). *Tao te ching*. National Braille Press.

Lee, H. Y. (1980). *The politics of the Chinese cultural revolution: A case study* (No. 17). University of California Press.

Lee, K. K. (1998). Confucian tradition in the contemporary Korean family. *Confucianism and the Family*, 249–266.

Lee, T. H. (2000). *Education in traditional China: A history* (Vol. 13). Brill.

Legge, J. (2009). *The Confucian analects, the great learning & the doctrine of the mean*. Cosimo Inc.

Leng, S. C. (1977). The role of law in the People's Republic of China as reflecting Mao Tse-Tung's influence. *Journal of Criminal Law and Criminology*, 356–373.

Lewis, M. E. (2009). *The early Chinese Empires* (Vol. 1). Harvard University Press.

Li, T., Yang, W., Zhang, H., & Cao, X. (2016). Evaluating the impact of transport investment on the efficiency of regional integrated transport systems in China. *Transport Policy, 45*, 66–76.

Lieberthal, K. (1995). *Governing China: From revolution through reform*. WW Norton.

Lin, Y. (2013). *My country and my people*. Read Books Ltd.

Lindley, A. F. (1866). *Ti-ping Tien-kwoh: The History of the Ti-ping Revolution* (Vol. 1). Day & son (limited).

Link, H., & Polak, J. (2003). Acceptability of transport pricing measures among public and professionals in Europe. *Transportation Research Record: Journal of the Transportation Research Board, 1839*, 34–44.

Litman, T. (1999). *The costs of automobile dependency*. Victoria Transportation Policy Institute.

Litman, T. (2002). Evaluating transportation equity. *World Transport Policy & Practice, 8*(2), 50–65.

Litman, T. (2012). *London congestion pricing: Implications for other cities*. Victoria Transport Policy Institute.

Little, D. (1989). *Understanding peasant China: Case studies in the philosophy of social science*. Yale University Press.

Liu, M. W. (1982). The Doctrine of the Buddha-Nature in the Mahāyāna Mahāparinirvāṇa Sūtra. *Journal of the International Association of Buddhist Studies, 5*(2), 63–94.

Liu, Q. (2022). Immobility: Surviving the COVID-19 outbreak. In *Human security in China* (pp. 133–154). Palgrave Macmillan.

Liu, Q., An, Z., Liu, Y., Ying, W., & Zhao, P. (2021a). Smartphone-based services, perceived accessibility, and transport inequity during the COVID-19 pandemic: A cross-lagged panel study. *Transportation Research Part D: Transport and Environment, 97*, 102941.

Liu, Q., Liu, Y., Zhang, C., An, Z., & Zhao, P. (2021b). Elderly mobility during the COVID-19 pandemic: A qualitative exploration in Kunming, China. *Journal of Transport Geography, 96*, 103176.

Liu, Q., Lucas, K., & Marsden, G. (2020). Public acceptability of congestion charging in Beijing, China: How transferrable are Western ideas of public acceptability? *International Journal of Sustainable Transportation, 15*(2), 97–110.

Liu, Q., Lucas, K., Marsden, G., & Liu, Y. (2019). Egalitarianism and public perception of social inequities: A case study of Beijing congestion charge. *Transport Policy, 74*, 47–62.

Liu, T., & Ceder, A. A. (2015). Analysis of a new public-transport-service concept: Customized bus in China. *Transport Policy, 39*, 63–76.

Liu, Y. (1998). *Origins of Chinese law: Penal and administrative law in its early development*. Oxford University Press.

Liu, Z., Li, R., Wang, X. C., & Shang, P. (2018). Effects of vehicle restriction policies: Analysis using license plate recognition data in Langfang, China. *Transportation Research Part A: Policy and Practice, 118*, 89–103.

Locke, J. (1690 [1978]). *Two Treatises of Government*. E. P. Dutton.

Loewe, M. (Ed.). (1993). *Early Chinese texts: A bibliographical guide* (No. 2). University of California Inst of East.

Loewe, M. (1994). Huang Lao thought and the Huainanzi. *Journal of the Royal Asiatic Society (Third Series), 4*(3), 377–395.

Loewe, M., & Shaughnessy, E. L. (1999). *The Cambridge history of ancient China: From the origins of civilization to 221 BC*. Cambridge University Press.

Loo, B. P. (1999). Development of a regional transport infrastructure: Some lessons from the Zhujiang Delta, Guangdong China. *Journal of Transport Geography, 7*(1), 43–63.

Lorge, P. (2006). *War, politics and society in early modern China, 900–1795*. Routledge.

Low, K. C. P. (2011). Confucianism versus Taoism. *Conflict Resolution & Negotiation Journal, 2011*(4), 111–127.

Lu, X. (1990). *Diary of a madman and other stories*. University of Hawaii Press.

Luo, C. (2004). Uncertainty during economic transition and household consumption behavior in Urban China. *Economic Research Journal, 4*, 010.

Lyon, A. (2008). Rhetorical authority in Athenian democracy and the Chinese legalism of Han Fei. *Philosophy and Rhetoric, 41*(1), 51–71.

MacFarquhar, R. (1997). *The origins of the cultural revolution* (Vol. 3). Oxford University Press.

MacFarquhar, R., & Mao, Z. (1989). *The Secret Speeches of Chairman Mao: From the Hundred Flowers to the Great Leap Forward*. Harvard University Press.

Major, J. S. (1993). *Heaven and earth in early Han thought: Chapters three, four, and five of the Huainanzi*. SUNY Press.

Marsden, G., & Stead, D. (2011). Policy transfer and learning in the field of transport: A review of concepts and evidence. *Transport Policy, 18*(3), 492–500.

McQuaid, R., & Grieco, M. (2005). Edinburgh and the politics of congestion charging: Negotiating road user charging with affected publics. *Transport Policy, 12*(5), 475–476.

Merry, S. E. (1990). *Getting justice and getting even: Legal consciousness among working-class Americans*. University of Chicago Press.

Miola, A. (2008). *Backcasting approach for sustainable mobility*. EUR—Scientific and Technical Research series—ISSN 1018-5593—ISBN 978-92-79-09189-6. Office for Official Publications of the European Communities Luxembourg.

Mok, L. W., & Wong, D. S. (2013). Restorative justice and mediation: Diverged or converged? *Asian Journal of Criminology, 8*(4), 335–347.

Moore, C. A. (1967). *The Chinese mind: Essentials of Chinese philosophy and culture*. University of Hawaii Press.

Morton, C., Schuitema, G., & Anable, J. (2011, January). Electric vehicles: Will consumers get charged up. In *Universities's Transport Study Group Conference*.

Mu, R., De Jong, M., & Koppenjan, J. (2011). The rise and fall of Public-Private Partnerships in China: A path-dependent approach. *Journal of Transport Geography, 19*(4), 794–806.

Muller, E. N., Seligson, M. A., & Midlarsky, M. I. (1989). Land inequality and political violence. *American Political Science Review, 83*(2), 577–596.

Needham, J., Wang, L., & Lu, G. D. (1963). *Science and civilisation in China*. Cambridge University Press.

Needham, J. (1981). *Science in traditional China: A comparative perspective*. Chinese University Press.

Newman, P., & Kenworthy, J. (1999). Costs of automobile dependence: Global survey of cities. *Transportation Research Record: Journal of the Transportation Research Board, 1670*, 17–26.

Nie, Y. (2017). Why is license plate rationing not a good transport policy? *Transportmetrica A: Transport Science, 13*(1), 1–23.

Ó Gráda, C. (2011). *Great Leap into Famine*. http://irserver.ucd.ie/bitstream/handle/10197/6378/WP11_03.pdf?sequence=1. Accessed 27 July 2019.

O'Brien, K. J., & Li, L. (2004). Suing the local state: Administrative litigation in rural China. *The China Journal, 51*, 75–96.

Oehry, B. (2010). *Critical success factors for implementing road charging systems*. OECD Publishing.

Park, H., Rehg, M. T., & Lee, D. (2005). The influence of Confucian ethics and collectivism on whistle blowing intentions: A study of South Korean public employees. *Journal of Business Ethics, 58*(4), 387–403.

Park, M., & Chesla, C. (2007). Revisiting Confucianism as a conceptual framework for Asian family study. *Journal of Family Nursing, 13*(3), 293–311.

Pines, Y. (2012). *The everlasting empire: The political culture of ancient China and its imperial legacy*. Princeton University Press.

Pines, Y. (2014). *Legalism in Chinese Philosophy* (Winter 2014 Edition, E. N. Zalta, Eds.). The Stanford Encyclopedia of Philosophy. http://plato.stanford.edu/archives/win2014/entries/chinese-legalism/. Accessed 27 July 2019.

Ping, L. (2001). The Influence of "Three Religions in One" on the Peasants' Spirit of Revolt—An Exploration in the Perspective of the Secret Societies in China. *Journal of Jiangsu Institute of Education, 2*, 019.

Posner, E. A. (2009). *Law and social norms*. Harvard University Press.

Pucher, J., Peng, Z., Mittal, N., Zhu, Y., Korattyswaroopam, N. (2007). Urban transport trends and policies in China and India: Impacts of rapid economic growth. *Transport Reviews, 27*(4), 379–410.

Pye, M. W., & Pye, L. W. (2009). *Asian power and politics: The cultural dimensions of authority*. Harvard University Press.

Raux, C., & Souche, S. (2004). The acceptability of urban road pricing: A theoretical analysis applied to experience in Lyon. *Journal of Transport Economics and Policy, 38*(2), 191–215.

Rawski, T. G., & Li, L. M. (1992). *Chinese history in economic perspective*. University of California Press.

Reilly, T. H. (2004). *The Taiping Heavenly Kingdom: Rebellion and the Blasphemy of Empire*. University of Washington Press.

Rickett, W. A., & Guan, Z. (2001). *Guanzi: Political, economic, and philosophical essays from early China, a study and translation*. Cheng & Tsui.

Rienstra, S. A., Rietveld, P., & Verhoef, E. T. (1999). The social support for policy measures in passenger transport: A statistical analysis for the Netherlands. *Transportation Research Part D: Transport and Environment, 4*(3), 181–200.

Riskin, C., Zhao, R., & Li, S. (2001). *China's retreat from equality: Income distribution and economic transition*. ME Sharpe.

Robinet, I. (1997). *Taoism: Growth of a religion*. Stanford University Press.

Russell, B. (2013). *History of western philosophy* (Collectors). Routledge.

Rye, T., Gaunt, M., & Ison, S. (2008). Edinburgh's congestion charging plans: An analysis of reasons for non-implementation. *Transportation Planning and Technology, 31*(6), 641–661.

Sailey, J. (1978). *The master who embraces simplicity: A study of the philosopher Ko Hung, AD 283–343*. Chinese Materials Center Inc.

Santos, G., & Shaffer, B. (2004). Preliminary results of the London congestion charging scheme. *Public Works Management & Policy, 9*(2), 164–181.

Saunders, J. P. (2005). The rise and fall of Edinburgh's congestion charging plans. *Proceedings of the Institution of Civil Engineers-Transport, 158*(4), 193–220.

Savvanidou, E., Zervas, E., & Tsagarakis, K. P. (2010). Public acceptance of biofuels. *Energy Policy, 38*(7), 3482–3488.

Schade, J., & Schlag, B. (2003). Acceptability of urban transport pricing strategies. *Transportation Research Part F: Traffic Psychology and Behaviour, 6*(1), 45–61.

Schade, J., & Baum, M. (2007). Reactance or acceptance? Reactions towards the introduction of road pricing. *Transportation Research Part A: Policy and Practice, 41*(1), 41–48.

Schade, J., & Schlag, B. (2000b). *Acceptability of urban transport pricing* (VATT Research Reports 72). Helsinki.

Schlag, B., & Teubel, U. (1997). Public acceptability of transport pricing. *IATSS Research, 21*, 134–142.

Schmöcker, J. D., Pettersson, P., & Fujii, S. (2012). Comparative analysis of proximal and distal determinants for the acceptance of coercive charging policies in the UK and Japan. *International Journal of Sustainable Transportation, 6*(3), 156–173.

Schneider, A. (2003). Reconciling history with the nation? Historicity, national particularity, and the question of universals. *Historiography East and West, 1*(1), 117–136.

Schuitema, G., Steg, L., & Forward, S. (2010). Explaining differences in acceptability before and acceptance after the implementation of a congestion charge in Stockholm. *Transportation Research Part A: Policy and Practice, 44*(2), 99–109.

Schuitema, G., & Steg, L. (2008). The role of revenue use in the acceptability of transport pricing policies. *Transportation Research Part F: Traffic Psychology and Behaviour, 11*(3), 221–231.

Schwarcz, V. (1986). *The Chinese enlightenment: Intellectuals and the legacy of the May Fourth Movement of 1919*. University of California Press.

Seidel, A. K. (1969). The image of the perfect ruler in early Taoist Messianism: Lao-tzu and Li Hung. *History of Religions, 9*(2/3), 216–247.

Shang, Y. (2017). *The book of Lord Shang: Apologetics of state power in early China*. Columbia University Press.

Shook, N. J., & Fazio, R. H. (2009). Political ideology, exploration of novel stimuli, and attitude formation. *Journal of Experimental Social Psychology, 45*(4), 995–998.

Silbey, S. S. (1998). *The common place of law: Stories from everyday life*. University of Chicago Press.

Sima, Q. (2011). *Records of the grand historian*. Columbia University Press.

Spence, J. D. (1996). *God's Chinese Son: The Taiping Heavenly Kingdom of Hong Xiuquan*. WW Norton & Company.

Steg, L. (2005). Car use: lust and must. Instrumental, symbolic and affective motives for car use. *Transportation Research Part A: Policy and Practice, 39*(2), 147–162.

Steg, L., Dreijerink, L., & Abrahamse, W. (2006). Why are energy policies acceptable and effective? *Environment and Behavior, 38*(1), 92–111.

Stokes, G., & Taylor, B. (1995). The public acceptability of sustainable transport policies: Findings from the British Social Attitudes survey. *PTRC-PUBLICATIONS-P*, 121–136.

Su, C., & Littlefield, J. E. (2001). Entering guanxi: A business ethical dilemma in mainland China? *Journal of Business Ethics, 33*(3), 199–210.

Suen, H., Cheung, S. O., & Mondejar, R. (2007). Managing ethical behaviour in construction organizations in Asia: How do the teachings of Confucianism, Taoism and Buddhism and Globalization influence ethics management? *International Journal of Project Management, 25*(3), 257–265.

Tzu, S. (2011). *The art of war*. Shambhala Publications.

Sun, X., Feng, S., & Lu, J. (2016). Psychological factors influencing the public acceptability of congestion pricing in China. *Transportation Research Part F: Traffic Psychology and Behaviour, 41*, 104–112.

Sun, Y., & Cui, Y. (2018). Evaluating the coordinated development of economic, social and environmental benefits of urban public transportation infrastructure: Case study of four Chinese autonomous municipalities. *Transport Policy, 66*, 116–126.

Sutter, R. G. (2012). *Chinese foreign relations: Power and policy since the Cold War*. Rowman & Littlefield Publishers.

Tang, S., & Lo, H. K. (2008). The impact of public transport policy on the viability and sustainability of mass railway transit—The Hong Kong experience. *Transportation Research Part A: Policy and Practice, 42*(4), 563–576.

Taylor, B., & Brook, L. (1998). Public Attitudes to transport issues: Findings from the British social attitudes surveys. *Transport Policy and the Environment*.

Tertoolen, G., Van Kreveld, D., & Verstraten, B. (1998). Psychological resistance against attempts to reduce private car use. *Transportation Research Part A: Policy and Practice, 32*(3), 171–181.

The Chinese Culture Connection. (1987). Chinese Values and the Search for Culture-Free Dimensions of Culture: The Chinese Culture Connection. *Journal of Cross-Cultural Psychology, 18*(2), 143–64.

Thorpe, N., Hills, P., & Jaensirisak, S. (2000). Public attitudes to TDM measures: A comparative study. *Transport Policy, 7*(4), 243–257.

Triandis, H. C. (1994). *Culture and social behavior*. Mcgraw-Hill Book Company.

Tylor, E. B. (2010). *Primitive culture: Researches into the development of mythology, philosophy, religion, art, and custom*. Cambridge University Press.

van Ess, H., Elman, B. A., Duncan, J. B., & Ooms, H. (2005). Rethinking confucianism, past and present in China, Japan, Korea, and Vietnam. *Monumenta Serica, 53*, 500–504.

Van Vuuren, D., Fengqi, Z., De Vries, B., Kejun, J., Graveland, C., & Yun, L. (2003). Energy and emission scenarios for China in the 21st century—Exploration of baseline development and mitigation options. *Energy Policy, 31*(4), 369–387.

Vermeer, E. B. (2004). Egalitarianism and the land question in China a survey of three thousand households in industrializing Wuxi and Agricultural Baoding. *China Information, 18*(1), 107–140.

Verplanken, B., Aarts, H., & Van Knippenberg, A. (1997). Habit, information acquisition, and the process of making travel mode choices. *European Journal of Social Psychology, 27*, 539–560.

Viegas, J. M. (2001). Making urban road pricing acceptable and effective: Searching for quality and equity in urban mobility. *Transport Policy, 8*(4), 289–294.

Wang, R. (2010). Shaping urban transport policies in China: Will copying foreign policies work? *Transport Policy, 17*(3), 147–152.

Weber, M., & Gerth, H. H. (1953). *The religion of China, Confucianism and Taoism*. Routledge and Kegan Paul.

Wilkinson, E. P. (2000). *Chinese history: A manual* (Vol. 52). Harvard University Asia Center.

Williams, R. (1983). *Culture and society, 1780–1950*. Columbia University Press.

Wong, Y., & Tsai, J. (2007). Cultural models of shame and guilt. *The self-conscious emotions: Theory and research*, 209–223.

Wong, K. K. (2003). The environmental awareness of university students in Beijing China. *Journal of Contemporary China, 12*(36), 519–536.

Wright, A. F. (1960). *The Confucian Persuasion*. Stanford University Press.

Wu, J. Y., & Xiao, Y. (2001). Seeing the Chinese gardens through the idea of the Chinese traditional culture. *Journal of Chinese Landscape Architecture, 3*, 037.

Wu, X. (2010). Economic transition, school expansion and educational inequality in China, 1990–2000. *Research in Social Stratification and Mobility, 28*(1), 91–108.

Xiao, J., Zhou, X., & Hu, W. M. (2017). Welfare analysis of the vehicle quota system in China. *International Economic Review, 58*(2), 617–650.

Xu, X. (2003). *The Jews of Kaifeng, China: History, culture, and religion*. KTAV Publishing House Inc.

Yamamoto, K. (1974). *The Mahayana Mahaparinirvana-sutra: A Complete Translation from the Classical Chinese Language* (3 vols). Karinbunko 1973–1975. PDF version online (ed. and rev. Tony Page). http://info.stiltij.nl/publiek/meditatie/soetras/mahaparinirvana.pdf

Yang, D. T. (2008). China's agricultural crisis and famine of 1959–1961: A survey and comparison to soviet famines. *Comparative Economic Studies, 50*(1), 1–29.

Yang, J. (2012). *Tombstone: The great Chinese famine, 1958–1962*. Macmillan.

Yang, X., Jin, W., Jiang, H., Xie, Q., Shen, W., & Han, W. (2017). Car ownership policies in China: Preferences of residents and influence on the choice of electric cars. *Transport Policy, 58*, 62–71.

Yao, X. (2000). *An introduction to Confucianism*. Cambridge University Press.

Yates, R. D. (1995). State Control of Bureaucrats under the Qin: Techniques and Procedures. *Early China, 20*, 331–365.

Yip, K. S. (2004). Taoism and its impact on mental health of the Chinese communities. *International Journal of Social Psychiatry, 50*(1), 25–42.

Yu, N., De Jong, M., Storm, S., & Mi, J. (2012a). The growth impact of transport infrastructure investment: A regional analysis for China (1978–2008). *Policy and Society, 31*(1), 25–38.

Yu, N., de Roo, G., De Jong, M., & Storm, S. (2016). Does the expansion of a motorway network lead to economic agglomeration? Evidence from China. *Transport Policy, 45*, 218–227.

Zhang, L., Zhang, J., Duan, Z. Y., & Bryde, D. (2015). Sustainable bike-sharing systems: Characteristics and commonalities across cases in urban China. *Journal of Cleaner Production, 97*, 124–133.

Zhang, X., Bai, X., & Zhong, H. (2018). Electric vehicle adoption in license plate-controlled big cities: Evidence from Beijing. *Journal of Cleaner Production, 202*, 191–196.

Zhang, X., Fan, S., Zhang, L., & Huang, J. (2004). Local governance and public goods provision in rural China. *Journal of Public Economics, 88*(12), 2857–2871.

Zhang, Y. B., Lin, M. C., Nonaka, A., & Beom, K. (2005). Harmony, hierarchy and conservatism: A cross-cultural comparison of Confucian values in China, Korea, Japan, and Taiwan. *Communication Research Reports, 22*(2), 107–115.

Zhao, D. (2015). *The Confucian-Legalist State: A new theory of Chinese history*. Oxford University Press.

Zhao, G. (1986). *Man and land in Chinese history: An economic analysis*. Stanford University Press.

Zhou, N., Levine, M. D., & Price, L. (2010). Overview of current energy-efficiency policies in China. *Energy Policy, 38*(11), 6439–6452.

Zweig, D. (1983). Opposition to change in rural China: The system of responsibility and people's communes. *Asian Survey, 23*(7), 879–900.

余英时. (2003). *中国思想传统的现代诠释*. 南京: 江苏人民出版社. (in Chinese. Yu, Y. S. (2003). *Zhong Guo Si Xiang Chuan Tong De Xian Dai Quan Shi*. Jiangsu People Publishing, LTD.

司马谈, & 司马迁. (1959). 论六家之要指. 北京: 中华书局. (in Chinese. Sima, T. & Sima, Q. (1959). *Lun Liu Jia Zhi Yao Zhi*. Chung Hwa Book Co.)

熊伟. (1938). 从先秦学术思想变迁大势观测⟨老子⟩的年代. *古史辨, 6*, 566–597. (in Chinese. Xiong, W. (1938). Cong Xian Qin Xue Shu Si Xiang Bian Qian Da Shi Guan Ce 'Laozi' De Nian Dai. *Gu Shi Bian, 6*, 566–597).

CHAPTER 3

Research Design and Methodology

3.1 Introduction

This chapter provides a detailed account of methods adopted in this research. Building upon the literature that spans the public acceptability of road pricing policies, Chinese culture, and China's political fields, this study bridges the gaps identified in the earlier review of the literature. Section 3.2 commences the narrative with an overview of the research process and discusses the relevance and application of both qualitative and quantitative methods to the research. Then, the narrative illustrates how the research progressed at each stage: stakeholder interviews in Sect. 3.3, focus groups in Sect. 3.4, and an attitudinal survey in Sect. 5. Lastly, Sect. 3.6 introduces ethical considerations.

3.2 Research Strategy

3.2.1 Overall Research Design

To meet the research aim, I adopted a mixed-methods approach for this research (Dahlberg & McCaig, 2010). Practically, qualitative data was needed to understand the complex nature of the public acceptability issue and people's concerns about the proposed scheme. Furthermore, a framework for assessing public acceptability in the Chinese context would be proposed by using qualitative analysis. Quantitative data was then needed to collect measurable public attitudes towards congestion charging which

Q. Liu, *Public Acceptability of Congestion Charging in China*,
https://doi.org/10.1007/978-981-19-0236-9_3

would first verify whether the framework can reflect the causal relationship between public acceptability and its determinants, and second identify key factors that influence public acceptability in the Chinese context.

Although qualitative research has been criticised by some who favour a positivist approach to research for lack of transparency about the research process (see Denzin & Lincoln, 1998) and being anecdotal (see Ritchie et al., 2013), qualitative approaches are preferable for deep explorations of people's personal experiences, inner feelings, emotions, perceptions and cognitive processes, data for which are difficult to gather from a closed question survey (Maxwell, 2012). Also, qualitative approaches are used to undertake the initial exploration of the issues associated with a given topic to gain meaningful preliminary insights into the nature of a problem when there is little information and few certainties about said nature. Furthermore, in follow-up explanations of the inferences from modelled analyses, researchers can use qualitative data to explore causal factors and interpret under-explained anomalies in the data.

Quantitative approaches (see Cresswell, 1994) can be used to develop explanatory models that can lead to theories of cause and effect. Also, the effects of the researcher's personal beliefs on findings can be limited to a minimum. However, quantitative methods are constrained by standards that may result in an artificial categorization of phenomena because the context within which the data was obtained may be buried underneath the statistical analysis (e.g., Punch, 2013; Sale et al., 2002).

Since the aim of the research is to determine whether the Western notion of public acceptability is transferrable to the Chinese context, I considered it inappropriate to adopt a Western context-based framework to conduct a survey in China directly. The logic here is that one could not know whether Chinese people think differently from Westerners or whether the policy was more (or less) acceptable to them. Therefore, there had to be a two-step process. Arguably, an in-depth understanding of the public acceptability issue from both policymakers' and lay citizens' perspectives can only be meaningfully gained through qualitative explorations.

I adopted qualitative interviews and focus groups as a means for answering different research questions. Figure 3.1 shows the stepwise research design for each research question. First, I conducted interviews with 12 stakeholders, including cadres, retired cadres, planners and scholars who served as policymaking advisers to explore whether and why public acceptability matters in the Chinese context. Next, I conducted

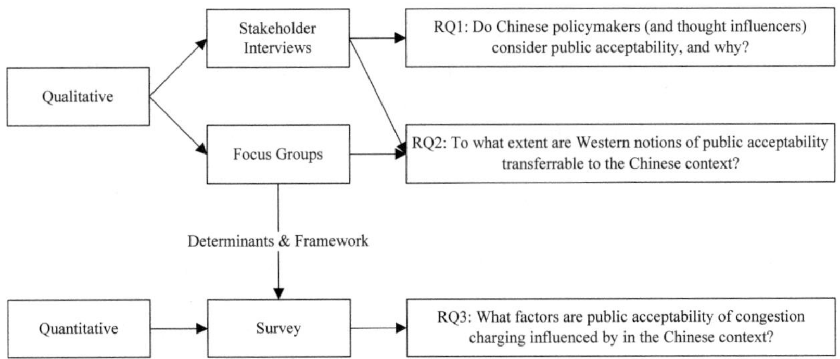

Fig. 3.1 Methodology flow chart

nine focus groups (73 participants) to explore key determinants of public acceptability of congestion charging in the Chinese context. I used the results from the focus groups to configure the design of an attitudinal survey. Also, it provided the context within which to interpret the findings from the questionnaire survey. Lastly, I conducted a randomly sampled survey (i.e., a quantitative device) with 1,104 valid responses to verify the framework and analyse public acceptability of congestion charging in Beijing. I develop the research process for each stage in the following three sections.

The research questions posed in this study could only be answered when qualitative and quantitative methods were used together. However, unlike some commonly practised mixed-method approaches that merely regarded qualitative data as supportive material for quantitative evidence (e.g., Silverman, 2015), the two methods were equally important in this study.

The following sections describe each stage of the research and discuss how they were used to answer the RQs.

3.2.2 *Case Selection*

Case selection is a challenging endeavour (Gerring, 2006). Since this case study aimed at elucidating the features of a broader population, it is no exception. Beijing was chosen in this study for three main reasons. First, both traffic congestion and smog are pervasive problems in many post-reform Chinese cities, but not all of them are considering congestion charging as a policy intervention. Hence, the city of Beijing was selected to reflect a city with the policy intention of congestion charging already in circulation and, thus, a population of potential adopters of congestion charging policies. Second, Beijing is highly likely to be the first Chinese adopter of congestion charging because several official documents have announced the implementation of congestion charging in Beijing since 2011. Beijing almost always performs as a heroic trailblazer of government-led interventions and a touchstone of new policy ideas,[1] and policies implemented in Beijing usually diffuse across the country rapidly. Third, since Beijing houses a large number of migrants, including people originally from other big cities and rural areas, this case can be said to reflect what an acceptable policy means to the Chinese public as a whole. Therefore, the case of Beijing is arguably the most appropriate of all major Chinese cities for the understanding of the public acceptability of congestion charging in the Chinese context.

3.3 Stakeholder Interviews

3.3.1 Abductive Research Strategy

The method used to answer RQ1 involved semi-structured interviews with key stakeholders. Semi-structured interviews are "conversation[s] with a purpose" (Burgess, 2002), which are used to generate rich, in-depth data relevant to answering research questions (e.g., Kvale & Brinkmann, 2008; Mason, 2017). Thus, qualitative interviewing aimed at constructing a shared knowledge based on participants' experiences and ideas of a specific topic (Turner, 2010; Weiss, 1995) was the most suitable method for answering the first RQ.

An *abductive research strategy* was adopted to generate interpretations of policymakers' concerns about public acceptability. The idea of

[1] Other pioneers are Shanghai, Guangzhou and Shenzhen. However, since one of the barriers to implementing congestion charging is a lack of legal basis in P.R. China (according to the constitution, only the National People's Congress have the right to levy a tax whilst local People's Congresses and local governments do not have that right; also, according to the current law, the road toll can only be charged for travelling on toll highways and loan returning toll highways, urban roads are non-chargeable). Beijing is much more likely to overcome the legislative barriers compared to all the other cities because of its political importance and its iconic representation of the Central.

abduction refers to a form of inference that seeks to find the most likely explanation for observations (e.g., Josephson & Josephson, 1996; Walton, 2001). Although abductive research strategy was originally used to generate hypotheses in the natural sciences, it has been widely used as a method of theory construction in the social sciences (Blaikie, 2007; Blaikie, 2010; Lewis-Beck et al., 2003; see also Dubois & Gadde, 2002; Dunne & Dougherty, 2016; Lipscomb, 2012; Thorkildsen et al., 2013). Unlike deductive and inductive approaches, this strategy yields the most likely conjecture based on observation but does not positively verify the generated theory, therefore allowing a remnant of uncertainty (e.g., Danermark et al., 2005). This strategy fits well with the first research question, which is whether and why policymakers consider public acceptability in the Chinese transport policy context.

First, although public acceptability has been extensively studied in Western literature, it is necessary to research whether and how the notion is transferrable to an authoritarian state. Second, the abductive research strategy gives attention to meanings, interpretations, motives, and intentions that help to identify the underlying causes that constitute the objectives of the research (Blaikie, 2010). Third, as evidence from different sectors of the society presents, cadres are highly likely to give ambiguous bureaucratic responses that have to be interpreted, and the policymaking process in China, especially cadres' motivations for considering a particular issue, is always shrouded in a fog (see Shen, 2012; Wu, 2015a, b; Zhang, 2006; Zhao, 1993). Consequently, the research could not directly verify the results of the analysis but had to rely on the interpretation of policymakers' viewpoints on public acceptability as corroborated by evidence from the focus group discussions and the literature from other fields.

The research process followed the practical steps for an abductive research strategy in social science suggested by Ong (2012).

1. A general formulation of the research objective
2. Review of relevant literature. Unlike grounded theory, which discourages conducting literature reviews before data collection (Glaser & Strauss, 1967; Strauss, 1987; see also Dunne, 2011; Ramalho et al., 2015), relevant literature is reviewed. In this study, except for those related to public acceptability of transport policies in the Western context and the public attitude towards public policies in the Chinese context, three bodies of literature were reviewed

prior to the abductive approach: the political logic of contemporary China (e.g., Dickson, 2000; Fewsmith, 2013; Shirk, 1993), Chinese civil society (e.g., Brook & Frolic, 2015; Ma, 1994; Tu, 2016), and the history of Chinese peasant revolts (e.g., Bianco, 2001; Chu & Lee, 1994; Hartford & Goldstein, 2016). Since it was problematic to assure the relevance of reviewed literature at the early stage of the research, a literature review was conducted in parallel with the interviews.

3. Regular involvement with the social actors' world and becoming one part of their world (Sect. 3.2)
4. Using sensitising concepts as a guide to doing the investigation while being as non-directive as possible
5. Identification of concepts and categories that keep recurring in the discussions
6. Trying to explore the meanings of these concepts and categories, continuously proceeding throughout the fieldwork
7. Recording comments and behaviours related to these concepts
8. Refinement of the problem to be studied herein by slightly modifying interview questions according to previous interviews, follow-up literature review, and the expertise of the interviewee.
9. Test concepts and categories identified from the conversation with one social actor with other social actors. For example, key motivations to consider public acceptability suggested by participants of the pre-interview exercises and official interviewees were tested with other official interviewees and academics. Officials' opinions on issues related to information were tested with academics and planners.
10. Relevant literature on social actors' concepts and categories and their relevance to the problem to be studied
11. Establishment of a theory to explain social actors

3.3.2 *Information Gathering & Participant Engagement Exercise*

The abductive approach requires regular involvement by the researcher with the social actors to become part of the social actors' world. However, the standard was impractical for this study because I intended to interview high-level cadres whose everyday activity I could not be extensively involved with; nor could I observe it. Therefore, an information gathering and participant engagement exercise, which lasted 4 months, was conducted to achieve involvement with those who had had experiences similar to those of the intended interviewees. The exercise consisted of three main parts: (a) regular contact with one transport scholar, one public policy scholar, two relatively low-level cadres, one retired high-level cadre, and one journalist who had expertise in interviewing high-level cadres via several mobile social media apps from June to September 2016; (b) short informal conversations with six people who worked in local government in different provinces (four of them are grassroots cadres) and three people who worked in different public institutions; and (c) three online discussions with those who had previously expressed ideas about congestion charging on social media (fifteen participants in total). In addition, the online discussions were also used as the first step in the recruiting process for the focus groups.

The information gathering and participant engagement exercises were crucial to the quality of the stakeholder interviews. First, to interpret concepts and categories mentioned by official interviewees, I had to be conversant with the language used in official discourse.[2] This was particularly important not only because it helped me to better communicate with the interviewees, but more importantly, to detect the differences between their own ideas and those promulgated in the language of officialdom.[3] Second, grassroots cadres and people who worked in public institutions were asked to express their opinions about whether and why policymakers considered the public acceptability issue. The cadres and other people were selected because of their position in the political system. On the one hand, I could approach them with relative ease since most of them identified themselves as lay citizens; on the other hand, all of them were insiders. These conversations provided substantial content regarding China's policymaking, and much of it was used in questions and as evidence in four of twelve stakeholder interviews. Third, I undertook these online discussions to glimpse at lay citizens' views about congestion

[2] This is because of the big difference between the official and public discourse. A word may have entirely different interpretations depending on who is using that word and in what condition the word is used. See Tong (2009), Nordin & Richaud (2014) for more information about the differences.

[3] Since cadres, especially high-level cadres, have to play by the rules of the official language game. This was found in the pilot study that grassroots cadres were seemingly much franker to the researcher. Higher level cadres, including the retired one, used the official language. See Holbig (2013) for more information about the language game cadres play.

charge, which allowed the researcher to think about their concerns when interviewing stakeholders. These informal conversations with lower-level cadres and online discussions with lay citizens were also intended to be an evidence collection tool; however, most of this evidence turned out to be hearsay or anecdotal, which can hardly qualify for use in stakeholder interviews. Therefore, these online discussions were only used as evidence for people's perceptions of political corruption in one stakeholder interview.

I revised the topical interview outline seven times pursuant to advice from online discussion. The final interview outline was sent to the retired cadre and the journalist to confirm that these topics were not too sensitive to discuss with cadres and check that key issues relevant to the study were included. In addition, I discussed a shortlist of follow-up, challenging questions repeatedly with all of those whom I contacted regularly. These challenging questions (see Appendix 4) were prepared to deal with cases where official interviewees persisted in playing the official language game, for example, talking in a bombastic way and using well-prepared ideological language to respond. Of course, I had to pose these challenging questions tactfully; otherwise, I could have made the challenge of obtaining information from official interviewees more difficult.

Most of the short informal conversations with people who worked in local governments and public institutions were undertaken in September 2016 (three conducted in person, five conducted by telephone, one conducted by using social media app). One of the online discussions was conducted in July 2016, and the other two were conducted in September 2016. These conversations and the online discussions were used as evidence supporting some challenging questions instead of modifying the interview outline.

3.3.3 Interview Design

Semi-structured interviews were selected for this study because, by its nature, the abductive research strategy is a "progressive deepening" process. Semi-structured interviews are more efficient than other approaches for abductive reasoning since they allow for the emergence of unexpected topics (Flick, 2018; Punch, 2013). Although I had conducted a literature review before the interviews, it was still difficult to ascertain the relevance of the reviewed literature. Hence, I avoided preparing detailed questions that focused on particular aspects of public acceptability. Also, since too many questions can inevitably implant the intended logic of the research into the interviewees' narratives (Bryman, 2016), thereby considerably diminishing the quality of interviews, my protocol emphasised primary topics instead of a long list of questions. The topics prepared for cadres included (see Appendix 4): (a) "do you personally think about public acceptability"; (b) "why do you think public acceptability is important (or not)"; and (c) "what role does public acceptability play in the policymaking process". Planners and academics were asked to explain their roles in the policymaking process, but their first topic was "do you think public acceptability is considered by policymakers".

Face-to-face interviews are preferable because telephone interviews are often less effective (Novick, 2008; Trier-Bieniek, 2012). Since the time I had available to complete the interviews was limited, I confirmed the cadres' participation in the study before May 2016 and scheduled all of the interviews before September 2016. Interviews with the two former cadres had to be conducted via Skype since they were based in different countries. Most of the face-to-face interviews were conducted in the participants' offices except for two that were conducted in tearooms[4] and one that was conducted in the participant's apartment.

3.3.4 Selection of Interviewees

The quality of the research findings would depend upon the quality of the data, and, therefore, interviewees had to be screened carefully. The most suitable people to answer the first research question were cadres who had been directly involved in transport policymaking in Beijing, including cadres in Beijing Municipal Commission of Transport, Beijing Traffic Management Bureau, Beijing Municipal Commission of Development and Reform, Beijing Municipal Ecological Environmental Bureau, Beijing Municipal Bureau of Finance and the Beijing Municipal Party Committee. Because of Beijing's capital city status, cadres in ministries and other national-level commissions could also be involved in the policymaking. Thus, cadres in relevant state organs were also considered as suitable interviewees, including cadres in the Ministry of Transport, Ministry of Housing and Urban–Rural Development, Ministry of Ecology and Environment, Ministry of Science and Technology, National Development and

[4] an establishment which primarily serves tea and other light refreshments.

Reform Commission, Ministry of Public Security, Central Comprehensively Deepening Reforms Commission,[5] and the Central Party School of the CPC. Since it was not clear who would be in charge of the policymaking for congestion charging, the relevant cadre was not known. We attempted to find the highest-level cadres possible because low-level cadres could not make final decisions even if they were involved in the policymaking. Therefore, I regarded high-level cadres as better suited to address RQ1 than low-level cadres.

Eleven cadres who had worked in the aforementioned organs of government were contacted via personal connections. Their administrative levels ranged from 14 (Deputy-Bureau-Director level) to 8 (Provincial-Ministerial level).[6] Eight of them confirmed participation before May 2016, but one decided not to participate until later in July; another could not participate because he was not in the office when the interviews were conducted. Finally, six cadres ranked from 13 (Deputy-Bureau-Director level) to 8 (Provincial-Ministerial level) participated in stakeholder interviews.

Other social actors were also invited to participate in the study, including two former cadres, two academics, and two planners in Beijing. The two former cadres were sufficiently knowledgeable to answer the first research question. Although they had not been directly involved in transport policymaking, they were familiar with the policymaking process in China in general. Furthermore, they both had the experience of working with Party leaders; hence, they were also regarded as insiders to the system. In addition, they could express opinions more frankly as they were no longer "within the system"; therefore, interviews with these persons were arranged following all the face-to-face interviews in order to validate the interpretations of whether public acceptability is an issue in the policymaking.

There are clearly limitations to the interviewed sample. It is difficult to invite people to discuss the importance of public opinions because not every invitee will be willing to discuss the issue and may have to be excluded even though such invitee may have an important role in decision-making. These people may simply see public acceptability as not

[5] known as the "Central Leading Group for Comprehensively Deepening Reforms" when the research was conducted. It is a policy formulation and implementation body set up under the Politburo of the CPC.

[6] Cadre administrative level rages from 1 (state-leader level) to 27 (office worker).

especially relevant. Therefore, these are not representative of the full range of opinions on this matter, but nonetheless, participants are exposed to these other actors in their daily work and so will provide assessments that are informed by more than their own world views. Hence, this helps to understand the decision-making context in which the rest of the research sits.

A broader range of actors was considered to be involved in policymaking in the West, such as civil society organisations (e.g., Castells, 2008; Steffek et al., 2007), academics (e.g., Dyson & Maes, 2017; Kuklick, 2013), think tanks (e.g., Rich, 2005; Weaver, 2017), and planners (e.g., Lyons & Davidson, 2016). However, it is ambiguous what roles these social actors play in the Chinese context (see Bottelier, 2018; Goldman, 1981; Han, 2018a, b); notwithstanding, academics and planners were interviewed to explore their roles in policymaking because their comments on cadres' consideration of public acceptability were still valuable even if they played insignificant roles in policymaking. Two academics were selected because of their rich experience as advisers to the government. Two planners were chosen for pragmatic reasons, being that they were the only two people willing to talk about this issue among the 18 planners that I contacted.

3.3.5 *Undertaking and Analysing Stakeholder Interviews*

Key challenges and strategies to overcome these challenges are:

1. The interviewer may expect the interviewees to answer questions in a particular way, confirming the hypotheses, especially when conjectures had been made after several interviews. Therefore, I must always remind myself to remain open to new ideas and to be patient.
2. As topics in this study were somehow sensitive to official interviewees, interviewees were sounded out about their general attitudes towards the contemporary transport policymaking at the beginning of the interviews. Thus, I had to start with value-neutral questions, such as a description of a process, goals of some reforms which are widely deemed as successful, and sometimes their own achievements in their political career. Issues such as social inequity and corruption were avoided in the first 20 min. The researcher also avoided asking

for opinions directly but attempted to use evidence[7] that was politically less sensitive to stimulate interviewees to express their own opinions voluntarily.

3. As expected, some cadres persistently played the official language game at the beginning of their interviews. Challenging questions prepared during the pilot study were effective in encouraging them to express more personal opinions.
4. New topics continued to emerge with saturation finally reached the ninth interview; and the literature review was conducted in parallel with the interviews.

A total of twelve interviews were conducted (shown in Table 3.1). Each interview lasted an average of 114 min and ranged from 82 to 156 min. All interviews were recorded. As the abductive research strategy requires, exploring the meaning of concepts and categories was a continuous process. Thus, each interview was briefly coded and analysed immediately following an interview. Comments associated with the core concepts were documented to refine and narrow the problem. These analyses, therefore, allowed the researcher to modify the interview questions before each interview and test concepts and categories identified expressed by one interviewee on other interviewees. Although participants of the pilot study might be fairly helpful at this stage, they were not informed about stakeholder interviews for ethical reasons. The recordings of interviews were transcribed after all the interviews were completed. I translated the transcripts of interviews, as well as the notes, and completed a round of manual coding. This coding resulted in a list of concepts and categories that I used in an effort to interpret each transcript. I used the software package NVivo 11 to organise, code, categorise and visualise the data. The coding process has been independently completed by Qiyang Liu and was discussed with experts with various backgrounds. Two lists of codes (820 codes and 663 codes, respectively) were generated compared. After deliberation, 31 concepts and categories emerged (Appendix 6).

[7] from Western media or evidence collected from the pilot study. The researcher also needs to sound out the interviewee at the beginning since using evidence from Western media can be annoying for some cadres and grassroots cadres' ideas collected from the pilot study were not considered as solid evidence sometimes.

Table 3.1 Interviewees & Interviews

	Type	*Ranking**	*Gender*	*Party affiliation*	*Duration (min)*
Interviewee 1	Academic, Cadre	13	Male	Non-CCP	143
Interviewee 2	Academic		Female	Non-CCP	119
Interviewee 3	Cadre	11	Male	CCP	98
Interviewee 4	Academic, Cadre	9	Male	CCP	91
Interviewee 5	Academic		Male	CCP	106
Interviewee 6	Academic, Cadre	10	Male	CCP	111
Interviewee 7	Cadre	8	Male	CCP	82
Interviewee 8	Planner		Female	Non-CCP	97
Interviewee 9	Planner		Male	CCP	102
Interviewee 10	Academic, Cadre	12	Male	CCP	125
Interviewee 11	Academic, Former Cadre		Male	Former CCP	156
Interviewee 12	Academic, Former Cadre		Male	Former CCP	139

*Ranking 7–8: Provincial-Ministerial level, ranking 9–10: Sub-Provincial (Ministerial) level, ranking 11–12: Bureau-Director level, ranking 13–14: Deputy-Bureau-Director level, see Børdsgaard & Chen (2009a, b) for more information.

Several rounds of analyses were conducted after coding and thematising, including themes linking selection of representative quotations and establishment of theories that can interpret the data.

3.4 Focus Group Discussions

3.4.1 Hypothetical Cordon-Based Charging Scheme

Beijing, the capital of the People's Republic of China and the capital of five ancient dynasties,[8] is not only well known for its political prominence but also for its historical and cultural richness. After the four smaller downtown urban districts within the 2nd ring road were merged into two districts in July 2010, the municipality is now composed of 16 urban

[8] Namely, Yan, Jin, Yuan, Ming, Qing. See Twitchett & Fairbank (1978) for more information.

districts and two counties. The urban area of Beijing is structured around a series of ring roads that start from the 2nd ring road close to where the Beijing city walls stood (see Visser, 2004; Zhang, 2008) and expand to the 6th ring road. The ring roads play an important role in setting the hypothetical cordon and the focus group recruitment. I selected the 3rd ring road as the hypothetical cordon and the boundary between participants residing in the inner and outer city.

The 2nd ring road is a rough boundary of Beijing's old city (see Li et al., 2005), where a large number of historical sites are distributed, and the inner-city core area, where the most important national party and government organs are housed. This study regarded the 3rd ring road as the boundary of the inner Beijing core area for two reasons. First, the 3rd ring road connects the inner urban districts (Zhang, 2001). Second, these boundaries were drawn to classify different groups of participants. In this regard, the 2nd ring road cannot be a purposeful line because only a few people reside in this area; most of the land within the 2nd ring road is occupied by historical sites and buildings that house different levels of government (Yang, Cai, et al., 2013).

The 4th ring road had been intended as the urban–rural boundary when it was completed in 2001 (Mu et al., 2012; Yang et al., 2013). However, given the rapid urbanisation process, it can no longer serve as a proper dividing line between urban and rural areas. The 5th ring road, which opened in 2003, connects key sub-centres in outer city areas, while the 6th ring road, which opened in 2009, connects main central towns (Yang, Cai, et al., 2013). I considered the 5th ring road as the rough boundary between urban and rural Beijing for this study. It was the most practical line to divide the participants into inner and outer Beijing residents because 51% of Beijing residents lived outside the fifth ring road, and most new migrants tended to live in this area (Chinanews, 2015).

Since the congestion policy for Beijing was still at the planning stage when focus groups were conducted, the participants could not have a shared understanding of the policy, although they might have a very rough idea of what the term "congestion charging" meant in broad terms. Therefore, I provided brief information about four different types of charging schemes, based around the Ring Road System (Small & Gómez-Ibáñez, 1998) in the participant information sheet to help the participants to understand more about congestion charging.

I introduced a hypothetical cordon-based charging scheme as the basis for discussion. The cordon-based pricing scheme was selected for several reasons: (a) cordon-based charging is the most widely implemented and studied type of charging (e.g., Börjesson & Kristoffersson, 2015, 2018; May et al., 2002;); (b) electronic urban tolling schemes have been implemented mostly in Norway (Ieromonachou et al., 2006); (c) the idea of single facility congestion charging, mostly implemented in North America (e.g., Dahlgren, 2002), is similar to toll roads that are prevalent in China; and (d) although the optimal toll level for area-based charging schemes was found to be higher than cordon-based charging (Maruyama & Harata, 2006), area-based charging is less practical and generates more inequitable results than cordon-based ones (Maruyama & Sumalee, 2007).

As shown in Fig. 3.2, the area within the 3rd ring road was selected as the charging zone for this study because the area between the 2nd and the 3rd ring road is the most congested zone in Beijing (Beijing Transport Research Centre, 2011). A simple hypothetical charging was introduced to the participants since complex charging (Wu et al., 2017) would be difficult for participants to understand. Moreover, the purpose of conducting focus groups was to engage participants in a discussion on congestion charging instead of on the precise details of any specific charging strategy. Evidently, the complexity of the proposed scheme can directly influence its acceptability (e.g., Francke & Kaniok, 2013; Gaunt et al., 2007; Hysing et al., 2015); hence, not only did I inform the participants that 50 CNY would be charged for driving a car within the charging zone between 7:00 and 18:00 on weekdays but that different charging schemes were also provided in the information sheet including different charges (10 CNY, 20CNY, 50CNY). The facilitator highlighted the fact that the price and the charging zones were hypothetical, and, thus, the participants were encouraged to discuss the types and levels of charging that would be most acceptable.

3.4.2 Conducting and Analysing Focus Groups

I utilised a three-step recruiting process because Chinese people are generally unwilling to participate in activities that involve face-to-face discussions with strangers. The idea of recruiting can be described as "inviting acquaintances of strangers".

First, I organised three online discussions via social media apps with 15 people who had expressed their ideas about the congestion charge policy

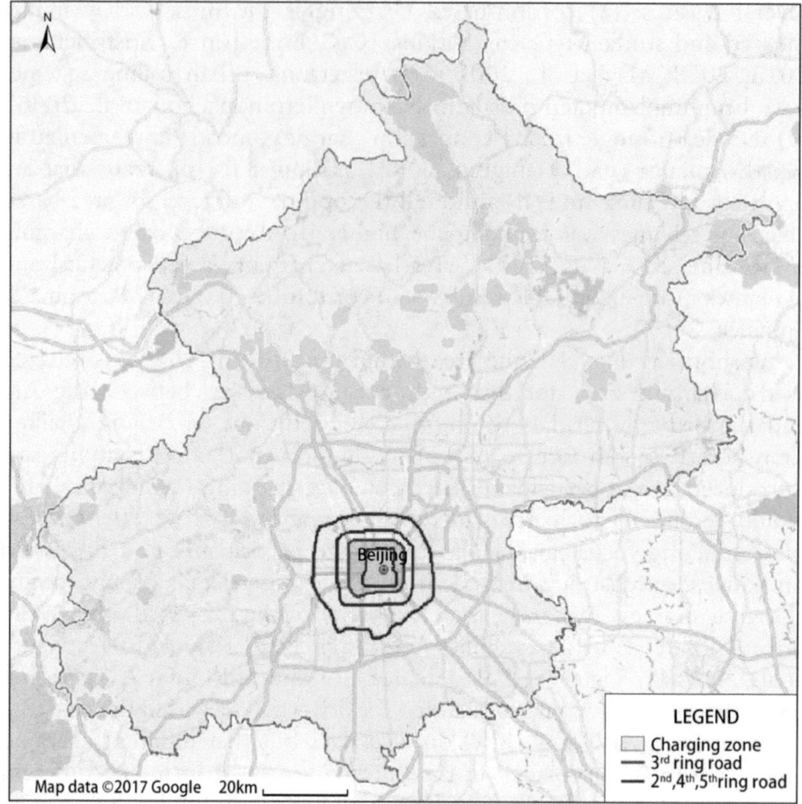

Fig. 3.2 The hypothetical charging zone within the metropolitan area of Beijing

on social media. There were four to seven participants (one person participated in two discussions) for each online discussion, and the duration of each discussion was more than an hour. This step targeted people who were willing to express opinions in a group discussion. These people were asked to introduce the research to their acquaintances in Beijing and invite their acquaintances to participate instead of directly participating in focus group discussions because half of the participants did not live in Beijing and so were not in scope for the main study. 58 people were recruited after this step.

However, most of them were young people who lived within the third ring road. To control for sample selection bias in the second step of the recruiting process, I asked these people to invite intentionally some particular groups of people who were more difficult for me to access, such as the elderly, people with low incomes, and new migrants who lived outside the 5th ring road (especially in urban villages[9]). Another 77 people were recruited after this step. Participants from the online pilot discussion were not invited to join in the final focus group discussions even if they were Beijing residents because I was concerned that they might dominate the follow-up discussion since they had previously discussed the issues.

I conducted an additional focus group with taxi and bus drivers after finishing the other eight focus groups. Unexpectedly, most professional drivers who talked with me wanted a congestion charge, although the majority of people in the initial eight groups held a negative opinion about the policy. To figure out the cause of such a phenomenon, I ran an additional focus group with three taxi drivers, two bus drivers and a staff member in a subway station.

Eventually, 73 participants were selected from 135 candidates, and another eight people were selected as alternative candidates. The grouping process proceeded in parallel with the recruiting. The grouping process had to guarantee that participants in one group did not meet each other before the focus group discussion took place. The results of the recruiting and grouping process are shown in Table 3.2, and the distribution of focus group participants is shown in Fig. 3.3.

There were two main barriers to conducting focus groups in this study. More generally, Chinese people are often totally quiet when sitting in a room full of strangers. Therefore, two undesirable situations can occur: a few participants dominate the discussion, or everyone remains uncommunicative. Particularly, in this case, people might not be confident enough to talk since a policy was to be discussed. To overcome these barriers, I adopted a "stimulator" strategy to encourage people to express ideas more freely.

I carried out a short informal conversation (15–30 min online or face-to-face) with every participant before focus group participation to make

[9] Urban villages (城中村, chengzhongcun) are villages that appear on both the outskirts and the downtown segments of major Chinese cities. They are surrounded by skyscrapers, transport infrastructures, and other urban constructions. Urban villages are a unique phenomenon that formed part of China's urbanisation.

Table 3.2 Cluster of participants

	Old To Beijing				*New Settlers*				*Additional*
	Inner City (inside the 3rd ring road)		*Outer City (outside the 3rd ring road)*		*Inner City*		*Outer City*		*Bus & Taxi Drivers*
	Young (<45)	*Elder (>45)*	*Young*	*Elder*	*Young*	*Elder*	*Young*	*Elder*	
Sample Size	9	8	6	6	10	9	11	8	6
					Former Rural *hukou*[*] Holders				
					1	2	4	3	

[*]*hukou* (户口) is a system of household registration used in mainland China. Due to its connection to social programs provided by the government, which assigns benefits based on agricultural and non-agricultural residency status (often referred to as rural and urban), the hukou system is sometimes likened to a form of caste system.

the participants feel comfortable and confident in expressing their own opinions about the policy and sounding out each of the other participants on their views. Those who held relatively extremist views were noted down. These people would serve stimulators if participants were uncommunicative at the beginning of discussions. Vocal participants found it easier to express their opinions and argue against each other because of the stimulator. This strategy seemed to be effective, as all participants actively joined in the subsequent discussions (for the use of this strategy, see also Liu et al., 2021; Liu, 2022).

I, as the moderator who collected the data, would have an unavoidable influence on participants and, thereby, affected the quality of data. Therefore, I remained as neutral as possible in terms of dress and body language in posing the three questions, which were "what do you think about the policy", "what benefits and problems might it bring" and "what are your expectations". A question about revenue allocation was asked at the end of each group since the literature identified this as one of the key determinants of public acceptability (e.g., Eliasson & Mattsson, 2006).

Each discussion lasted an average of 104 min, ranging from 86 to 145 min. I recorded, transcribed, and translated all conversations into English and then analysed the data inductively (for the analytical process,

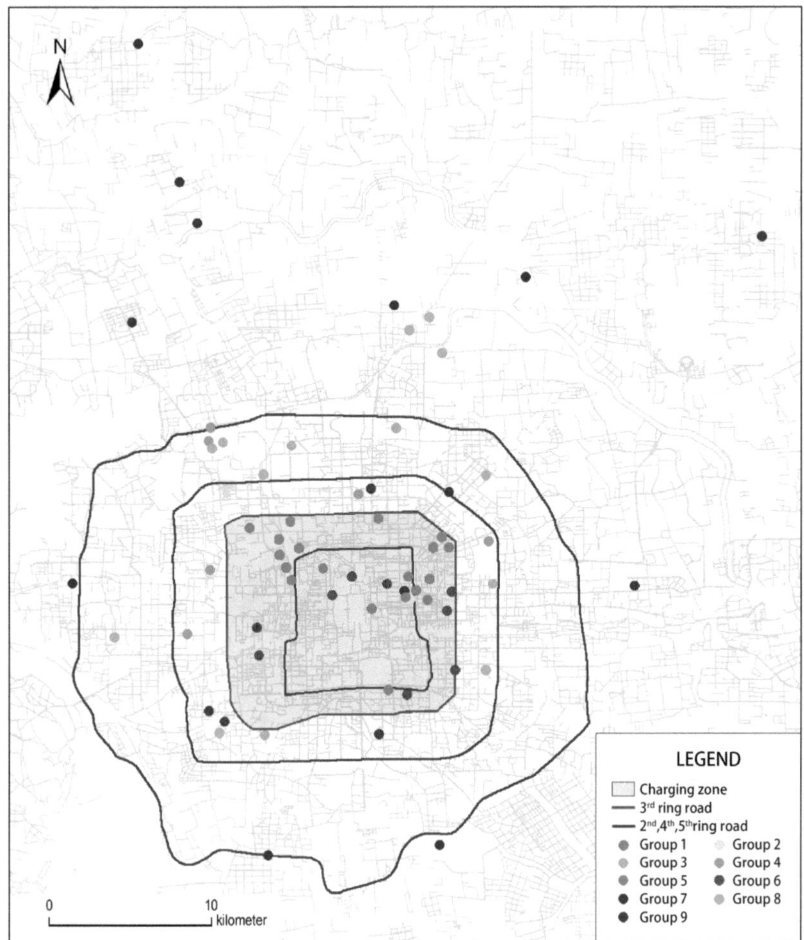

Fig. 3.3 The distribution of focus group participants

see Burnard, 1991; Charmaz, 2014; Glaser & Strauss, 1967; Thomas, 2006). I completed one round of manual coding, clustered the codes into categories, and then used the list of categories to go through the transcripts. I completed another two rounds of coding by using the software NVivo 11, which generated 1,074 codes and 23 themes (see Appendix 7).

I performed additional analysis, including linking themes, selecting representative quotations, and generating theories grounded in the data. These analytical processes were discussed further with two groups of peers from various academic institutions to ensure their reliability and validity (e.g., Creswell & Miller, 2000; Golafshani, 2003).

3.5 Attitude Survey

3.5.1 Survey Design

Based on a comprehensive review of the literature (Chapter 2) and qualitative explorations conducted prior to the survey (Chapters 4 & 5), I proposed a framework to organise determinants of public acceptability (shown in Fig. 3.4). I selected three to five quotes from focus group

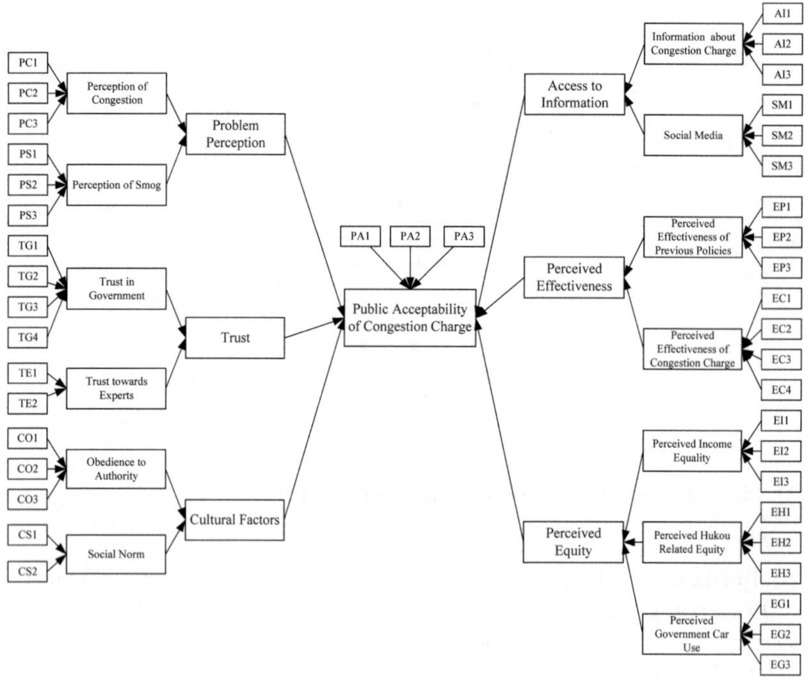

Fig. 3.4 Framework for analysing public acceptability in the Chinese context

participants that corresponded to the emerging main themes and assigned them to their relevant theoretical constructs.

Among them, some constructs were asked in a similar way to Western methods to test whether those constructs are relevant, including problem perception, perceived effectiveness, and acceptability of congestion charging. For instance, four participant statements reflect the determinant "perceived effectiveness of congestion charging". These four statements were:

1. A policy that has been successfully implemented in foreign countries could be effective in China.
2. Congestion charging can effectively alleviate the congestion problem in Beijing.
3. Congestion charging can effectively alleviate the smog problem in Beijing.
4. People will use cars less because of the congestion charging.

Statements for others of the 13 determinants were more culturally specific but nonetheless properly reflected the way Chinese respondents perceived transport inequities, trust issues, and social conformity. For instance, for the determinant "income inequity", I found five assertions that reflected the construct. These were;

1. The policy is inequitable to poorer car users.
2. The policy will cause more social inequities.
3. The policy will deprive poorer car owners of the right to use cars.
4. The policy intentionally makes driving another privilege of the rich.
5. Rich people will not be influenced by the policy.

I ultimately selected 78 representative statements to form an initial pilot survey.

Statements were organised to be evaluated by the participant through a 6-point Likert scale (1 = strongly disagree; 6 = strongly agree). There is an ongoing debate among researchers concerning the number of choices in a Likert scale because this decision can alter the results considerably (Garland, 1991). Likert scales can be categorised into two types: odd-numbered and even-numbered, providing or not providing for a mid-point (Brown, 2000). This is important for this study since Chinese respondents were highly likely to give a neutral response to questions relating to a policy. A middle point, therefore, is not only a legitimate way to be absentminded but also an option for non-commitment in political equivocation. Many researchers are inclined to keep the neutral option by using 5-point or 7-point Likert scales; they believe respondents might truly feel neutral about the question (e.g., Randall & Fernandes, 1991). However, the question remains as to whether the neutral option truly expresses a neutral position. Matell and Jacoby (1972) found that the usage of the middle point dramatically decreases with an increasing number of options, which implies that those who chose the middle point were not expressing neutrality. Raaijmakers et al. (2000) discovered that neutral responses more frequently express "don't know" rather than a neutral position. Moreover, Chomeya (2010) has shown that 6-point Likert scales have higher reliability than 5-point scales. Therefore, a 6-point Likert format was a proper and practical method for the purposes of this study.

I refined the statements in the final survey through the use of an online pilot survey that I conducted in September 2017 for 126 respondents with a background in psychology, sociology, or political science. Cronbach's α values for each construct were calculated to test the internal consistency. I took 0.7 as the acceptable level of internal consistency (Tavakol & Dennick, 2011). Items were eliminated if removing the items increased the Cronbach's α value to an acceptable level. Additionally, based upon feedback from pilot survey participants, I eliminated some items because they were ambiguous, misleading or politically sensitive.

The shortened survey with 49 attitudinal questions was administered in November 2017 (Appendix 5). Hard-copy questionnaires were distrubuted at commercial areas, bus stops, city parks, and residential areas in various districts of Beijing, whereas the online survey was distributed through social media. The collection of data yielded a final sample of 1,104 valid responses.

3.5.2 *Survey Data*

Table 3.3 reports the socio-demographic information of the sample. The sample is compared to the Beijing population in general (Beijing Municipal Bureau of Statistics, 2017). People residing outside the fifth ring road reflect a much larger population (51%) than the sample (23.9%), whereas the sample has more people living within the third ring road (33.8%) and

Table 3.3 Socio-demographic information for the sample

		Frequency	*Percentage*	*Beijing*
Heard about the CC	Yes	1060	96.0	
	No	44	4.0	
Age	18–30	342	31.0	24.6
	31–45	336	30.4	26.4
	46–60	285	25.8	21.8
	Above 60	141	12.8	14
Gender	Male	552	50.0	51.6
	Female	552	50.0	48.4
Annual Household Income (CNY)	<120 k	430	38.9	
	120 k-1 m	531	48.1	
	>1 m	143	13.0	
Pekingese/migrants	Pekingese	468	42.4	
	Migrants	636	57.6	
Residential area	six inner-city districts (inside the 3rd ring road)	373	33.8	18.8
	six inner-city districts (outside the 3rd ring road)	467	42.3	30.2
	other districts	264	23.9	51
Car ownership	Car Owner	755	68.4	
	Non-car owner	349	31.6	

between the third and fifth ring road (42.3%) than does the Beijing population (18.8% and 30.2% respectively). Therefore, the sample may contain more Pekingese and more wealthy people than the broader Beijing population, the reason being that housing prices inside the third ring road are rather high, and 51.6% of the permanent migrant population reside outside the fifth ring road (People's Daily, 2015). For a city the size of Beijing, it is difficult to obtain representative samples. In this case, the focus is on understanding the extent to which acceptability constructs matter rather than in determining some kind of pan-Beijing response; thus, this study deems the sample, despite its size and slight bias, to be adequate for purposes of the research performed.

3.5.3 Analytical Approach

According to Koufteros (1999), Koufteros et al. (2001), and Golob (2003), the analytical approach included an exploratory factor analysis

(EFA), a confirmatory factor analysis (CFA), and the testing of the structural model (shown in Fig. 3.5).

Structural equation modelling (SEM) is a form of causal modelling that includes a set of mathematical and statistical models that fit structures of constructs to data (Kaplan, 2008). SEMs are widely used in social sciences to represent the causal influences of exogenous variables on endogenous variables and the causal relationship between different endogenous variables (Baumgartner & Homburg, 1996; Cuttance & Ecob, 2009; Hancock, 2003; MacCallum & Austin, 2000; McQuitty, 2004; Shah & Goldstein, 2006). SEMs specify and estimate models of linear relationships among variables. This technique is usually considered as a confirmatory method, although some recent studies have applied an exploratory SEM approach (e.g., Asparouhov & Muthén, 2009; Marsh et al., 2010, 2014). Some special cases of SEM are commonly used in practice, such as path analysis, factor analysis and canonical correlation analysis (e.g., Cudeck & MacCallum, 2012; McDonald, 1996; Hardoon

Exploratory Study （n=1104）

- Corrected Item-Total Correlations >0.35
- Within block Factor Analysis
- Exploratory Factor Analysis of entire set
- Reliability test: Cronbach' s alpha>0.7

↓

Confirmatory Study (n=1104)

- t-value for each loading, significance
- Goodness-of-Fit indices
  - $X^2/df<3$
  - GFI, AGFI, CFI>0.9
  - SRMR<0.5
  - RMSEA<0.6
- Discriminant validity, squared correlation vs. AVE

↓

Test of Structural Model (n=1104)

- Goodness-of-Fit indices
- T-values of structural coefficients, significance

Fig. 3.5 General analytical approach

et al., 2004). A full SEM is composed of three sets of equations: (a) a measurement model for latent variables, (b) a measurement model for measured variables, and (c) a structural model. SEMs with a measurement model for latent variables focus on latent variables instead of observed ones that play the role of indicators of unobserved constructs.

Here, we only present a brief introduction to the methods used in each step of the analytical approach. (See the description of the SEM method and criterion selections in Chapter 6.) In this research, we first employed an exploratory study to identify latent variables underlying the complete set of items (implemented in the SPSS package). Corrected item-total correlations were used to eliminate items that were inconsistent with the average behaviour of the other items in the set (Howard & Forehand, 1962). A within-block factor analysis was conducted before subjecting all items to check the within-block dimensionality (Houston, 2004; Schlegel et al., 2012).

I next conducted an exploratory factor analysis (EFA) of the entire set of variables to extract main factors. I used principal axis factoring (PAF) because my focus was to identify latent variables that contributed to the common variance (Kline, 1998; Widaman, 1993;). Cronbach's alpha values for each construct were used to evaluate reliability after the EFA.

The EFA is usually considered as a preliminary analysis because the unidimensionality cannot be directly assessed. Therefore, experts have suggested that the CFA should be employed to test whether the data confirm the generated model (e.g., Garver & Mentzer, 1999; Lu et al., 2007). AMOS 20 was used to conduct the CFA in this study.

Convergence validity is assessed by t-values, which represent the parameter estimate divided by its standard error (Dunn et al., 1994). The t-values are shown as critical ratios in the AMOS outputs. An absolute value of the critical ratio greater than 1.96 indicates statistical significance (Byrne, 2016). Item reliability is estimated by R2 values. R2 values greater than 0.50 imply acceptable reliability (Bollen, 1989). The R2 values are shown as squared multiple correlations in AMOS outputs.

I employed SEM to specify the causal relationship between determinants and public acceptability. To test hypotheses, I evaluated structural models. Multiple goodness-of-fit measures provided by AMOS 20 were used to assess the fit of the structural model to the observed data, including normed Chi-square, GFI, AGFI, SRMR, RMSEA, NFI, and CFI (Hooper et al., 2008). If the model adequately fits the data, hypotheses will be tested by evaluating t-values of the structural coefficients.

3.6 Ethical Considerations

Ethical approval was obtained from the University of Leeds (AREA 16–003, see. Appendix 3).

The main ethical considerations concerned stakeholder interviews. Sensitive topics would be discussed in the interviews, including topics related to political factors. First, to protect myself and the interviewees invited by using personal connections, I carefully selected comments on sensitive topics to avoid unnecessary political pressure on myself or the interviewees. Since two former cadres were interviewed to verify concepts and categories from other perspectives, there may be some instances where I might feel that material could be interpreted as a criticism of the government, which President Xi has prohibited. The use of such quotations without rephrasing direct criticisms on sensitive topics might be considered politically outrageous and unacceptable behaviour, which could endanger those involved in the study, including its author. Therefore, such quotations were somewhat rephrased but with the participants' intent intact. The rephrased quotations were sent back to the interviewees to check if the rephrased version altered their original meanings. Second, people who participated in the pilot study were not informed about the stakeholder interviews. Third, I performed three rounds of anonymisation to make sure the data could not be traced back to individual persons. Fourth, data was fully anonymized prior to translation, and the translators were informed that they were not allowed to keep the data. Lastly, the original data was securely stored in a locked cabinet in a place known to only two people, and the anonymised data were deposited in the University of Leeds Research Data Repository. Focus group participants also faced the problem of expressing their own opinions about a policy with which most were unfamiliar. Therefore, the participants were guaranteed that the research data would be used only for research purposes and totally anonymised. Thanks to the recruiting process adopted, I was able to gain participants' trust to the degree that could influence the quality of focus groups in this case. There were three measures taken to deal with issues of anonymity. First, participants' names were removed. Second, information that could help identify people was anonymized, including job title, age, gender, length of service, membership in clubs, geographical information, organisations units and groups, and strongly expressed opinions. Third, inside information that could lead to the identification of individuals was not to be used before having been made accessible to the public.

Participants were given the right to withdraw from participation. Interviewees and participants of focus groups could withdraw their data before the results were published. Such data would be destroyed after they had formally decided to withdraw from participation.

There were fewer ethical issues with the attitude survey. Although survey respondents also needed to answer questions about a policy, these answers were fully anonymised. The survey respondents were also guaranteed their data would only be used for research purposes. The original paper questionnaires would be securely stored in a locked cabinet in my home, and the anonymised data would be deposited in the University of Leeds Research Data Repository.

3.7 Conclusion

This chapter has presented the methodological approach adopted in this study, starting with the research strategy in general, including an introduction of key research questions and the research methods to answer each of them. Detailed research methods were presented in three sections: stakeholder interviews in Sect. 3.3, focus groups in Sect. 3.4, and attitude survey in Sect. 3.5. The next three chapters will outline the results from each research method that I used in attempting to answer the RQs.

References

Asparouhov, T., & Muthén, B. (2009). Exploratory structural equation modeling. *Structural Equation Modeling: A Multidisciplinary Journal, 16*(3), 397–438.

Baumgartner, H., & Homburg, C. (1996). Applications of structural equation modeling in marketing and consumer research: A review. *International Journal of Research in Marketing, 13*(2), 139–161.

Beijing Transportation Research Centre. (2011). *Urban Road Traffic Performance Index* (DB11/T 785–2011). (in Chinese).

Bianco, L. (2001). *Peasants without the party: Grass-roots movements in twentieth-century China*. ME Sharpe.

Blaikie, N. (2007). *Approaches to social enquiry: Advancing knowledge*. Polity.

Blaike, N. (2010). *Designing social research: The logic of anticipation* (2nd ed.). Oxford.

Bollen, K.A. (1989). *Structural equations with latent variables*. Wiley-Interscience Publication.

Børdsgaard, K. E., & Chen, G. (2009a, December). *China's attempt to professionalize its civil service* (EAI Background Brief No. 494).
Børdsgaard, K. E., & Chen, G. (2009b, December). *China's civil service reform: An update* (EAI Background Brief No. 493).
Börjesson, M., & Kristoffersson, I. (2015). The Gothenburg congestion charge. Effects, design and politics. *Transportation Research Part A: Policy and Practice, 75*, 134–146.
Börjesson, M., & Kristoffersson, I. (2018). The Swedish congestion charges: Ten years on. *Transportation Research Part A: Policy and Practice, 107*, 35–51.
Bottelier, P. (2018). *Economic policy making in China (1949–2016): The role of economists*. Routledge.
Brook, T., & Frolic, B. M. (2015). *Civil society in China*. Routledge.
Brown, J. D. (2000). What issues affect Likert-scale questionnaire formats. *Shiken: JALT Testing & Evaluation SIG Newsletter, 4*(1), 27–33.
Bryman, A. (2016). *Social research methods*. Oxford University Press.
Burgess, R. G. (2002). *In the field: An introduction to field research*. Routledge.
Burnard, P. (1991). A method of analysing interview transcripts in qualitative research. *Nurse Education Today, 11*(6), 461–466.
Byrne, B. M. (2016). *Structural equation modeling with AMOS: Basic concepts, applications, and programming*. Routledge.
Castells, M. (2008). The new public sphere: Global civil society, communication networks, and global governance. *The ANNALS of the American Academy of Political and Social Science, 616*(1), 78–93.
Charmaz, K. (2014). *Constructing grounded theory*. Sage.
Chinanews. *Half of Beijing's population live far from downtown*. http://www.ecns.cn/cns-wire/2015/05-22/166429.shtml. Accessed 27 July 2019.
Chomeya, R. (2010). Quality of psychology test between Likert scale 5 and 6 points. *Journal of Social Sciences, 6*(3), 399–403.
Chu, C. C., & Lee, R. D. (1994). Famine, revolt, and the dynastic cycle. *Journal of Population Economics, 7*(4), 351–378.
Cresswel, J. W. (1994). *Research design: Qualitative and quantitative approaches*. Amerika: SAGE Publications.
Creswell, J. W., & Miller, D. L. (2000). Determining validity in qualitative inquiry. *Theory into Practice, 39*(3), 124–130.
Cudeck, R., & MacCallum, R. C. (Eds.). (2012). *Factor analysis at 100: Historical developments and future directions*. Routledge.
Cuttance, P., & Ecob, R. (Eds.). (2009). *Structural modeling by example: Applications in educational, sociological, and behavioral research*. Cambridge University Press.
Dahlberg, L., & McCaig, C. (Eds.). (2010). *Practical research and evaluation: A start-to-finish guide for practitioners*. Sage.

Dahlgren, J. (2002). High-occupancy/toll lanes: Where should they be implemented? *Transportation Research Part A: Policy and Practice, 36*(3), 239–255.

Danermark, B., Ekstrom, M., & Jakobsen, L. (2005). *Explaining society: An introduction to critical realism in the social sciences*. Routledge.

Denzin, N. K., & Lincoln, Y. S. (Eds.). (1998). *Collecting and interpreting qualitative materials*. Sage.

Dickson, B. J. (2000). Cooptation and corporatism in China: The logic of party adaptation. *Political Science Quarterly, 115*(4), 517–540.

Dunne, C. (2011). The place of the literature review in grounded theory research. *International Journal of Social Research Methodology, 14*(2), 111–124.

Dunne, D. D., & Dougherty, D. (2016). Abductive reasoning: How innovators navigate in the labyrinth of complex product innovation. *Organization Studies, 37*(2), 131–159.

Dunn, S. C., Seaker, R. F., & Waller, M. A. (1994). Latent variables in business logistics research: Scale development and validation. *Journal of Business Logistics, 15*(2), 145.

Dubois, A., & Gadde, L. E. (2002). Systematic combining: An abductive approach to case research. *Journal of Business Research, 55*(7), 553–560.

Dyson, K., & Maes, I. (Eds.). (2017). *Architects of the Euro: Intellectuals in the Making of European Monetary Union*. Oxford University Press.

Eliasson, J., & Mattsson, L. G. (2006). Equity effects of congestion pricing: Quantitative methodology and a case study for Stockholm. *Transportation Research Part A: Policy and Practice, 40*(7), 602–620.

Fewsmith, J. (2013). *The logic and limits of political reform in China*. Cambridge University Press.

Flick, U. (2018). *An introduction to qualitative research*. Sage.

Francke, A., & Kaniok, D. (2013). Responses to differentiated road pricing schemes. *Transportation Research Part A: Policy and Practice, 48*, 25–30.

Garland, R. (1991). The mid-point on a rating scale: Is it desirable. *Marketing Bulletin, 2*(1), 66–70.

Garver, M. S., & Mentzer, J. T. (1999). Logistics research methods: Employing structural equation modeling to test for construct validity. *Journal of Business Logistics, 20*(1), 33–57.

Gaunt, M., Rye, T., & Allen, S. (2007). Public acceptability of road user charging: The case of Edinburgh and the 2005 referendum. *Transport Reviews, 27*(1), 85–102.

Gerring, J. (2006). *Case study research: Principles and practices*. Cambridge university press.

Glaser, B. G., & Strauss, A. L. (1967). *Discovery of grounded theory: Strategies for qualitative research*. Wiedenfeld and Nicholson.

Golafshani, N. (2003). Understanding reliability and validity in qualitative research. *The Qualitative Report, 8*(4), 597–606.

Goldman, M. (1981). China's Intellectuals. *Index on Censorship, 10*(6), 85–89.

Golob, T. F. (2003). Structural equation modeling for travel behavior research. *Transportation Research Part B: Methodological, 37*(1), 1–25.

Han, R. (2018a). *Contesting cyberspace in China: Online expression and authoritarian resilience*. Columbia University Press.

Han, R. (2018b). Withering gongzhi: Cyber criticism of Chinese public intellectuals. *International Journal of Communication, 12*, 1966–1987.

Hancock, G. R. (2003). Fortune cookies, measurement error, and experimental design. *Journal of Modern Applied Statistical Methods, 2*(2), 293–305.

Hardoon, D. R., Szedmak, S., & Shawe, J. (2004). Canonical correlation analysis: An overview with application to learning methods. *Neural Computation, 16*(12), 2639–2664.

Hartford, K., & Goldstein, S. M. (2016). *Single sparks: China's rural revolutions*. Routledge.

Holbig, H. (2013). Ideology after the end of ideology. China and the quest for autocratic legitimation. *Democratization, 20*(1), 61–81.

Hooper, D., Coughlan, J., & Mullen, M. (2008). Structural equation modelling: Guidelines for determining model fit. *Electronic Journal of Business Research Methods, 6*(1), 53–60.

Houston, M. B. (2004). Assessing the validity of secondary data proxies for marketing constructs. *Journal of Business Research, 57*(2), 154–161.

Howard, K. I., & Forehand, G. A. (1962). A method for correcting item-total correlations for the effect of relevant item inclusion. *Educational and Psychological Measurement, 22*(4), 731–735.

Hysing, E., Frändberg, L., & Vilhelmson, B. (2015). Compromising sustainable mobility? The case of the Gothenburg congestion tax. *Journal of Environmental Planning and Management, 58*(6), 1058–1075.

Ieromonachou, P., Potter, S., & Warren, J. P. (2006). Norway's urban toll rings: Evolving towards congestion charging? *Transport Policy, 13*(5), 367–378.

Josephson, J. R., & Josephson, S. G. (Eds.). 1996. *Abductive inference: Computation, philosophy, technology*. Cambridge University Press.

Kaplan, D. 2008. *Structural equation modeling: Foundations and extensions*. Sage Publications.

Kline, R. B. (1998). *Principles and practice of structural equation modeling*. Guilford Press.

Koufteros, X. A. (1999). Testing a model of pull production: A paradigm for manufacturing research using structural equation modeling. *Journal of Operations Management, 17*(4), 467–488.

Koufteros, X., Vonderembse, M., & Doll, W. (2001). Concurrent engineering and its consequences. *Journal of Operations Management, 19*(1), 97–115.

Kuklick, B. (2013). *Blind oracles: Intellectuals and war from Kennan to Kissinger*. Princeton University Press.

Kvale, S., & Brinkmann, S. (2008). *InterViews: Learning the craft of qualitative research interviewing*. Sage Publications.

Lewis-Beck, M., Bryman, A. E., & Liao, T. F. 2003. *The Sage encyclopedia of social science research methods*. Sage Publications.

Li, F., Wang, R., Paulussen, J., & Liu, X. (2005). Comprehensive concept planning of urban greening based on ecological principles: A case study in Beijing China. *Landscape and Urban Planning, 72*(4), 325–336.

Lipscomb, M. (2012). Abductive reasoning and qualitative research. *Nursing Philosophy, 13*(4), 244–256.

Liu, Q. (2022). Immobility: Surviving the COVID-19 outbreak. In *Human security in China* (pp. 133–154). Palgrave Macmillan.

Liu, Q., Liu, Y., Zhang, C., An, Z., & Zhao, P. (2021). Elderly mobility during the COVID-19 pandemic: A qualitative exploration in Kunming, China. *Journal of Transport Geography, 96*, 103176.

Lu, C. S., Lai, K. H., & Cheng, T. E. (2007). Application of structural equation modeling to evaluate the intention of shippers to use Internet services in liner shipping. *European Journal of Operational Research, 180*(2), 845–867.

Lyons, G., & Davidson, C. (2016). Guidance for transport planning and policymaking in the face of an uncertain future. *Transportation Research Part a: Policy and Practice, 88*, 104–116.

Ma, S. Y. (1994). The Chinese discourse on civil society. *The China Quarterly, 137*, 180–193.

MacCallum, R. C., & Austin, J. T. (2000). Applications of structural equation modeling in psychological research. *Annual Review of Psychology, 51*(1), 201–226.

Marsh, H. W., Lüdtke, O., Muthén, B., Asparouhov, T., Morin, A. J., Trautwein, U., & Nagengast, B. (2010). A new look at the big five factor structure through exploratory structural equation modeling. *Psychological Assessment, 22*(3), 471–491.

Marsh, H. W., Morin, A. J., Parker, P. D., & Kaur, G. (2014). Exploratory structural equation modeling: An integration of the best features of exploratory and confirmatory factor analysis. *Annual Review of Clinical Psychology, 10*, 85–110.

Maruyama, T., & Harata, N. (2006). Difference between area-based and cordon-based congestion pricing: Investigation by trip-chain-based network equilibrium model with nonadditive path costs. *Transportation Research Record: Journal of the Transportation Research Board, 1964*, 1–8.

Maruyama, T., & Sumalee, A. (2007). Efficiency and equity comparison of cordon-and area-based road pricing schemes using a trip-chain equilibrium model. *Transportation Research Part A: Policy and Practice, 41*(7), 655–671.

Mason, J. (2017). *Qualitative researching*. Sage.

Matell, M. S., & Jacoby, J. (1972). Is there an optimal number of alternatives for Likert-scale items? Effects of testing time and scale properties. *Journal of Applied Psychology, 56*(6), 506.

Maxwell, J. A. 2012. *Qualitative research design: An interactive approach*. Sage publications.

May, A. D., Liu, R., Shepherd, S. P., & Sumalee, A. (2002). The impact of cordon design on the performance of road pricing schemes. *Transport Policy, 9*(3), 209–220.

McDonald, R. P. (1996). Path analysis with composite variables. *Multivariate Behavioral Research, 31*(2), 239–270.

McQuitty, S. (2004). Statistical power and structural equation models in business research. *Journal of Business Research, 57*(2), 175–183.

Mu, X. D., Liu, H. P., & Xue, X. J. (2012). Urban growth in Beijing from 1984–2007 as gauged by remote sensing. *Journal of Beijing Normal University, 48*, 81–85.

Nordin, A., & Richaud, L. (2014). Subverting official language and discourse in China? Type river crab for harmony. *China Information, 28*(1), 47–67.

Novick, G. (2008). Is there a bias against telephone interviews in qualitative research? *Research in Nursing & Health, 31*(4), 391–398.

Ong, B. K. (2012). Grounded Theory Method (GTM) and the Abductive Research Strategy (ARS): A critical analysis of their differences. *International Journal of Social Research Methodology, 15*(5), 417–432.

People's Daily. (2015). *Beijing authority reveal the population distribution of Beijing for the first time*. [Online]. http://politics.people.com.cn/n/2015/0522/c1001-27039783.html. Accessed 27 July 2019 (in Chinese).

Punch, K. F. 2013. *Introduction to social research: Quantitative and qualitative approaches*. Sage.

Raaijmakers, Q. A., Van Hoof, J. T. C., t Hart, H., Verbogt, T. F., & Vollebergh, W. A. (2000). Adolescents' midpoint responses on Likert-type scale items: Neutral or missing values? *International Journal of Public Opinion Research, 12*, 208–216.

Ramalho, R., Adams, P., Huggard, P., & Hoare, K. (2015, August). Literature review and constructivist grounded theory methodology. In *Forum: Qualitative social research* (Vol. 16, No. 3, pp. 1–13). Freie Universität Berlin.

Randall, D. M., & Fernandes, M. F. (1991). The social desirability response bias in ethics research. *Journal of Business Ethics, 10*(11), 805–817.

Rich, A. (2005). *Think tanks, public policy, and the politics of expertise*. Cambridge University Press.

Ritchie, J., Lewis, J., Nicholls, C. M., & Ormston, R. (Eds.). 2013. *Qualitative research practice: A guide for social science students and researchers*. Sage.

Sale, J. E., Lohfeld, L. H., & Brazil, K. (2002). Revisiting the quantitative-qualitative debate: Implications for mixed-methods research. *Quality and Quantity, 36*(1), 43–53.

Schlegel, K., Grandjean, D., & Scherer, K. R. (2012). Emotion recognition: Unidimensional ability or a set of modality-and emotion-specific skills? *Personality and Individual Differences, 53*(1), 16–21.

Shah, R., & Goldstein, S. M. (2006). Use of structural equation modeling in operations management research: Looking back and forward. *Journal of Operations Management, 24*(2), 148–169.

Shen, Z. (2012). *Mao, Stalin and the Korean War: Trilateral communist relations in the 1950s*. Routledge.

Shirk, S. L. (1993). *The political logic of economic reform in China* (Vol. 24). University of California Press.

Silverman, D. (2015). *Interpreting qualitative data*. Sage.

Small, K. A., & Gómez-Ibáñez, J. A. (1998). Road pricing for congestion management: The transition from theory to policy. In K. J. Button & E. T. Verhoef (Eds.), *Road pricing, traffic congestion and the environment: Issues of efficiency and social feasibility* (pp. 213–246). Edward Elgar.

Steffek, J., Kissling, C., & Nanz, P. (Eds.). (2007). *Civil society participation in European and global governance: A cure for the democratic deficit?* Springer.

Strauss, A. L. (1987). *Qualitative analysis for social scientists*. Cambridge University Press.

Tavakol, M., & Dennick, R. (2011). Making sense of Cronbach's alpha. *International Journal of Medical Education, 2*, 53–55.

Thomas, D. R. (2006). A general inductive approach for analyzing qualitative evaluation data. *American Journal of Evaluation, 27*(2), 237–246.

Thorkildsen, K. M., Eriksson, K., & Råholm, M. B. (2013). The substance of love when encountering suffering: An interpretative research synthesis with an abductive approach. *Scandinavian Journal of Caring Sciences, 27*(2), 449–459.

Tong, J. (2009). Press self-censorship in China: A case study in the transformation of discourse. *Discourse & Society, 20*(5), 593–612.

Trier-, A. (2012). Framing the telephone interview as a participant-centred tool for qualitative research: A methodological discussion. *Qualitative Research, 12*(6), 630–644.

Tu, F. (2016). WeChat and civil society in China. *Communication and the Public, 1*(3), 343–350.

Turner, D. W., III. (2010). Qualitative interview design: A practical guide for novice investigators. *The Qualitative Report, 15*(3), 754–760.

Twitchett, D. C. & Fairbank, J. K. (Eds.). 1978. *The Cambridge History of China*. Cambridge University Press.

Visser, R. (2004). Spaces of disappearance: Aesthetic responses to contemporary Beijing city planning. *Journal of Contemporary China, 13*(39), 277–310.

Walton, D. (2001). Abductive, presumptive and plausible arguments. *Informal Logic, 21*(2), 141–169.

Weaver, R. (2017). *Think tanks and civil societies: Catalysts for ideas and action.* Routledge.

Weiss, R. S. 1995. *Learning from strangers: The art and method of qualitative interview studies*. Simon and Schuster.

Widaman, K. F. (1993). Common factor analysis versus principal component analysis: Differential bias in representing model parameters? *Multivariate Behavioral Research, 28*(3), 263–311.

Wu, G. (2015a). *China's Party Congress: Power, legitimacy, and institutional manipulation*. Cambridge University Press.

Wu, G. (2015b). *Paradoxes of China's Prosperity: Political Dilemmas and Global Implications*. World Scientific.

Wu, K., Chen, Y., Ma, J., Bai, S., & Tang, X. (2017). Traffic and emissions impact of congestion charging in the central Beijing urban area: A simulation analysis. *Transportation Research Part D: Transport and Environment, 51*, 203–215.

Yang, P., Ren, G., & Liu, W. (2013). Spatial and temporal characteristics of Beijing urban heat island intensity. *Journal of Applied Meteorology and Climatology, 52*(8), 1803–1816.

Yang, Z., Cai, J., Ottens, H. F. L., & Sliuzas, R. (2013). *Beijing. Cities, 31*, 491–506.

Zhang, J. (2001). *Beijing urban plan and constructions 50 years*. China's Bookstore. (in Chinese).

Zhang, X. (2006). Fiscal decentralization and political centralization in China: Implications for growth and inequality. *Journal of Comparative Economics, 34*(4), 713–726.

Zhang, Y. (2008). Steering towards growth: Symbolic urban preservation in Beijing, 1990–2005. *Town Planning Review, 79*(2–3), 187–208.

Zhao, S. (1993). Deng Xiaoping's southern tour: Elite politics in post-Tiananmen China. *Asian Survey, 33*(8), 739–756.

CHAPTER 4

Acceptability in the Chinese Context: Exploratory Interviews

4.1 Introduction

As asserted in Chapter 2, it is unclear whether and to what extent Western notions of acceptability apply in the Chinese context. There are no formal laws or official documents indicating how lay citizens could participate in policymaking processes in the Chinese context (Peters & Zhao, 2017). Due to China's government–citizen relations (discussed in Sect. 2.3), the ways in which policymakers consider public acceptability is probably different from that in a democracy.[1] Therefore, this chapter will

[1] There is no consensus on how to define democracy and the practice is altogether different, especially in new democracies. Even the three commonly acknowledged foundations of democracy—legal equality, political freedom, and rule of law (see Weingast, 1997; Diamond & Morlino, 2005), are sometimes absent (see Cheesman, 2015; Fukuyama, 2015). But nevertheless, they are forms of government where the citizens exercise power by voting. Or, as Popper defined, they offer opportunities for the people to oust their leaders without a revolution (Popper, 2012, see also. Jarvie et al., 2006). In this sense, such government has never existed in Mainland China throughout the history. This, however, does not imply a "romanticism" of democracy (see Epstein, 2017; Gilley, 2009). Democracy, or the practice of democracy, has been criticised by many political thinkers, and have been facing crisis since the very early stage (see Dahl, 1973; Hoppe, 2018; Manin, 1997; Michels, 1962; Nietzsche, 2002). I have personally noticed more criticism of democracy after the rise of Trump, Brexit, and other "black swan events" (e.g., Dahlgren, 2018; McCoy et al., 2018; Muis & Immerzeel, 2017; Parmar, 2017). This is probably the biggest challenge for this study is to stop comparing the China's system with Western systems which I am quite unfamiliar with.

Q. Liu, *Public Acceptability of Congestion Charging in China*,
https://doi.org/10.1007/978-981-19-0236-9_4

illustrate how Chinese policymakers consider public acceptability. It does so by drawing on the analysis of 12 interviews with officials, academics, and planners (shown in Table 3.1), as set out in Sect. 3.3. This will address the first RQ: Do policymakers consider public acceptability, and why?

Since an abductive approach was applied to answer this question, stakeholder interviews were conducted in parallel with a literature review on contextual factors related to public acceptability in the Chinese context. These interviews helped to guide the reading of relevant literature and conceptual thinking about how the focus groups and survey were designed.

This chapter starts with reporting the most direct answer to the question in Sect. 4.2, including (a) whether policymakers consider public acceptability (Sect. 4.2.1) and (b) reasons to consider public acceptability in policymaking (Sect. 4.2.2). Political factors discussed by interviewees are reported in Sect. 4.3. Section 4.3.1 presents the theoretical basis of considering public acceptability in China's polity; Sect. 4.3.2 manifests corruption and corrupt cadres as barriers to considering public acceptability; Sect. 4.3.3 shows different opinions about access to information, social media, and media control; Sect. 4.3.4 demonstrates why these fragmented and seemingly "local" problems can undermine the regime. In Sect. 4.4, I introduce two main cultural factors that influence policymakers' perceived importance of public accessibility: lay people's obedience and the supremacy of the rulers.

4.2 Why Do They Care?

4.2.1 Do Policymakers Consider Public Acceptability?

Most of the interviewees, including all cadres in state organs, local authorities and universities, stated that policymakers consider public acceptability an important issue. However, academics without administrative positions and planners, especially non-Communist Party members, were doubtful that it was true.

According to most of the cadres, public acceptability was deemed to be a more important issue than the effectiveness of one particular policy. For example:

> Public acceptability is a different issue [...] it is more important than the three detailed or practical issues (about congestion charging). [...] All policymakers are facing this issue. So, it's more of a fundamental principle for policy-making in general. We have to consider the people. It's derived from the governing idea of the CPC. We are a People's Party [laugh]. (Interviewee 3)

Although cadres made efforts to explain how important public acceptability is for policymakers and how they themselves attempted to listen to the public, there is no institutional requirement or process that incorporates acceptability. It is always the policymakers' personal experiences, perceptions, and attitudes that determine whether the voice of the public should be heard.

> All politicians do pay attention to public acceptability, but the communication channel provided by the government may not thoroughly reflect the voice of the public. The officials will need to make independent judgments on the public's resistance, and they will evaluate the public's basic rights and interests based on their own experience. (Interviewee 1)

It is evident that these judgments are subjective evaluations based on limited information—some based on an informal chat with lay citizens, some on checking comments on social media, and some on expert advice. Since public opinion highly depends on cadres, all interviewees thought it common that policymakers ignored public acceptability in the policymaking process, especially at the grassroots level.

> But these cadres don't care about the inculcation of our Party central committee. Who cares about public acceptability? Who cares about the people? [...] A lot of them. A lot of them don't even know what is public acceptability. What are people? Who cares? They just care about their black gauze hat (political career). They just care about the money. (Interviewee 5)

4.2.2 *Reasons for Considering Public Acceptability*

Cadres considered public acceptability for different reasons. First, almost all cadres mentioned in the first place consider public acceptability a basic requirement for Chinese policymakers because it is the governing idea of the CCP.

> Broadly speaking, considering public acceptability is an instinct of every member of the Communist Party. The core of our governing idea is "The Party is built for the public, and it exercises state power for the people." [...] Thus, the importance of considering public acceptability throughout the whole policy-making process and the implementation of the policy is decided by the essence of our Party. (Interviewee 7)

However, there is neither a practical guideline for policymaking that carries out this governing idea nor a criterion for assessing cadres' performance based on this governing idea. Interestingly, most of the cadres also mentioned "self-cultivation" or "self-discipline" of a Communist when they talked about the governing idea of the CCP. Therefore, this concern for public acceptability depends on cadres' socialist ideology and theoretical knowledge of Chinese Marxism–Leninism.

Other reasons for considering public acceptability were more practical. For example, some interviewees thought public acceptability is more important for policymakers than ever because manipulation of public opinion has become more difficult in the information era.

> Information spreads out quickly through social media, and it may cause mass Internet incidents or mass disturbances. No matter how strictly the officials prohibit the spread of some embarrassing news, there are always some ways to get exposed. So that is one part of the reason why public acceptability is important for policymakers to be concerned about. (Interviewee 1)

Five interviewees thought that cadres consider public acceptability for the sake of social stability maintenance. Since there has been a steady upsurge of large-scale mass incidents in China since the 1990s (Tong & Lei, 2010), cadres have been compelled to consider whether people would rise up in social unrest because of the proposed policy. For example:

> Most cadres want to be promoted. These kinds of riots and social disorders will be political stains for politicians. So, in that case, cadres will pay attention to this issue somehow. (Interviewee 6)

These concerns for public acceptability can be of two main types: concerns derived from theoretical socialist ideology and pragmatic concerns caused by low public acceptability that might end up producing mass incidents that would significantly influence cadres' political careers. Even if the first type of concern was considered tokenism by some interviewees as it does not impose actual constraints on cadres, there is no doubt that the second type of concern is closely related to cadres' personal interests. However, cadres' concerns for public acceptability seem to be motivated not by a need to achieve a higher acceptance but to avoid radical rejections.

4.2.3 Acceptability & Acceptance in the Chinese Context

Most of the interviewees supposed public acceptability or public acceptance of policies in China to be much greater than in the West. It is not clear whether it is acceptability (simplified Chinese: 接受度) or acceptance (simplified Chinese: 接受度) they referred to during the interviews because these two words are translated identically in Chinese. These language ambiguities underlie traditional Chinese philosophies (discussed in Sect. 2.3.1). However, certain signs showed that this word had different meanings on occasion. Some interviewees were aware of the subtle difference between acceptability and acceptance and tried to use "the likelihood that a proposed policy is accepted by the public" to explain acceptability.

> Different purpose. In order to implement a new policy, we need to consider the likelihood that a proposed policy is accepted by the public. But like I said, we need to think about this issue over a longer term, considering that actual acceptance is for policies that we want to implement in the future. We need to know to what extent they are satisfied or unsatisfied with this policy. (Interviewee 6)

Interviewees indicated that the acceptance of policies after the implementation was sometimes reported by newspapers, and it seems the government pays more attention to this; rarely reported is how people think about a policy that is still in the planning stage. However, the real public opinions about a policy may not be reflected by looking at the acceptance or satisfaction of policies in practice because lay citizens do not have feasible routes to object to a policy. Therefore, even high acceptance of a policy could be a hidden danger for the government. Most of the interviewees recognised this problem:

> Maybe it is not obvious if we look at the result of accepting a policy, but if we look at the processing of accepting the policy and what people are

> doing after the policy is accepted, we could find it is entirely different. [...] In China, we can hardly find people saying no to a policy in public because the policy violated their interests. In most cases, even if they know their own interests were violated, they still tend to obey, to do exactly what they are asked to do. So, if you do a survey and get a very positive result, it may not actually mean that this policy is accepted by most of Chinese people. (Interviewee 3)

There are three reasons why the importance of acceptability is seemingly ignored by cadres, although the acceptance or the satisfaction of policies are conventionally reported. First, according to four interviewees, high acceptance of policies is usually reported for propaganda purposes to praise the wisdom of decision-makers. Second, the Chinese notion of acceptance is different from the Western one. For example:

> Europeans could and should accept something is because they have the right to refuse it, for example, the Brexit. No matter how these politicians, scholars, and elite persuade the public or threaten the public, they (lay citizens in democracies) choose to leave. Chinese people don't have such a right. What they can choose is to accept it with pleasure or with a complaint. (Interviewee 5)

> Chinese people's acceptance is not choosing. They don't choose to accept something. Chinese people have a very clear social identity or social position. When I'm in this position, I will do these things; otherwise, I will not. That makes China stable. (Interviewee 10)

In short, individual-level acceptance in the Western context is a result of choice based on self-interest, whilst acceptance is a social, identity-based action in the Chinese context. Therefore, people usually do not have other choices in particular social positions.

Third, reaction to unacceptable policies in the Chinese context is more binary, and major social uprisings are usually not trivial and can be easily suppressed.

> So, the real problem is to distinguish what kind of action people will undertake when they feel the proposed policy is truly unacceptable. A really 'unacceptable' policy means the public is going to rise in rebellion. (Interviewee 1)

Another interviewee (interviewee 8) thought policymakers should not care much about whether people complain about a policy because complaining does not mean the policy is unacceptable. In this case, it is quite unlikely that implementing a transport policy can result in large-scale social unrest; therefore, implementing any single transport policy cannot be unacceptable for the public.

On the one hand, high-level cadres recognise the potential importance of public acceptability, but, in reality, this recognition tends to be expressed only in rare social uprisings. Transport projects are not seen to be likely to result in such grave consequences. There appear to be no formal mechanisms or practices to try and establish public acceptance. Discourse from high-level cadres suggested this is unimportant because the Party philosophy is for the people. Acting in the public interest is then left to the discretion of the cadres (see Sect. 4.3.1).

However, changes in the way public policies have been made might suggest increasing concerns about public acceptability by cadres. The ideological, vague statement of acting for the People may be facing more practical concerns (Foley et al., 2018; He et al., 2016; Hillman & Tuttle, 2016; Li et al., 2016; Sun et al., 2016; Wallace & Weiss, 2015; Wasserstrom, 2018), which is an inevitable result of a series of political and social problems that I elaborate on in the following sections.

4.3 Political Factors

4.3.1 *"To Serve the People"*

Almost every interviewee talked about, and many of them mentioned in the first place, the governing idea of the CCP "to serve the people" (simplified Chinese: 为人民服务) when they were asked about considering public acceptability. This general agreement shows the importance of seeing socialist ideology as the theoretical basis for public acceptability in the Chinese context. Because of the socialist ideology, nobody directly admitted that public acceptability of transport policies may not always deserve attention from cadres. All interviewees indicated that public acceptability should be a major concern for policymakers.

> The ultimate purpose of the CPC, you can find it in almost every most important official document, is to serve Chinese people. It's written there. [...] On the 18th National Congress of the Communist Party of China,

> the Party central committee and the State Council of P.R. China emphasize it again, the Party should consider 'Benefit of The People Is Higher Than All' (simplified Chinese: 人民的利益高于一切) as the starting point and finishing point of policymaking. (Interviewee 4)

Their disagreement on this issue was whether this governing idea is merely a theory or is carried out in practice. All official interviewees thought the idea is used in practice but cannot be dogmatically implemented in the policymaking process:

> We policymakers should not stubbornly stick to the literal meaning of "serving the people." Practically, our work is to make sure we can protect the interests of the great majority of the people, not each one of them. Nowadays, we can see many people complain about the government and the Party. We should listen to them, but we should not allow those noises to cloud our own judgment. I believe the majority of people are still quite satisfied with our administration. (Interviewee 7)

Such statements are not merely pragmatic modifications of the theory of "serving the people" in practice but also have a theoretical justification that allows policymakers to ignore or even oppress some particular population groups.

> People'[2] in China, is not a biological term or a sociological term, it is a political term. You are not born to be one of the People. You need to prove you belong to the People and are not an enemy of the People by your actions. Or in other words, whether you are one of the People or one of the enemies of the People is decided by the Party. (Interviewee 12)

This is in line with previous studies interpreting the term "the People" in the Chinese context (e.g., Levenson, 1968). According to Mao's theory of People's Democratic Dictatorship (simplified Chinese: 人民民主专政), which is a phrase incorporated into the Constitution of the People's Republic of China, the CPC represents the people but may use powers against reactionary forces (Mao, 2014; see also Steiner, 1950). The main ideas of this theory could be summarised as the following: (a) "the

[2] People and human beings are the same word in Chinese (人).

People" is different from "all citizens" declared by the bourgeois; (b) the main body of "the People" should always be the much larger proletariat; (c) the domain of "the People" is ever-changing depending on the judgment of the Party or its leader; (d) the People are the creators of history; but (e) the People need to be represented and cultivated.[3] This is a starting point to understand the relationship between lay citizens and the government and, therefore, of particular importance to understand how and why policymakers concern themselves about public acceptability in the Chinese context.

Since "the People" is an ambiguous political term, many interviewees thought "to serve the people" is merely a slogan.

> If they care about the people, if they reach the Central Committee's requirement; what they need to do is to make the policy more effective, more acceptable. Have you heard about someone who serves you but doesn't allow you to talk, doesn't allow you to express your ideas? I serve you, but I don't care about what you want. What kind of service is it? [...] If you ask those cadres, they will be all apple polishing. "Our Party, our government, serves the people; we think what they think, do what they want." [...] Shameless. Yes, the government should be like that, but what did they do, what are they doing? [...] If they think about the people, why should they use unscrupulous divisive tactics to treat the people? (Interviewee 5)

This is connected to ill-trained or corrupt cadres and, more generally, to political corruption in China since most of the interviewees, including all of the official interviewees who called into question the implementation of "to serve the people" mentioned corruption when they talked about this governing idea.

[3] This was first proposed in the "On The People's Democratic Dictatorship" (simplified Chinese: 论人民民主专政) speech given in commemoration of the 28th anniversary of the founding of the Chinese Communist Party, 30 June 1949. See related discussions about People's Democratic Dictatorship in Selected works of Mao Tse-tung (in Chinese), People's Publishing House, Vol. 1, 1991, pp. 142, 240; Vol. 2, 1991, pp. 637, 690–691; Vol. 3, 1991, 1005; Vol. 4, 1991, pp. 1215, 1412–1413; Vol. 5, 1977, pp. 366–367.

4.3.2 Corruption

Corruption was mentioned by every interviewee; some only intimated that corrupt cadres are always involved in the public acceptability issue, and political corruption is one of the major reasons that public acceptability has not been considered, while most of the interviewees gave detailed and lengthy discussions about corruption. Corruption was also one of the main topics in focus group discussions (see Sect. 5.5.1); hence, the topic was included under the "trust" construct of the survey, the results of which I discuss further in Sects. 6.2.2.5 and 6.3.2.4. It is commonly perceived that corrupt cadres do not think about public acceptability because they only care about their political careers and money. Cadres, especially higher-level cadres and older CCP members, showed a great deal of concern over this issue.

> I feel grievous that corrupt cadres and indolent cadres have already significantly influenced our Party's image among the people. (Interviewee 7)

Some interviewees stated that nationwide corruption had come along with the Economic Reform.

> Actually, cadres started being corrupted since the implementation of the Reform and Opening-up Policy. When 1980, I, as the leader of our department, accompanied many cadres from Guangdong Province to meet a visiting group of representatives of the Swiss Bank. Many cadres were there; I think about one hundred cadres at different levels—provincial level, municipal level, some are even county-level cadres. I remember at that time that they continuously asked about how to open an account in the Swiss Bank, how to transfer money to the Swiss Bank, and a lot of other details. [...] Only after I visited Europe, I found that many of these corrupt cadres' family members have already lived in Western countries. I suddenly realized that actually these cadres started thinking about these issues at the very beginning of our economic reform. (Interviewee 11)

All of the interviewees agreed that nationwide corruption led to people's perception of social injustice because many people used dishonest ways to become rich, such as power-for-money deals and the embezzlement and transfer of state-owned assets by the institution under transformation through secretly sharing assets after the Economic Reform. These phenomena have been widely reported and studied since1990s (e.g.,

Ding, 2000; Smyth, 2000; Sun, 1999; White, 1996; Woo, 1999; Zhu, 2008). Corrupt cadres were deemed as one of the most daunting challenges for the CCP because they brought about a low level of trust in government and widespread public dissatisfaction with the CCP. The low level of trust was thought to have knock-on effects leading to the way the public would view a congestion charge.

> Corrupt cadres constitute one of the main reasons that Chinese people cannot trust the government. The congestion charge will absolutely be considered as a new method of grabbing money from working people. (Interviewee 2)

Many interviewees perceived corruption as an institutional problem because the CCP and the cadres, as the representatives of the CCP, have unlimited power.

> President Xi also said, at the plenary session of the Central Discipline Inspection Commission on January 22, 2013, "Power should be contained within a cage of regulation." Also, on March 26, 2013, Premier Li said, "Power should be executed with caution and responsibility." What do they mean? Corruption is not because of cadres' personalities or some other reasons. It's not because of these individuals; it's because they have unlimited power. Absolute power absolutely leads to corruption. (Interviewee 5)

Although interviewees, especially members of the CCP, repeatedly emphasised the determination of the central committee to fight against corruption[4] (see also Xinhua, 2014, 2015), the perception came from a large number of corrupt cadres who were the actual policymakers of public policies that influence people's everyday lives. Therefore, corrupt cadres are at the core of the issues as to whether and why public acceptability had not been sufficiently considered in the contemporary transport policymaking.

[4] Xi used "where a man has to cut off his own snake-bitten wrist to save his life" (simplified Chinese: 壮士断腕) to describe his determination of the Anti-corruption Campaign when addressing the third plenary session of the CPC Central Commission for Discipline Inspection (CCDI) in January, 2014 and "no border and no taboo, but zero tolerance" at a key meeting during the fifth plenary session of the 18th CPC CCDI in January, 2015.

Interestingly, most of the interviewees made a distinction between high-level and low-level cadres (or, more directly, leading comrades of the central committee and local cadres). Not only official interviewees but also those who considered themselves as lay citizens thought public acceptability is an important political concern for high-level cadres since negative consequences caused by a lack of considering public acceptability may influence the legitimacy of the CCP. For high-level cadres, public acceptability of the policy and how people would react to the policy are perhaps of greater importance than the effectiveness of any particular policy.

> The legitimacy of the CPC is derived from an "irresistible historical tide." The CPC was chosen by Chinese people. [...] So the Party should serve the people and represent the interests of the people. I think high-level leaders are seriously considering the problem. And I think that could let them think about public acceptability more than ever. (Interviewee 4)
>
> You see, high-level cadres care about this issue because they need to think about the ruling position of the CPC, [...] in my opinion, high-level cadres, those who are in the central committee of the CPC, they do care, they care about this issue very much. (Interviewee 9)

Meanwhile, all of the interviewees criticised low-level cadres and local cadres. Most interviewees thought low-level cadres had rarely shown concern for the public in the policymaking process.

> But a lot of local cadres, especially those who want to have greater political achievements, have not rid themselves of that bad habit yet. But these policies actually are closely related to our daily lives. Many projects were approved very quickly, without anyone listening to the voice of the People. Policies were implemented without investigating public attitudes. That's very common. (Interviewee 10)
>
> Well, I think I could tell you very frankly that many of them don't (think about public acceptability). They don't even know what the People means. They think about nothing but power and money. (Interviewee 6)
>
> The result is a bad transport system but what led to the result is something else. Drivers' money for licenses was grabbed by local cadres. If the provincial government wanted to solve the problem, then they would have to interfere with those corrupt cadres. However, corrupt cadres in county-level governments also have connections with corrupt cadres in the

> provincial government. They need to protect each other. As a result, they decide to give up making that policy. (Interviewee 2)

As Lee and Zhang (2013) discussed, as the front line of governance for the authoritarian state, grassroots cadres' behaviours, interests and motivations are limited by their levels in the state machinery. Furthermore, grassroots cadres have adequate flexibility and autonomy based on the institutional logic of the CCP (e.g., Zhou, 2010). There is much evidence showing that corruption, especially at the grassroots level, is extremely common (e.g., Cai, 2003, 2008; King et al., 2013; Li, 2004; Perry, 2001). These low-level cadres, therefore, directly influence the Party's reputation, which produces a breakdown of trust in government. I report on this in Sect. 5.5.1.

The above-mentioned evidence shows that public acceptability of policies is an increasingly important concern of higher-level cadres and probably even more important for the Party leaders because the differences between CCP, China, the government, and its cadres are unclear to the public.

The distinctions between Party, government, and country have been blurred (Brødsgaard, 2012; Pye, 1990). According to some interviewees, congestion charging as a transport policy is merely an issue of governance—the Party plays a less important role than the government in making such a policy. However, it is the Party's image that will be tarnished by public discontent with unacceptable policies attributable to the blurred boundary between the Party and the government.

> People always say, "the Communist Party did it again." (Interviewee 8)

Moreover, lay citizens consider cadres as the "docile tools of the Party (simplified Chinese: 党的驯服工具)" and, therefore, apparently the representatives of the Party.

> There is no doubt that the public considers those cadres are representatives of the Party and that the Party assigns those cadres to rule the people. It is beyond all doubt, a deeply ingrained thought. (Interviewee 1)

Although Liu's[5] theory of "docile tool" (Liu, 1939; see also Boorman, 1963) was rarely seen in official documents, as it was criticised during the Great Cultural Revolution (Dittmer, 2015; Harding, 1971), it has remained an inseparable component of the CCP's ideology; for example, "each Party member should completely submit himself to the interests of the Party and self-sacrificingly devote himself to the public duty. He should forego all personal aims and private considerations which conflict with the Party's interests" (Liu, 1991; see also Dittmer, 1981; Jin, 1993; Yu, 2016). Unsurprisingly, cadres at all levels would be regarded as the embodiment of the CCP at the grassroots level and as practitioners who implement the guidelines of the Central Committee of the CCP.

However, many official interviewees indicated that local governments and cadres do not always follow the guidance of the central committee.

> Local governments have become relatively independent; then, they will have their independent interests. Sometimes, these interests may not be in line with the central government's guidance. That's why we see some local cadres, including high-level local cadres, do not follow the guidance of our central committee but persist in their old ways. (Interviewee 7)

Interviewees considered these changing central–local relations as the result of fiscal decentralisation and the reform of the classified taxation system. This is in agreement with previous research about political and economic reform in the post-Mao era (e.g., Bardhan, 2002; Wong, 1991; Zhang, 2006; Zhang & Zou, 1998). Thus, the congestion charging, as a new source of revenue, might be very attractive to local cadres. In this

[5] Liu Shaoqi was the First Vice Chairman of the Communist Party of China from 1956 to 1966 and Chairman of the People's Republic of China from 1959 to 1968. He held very high positions in Communist China's leadership for some twenty years and was commonly considered as the successor to Mao. He is believed to be the apostle of the so-called Mao Zedong Thought (毛泽东思想, also called Maosim) and the instigator of Mao's cult of personality (see Gao, 2000). However, although he was the one who first systematically argued the Mao Zedong Thought, put the Mao Zedong Thought into the Constitution of the Chinese Communist Party, and clearly stated that the Mao Zedong Thought must be the guideline of everything in the CCP (毛泽东思想作为全党一切工作的指导方针), he was labelled by Mao the "commander of China's bourgeoisie headquarters"(资产阶级司令部的黑司令), "Khrushchev sleeping by our side" (睡在身边的赫鲁晓夫), "China's foremost capitalist-roader" (头号走资派), and a traitor to the revolution in 1968 and then, purged, imprisoned, and tortured to death during the Cultural Revolution (see Dittmer, 1974).

circumstance, they may pay less rather than more attention to whether the policy is acceptable to the public.

There were two main reasons why low-level cadres did not consider the public: the weakening socialist ideology and the cadres' political careers. Most of the interviewees who in fact mentioned the governing idea suggested that the Socialist ideology, as the theoretical foundation for considering the public, has evaporated.

> You know ideology used to be one of the most powerful weapons of our Party, especially during Mao's time. [...] Most of them (younger generation cadres) are indifferent to the ideology; they only think about their personal interests. [...] Thus, public opinions are usually considered as an impediment to their political career advancement. (Interviewee 4)

Unlike the unwavering ideology at the grassroots level in Mao's time (e.g., Lu, 2004; Schurmann, 1971), the official ideology in post-Mao China has been usually regarded as a dogmatic disguise for its capitalist nature in the literature on contemporary China (e.g., Fukuyama, 1989, 2012; Kraus, 1991; Misra, 1998). Although some scholars have argued that the political elites have been attempting to rebuild the official ideology (e.g., Holbig, 2008, 2009; Holbig & Gilley, 2010; Yang, 2014). Socialist ideology, it has been argued, is no longer a shared belief in Chinese society (e.g., Holbig, 2013; Zhao & Belk, 2008). Since it is merely a matter of performing according to the rules of the official language system (see Link, 1992), socialist theories, such as "to serve the people" can hardly urge low-level cadres to think about the public. Their political career is the most important and pragmatic motivation for low-level cadres to consider public acceptability.

> Well, but nowadays, some cadres, you know they just want to be promoted fast; they don't give a damn about the people. Everything they do is for their political career. (Interviewee 3)

Many interviewees mentioned cadres' enthusiasm over short-term political achievements to explain why being promoted is the ubiquitous motivation for cadres (see also Chan, 2004; Edin, 2003; Guo, 2008, 2009; Kou & Tsai, 2014; Steidlmeier, 1999; Sun, 2004). However, cadres do not have to think about public opinion due to China's cadre appointment system.

> Western politicians' power comes from the people. They are elected. [...] However, in China, cadres' power is not from the people. People can give them nothing but trouble. They are not elected to be a cadre; they are not elected because of their ideas and plans. They are appointed by higher-level Party organisations; they are appointed by higher-level cadres. Chinese cadres are only responsible to their superiors, not to their inferiors. So, the first and foremost rule of being a Chinese cadre is to be submissive to your superiors. (Interviewee 12)

Predictably, public opinion plays a negligible role in the cadre management system. Therefore, practically, it is highly unlikely that low-level cadres would be motivated to consider public acceptability of congestion charges without pressure from their superiors.

In summary, the governing philosophy is for the people, but this philosophy is not acted upon in practice through engagement or feedback mechanisms. Whilst there is some overarching concern from senior politicians that the CPC needs to act for the people sufficiently to avoid uprisings and future problems, this concern does not trickle down to the lower level government. At a local and provincial level, there appears to be widespread corruption and little interest in considering the public compared with personal advancement. The behaviour of the ruling class more generally could have a significant impact on how the public views new public policies such as congestion charging. There is not necessarily a belief that new policies are indeed for "the people." These corrupt low-level cadres and their lack of concern about the public have reduced public trust and confidence in government and roused people's resentment, thereby considerably undermining the CCP regime's legitimacy (see Chen, 2013; Li, 2012; Pei, 2012). This is why official interviewees, especially high-level cadres, attached great importance to a lack of concern about public acceptability at the grassroots level.

4.3.3 Access to Information

Information was one of the most frequently mentioned themes, and these concerns about information were different from those reported in the literature. Interviewees extensively discussed various topics related to information, including access to information, exchange of ideas, information from official sources, information from social media, information transparency, propaganda, and media control. Focus group discussions targeted information and access to it (see Sect. 5.3), and I included it under the "information" construct of the survey, the results of which I discuss in Sects. 6.2.2.3 and 6.3.2.4

First, interviewees had different opinions about whether providing information at the planning stage may help gain public support for congestion charging. Some thought information can help the public to understand the policy better and, therefore, make the policy more acceptable; others emphasised that policymaking must be based on China's realities. China's realities is a commonly used term in China's official language (e.g., Choi, 2011; Saich, 2010), and it usually implies differences between the Chinese and Western contexts. Therefore, this case suggests that Chinese policymakers do not need to provide access to information.

Second, those who valued public opinions found no effective means for exchanging ideas; therefore, it is difficult for both policymakers and the public to get useful information from each other. On the one hand, citizens cannot get enough information about a policy that is still at the planning stage; on the other hand, cadres can hardly listen to the public even if they are willing to.

> We policymakers may not have any chance to know what the people think. Sometimes, it's not really true that we don't want to consider the public acceptability issue, sometimes maybe we cannot know their true opinion, or even worse, sometimes we get fake public opinions. (Interviewee 3)

Although there are several official ways to collect ideas from the public, such as public hearings and the petitioning system, these have proved to be ineffective in collecting ideas and hearing complaints from individuals. Many interviewees regarded public hearings as "going through the motions", as the public is rarely asked to participate in these so-called public hearings. Moreover, the petitioning system, which has been relied upon since 1949, has never been an effective means for dealing with public complaints (e.g., Michelson, 2007; Minzner, 2006). It was widely reported that local governments have been violently responding to petitioners, such as intercepting citizens before they could appeal in Beijing and imprisoning large numbers of petitioners in illicit detention facilities (Hurst et al., 2014; Li, 2008; Li & O'brien, 2008; Li et al., 2012; Michelson, 2008).

Third, social media have become an important source of information (and fabricated information) for the public. Most interviewees mentioned social media as an effective way to get information and express opinions. However, many official interviewees were worried about fabricated information on social media. It is noteworthy that whether the information should be fabricated or not dominantly depends on how the government defines the information; pervasively, information officially announced as "fabricated" is later proven to be the truth, mostly along with relative cadres' fall from power (for example the case of Bo Xilai, see Broadhurst & Wang, 2014). Therefore, in most cases, even if the information from unofficial sources is incredibly unreasonable, lay citizens are still more willing to believe or enjoy fake news than information from official sources. Such willingness implies a low level of trust in government, which I discuss in Chapter 5. Interviewees thought such fabricated information can bring about unnecessary complaints about the proposed scheme and make the policy more unacceptable to the public.

> People can get much more information nowadays thanks to the fast development of social media. However, a large percentage of that information is rumours; some are even ridiculous lies. But the public is always willing to believe such fake news. For example, there are several popular versions of the congestion charge in Beijing now; however, I myself know none of these plans. The public talks about these rumours as if they are really going to happen and criticise the government based on those ridiculous plans. So, of course people can get much more information now, but how much of it is real? (Interviewee 3)

Most interviewees thought social media today urge cadres to think about public acceptability since information spreads fast on social media.

> Information spread out quickly through social media such as WeChat, and it may cause mass internet incidents or mass disturbances. No matter how strictly the officials prohibit the spread of some embarrassing news, the media always find a way to expose it. So that is one part of the reason why public acceptability is important for policymakers, more than ever. (Interviewee 1)

Fourth, information from official and unofficial sources always tells different stories.

> According to an online survey by Sina, only 14% of people support the traffic restriction based on the last digit number. And there is another online survey by Xinhua, more than 60% of people are against it. […] there is an official survey conducted by Beijing Transportation Development & Research Centre. They said more than 80% of car owners support this policy. And there is a company called Zero point that did a survey authorized by the government. Their result is that 90% of the respondents support the traffic restriction. (Interviewee 4)

Five interviewees suggested that people are more willing to believe information presented on social media than on traditional media and that traditional propaganda has become less effective at present. It is interesting that all official interviewees frequently mentioned the word "propaganda" or "guiding public opinion" during the interviews, while few mentioned access to information. Propaganda was one of the principal concerns for cadres, and enhancing propaganda was perceived as one of the most effective ways to increase public acceptability. This fits with literature on contemporary China (e.g., Brady, 2009; Brady & Wang, 2009; Chen, 2003; Creemers, 2017; Tang & Iyengar, 2011).

Fifth, the Party is still highly capable of media control and guiding public opinion. Media control plays a vital role in China's polity (e.g., Li, 2000; Shambaugh, 2007; Stockmann & Gallagher, 2011; Tong, 2010). Some interviewees were very confident about CCP's capability of media control. They suggested that although the Party worried about social media at the beginning, it found that social media are actually easier to control than are traditional media. Moreover, the Party perceived it to be more effective to guide and manipulate public opinion through social media than through traditional media.

> The government is still highly capable of preventing the dissemination of this information. […] Some people might think social media is dangerous for our Party, the Party used to worry about this too, but then we find that our concern is misplaced. […] Several years ago, people who circulated rumours through social media were put in jail, but our government doesn't do that much anymore. […] We still control the press. […] We provide useful information and filter harmful information to maintain the stability of our society like every country in the world. (Interviewee 7)

Media control was also regarded as an alternative or perhaps a much-preferred way to deal with low public acceptability in the Chinese context.

Some interviewees suggested that media control could be a more effective way to avoid mass incidents, which is the practical motivation for considering public acceptability.

> Of course, no cadre wants social disorders, but actually they have many other methods to deal with this. Their political career may be influenced but they will not be politically dead unless the social disorder is very influential, for example, foreign media involved. They might think that controlling the spread of information is much easier than making people happy. (Interviewee 3)

This fits well in the literature on Chinese media and censorship (e.g., Fu et al., 2013; King et al., 2013; MacKinnon, 2008; Qiu, 1999; Tong, 2009). The interviewees pointed to an increased role of information in policy discourse, regardless of any official sanction. If anything, the weight of opinion was that the potential for bottom-up or "fake news" limited the benefits which would be achieved from greater government efforts to communicate. It is not clear which information the public believes. This question is further explored in the focus groups and the survey (see Sects. 5.3, 6.2.2.2, and 6.3.2.4).

4.3.4 Interconnectedness of Policies

Official interviewees repeatedly highlighted the "interconnectedness of policies" and the "big picture" as one of the most crucial reasons underlying high-level cadres' intention to consider public acceptability. To put the issue straightforwardly, the acceptability of one policy is related to people's experience and perceptions of policies implemented previously. An extremely unacceptable local policy can be especially dangerous to higher-level governments and ultimately undermine the regime. Although this issue was of concern only to the high-level cadres in our stakeholder, evidence from focus groups corroborates this as lay citizens repeatedly talked about previous policies, which were perceived mostly as extremely ineffective and consequently, making them to think that congestion charging would definitely fail to alleviate any problem. Relevant discussions around previous policies are presented in Sect. 5.4.1, and this issue was tested by the survey under the "perceived effectiveness of previous policies" construct, the results of which are discussed further in Sects. 6.2.2.3 and 6.3.2.4.

The interactions between congestion charging and other previous policies were rarely investigated in the literature, which implies that the acceptance of previous policies may not play an important role in the Western context. However, it is an important reason for considering public acceptability in the Chinese context—discontent with the government tends to accumulate because of the increasing energy that must be available over time to people who have to endure policies, especially bad ones.

> When the policy comes to people's minds, it does not come alone. It comes along with the memories of all the unsolved problems, social inequality, and lost personal interests caused by previous policies. (Interviewee 10)

Public acceptability of congestion charging, therefore, should be regarded as a result of accumulated positive and negative attitudes towards the government instead of a relatively independent attitude towards this particular policy. The following quotation shows how accumulated discontent makes congestion charging more unacceptable.

> Last year the government implemented a new housing policy which violated my personal interests. I was quite disappointed but didn't say a word. Months ago, they revised the tax policy. I started complaining because I am going to pay quite some money. Yesterday, I just heard that the local government planned to invest in the chemical industry. Several new factories will be built around my apartment. I got very angry about the new plan, but I decided to endure it again. And now, you bring your congestion charge. Tax me again? Should I endure it again? (Interviewee 8)

Theoretically, the idea of interconnectedness is firmly embedded in dialectical materialism (Mao, 1965; Marx, 1976), in which every individual Chinese is systematically indoctrinated through course content beginning in elementary school (Li et al., 2004; Reed, 1995). Most of the interviewees did not perceive the public acceptability of congestion charging as an independent issue or merely an issue of transport but tended to put the issue in a broader context, considering the public acceptability of policies and public attitude towards the government in general. This makes sense in a context where there is no prospect of a referendum or objection to a specific scheme such as could occur in the West. Therefore, in the Chinese context, one would not expect the effectiveness of the policy to be strongly directly connected to acceptability. By contrast, it would be more important to trust that the government will do the right thing.

4.4 Cultural Factors

Certainly, these political factors influence the nature of the public acceptability issue in the Chinese context, but, nonetheless, political factors alone cannot thoroughly explain (a) why public acceptability of policies could be marginalised by grassroots cadres for so long, and (b) why higher-level cadres were particularly sensitive about this issue and assigned to it a heightened level of vigilance. This Section elaborates how cultural factors make public acceptability in an authoritarian state like China different from that in democracies.

A large variety of cultural factors were discussed during the interviews, including obedience, the cult of personality, the unwillingness to express opinions in public, a lack of civic awareness, the unwillingness to change, being hypocritical, being indifferent to others, *mianzi* (face-saving), *chaxu geju* (differential mode of association), and a lack of civic trust.[6] This section focuses on the first three of these factors, as the remaining factors are not directly related to this topic.

The three factors helped in conducting focus group discussions and designing the survey. Obedience to and the supremacy of the rulers were further discussed in focus groups (see Sect. 5.7); the topics were included under the "obedience to authority" construct of the survey, the results of which are discussed in Sects. 6.2.2.6 and 6.3.2.4. Further, I considered unwillingness to express opinions in public when organising focus group discussions (see the "stimulator" strategy, Sect. 3.4.3).

4.4.1 *Obedience*

It is interesting that interviewees, most of the time, used *to accept* as a synonym for *to obey* or *to endure*. The term *to accept*, in the Western context, is to make a favourable response to an offer. In other words, it is an initiative act to approve or consent to a proposed scheme with favour. However, it is evident that the term is interpreted differently in the

[6] The trust here is different from other "trust" in the thesis. It is more about the relationship between lay citizens. About civic trust and civic honesty see Cohn et al. (2019).

Chinese context. The interviews suggested a meaning along the lines of the ability *to endure* an unfavourable offer or the degree to which people are willing to *obey* authority, as such being more similar to the Western term *tolerate*. For example:

> In China, we can hardly find someone saying no to a policy because the policy violated their interests. In most cases, even if they know their own interests were seriously violated, they still tend to obey. [...] Maybe they just endure another terrible policy. (Interviewee 3)

Some interviewees thought the root of this obedience is the authoritarian government, which imposes great pressure on the public. Lay citizens have to obey the authority SIMPLY because it is too risky not to obey. Most interviewees considered that obedience to authority is more of a Chinese people's cultural gene, evolving from Confucianist thoughts. Interviewees regarded obedience as the core of the Confucianist notion of family, which plays an essential role in the Confucianist ethical system. Therefore, as interviewee 2 stated:

> This obedience should not be considered as a result of Confucian brainwash. Because the obedience is not passive, it is a common choice of Chinese people and a result of self-cultivation. People who do not know how to obey could accomplish nothing. In the long term, it is Chinese ethics that maintain social order. (Interviewee 2)

According to some interviewees, traditional Confucianist values, as already described in the literature review, have been playing an increasingly important role since the beginning of the new century. Unlike Mao's criticism of Confucianism during the Cultural Revolution (e.g., Gregor & Chang, 1979; Zhang & Schwartz, 1997), Confucianism has come back into official discourses (e.g., Billioud, 2007; Yu, 2008; Zhao, 1998). It has been developed in Hu's socioeconomic vision "Harmonious Society" (Guo & Guo, 2008) and advocated as the cornerstone of CCP's Core Socialist Values (Guo, 2014).

Although interviewees showed disagreements about the "revival of Chinese traditional virtues" movement, they all indicated or implied that the larger political purpose of the government's support for this movement is to maintain social and political stability, which corroborates earlier evidence discussing the purpose of the contemporary revival of

Confucianism (e.g., Cheung, 2012; Dai, 2018; Pang, 2014; Wu, 2014; Yu, 2008). Therefore, Confucianism, as a tool for cultural cultivation (Billioud & Thoraval, 2007), significantly contributes to Chinese people's obedience to authority.

Second, interviewees considered obedience as a shared trait of collectivist societies (see also Konsky et al., 2000; Sabatier & Lannegrand-Willems, 2005; Triandis, 1988). In such a society, individuals, as small parts of the society, are usually encouraged to think about the society as a whole instead of in terms of their personal interests.

> Our culture is a collectivist culture. We don't pay much attention to personal choices; group interests or collective interests are what we care about. So, in this case, personal interests are always something to be sacrificed. Sometimes people are forced to do so, but sometimes it is their will to self-sacrifice. (Interviewee 4)

Third, some interviewees indicated that obedience to authority is an inevitable outcome of Stalinism. These interviewees deemed the influence of Stalinism to be more influential than traditional Confucianism because, during the Cold War, obedience to authority was also a common phenomenon in eastern European countries (e.g., Hopf, 2012; Mastny, 1998; Wettig, 2008; Whitfield, 1996), which have by no means been influenced by Confucianist values.

> It is partly because of our autocratic culture, but more importantly, it is because of our Socialist culture. [...] Chinese people don't have such kind of rights (to reject a proposed scheme). What they can choose is to accept it with pleasure or with a complaint. [...] When people peacefully request their political appeals at Tiananmen Square and a lot more occasions, what happened? Facts are more eloquent than words. (Interviewee 5)

However, if, as almost all interviewees mentioned, the Chinese people are that obedient, public acceptability should not be an issue whatsoever because the public neither has the right to reject an unacceptable policy nor is willing to consider whether the policy is favourable or not. In fact, all interviewees are aware of the importance of the people's attitude, especially official interviewees and academics, who are involved in policymaking processes.

All interviewees believed that Chinese and Western peoples would react differently to unacceptable policies. Some interviewees indicated that there is a compromise mechanism in Western countries that allows different interest groups to make an agreement, adjusting conflicting ideas and interests. However, it is quite the opposite way in China, as, for instance, one scholar noted:

> There is a duality in the Chinese people: sometimes they are docile while sometimes they turn into mobs. Our national character is just like China's mother river, the Yellow River. Under the constraints of strong embankments, it could be quite docile; once the embankments burst, it becomes cruel, brutal, and destructive. (Interviewee 4)

Even if a proposed scheme is unacceptable to the public, it is still highly likely that the Chinese people will appear to be obedient and calm compared to Western people. However, once their dissatisfactions accumulate to a certain degree, all the pent-up anger and resentment will break out. Most interviewees found that this type of extreme reaction makes it difficult for policymakers to investigate the resentment hidden under a seemingly high acceptance rate.

4.4.2 Supremacy of the Rulers

Confucianist values undoubtedly attracted Western researchers' attention when they studied the Chinese context (e.g., Farh & Cheng, 2000; Yan & Sorenson, 2006). However, it is common that the traditional Chinese schools of thought are simplified to the Confucianism. This oversimplified interpretation of traditional Chinese culture may result in a lack of consideration about the effects of other schools of thought and the interactions between them (see Sect. 2.3.1).

The supremacy of the rulers, originally derived from the Legalist school (see Sect. 2.3.1.3), was mentioned as another important reason why public acceptability is not necessarily a major concern for policymakers in the Chinese context. On the one hand, the supremacy of the rulers reflects an attachment relationship between lay citizens and officials throughout Chinese history.

> In our history, local officials were called as fathers and mothers of ordinary people. [...] Ordinary people were heavily dependent on officials. Whatever these officials said, ordinary people would be regarded as something right,

> something that had to be done, and orders that needed to be obeyed. (Interviewee 3)

Some interviewees indicated this attachment relationship was caused by the "servility" or "slavery" of Chinese people, which has been criticised since the New Culture Movement in the 1910s and 1920s (e.g., Chen, 2007; Schwarcz, 1986). Lu Xun's forthright summary of the Chinese history was mentioned by half of the interviewees as the most precise description of this servility:

1. The era of longing, but failing, to become slaves
2. The era of provisionally securing status as slaves (Lu, 2017)

On the other hand, the ruling class makes efforts to convince the public that lay citizens are incapable of making the right decision, thereby discouraging them from thinking about proposed schemes and participation in policymaking.

> For thousands of years, the ruling classes devoted themselves to strengthening the idea of the supremacy of rulers. [...] they (the public) believe policymakers are much smarter than themselves and made the best choices for society. (Interviewee 6)

Obviously, this supremacy of the rulers could enhance blind obedience to authority, which is one of the major causes of the cult of personality in Mao's time (Leese, 2011; Schrift, 2001). Obedience to authority and supremacy of the rulers complement each other. Together, they reinforce the cadres' lack of consideration for public acceptability.

4.4.3 *Unwillingness to Express Opinions in Public*

The above-mentioned two cultural factors explain why it is possible for low-level cadres to ignore the public acceptability of policies. In this section, I argue that even if cadres are willing to consider this issue, it can still be difficult to collect ideas from the public.

Lay citizens are unwilling to express opinions in public and that this, in turn, acts as a major barrier for policymakers in considering public acceptability.

> A bit of interesting news [...] BBC journalists in Beijing find it extremely hard to interview people on the street. Those citizens told the journalists that they cannot answer questions because if they do so, they might be asked for a cup of tea.[7] This journalist said that gathering people's opinions in Beijing is like a hungry lion hunting sheep on a grassless land. (Interviewee 4)

Furthermore, most official interviewees indicated that Chinese people tend to express fake opinions, especially when they were asked by official media. Interviewees claimed that the results of official surveys are always opposite to those of online surveys conducted by mass media. They thought online survey results are more likely to represent real public opinions, whereas official survey results are usually used as evidence supporting official statements, such as that citizens are satisfied with a new policy. However, this judgement is still highly subjective since none of the interviewees had an effective way to detect fake opinions.

At present, Chinese netizens more actively participate in online discussions about politically sensitive issues (Clark, 2012; Lei, 2013; Yang & Jiang, 2015); however, most interviewees from officialdom were cautious and dubious about online comments, which are usually hostile (see also Leibold, 2011; Tong & Lei, 2013a, b). Interviewees intimated that complaints were generally regarded as a way to release pressures in everyday life and that satires were regarded as self-amusement instead of dissatisfaction with the government, a claim also made by the two planners who perceived themselves as lay citizens.

> I feel they (cadres) don't care much about whether we are complaining or not because, you know, many people complain about everything. For example, me, hee hee. (Interviewee 8)

[7] Since 2007, Chinese netizens have started using the term "tea talk" or "forced to drink tea" (simplified Chinese: 被喝茶) to describe interrogations by the internal security police. A person can be called for a cup of tea due to different reasons, such as sharing sensitive information from unofficial channels. Different forms of police harassment related to tea talks include home surveillance, house arrest, and kidnapping (e.g., Advox, 2013; BBC, 2013).

This unwillingness to express opinions was considered to be the result of obscurantism.[8] Interviewees explained that lay citizens may not dare to talk about their ideas about policies because they feel their ideas are not professional. Moreover, they said, the government and its experts deliberately discourage the public from acquiring information about proposed policies. Self-censorship was mentioned as a main cause of the seeming "unwillingness to express opinions". Some interviewees argued that Chinese people's opinions depend on the nature of the conversation and audiences. People would automatically self-censor sensitive comments when they are talking. These interviewees suggested that most Chinese people are hypocritical. For example:

> I think Chinese people are always wearing three masks. What they say, what they act, and what they think are quite different. (Interviewee 2)

This view agrees with the literature that shows the important role of self-censorship in China (e.g., Esarey & Xiao, 2011; Hassid, 2008; Weber & Jia, 2007). Also, it is worth noting that the obscurantist ruling class policy is also one part of the tradition of Chinese culture as obscurantism has been practised by the ruling classes for thousands of years (see also Friedman, 2016; Hsiao, 1976; Wang, 2017).

Due to the unwillingness to express opinions and the likely more common habit of expressing politically correct views in public or extremist opinions online, it is rather difficult for policymakers to understand people's concerns about a proposed scheme. This may also have implications for the research design pursued in this thesis, as discussed in Sects. 3.4 and 3.5. Consequently, policymakers have to make subjective judgments about public acceptability and maybe even about the acceptance of policies.

[8] *Obscurantism* is the practice of deliberately presenting information in a recondite manner, designed to forestall further understanding (see Nietzsche, 1996; Schopenhauer, 1998). Since it restricts knowledge to a small group of people—the ruling class, it is commonly considered anti-democratic (see Elster, 2011; Good, 2003; Wright et al., 1992 see also Ho, 1945).

4.5 Summary and Conclusions

In summary, interviews with public officials helped to elucidate the overarching nature of the public acceptability of congestion charging in the Chinese context and echoed many of the issues that had been noted in the literature about Chinese culture and the way in which this might influence how Chinese people think about public policies and the manifestations of public acceptability of these.

Figure 4.1 presents the mechanism of policymakers' concern about public acceptability in the Chinese context. In general, there are multiple barriers for policymakers to consider public acceptability, but only a few factors urge them to do so.

Most of the research investigated the public acceptability of road pricing schemes in the democratic polity; however, there is little research exploring this issue in an authoritarian regime such as China. Some

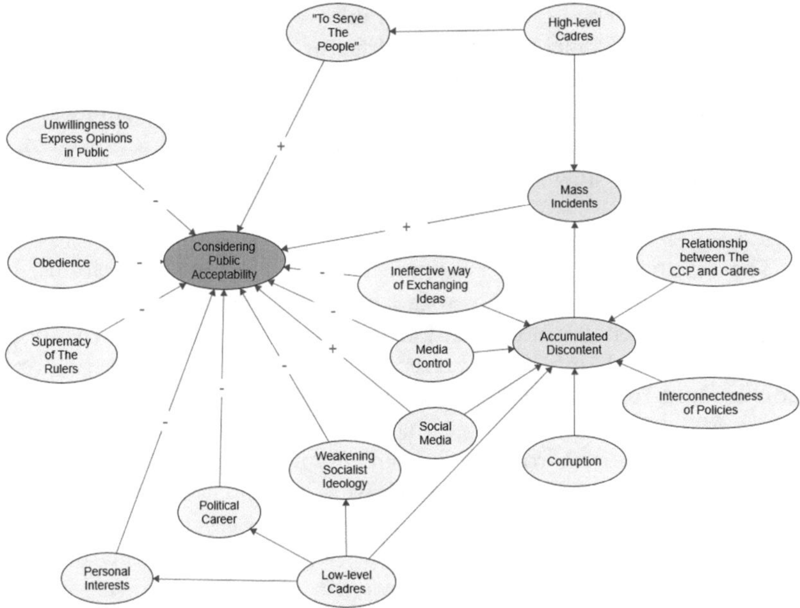

Fig. 4.1 Policymakers' concern about public acceptability

scholars have attempted to analyse public acceptability of transport policies in the Chinese context recently (Chen & Zhao, 2013; Jia et al., 2017; Song, 2015; Sun et al., 2016), which implies that public acceptability has attracted some attention. However, all of this research dogmatically applied Western-based frameworks to analyse Chinese policies, except for Chen and Zhao (2013).

Public acceptance is different from acceptability, but these terms are ambiguously used in official discourse. For various reasons, the state is not accustomed to asking for public views, and the public is equally unused to giving them. As the summary in Fig. 4.1 suggests, even were there to be a perceived need to ask about public acceptance, there are some important reasons why the interpretation of any answers would be difficult: (a) low levels of trust in government, fuelled partly by corrupt cadres; (b) traditional Chinese values of servitude and endurance of policy; and (c) a tendency, therefore, to reflect dissatisfaction via occasional uprisings rather than issue-specific actions.

In this chapter, I argued that public acceptability of congestion charging in the Chinese context is different from that in a democracy. Policymakers in democracies need to consider public acceptability because they need public support to implement the policy. However, Chinese policymakers are concerned about public acceptability because it is likely that a low level of acceptability can result in mass incidents, which will ruin the cadres' political career and significantly undermine the image of the CCP.

The results of stakeholder interviews had important implications for the design of the focus groups with lay citizens, the design of the public survey, and the choice of the SEM analytical approach. Because the motivation for considering public acceptability in this context is to avoid troubles and risks instead of obtaining public support, the public may have s different interpretation of what the government should deliver and different expectations from the implementation of the policy, and these differences have to be explored via focus group discussions. Also, it was necessary to ascertain what people really meant by certain terms in order to design a questionnaire. This is one of the reasons to consider using an SEM approach, as this approach allows the relationships to self-identify rather than to presume a model form from which it may be unclear what elements might be related to each other in the formulation of opinions in this context.

References

Advox. (2013). *China: Bloggers "Forced to Drink Tea" with Police* [Online]. https://advox.globalvoices.org/2013/02/19/china-bloggers-forced-to-drink-tea-with-police/. Accessed 27 July 2019.

Bardhan, P. (2002). Decentralization of governance and development. *Journal of Economic Perspectives, 16*(4), 185–205.

BBC. (2013). *Tea? Reining in dissent the Chinese way* [Online]. https://www.bbc.co.uk/news/world-asia-china-21027416. Accessed 27 July 2019.

Billioud, S. (2007). Confucianism, "cultural tradition" and official discourses in China at the start of the new century. *China Perspectives, 2007*(3), 50–65.

Billioud, S., & Thoraval, J. (2007). Jiaohua: The Confucian revival in China as an educative project. *China Perspectives, 2007*(4), 4–20.

Boorman, H. L. (1963). How to be a good Communist: The political ethics of Liu Shao-Ch'I. *Asian Survey,* 372–383.

Brady, A. M. (2009). *Marketing dictatorship: Propaganda and thought work in contemporary China*. Rowman & Littlefield Publishers.

Brady, A. M., & Wang, J. (2009). China's strengthened new order and the role of propaganda. *Journal of Contemporary China, 18*(62), 767–788.

Broadhurst, R., & Wang, P. (2014). After the Bo Xilai trial: Does corruption threaten China's future? *Survival, 56*(3), 157–178.

Brødsgaard, K. E. (2012). Politics and business group formation in China: The Party in control? *The China Quarterly, 211*, 624–648.

Cai, Y. (2003). Collective ownership or cadres' ownership? The non-agricultural use of farmland in China. *The China Quarterly, 175*, 662–680.

Cai, Y. (2008). Local governments and the suppression of popular resistance in China. *The China Quarterly, 193*, 24–42.

Chan, H. S. (2004). Cadre personnel management in China: The nomenklatura system, 1990–1998. *The China Quarterly, 179*, 703–734.

Cheesman, N. (2015). *Opposing the rule of law*. Cambridge University Press.

Chen, N. (2003). From propaganda to public relations: Evolutionary change in the Chinese government. *Asian Journal of Communication, 13*(2), 96–121.

Chen, X. (2007). *From the May Fourth Movement to Communist Revolution.* SUNY Press.

Chen, X. (2013). The rising cost of stability. *Journal of Democracy, 24*(1), 57–64.

Chen, X., & Zhao, J. (2013). Bidding to drive: Car license auction policy in Shanghai and its public acceptance. *Transport Policy, 27,* 39–52.

Cheung, K. C. K. (2012). Away from socialism, towards Chinese characteristics: Confucianism and the futures of Chinese nationalism. *China Information, 26*(2), 205–218.

Choi, Y. (2011). The evolution of "socialism with Chinese characteristics": Its elliptical structure of socialist principles and China's realities. *Pacific Focus, 26*(3), 385–404.

Clark, P. (2012). *Youth culture in China: From red guards to netizens*. Cambridge University Press.

Cohn, A., Maréchal, M. A., Tannenbaum, D., & Zünd, C. L. (2019). Civic honesty around the globe. *Science, 8712*(June), 1–9.

Creemers, R. (2017). Cyber China: Upgrading propaganda, public opinion work and social management for the twenty-first century. *Journal of Contemporary China, 26*(103), 85–100.

Dai, Z. (2018). Chairman Xi Jinping animated online videos: Representation of paternalistic leadership in a postmodern age. *Chinese Studies, 7*(2), 183–196.

Dahl, R. A. (1973). *Polyarchy: Participation and opposition*. Yale University Press.

Dahlgren, P. (2018). Media, knowledge and trust: The deepening epistemic crisis of democracy. *Javnost—The Public, 25*(1–2), 20–27.

Diamond, L., & Morlino, L. (Eds.). (2005). *Assessing the quality of democracy*. JHU Press.

Ding, X. L. (2000). The illicit asset stripping of Chinese state firms. *The China Journal, 43,* 1–28.

Dittmer, L. (1974). *Liu Shao-Chi and the Chinese cultural revolution: The politics of mass criticism* (No. 10). University of California Press.

Dittmer, L. (1981). Death and transfiguration: Liu Shaoqi's rehabilitation and contemporary Chinese politics. *The Journal of Asian Studies, 40*(3), 455–479.

Dittmer, L. (2015). *Liu Shaoqi and the Chinese cultural revolution*. Routledge.

Edin, M. (2003). State capacity and local agent control in China: CCP cadre management from a township perspective. *The China Quarterly, 173,* 35–52.

Elster, J. (2011). Hard and soft obscurantism in the humanities and social sciences. *Diogenes, 58*(1–2), 159–170.

Epstein, W. (2017). *The masses are the ruling classes: Policy romanticism, democratic populism, and social welfare in America*. Oxford University Press.

Esarey, A., & Xiao, Q. (2011). Digital communication and political change in China. *International Journal of Communication, 5,* 298–319.

Farh, J. L., & Cheng, B. S. (2000). A cultural analysis of paternalistic leadership in Chinese organizations. *Management and organizations in the Chinese context* (pp. 84–127). Palgrave Macmillan.

Foley, K., Wallace, J. L., & Weiss, J. C. (2018). The political and economic consequences of Nationalist protest in China: The 2012 Anti-Japanese demonstrations. *The China Quarterly, 236,* 1131–1153.

Friedman, E. (2016). *National identity and democratic prospects in socialist China*. Routledge.

Fu, K. W., Chan, C. H., & Chau, M. (2013). Assessing censorship on microblogs in China: Discriminatory keyword analysis and the real-name registration policy. *IEEE Internet Computing, 17*(3), 42–50.

Fukuyama, F. (1989). The end of history? *The National Interest, 16,* 3–18.

Fukuyama, F. (2012). The patterns of history. *Journal of Democracy, 23*(1), 14–26.

Fukuyama, F. (2015). Why is democracy performing so poorly? *Journal of Democracy, 26*(1), 11–20.

Gao, H. (2000). *How did the Sun rise over Yan'an?* The Chinese University of Hong Kong Press (in Chinese).

Gilley, B. (2009). Is democracy possible? *Journal of Democracy, 20*(1), 113–127.

Good, K. (2003). Democracy and the control of elites. *Journal of Contemporary African Studies, 21*(2), 155–172.

Gregor, A. J., & Chang, M. H. (1979). Anti-Confucianism: Mao's last campaign. *Asian Survey, 19*(11), 1073–1092.

Guo, G. (2009). China's local political budget cycles. *American Journal of Political Science, 53*(3), 621–632.

Guo, J. (2014). *Interpretation of the basic content of core socialist values*. People's Publishing House (in Chinese).

Guo, S., & Guo, B. (Eds.). (2008). *China in search of a harmonious society*. Lexington Books.

Guo, Y. (2008). Corruption in transitional China: An empirical analysis. *The China Quarterly, 194*, 349–364.

Harding, H. (1971). China: Toward revolutionary pragmatism. *Asian Survey, 11*(1), 51–67.

Hassid, J. (2008). Controlling the Chinese media: An uncertain business. *Asian Survey, 48*(3), 414–430.

He, G., Mol, A. P., & Lu, Y. (2016). Public protests against the Beijing-Shenyang high-speed railway in China. *Transportation Research Part D: Transport and Environment, 43*, 1–16.

Hillman, B., & Tuttle, G. (Eds.). (2016). *Ethnic conflict and protest in Tibet and Xinjiang: Unrest in China's west*. Columbia University Press.

Ho Chi Minh. (1945, September 2). *Declaration of Independence of the Democratic Republic of Vietnam*. [Online]. http://www.chinhphu.vn/cttdtcp/en/about_vietnam01.html. Accessed 20 March 2019.

Holbig, H. (2008). Ideological reform and political legitimacy in China: Challenges in the post-Jiang era. In *Regime legitimacy in contemporary China* (pp. 27–48). Routledge.

Holbig, H. (2009). Remaking the CCP's ideology: Determinants, progress, and limits under Hu Jintao. *Journal of Current Chinese Affairs, 38*(3), 35–61.

Holbig, H. (2013). Ideology after the end of ideology. China and the quest for autocratic legitimation. *Democratization, 20*(1), 61–81.

Holbig, H., & Gilley, B. (2010). Reclaiming legitimacy in China. *Politics & Policy, 38*(3), 395–422.

Hopf, T. (2012). *Reconstructing the Cold War: The early years, 1945–1958*. Oxford University Press.

Hoppe, H. H. (2018). *Democracy—The God that failed: The economics and politics of monarchy, democracy and natural order*. Routledge.

Hsiao, K. C. (1976). Legalism and autocracy in traditional China. *Chinese Studies in History, 10*(1–2), 125–143.

Hurst, W., Liu, M., Liu, Y., & Tao, R. (2014). Reassessing collective petitioning in rural China: Civic engagement, extra-state violence, and regional variation. *Comparative Politics, 46*(4), 459–482.

Jarvie, I. C., Milford, K., & Miller, D. W. (Eds.). (2006). *Karl Popper: A centenary assessment volume I*. Ashgate Publishing Ltd.

Jia, N., Zhang, Y., He, Z., & Li, G. (2017). Commuters' acceptance of and behavior reactions to license plate restriction policy: A case study of Tianjin, China. *Transportation Research Part D: Transport and Environment, 52,* 428–440.

Jin, G. (1993). Socialism and tradition: The formation and development of modern Chinese political culture. *The Journal of Contemporary China, 2*(3), 3–17.

King, G., Pan, J., & Roberts, M. E. (2013). How censorship in China allows government criticism but silences collective expression. *American Political Science Review, 107*(2), 326–343.

Konsky, C., Eguchi, M., Blue, J., & Kapoor, S. (2000). Individualist-collectivist values: American, Indian and Japanese cross-cultural study. *Intercultural Communication Studies, 9*(1), 69–84.

Kou, C. W., & Tsai, W. H. (2014). "Sprinting with small steps" towards promotion: Solutions for the age dilemma in the CCP cadre appointment system. *The China Journal, 71,* 153–171.

Kraus, W. (1991). *Private business in China: Revival between ideology and pragmatism*. University of Hawaii Press.

Lee, C. K., & Zhang, Y. (2013). The power of instability: Unraveling the microfoundations of bargained authoritarianism in China. *American Journal of Sociology, 118*(6), 1475–1508.

Leese, D. (2011). *Mao Cult: Rhetoric and ritual in China's cultural revolution*. Cambridge University Press.

Lei, Y. W. (2013). The political consequences of the rise of the Internet: Political beliefs and practices of Chinese netizens. In *Political communication in China* (pp. 37–68). Routledge.

Leibold, J. (2011). Blogging alone: China, the internet, and the democratic illusion? *The Journal of Asian Studies, 70*(4), 1023–1041.

Levenson, J. R. (1968). *Confucian China and its modern fate: A trilogy*. University of California Press.

Li, C. (2012). The end of the CCP's resilient authoritarianism? A tripartite assessment of shifting power in China. *The China Quarterly, 211,* 595–623.

Li, J. (2000). *Power, money, and media: Communication patterns and bureaucratic control in cultural China*. Northwestern University Press.

Li, L. (2004). Political trust in rural China. *Modern China, 30*(2), 228–258.

Li, L. (2008). Political trust and petitioning in the Chinese countryside. *Comparative Politics, 40*(2), 209–226.

Li, L., Liu, M., & O'Brien, K. J. (2012). Petitioning Beijing: The high tide of 2003–2006. *The China Quarterly, 210*, 313–334.

Li, L., & O'brien, K. J. (2008). Protest leadership in rural China. *The China Quarterly, 193*, 1–23.

Li, P., Zhong, M., Lin, B., & Zhang, H. (2004). Deyu as moral education in modern China: Ideological functions and transformations. *Journal of Moral Education, 33*(4), 449–464.

Li, T., Yang, W., Zhang, H., & Cao, X. (2016). Evaluating the impact of transport investment on the efficiency of regional integrated transport systems in China. *Transport Policy, 45*, 66–76.

Link, P. (1992). *Evening chats in Beijing: Probing China's predicament*. W. W. Norton.

Liu, Shao-chi. (1939/1972). How to be a good communist. In *Essential works of Chinese communism* (2nd ed., W. Chai, Ed., pp. 133–151). Bantam Books.

Liu, S. (1991). *Selected works of Liu Shaoqi*. Foreign Languages Press.

Lu, X. (2004). *Rhetoric of the Chinese cultural revolution: The impact on Chinese thought, culture, and communication*. University of South Carolina Press.

Lu, X. (2017). *Jottings under lamplight*. Harvard University Press.

MacKinnon, R. (2008). Flatter world and thicker walls? Blogs, censorship and civic discourse in China. *Public Choice, 134*(1–2), 31–46.

Manin, B. (1997). *The principles of representative government*. Cambridge University Press.

Mao, T. (1965). *On contradiction*. Foreign Languages Press.

Mao, T. (2014). *Selected works of Mao Tse-tung*. Elsevier.

Marx, K. (1976). *Capital volume I*. Penguin Books.

Mastny, V. (1998). *The Cold War and Soviet insecurity: The Stalin years*. Oxford University Press.

McCoy, J., Rahman, T., & Somer, M. (2018). Polarization and the global crisis of democracy: Common patterns, dynamics, and pernicious consequences for democratic polities. *American Behavioral Scientist, 62*(1), 16–42.

Michels, R. (1962). *Political parties: A study of the oligarchical tendencies of modern democracy*. Collier Books.

Michelson, E. (2007). Climbing the dispute pagoda: Grievances and appeals to the official justice system in rural China. *American Sociological Review, 72*(3), 459–485.

Michelson, E. (2008). Justice from above or below? Popular strategies for resolving grievances in rural China. *The China Quarterly, 193*, 43–64.

Minzner, C. F. (2006). Xinfang: An alternative to formal Chinese legal institutions. *Stanford Journal of International Law, 42,* 103–180.

Misra, K. (1998). *From post-Maoism to post-Marxism: The erosion of official ideology in Deng's China*. Psychology Press.

Muis, J., & Immerzeel, T. (2017). Causes and consequences of the rise of populist radical right parties and movements in Europe. *Current Sociology, 65*(6), 909–930.

Nietzsche, F. (1996). *Nietzsche: Human, all too human: A book for free spirits.* Cambridge University Press.

Nietzsche, F. (2002). *Nietzsche: Beyond good and evil: Prelude to a philosophy of the future*. Cambridge University Press.

Pang, Q. (2014). The "two lines control model" in China's state and society relations: Central State's management of Confucian revival in the new century. *International Journal of China Studies, 5*(3), 627–655.

Parmar, I. (2017). The legitimacy crisis of the US elite and the rise of Donald Trump. *Insight Turkey, 19*(3), 9–22.

Pei, M. (2012). Is CCP rule fragile or resilient? *Journal of Democracy, 23*(1), 27–41.

Perry, E. J. (2001). Challenging the mandate of heaven: Popular protest in modern China. *Critical Asian Studies, 33*(2), 163–180.

Peters, B. G., & Zhao, Y. (2017). Local policy-making process in China: A case study. *Journal of Chinese Governance, 2*(2), 127–148.

Popper, K. (2012). *The open society and its enemies*. Routledge.

Pye, L. W. (1990). China: Erratic state, frustrated society. *Foreign Affairs, 69*(4), 56–74.

Qiu, J. L. (1999). Virtual censorship in China: Keeping the gate between the cyberspaces. *International Journal of Communications Law and Policy, 4*(1), 25.

Reed, G. G. (1995). Moral/political education in the People's Republic of China: Learning through role models. *Journal of Moral Education, 24*(2), 99–111.

Sabatier, C., & Lannegrand-Willems, L. (2005). Transmission of family values and attachment: A French three-generation study. *Applied Psychology, 54*(3), 378–395.

Saich, T. (2010). *Governance and politics of China*. Macmillan International Higher Education.

Schopenhauer, A. (1998). *On the basis of morality*. Hackett Publishing.

Schrift, M. (2001). *Biography of a Chairman Mao badge: The creation and mass consumption of a personality cult*. Rutgers University Press.

Schurmann, F. (1971). *Ideology and organization in Communist China*. University of California Press.

Schwarcz, V. (1986). *The Chinese enlightenment: Intellectuals and the legacy of the May Fourth Movement of 1919*. University of California Press.

Shambaugh, D. (2007). China's propaganda system: Institutions, processes and efficacy. *The China Journal, 57,* 25–58.

Smyth, R. (2000). Asset stripping in Chinese state-owned enterprises. *Journal of Contemporary Asia, 30*(1), 3–16.

Song, S. (2015). Should China implement congestion pricing? *Chinese Economy, 48*(1), 57–67.

Steidlmeier, P. (1999). Gift giving, bribery and corruption: Ethical management of business relationships in China. *Journal of Business Ethics, 20*(2), 121–132.

Steiner, H. A. (1950). The people's democratic dictatorship in China. *Western Political Quarterly, 3*(1), 38–51.

Stockmann, D., & Gallagher, M. E. (2011). Remote control: How the media sustain authoritarian rule in China. *Comparative Political Studies, 44*(4), 436–467.

Sun, C., Yuan, X., & Xu, M. (2016). The public perceptions and willingness to pay: From the perspective of the smog crisis in China. *Journal of Cleaner Production, 112,* 1635–1644.

Sun, Y. (1999). Reform, state, and corruption: Is corruption less destructive in China than in Russia? *Comparative Politics, 32*(1), 1–20.

Sun, Y. (2004). *Corruption and market in contemporary China*. Cornell University Press.

Tang, W., & Iyengar, S. (2011). The emerging media system in China: Implications for regime change. *Political Communication, 28*(3), 263–267.

Tong, J. (2009). Press self-censorship in China: A case study in the transformation of discourse. *Discourse & Society, 20*(5), 593–612.

Tong, J. (2010). The crisis of the centralized media control theory: How local power controls media in China. *Media, Culture & Society, 32*(6), 925–942.

Tong, Y., & Lei, S. (2010). Large-scale mass incidents and government responses in China. *International Journal of China Studies, 1*(2), 487–508.

Tong, Y., & Lei, S. (2013a). *Social protest in contemporary China, 2003–2010: Transitional pains and regime legitimacy*. Routledge.

Tong, Y., & Lei, S. (2013b). War of position and microblogging in China. *Journal of Contemporary China, 22*(80), 292–311.

Triandis, H. (1988). Collectivism v. individualism: A reconceptualisation of a basic concept in cross-cultural social psychology. In *Cross-cultural studies of personality, attitudes and cognition* (pp. 60–95). Palgrave Macmillan.

Wallace, J. L., & Weiss, J. C. (2015). The political geography of nationalist protest in China: Cities and the 2012 anti-Japanese protests. *The China Quarterly, 222,* 403–429.

Wang, F. L. (2017). *The China order: Centralia, World Empire, and the nature of Chinese power*. SUNY Press.

Wasserstrom, J. N. (2018). *Popular protest and political culture in modern China*. Routledge.
Weber, I., & Jia, L. (2007). Internet and self-regulation in China: The cultural logic of controlled commodification. *Media, Culture & Society, 29*(5), 772–789.
Weingast, B. R. (1997). The political foundations of democracy and the rule of the law. *American Political Science Review, 91*(2), 245–263.
Wettig, G. (2008). *Stalin and the Cold War in Europe: The emergence and development of East-West conflict, 1939–1953*. Rowman & Littlefield.
White, G. (1996). Corruption and market reform in China. *IDS Bulletin, 27*(2), 40–47.
Whitfield, S. J. (1996). *The culture of the Cold War*. JHU Press.
Wong, C. P. (1991). Central–local relations in an era of fiscal decline: The paradox of fiscal decentralization in post-Mao China. *The China Quarterly, 128*, 691–715.
Woo, W. T. (1999). The real reasons for China's growth. *The China Journal, 41*, 115–137.
Wright, E. O., Levine, A., & Sober, E. (1992). *Reconstructing Marxism: Essays on explanation and the theory of history*. Verso.
Wu, S. (2014). The revival of Confucianism and the CCP's struggle for cultural leadership: A content analysis of the People's Daily, 2000–2009. *Journal of Contemporary China, 23*(89), 971–991.
Xinhua. (2014). *Xi promises harsher anti-corruption drive* [Online]. http://www.globaltimes.cn/content/837556.shtml. Accessed 27 July 2019.
Xinhua. (2015). *Xi calls for more anti-corruption efforts despite achievements* [Online]. http://www.china.org.cn/china/2015-01/14/content_34552119.htm. Accessed 27 July 2019.
Yan, J., & Sorenson, R. (2006). The effect of Confucian values on succession in family business. *Family Business Review, 19*(3), 235–250.
Yang, G. (2014). The return of ideology and the future of Chinese Internet policy. *Critical Studies in Media Communication, 31*(2), 109–113.
Yang, G., & Jiang, M. (2015). The networked practice of online political satire in China: Between ritual and resistance. *International Communication Gazette, 77*(3), 215–231.
Yu, K. (2016). Learning, training, and governing: The CCP's cadre education since the reform. *Journal of Chinese Governance, 1*(1), 41–54.
Yu, T. (2008). The revival of Confucianism in Chinese schools: A historical-political review. *Asia Pacific Journal of Education, 28*(2), 113–129.
Zhang, T., & Schwartz, B. (1997). Confucius and the cultural revolution: A study in collective memory. *International Journal of Politics, Culture, and Society, 11*(2), 189–212.

Zhang, T., & Zou, H. F. (1998). Fiscal decentralization, public spending, and economic growth in China. *Journal of Public Economics, 67*(2), 221–240.

Zhang, X. (2006). Fiscal decentralization and political centralization in China: Implications for growth and inequality. *Journal of Comparative Economics, 34*(4), 713–726.

Zhao, S. (1998). A state-led nationalism: The patriotic education campaign in post-Tiananmen China. *Communist and Post-Communist Studies, 31*(3), 287–302.

Zhao, X., & Belk, R. W. (2008). Politicizing consumer culture: Advertising's appropriation of political ideology in China's social transition. *Journal of Consumer Research, 35*(2), 231–244.

Zhou, X. (2010). The institutional logic of collusion among local governments in China. *Modern China, 36*(1), 47–78.

Zhu, J. (2008). Why are offices for sale in China? A case study of the office-selling chain in Heilongjiang Province. *Asian Survey, 48*(4), 558–579.

CHAPTER 5

The Complex Nature of Public Acceptability of Congestion Charging: What Should Be Considered in the Chinese Context?

5.1 Introduction

This chapter presents the results of the nine focus groups of lay citizens in different parts of Beijing to identify the key determinants of public acceptability of congestion charging in the Chinese context. As identified in the literature review and partially explored through the interviews with Chinese public officials, researchers have explored eight key determinants in the Western context, namely (a) problem perception (e.g., Gärling et al., 2008; Schade & Schlag, 2000), (b) access to understandable information (e.g., Francke & Kaniok, 2013; Litman, 2004; Rye et al., 2008), (c) perceived effectiveness (e.g., Ison, 2000; Taylor & Kalauskas, 2010; Winslott-Hiselius et al., 2009), (d) perceived equity (e.g., Bröcker et al., 2010; Fujii et al., 2004; Raux & Souche, 2004), (e) trust in government (e.g., Gaunt et al., 2007; Kim et al., 2013; McQuaid & Grieco, 2005), (f) social norms (e.g., Börjesson et al., 2012; Schade & Schlag, 2003), (g) personal freedom and privacy concerns (e.g., Hau, 1990; Jakobsson et al., 2000) and (h) revenue allocation and transparency (e.g., Farrell & Saleh, 2005; Hensher & Puckett, 2007; Thorpe et al., 2000). This chapter discusses whether these factors are appropriate to examine participants' concerns about congestion charging and whether Western-context-based frameworks can be applied to assess public acceptability in the Chinese context thereafter. This addresses the second objective of this research.

Q. Liu, *Public Acceptability of Congestion Charging in China*,
https://doi.org/10.1007/978-981-19-0236-9_5

Nine focus groups with 73 participants in total were conducted with a range of groups of lay citizens. The participants in the first eight groups were recruited based on three dimensions: Pekingese/migrants, inner/outer city residents and younger/older. The participants in the last group were employees in the public transport sector, including taxi and bus drivers and two people who worked in subway stations. All discussions (which lasted on average 104 minutes) were recorded, transcribed and analysed via four rounds of coding and other analyses carried out using NVivo11. The coding and thematising process are visualised in Appendix 7.

Figure 5.1 presents a word cloud of the 100 most frequently used words in all the focus group discussions. Stemmed words are grouped as one word in the word cloud. Some words were deleted when generating the figure (including conjunctions, prepositions, pronouns, classifiers, and some verbs, adjectives and adverbs such as think, well, actually) because of a lack of meaningfulness. This gives a general idea about the important discussion topics before the detailed analysis. Intuitively, issues relating to the government, equity, traffic congestion and smog are overwhelmingly

Fig. 5.1 Word Cloud (Focus Group)

important, while information, effectiveness and revenue management are less so. These topics are more fully explored in the following sub-sections of this chapter.

This chapter presents the following topics discussed in focus groups: problem perceptions (Sect. 5.2); access to information (Sect. 5.3); perceived effectiveness (Sect. 5.4), which includes the perceived effectiveness of previous policies (Sect. 5.4.1) and perceived effectiveness of congestion charging (Sect. 5.4.2); trust issues (Sect. 5.5), which consists of trust in government (Sect. 5.5.1), trust towards experts (Sect. 5.5.2) and the impact of trust on other determinants of public acceptability (Sect. 5.5.3); perceived social inequity issues (Sect. 5.6) and cultural factors (Sect. 5.7).

5.2 Problem Perceptions

According to the literature, public acceptability of congestion charging schemes is influenced by perceptions of the problems that may be alleviated by implementing such a scheme, such as congestion and air pollution (e.g., Gärling, 2007; Schade & Schlag, 2000). However, it is interesting that the traffic congestion problem was only cursorily mentioned during group discussions, while air pollution, particularly smog, was intensely discussed.

Nowadays, smog is perceived as one of the most serious problems for Beijing residents.

> It would be no exaggeration to say that smog is threatening our life. I mean everyone. You can't feel that if you are not in Beijing: the smog problem is the problem of survival. (Female, younger than 45, new migrant, inner Beijing)

Traffic congestion did not receive much attention, because participants thought congestion is merely a matter of quality of life. Some participants arrived half an hour late because of traffic congestion and some wanted to leave before peak hours, but still, participants perceived congestion as much less serious than smog. It is indeed unpleasant driving a car during rush hour in Beijing, but there are still alternatives, although public transport is crowded and uncomfortable. However, smog is perceived as directly harmful for every Beijing resident.

> We are human: we need to breathe. That's unavoidable. The Chinese Academy of Science did a study; they said the life expectancy of people in North China is about 6 years shorter than people in South China. It is because of the pollution. It's a slow cumulative poison. And the point is you have to take it, you have to take it every minute. That's why it's good to solve the smog problem. (Female, older than 45, Pekingese, inner Beijing)

The high level of concern for smog was expected because reporter Chai Jing's film *Under the Dome* has aroused nationwide public concern about air pollution since 2013 (Hatton, 2015; Powers, 2016). Three main concerns about smog were discussed in the focus groups. Firstly, participants were concerned about health risks in general.

> I want to do something to make our city better. I do care about my health, my parents' health, and in the future my child. (Male, younger than 45, Pekingese, outer Beijing)

Secondly, older people attached greater importance to the smog problem, as all the older groups anxiously discussed this topic. Many of them pointed out the imperative of coping with smog because of the concern for future generations or Confucianist family values.

> I don't want my grandchild growing up in an ugly and smelly city. I don't want him growing up in fear that they may someday die because of this harmful air. I don't want him to envy other children in Western countries because there's no smog in their country. (Male, older than 45, Pekingese, outer Beijing)

Moreover, participants in three groups sparked extensive debate about air pollution-induced migration. According to them, fleeing from nationwide smog has become one of the most important considerations for emigration.

> As a mother, I can feel what you feel. I sent my child to the UK. I told her not to come back until they solve the smog problem. We have breathed this toxic air for years, and I don't want my daughter, her children to breathe this anymore. No more. (Female, older than 45, Pekingese, inner Beijing)

Thirdly, smog is in marked contrast to older Pekingese's memories of fresh air and the blue sky. Therefore, alleviating the smog problem was a frequently mentioned expectation of implementing a congestion charge in Beijing.

> But before that, I think it's worth trying this policy because I wish we could have fresh air. I want our fresh air back. […] I remember the air was quite good 20 years ago. I can't say it's as good as Tibet, but at least as good as South China. But now, you see. So I wish this policy could be successful and bring back our fresh air. (Male, older than 45, Pekingese, outer Beijing)

These results showed a high public awareness of smog pollution, which elaborates previous research (Sun et al., 2016; Wang et al., 2016). Nevertheless, it is questionable whether this awareness can be generalised to environmental awareness. Environmental awareness usually refers to being aware of a series of environmental threats in the literature, including climate change, energy consumption, pollution, water scarcity and deforestation (e.g., Gadenne et al., 2009; Hartmann & Apaolaza-Ibáñez, 2012; Koop & Tole, 2001; Lorenzoni et al., 2007; Tang et al., 2013; Wong, 2003). Wider environmental issues, such as climate change and emissions, were also taken into consideration to assess environmental awareness in previous research on the public acceptability of congestion charging (Eliasson & Jonsson, 2011; Kim et al., 2013). However, participants' environmental concerns were confined to smog. Other related environmental issues were never mentioned during the discussions. On the one hand, these results are in line with the literature showing that the extensively reported smog problem has effectively evoked public concerns (e.g., Ma, 2015; Wang, 2015, Yang & Huang, 2017); on the other hand, the results revealed that the participants lacked a systematic understanding of environmental problems; hence, they might underestimate the benefits of congestion charging such as emissions reductions. Consequently, it may be difficult to gain public support for the charge via stressing the environmental benefits suggested by Eliasson and Jonsson (2011).

Although traffic congestion did not appear to be a main topic during the discussions, this does not imply that participants did not perceive congestion as a serious problem. On the contrary, they did not talk much about traffic congestion, because there is a consensus that traffic congestion is a serious problem in Beijing, and most Beijing residents shared similar experiences of congestion. Moreover, more than half the participants did not expect the congestion charge to mitigate congestion problems, since they believed all the previously implemented policies had been unsuccessful in dealing with traffic congestion. The perceived effectiveness of congestion charging is presented in Sect. 5.4.

5.3 Access to Information

Before presenting the results for perceived effectiveness, it is worthwhile to look at what the participants thought about the access to relevant information, since it can be an important barrier to implementing a congestion charge (e.g., Clee, 2007; Francke & Kaniok, 2013; Rößger et al., 2008). Access to understandable information about the proposed scheme should have a significant impact on public acceptability because, theoretically, sufficient information is the basis for the public to consider the costs and benefits of the scheme. However, none of the participants thought they had enough information about congestion charging.

> Yeah, but they just talk about it (when the government will implement the congestion charge). They didn't take any further action after they talked about the policy. So I'm not sure whether the policy is really going to be implemented. We never know what they are going to do, hee hee. (Female, older than 45, Pekingese, outer Beijing)

Some participants argued that it is difficult for them to discuss the perceived effectiveness of congestion charging because of limited information.

> I think this (whether congestion charging can alleviate traffic congestion and/or smog) is way beyond our ability to discuss, because we don't have that kind of background. And we also don't have enough information to make that judgment. (Female, older than 45, Pekingese, inner Beijing)

However, many participants showed considerable knowledge about the congestion charge during discussions, as they touched upon many of the details of congestion charging that were not in the information sheet, including official announcements of the implementation of congestion charging before 2015, congestion charging policies implemented in Western cities, which were introduced in the information sheet, and experts' opinions about congestion charging. This shows that (a) the participants tended to know more about the policy, which was still at the planning stage and (b) many participants had acquired knowledge about congestion charging from various non-official sources. Yet none of them thought they had enough information about congestion charging. This is because the information that lay citizens have access to was perceived as biased.

> They don't let us know this kind of information (that congestion charging has little effect on air pollution), these negative things. They provide details about how they charge in other countries, but they will never tell us, "Look, this policy actually has no effect." (Male, older than 45, Pekingese, inner Beijing)

Biased information from official media had led to a mistrust of official information. Over half the participants indicated that information from official media is extremely unreliable.

> We (lay-citizens) always have different stories about the same thing. They (the government) always blame those people for fabricating and spreading rumours, but you (official media) are the origin of this fabrication, all right? You are the master of making fake news. [...] You don't tell us what happened and then you blame us for guessing? So, we all know there is a lot of fake news on social media, we know that. But what can we do? We can't get what we want from the official media. (Male, older than 45, Pekingese, inner Beijing)

Instead of the unreliable official information, participants clarified three alternative sources of information that they preferred. The most frequently mentioned information source was social media. Many participants, especially older people, stated that they no longer rely on official media thanks to the widely used app WeChat.

> I think this is about what information we could have. Nowadays, of course we have some more options to get information than before, because we can use WeChat. (Female, older than 45, Pekingese, outer Beijing)

There was both consensus and disagreement about fake news on social media. The participants reached a consensus that fabricated information on social media is pervasive. However, so-called fake news was deemed reliable by some participants, who regarded fabricated news as accurate predictions that have not yet been reported by official media. These people would regard information deleted by the government as the truth. This is consistent with literature on Chinese media (e.g., Gao, 2012; Navarria, 2016; Poell et al., 2014). The others thought they could not trust any information because of widely spread fake news from both official and non-official sources. Consequently, some of them pointed out that their acceptance of congestion charging will not be influenced by the accessibility of information.

Western media was mentioned as another important information source in the globalisation era. Western media played a special role in China by reporting embarrassing news that is not reported by the official media.

> This problem (smog) was reported by foreign media and then Chinese media had to report it. I think the American media reported this problem because the air smells strange in their embassy. I don't believe those people in environmental protection departments are not aware of this problem, but they just choose to cheat us. (Male, younger than 45, Pekingese, inner Beijing)

The most trustworthy information source for the participants was apparently inside information. For example, one of the participants talked about a congestion charge plan that people residing inside the third ring road do not need to pay:

> My friend. He has some friend in the Commission of Transport. He told me [… that] people who live inside the third ring road don't need to pay. (Male, older than 45, new migrant, inner Beijing)

After he claimed that the information was from a cadre in the Municipal Commission of Transport, all participants but one expressed a high level of trust towards this information. However, according to the stakeholder interviews, there was no concrete plan on the table when the focus group was conducted. In other words, most of the participants firmly believed in this fabricated inside information. It reflects lay-citizens' desire for inside information, which usually brings considerable benefits in contemporary China (see De Fond et al., 1999; Su & Fleisher, 1999; Zhou, 2000). Also, this obsession with inside information implies an inequity between those who have access to inside information and lay citizens, which is discussed in Sect. 5.6.

This evidence from focus group discussions verified the results reported in Sect. 4.3.4, suggesting that there is no effective way of exchanging ideas. On the one hand, it was derived from a lack of transparency and public engagement in the policymaking process; on the other hand, it embodied a low level of trust in government, which is discussed in Sect. 5.5. Due to a lack of information about congestion charging, the participants rarely thought about the policy from a cost–benefit trade-off perspective, and this influenced the way they perceived the effectiveness of congestion charging and social equity issues (Sect. 5.6).

5.4 Perceived Effectiveness

5.4.1 Perceived Effectiveness of Previous Policies

As discussed in Sect. 4.3.4, policies were deemed interconnected in the Chinese context. It is not surprising that perceived effectiveness of congestion charge was inextricably connected to perceived effectiveness of previous policies. Although some participants were willing to pay for a less congested city and better air quality, they questioned the effectiveness of the congestion charge, since most of transport policies implemented in Beijing were perceived as irrational and unsuccessful.

> I think I'm ready to pay. [...] I think now the problem is they have implemented a lot of policies that make us pay more and more to drive our cars, but we never see any improvements. That's the problem. [...] What about the license plate lottery? That's incredibly ferocious. (Female, younger than 45, Pekingese, inner Beijing)

Two policies were repeatedly criticised by the participants: the road space rationing policy, which was introduced during the 2008 Beijing Olympic Games, and the license plate lottery, which has been in place since 2012. These participants believed that neither traffic congestion nor air pollution has been alleviated by implementing these policies.

> I'm not a car user. I'm not directly influenced by the traffic restrictions or the lottery, but I don't see any benefit of these two policies. I can't see any changes. (Female, older than 45, new migrant, Inner Beijing)

Quite a few participants expressed strong discontent with previous transport policies and those who delivered and endorsed these policies.

> Look at all these policies they have implemented: which is effective? [...] Every time they want to implement a policy, they tell you how [obscenities] good it is, how [obscenities] effective it will be, how it can solve the problem. Then with our high expectation, they [obscenities] up again and again. (Male, younger than 45, Pekingese, Inner Beijing)

This discontent was derived from the tremendous difference between the official propaganda before the policy was implemented and the actual effectiveness and fairness that residents have perceived. Since similar strategies are adopted to propagate public policies, we use the Beijing license plate lottery policy as an example of how perceived effectiveness was formed.

The following propaganda tactics were used before the implementation of the license plate lottery (see also official propaganda before implementing the road space rationing policy: Xinhua, 2008): (a) presenting a vision for a promising future as a consequence of implementing the policy, (b) showing an overwhelming majority of people supporting the policy[1] (e.g., People's Daily, 2010), (c) expert endorsements (e.g., China Youth Daily, 2010) and (d) successful experience in foreign cities and foreigners' endorsements (e.g., Global Times, 2013). By using these tactics, the government generated a high public expectation of the policy before its implementation.

However, participants only mentioned the difficulty of getting a license and the social unfairness caused by the policy during the group discussions. Although scholars have substantiated that the policy has effectively retarded the growth in car ownership (e.g., Yang et al., 2014), this effect left almost all the participants unimpressed. There are three main reasons for this perception.

Firstly, the policy was introduced as an effective way to mitigate congestion by the official media before its implementation (People's Daily, 2010), whereas scholars explained, and the official media propagated that the policy merely slowed down the deteriorating congestion, since the traffic congestion index remained the same level after the implementation of this policy (China Daily, 2013). Besides, the inconsistency

[1] In this case, only 5.8% of the respondents disliked the license plate lottery.

of propaganda before and after the implementation of the policy led to a distrust of official media, which has claimed the effectiveness of congestion charging in foreign cities. This is presented in Sect. 5.5.

Secondly, the strongest feeling for the participants was not the retarded growth in car ownership but the extremely low possibility of getting a new license plate. According to the new reports, only one out of 1907 applicants can get a new license plate (JRJ, 2018).

> Probably you need to wait for 6 years to get that plate. [...] You may get rich tomorrow, but you definitely cannot get another plate tomorrow. You can make money day by day, you can work harder, but a plate, you know, you can do nothing. It's out of hand. (Male, older than 45, Pekingese, outer Beijing)

Compared to its effect on congestion alleviation, a series of social problems of the lottery has caused a greater impact on people's everyday life. For example, Liu et al. (2018) found that the lottery has caused a 35% reduction in births in households of lottery participants and a 6% reduction across Beijing, which had higher impacts on fertility than many other policies, including policies intentionally aimed at fertility.

Thirdly, many participants perceived this policy as inequitable to new migrants, who are basically excluded from owning a car.

> I'm kind of a little supportive because compared to the license plate lottery system, this policy (congestion charge) is not that unfair to us new migrants. [...] The license plate lottery system gives tremendous privileges to the Pekingese. It's extremely hard to own a car for those who are not originally from Beijing. (Female, older than 45, Pekingese, outer Beijing)

Moreover, some participants believed that political corruption is involved, and that privileged people can get plates much more easily than average people. It is interesting that none of the participants had any evidence to support this argument during the group discussions, but nevertheless, it was reported that the former director of the Beijing Traffic Management Bureau fraudulently sold license plates for money after the implementation of this policy (CNTV, 2012).

The plate-number-based traffic rationing policy received less criticism from the participants than the lottery because (a) the policy was first introduced as part of the policy package relating to the Beijing Olympic Games, which generated great enthusiasm and wide public support (Chen, 2012; Finlay & Xin, 2010; Zhou & Ap, 2009), (b) similar policies have been implemented in many Latin American cities, such as Mexico City and São Paulo (Davis, 2010; Mahendra, 2008;) and most importantly, (c) this policy is much less strictly enforced. According to Wang et al. (2014), rule-breaking behaviour is pervasive—almost half the people do not follow the restrictions.

Some participants also blamed Beijing subway's new fare policy. The new fare was adopted at the end of 2014, replacing the 2 CNY (£0.21) flat fare system (BBC, 2015). The cost of the average journey was effectively doubled by the new fare policy.

> It's like they raise the price of the subway. They said that the purpose of raising ticket price is to let more subway user to take buses. But in fact, obviously, they did not reach that goal. The subway system is as crowded as it used to be because they raised the ticket price of bus tickets at the same time. I guess they just want to drive away some new poor migrants who are struggling for survival. (Female, younger than 45, Pekingese, outer Beijing)

This is inconsistent with a previous study suggesting that the degree of dissatisfaction could be effectively dispelled over time (Zhang et al., 2017). It is probably because of the 5 months' data-collection span of the study, which could only reflect the change of satisfaction in the short term. Furthermore, around half the respondents were still dissatisfied with the new fare system 5 months after the policy was implemented, although the proportion of dissatisfied respondents dropped some 10% in the first 5 months. This inconsistency also elaborates the results in Sect. 4.2.3, suggesting that real public opinions about a policy may not be reflected by surveying satisfaction with the policy.

Participants expressed disappointment with some other policies that are not in the transport domain during the group discussion, such as housing policies, environmental policies and rural policies. This implies the interconnectedness of public acceptability, because no matter what a policy is, it will be perceived as a decision of the government (and ultimately the Party). Therefore, the public accessibility of a transport policy is not necessarily influenced by dissatisfaction with a previous transport policy, but with anything that is perceived to be related to the government. Attitudes towards these policies are further illustrated in Sect. 5.5.

People's perceptions of previous policies may influence the perceived effectiveness of congestion charging in two ways: (a) after years of witnessing unsuccessful efforts to alleviate traffic congestion and pollution, people tended to believe that these problem could never be alleviated, leading to an inherent mistrust of the effectiveness of congestion charging and (b) the ineffectiveness of and other social problems caused by previous policies led to a breakdown of trust in government, which inevitably resulted in public suspicion of the effectiveness of, and even the motivation for, congestion charging. This is further explained in Sect. 5.5.

5.4.2 *Perceived Effectiveness of Congestion Charging*

The perceived effectiveness of the proposed scheme is identified as one of the most important factors influencing public acceptability in the literature (e.g., Bartley, 1995; Jaensirisak et al., 2005; Taylor & Kalauskas, 2010) and it was one of the main concerns of focus group participants. Although most believed that the congestion charge cannot alleviate traffic congestion and smog problems, their perceptions of the effectiveness of the policy varied more than their perceptions of other issues.

5.4.2.1 *Perceived Effectiveness in General*

Some participants, especially younger people, thought congestion charging could be more acceptable to them if it could make a tangible difference.

> I expect it to be effective, really solve the problem as they said. Or maybe it doesn't have to be that effective, but at least some improvements we could see. I think that's enough for me. I think money is not a big problem. If it's too expensive, I can drive less; if it's still affordable for me, I'm willing to pay. But I hope it could solve the problem if we have to pay. (Female, younger than 45, Pekingese, inner Beijing)

Some participants anticipated that the congestion charge might effectively reduce private car use. These participants had less negative attitudes towards the policy during the group discussions.

> I think some people will not use cars that frequently, so less congestion. And I guess it could improve air quality to some extent. (Female, older than 45, Pekingese, inner Beijing)

> I think the congestion charge can force some people away from their cars. That's good. (Male, younger than 45, new migrant, Inner Beijing)

Those who had high expectations for the effectiveness of congestion charging mainly focused on two aspects: collective benefits and long-term effects.

> If you ask whether this policy is good for private car users, maybe the answer is negative; but if you ask whether this policy is good for the city, for Beijing, I think absolutely yes, it's very good for the city. Less congestion, less smog, who doesn't want it? So, I think we should look at long-term benefits; at least I think those car users should think about what they can get from the policy in a longer term. (Male, younger than 45, Pekingese, outer Beijing, taxi driver)

Apart from emphasising the benefits to the society as a whole, some participants mentioned benefits to Beijing, especially the Pekingese. This reflected their love for their hometown Beijing and a strong hometown identity. However, this hometown identity sometimes appeared rather xenophobic—some Pekingese participants blamed new migrants for their negative attitudes towards the congestion charge because they thought migrants are indifferent about Beijing.

> I think we Beijing people more or less think this policy is good for Beijing, good for this city. So although it will violate our personal interests, we kind of support it. Or at least we are not strongly against it. But those people who come from other places are not like this. [...] Like you said, they don't like it here, they consider Beijing as a big casino, they just come here, grab some money, and go back. [...] They are unwilling to make any contribution to this city. So, I guess those people actually hate this policy because they don't care (about Beijing). (Male, older than 45, Pekingese, outer Beijing)

Although these Pekingese participants' emotional judgements of new migrants reflected typical stereotypes of migrants (see also Afridi et al., 2015; Kwong, 2011; Li et al., 2006), some participants in each Pekingese group showed relatively positive attitudes towards the policy and expressed a willingness to pay for a smog mitigation plan because they believed the policy will deliver favourable outcomes for Beijing, whereas few migrant participants thought so.

Even though a few participants were, to some extent, confident about the effectiveness of congestion charging, most questioned whether the policy could alleviate traffic congestion and smog. Some participants refuted the argument that congestion charging can have long-term effects, because they believed the policy cannot even be effective in the short term.

> Can you explain to me, if we can't expect any short-term effect, how can you make sure there will be long-term effects? (Male, younger than 45, new migrant, inner Beijing)

Some participants were still doubtful about the effectiveness of congestion charging even if they thought the policy could have a short-term effect because they did not think a policy with only short-term effects should be regarded as effective.

> Yes, that (50 CNY/day) could be quite expensive. But maybe at first people will drive less, but later people will be familiar with this and start to use it more and more. So I guess it's a quite short-term thing. The policy cannot solve the problem: it just makes it seem less serious or maybe slows it down a little. I don't know if we can call it effective. (Male, older than 45, new migrant, outer Beijing)

Moreover, some participants argued that congestion charging will not reduce private car use, but encourage car use instead.

> I think it doesn't mean people will drive less. For example, if I have already paid for this, maybe I will use my car more. Because I have already paid. Maybe I don't have to use my car to go somewhere, but when I think about that, oh I've already paid, I will use my car. So actually it may encourage people who have already paid the charge to use cars more frequently. (Male, younger than 45, Pekingese, inner Beijing).

The participants discussed three main topics as factors influencing the perceived effectiveness of congestion charging: (a) a congestion charge as a policy that has been implemented in cities in many developed countries, (b) Beijing's urban planning and (c) the uniqueness of Beijing. Together with a prevalent disappointment with previous efforts intended to mitigate traffic congestion and smog, which was presented in Sect. 5.4.1, most of the participants showed a very low expectation of the effectiveness of congestion charging.

5.4.2.2 *The Implementation of Congestion Charging in Western Cities*

The implementation of congestion charging in Western cities was a bone of contention between the participants. Its implementation in famous Western cities significantly influenced participants' perceptions of the policy. One group of participants expected the policy to be effective because there are quite a few successfully implemented congestion charging policies in developed countries, whereas others thought policies successfully implemented in other countries had always failed in China, thereby questioning the transferability of the policy.

Successful experience of implementing congestion charging policies was regarded as a reasonable justification for implementing congestion charging in China.

> I think they want to implement this policy because this policy has been implemented in other countries, for example Singapore. (Female, older than 45, new migrant, inner Beijing)

For many participants, that the policy had been implemented in other countries was deemed an important reason to believe that the policy could be effective. Some participants found congestion charging unacceptable because they thought the policy had not been implemented in other countries.

> When I first heard about this policy, [...] I thought it's quite ridiculous. At that time, because we don't know if there are similar policies implemented in other countries, so I think the Communist Party just invented a new way to grab money from us. (Male, younger than 45, Pekingese, inner Beijing)

Moreover, some participants showed relatively higher confidence about congestion alleviation because of policies successfully implemented in developed countries, whereas they were concerned about its effectiveness in terms of smog alleviation, because congestion charging policies were not used as a tool for smog alleviation in other countries.

> I don't think it could solve the smog problem, but I think maybe it can alleviate congestion. Because it has been implemented in many Western countries, and it's very effective in Western countries, so I think it will work. But it cannot solve the smog problem because there is no smog

> problem in Western countries, so I think Western people never have this experience using this policy to solve smog problem. (Female, younger than 45, new migrant, outer Beijing)

Although these participants somehow showed positive attitudes towards congestion charging, it is evident that they had some reservations about its effectiveness. Words expressing uncertainty were frequently used when they talked about congestion charging as a successfully implemented policy in Western cities. On the contrary, those who did not believe the policy is transferable from the Western context to the Chinese context firmly believed that congestion charging cannot be as effective as it is in Western countries.

> Since many other policies implemented in developed countries are not very successful in China, I don't know if the road pricing could be effective. I think it's very hard to be effective, because of the fundamental conditions of the country. I can't tell why it will be not effective, and how it will go wrong, but I just feel something is wrong. (Female, older than 45, new migrants, outer Beijing)

This evidence also shows that the lack of trust in copying policies implemented in Western countries was derived from impressions about previous policies. Moreover, many participants mentioned "China's actual condition" as one of the reasons that policies transferred from Western countries cannot be effective in China.

> I think the most important thing is not whether this policy is reasonable, I think the most important thing is whether it is adaptable. Whether it could fit in the actual situation of China, of Beijing. We have copied tons of policies that have been implemented in Western countries. I don't think they are successful here. (Male, younger than 45, new migrant, inner Beijing)

It is worth noting that "China's actual condition" was mentioned as a vague and general concept that may refer to any differences between China and other countries. There was no clue that participants explicitly referred this to any particular condition that may lead to the non-transferability of Western policies. However, this term has a special meaning in the Chinese context. Firstly, it has been widely used as an excuse for anti-reform politics since the late Qing Dynasty (e.g., Chang, 2013; Warner, 2012). Secondly, it is derived from a sub-theory of the official ideology, Chinese Marxist thought—the primary stage of socialism, which contains several officially identified characteristics of the contemporary China (Brugger, 2018a; Fewsmith, 2016; Li, 1995a; Sun, 1995; Zhao, 2009). Thirdly, this term has also been widely used without substantive content by scholars and experts in many different domains (e.g., Chen, 2009; Jiang et al., 2016; Li et al., 2010). Consequently, a sense of universal uniqueness of China, which many participants suggested, has been engendered and significantly undermined people's perception of the transferability of Western concepts and policies.

A few older participants expressed hostility towards policies implemented in Western countries as responses to other participants' complaints about the effectiveness of policies successfully implemented in Western countries.

> We should not just focus on these mistakes; we need to look at those achievements, we should look at what we achieved. We should be proud of it. There is congestion in Western countries too, did they solve that? [...] There are problems in those capitalist countries too. (Male, older than 45, Pekingese, inner Beijing)

On the one hand, this implies that these participants did not believe traffic congestion can be mitigated by implementing congestion charging, because the problem has not been solved in developed countries; on the other hand, this sense of national pride reflects rising Chinese nationalism in the post-Tiananmen Era (Hughes, 2006; Johnston, 2017; Zheng, 1999). Although other participants did not explicitly express such an efficacious patriotic feeling, people's attitude towards a policy transferred from the West may be influenced by this state-led Chinese nationalism, which the patriotic education campaign aimed to achieve (e.g., Hyun & Kim, 2015; Waldron, 1995; Wang, 2008; Zhao, 2000, 2004).

5.4.2.3 Urban Planning

Apart from the two impression-based views on the transferability of congestion charging, a few participants also considered issues relating to the urban planning of Beijing. They thought traffic congestion in Beijing is unavoidable because of the urban planning.

> I visited Sweden once, London also, many times. I think even if these policies are successful in these countries, they may not be successful here. I

> mean, Beijing is bigger than those cities, and it looks different. You know, the density of some particular areas is extremely high, like Zhongguancun, Jianguomen, Tiantongyuan, and the Children's Hospital around the west 2nd ring road. So, there will be congestion on those roads. I think it's unavoidable. [...] I think our urban planning has been chaotic for decades. [...] I don't think a policy could be effective here even if it was proved to be effective in other countries, other cities. Even successful policies in Shanghai cannot be effective in Beijing. I don't know why, but that's what happened. Look, Shanghai is almost the same scale as Beijing, but there is less smog and less congestion in Shanghai. (Male, older than 45, Pekingese, inner Beijing)

Some participants believed congestion charging can only be effective if systematic changes in urban planning are made.

> Well, they (the government) say the policy is to solve congestion and smog problem. I don't believe that. [...] There seems no benefit at all. But I think maybe it could be a chance for the government to launch a replanning of the urban transport system in Beijing. [...] They must prepare a series of policies to solve this problem, otherwise it won't make any difference. So for now, I can only see problems. (Male, older than 45, new migrant, inner Beijing)

Some participants thought congestion has been significantly exacerbated by thousands of gated residential areas and *danwei* (socialist work-unit compounds) in Beijing, which are usually inaccessible for other people. Gated communities, especially those occupied by government organs at all levels and the armed forces, were discussed in many groups.

> I think the first thing is gated communities. We cannot go across those areas. For example, there is a gated community between a subway station and my home. But we are not allowed to go across the community, so every time I have to go around that area. It takes about 20 minutes more. It's OK, because I also want to live in a gated community. Safety, you know, and maybe kind of a social status. (Female, younger than 45, Pekingese, outer Beijing)

The anticipated negative effects of the gated community match those in previous studies on *danwei* and gated communities (e.g., Bray, 2005; Miao, 2003; Pow, 2009; Wang & Chai, 2009; Wei et al., 2016; Wu &

Webber, 2004). These studies mainly focus on factory-based communities of state-owned enterprises before the economic reform and gated communities after the reform. The *danwei* used to function as a basic unit of CCP's economic and social organization, which controls low-level cadres, monitors lay citizens and implements policies (Björklund, 1986; Lü & Perry, 1997). After the economic reform, many affiliated functions of state-owned enterprises were abolished due to enterprises shirking social responsibility for their employees, including housing provision and affiliated facilities such as schools and hospitals (Cai, 2002; Steinfeld, 1999; Wang et al., 2005). Therefore, factory-based community was merely mentioned to explain that gated communities are a feature of urban life in group discussions. Participants were concerned about government organ compounds, which are widely distributed in the congested inner Beijing region. However, to the author's knowledge, these communities have received little academic attention to date.

Some participants thought that Beijing is congested because of the planning of an over-centralised metropolis; thus, edge cities can more effectively alleviate traffic congestion.

> In my opinion, it's a good start that the Beijing municipality has moved some functional divisions to Tongzhou. It promotes the economic development of the peripheral regions and makes downtown Beijing less crowded. I think it's good to have several edge cities around Beijing, edge cities with specific functionalities. Thus, it's unnecessary to come to the city centre for everything, and then there's less congestion. (Male, younger than 45, Pekingese, outer Beijing)

The over-centralised Beijing is a legacy of the Soviet urban planning structure (Xie & Costa, 1993; Yeh & Wu, 1999). Moreover, although Beijing has undergone rapid urban expansion for 40 years (Li et al., 2013), high-quality public resources are still over-centralised (e.g., Liao & Wang, 2018; Postiglione, 2015). In addition, it is influenced by the uniqueness of Beijing.

5.4.2.4 *The Uniqueness of Beijing*

The uniqueness of Beijing was frequently discussed as the reason why policies implemented in the West are not applicable to China, and therefore a reason to question the effectiveness of congestion charging. The participants mentioned three main distinctive characteristics of Beijing:

Beijing's capital city status; its population size and population density compared to cities in which congestion charging policies have been implemented, such as London, Stockholm and Singapore; and its attractiveness to migrants.

Firstly, a few participants argued that Beijing's capital city status would, to some extent, guarantee the effectiveness of congestion charging. They thought policymakers have to be cautious about implementing congestion charging because policies implemented in Beijing have national impacts. These participants believe that policymakers will not implement the policy until they are sure it can effectively alleviate traffic congestion and smog.

> Beijing [...] is the capital of China. If bad things happen here, the whole country will be influenced. It's not like you implement a policy in Henan province. If [...] it's failed [...] the impact of that failed policy is within the province, or maybe even within the city. But if it failed in Beijing, that's a national issue, maybe international. So I think they don't dare, at least they need to be more certain of that. (Male, younger than 45, Pekingese, inner Beijing)

Secondly, the population size and population density in particular areas was repeatedly underlined to explain why the congestion charge cannot be effective.

> Yes, too many people. Look, there are about 25 million people in this city, if 1% (should be 10%) of people drive, then there are 2.5 million cars. If half of them stop using cars [...] due to the policy, which is impossible in my opinion, still over 1 million cars. There will be congestion if so many people live in this city. I think maybe it's more than a transport problem, I mean congestion. (Female, older than 45, new migrant, inner Beijing)

Thirdly, the large population size was deemed as an inevitable result of Beijing's attractiveness to migrants.

> They [...] come here, for whatever reasons, maybe go to the hospital, maybe, I don't know. I actually don't know why they like to come here. I think if I'm not born here, I'm unwilling to come to this crowded city, hee hee hee. (Male, younger than 45, Pekingese, outer Beijing)

Many capital cities are attractive to talented people (e.g., Haven-Tang et al., 2007; Krätke, 2004; Waley, 2007). However, the rapid growth of the urban population in China has been predominantly caused by rural–urban migrants (e.g., Bosker et al., 2012; Fan, 2007; Fu & Gabriel, 2012), and Beijing has been one of the top destinations for migration since 1985 (Shen, 2013). Scholars have extensively investigated factors influencing migration after the economic reform, such as unbalanced development between urban and rural areas, relaxed household registration, the rural land system and family reunion (Bosker et al., 2012; Goldstein & Guo, 1992; Liu et al., 2015; Zhao, 1999; Zhu, 2002). In addition, several participants stated that the increasing number of migrants is also a result of Chinese people's preference for going to the capital city.

> I think the more fundamental problem is our culture. Many Chinese people are so enthusiastic about coming into the capital city, where all money and power are. (Male, older than 45, Pekingese, outer Beijing)

It is noteworthy that those who believed that the population size of Beijing is the underlying cause of traffic congestion disparaged migrants in varying degrees, although some of them are migrants themselves. This is further discussed in Sect. 5.5.

In summary, the overwhelming predominance of focus group participants distrusted the effectiveness of congestion charging, which is in line with evidence from the West (e.g., Jones, 1998). I identified four main factors that undermined the perceived effectiveness of congestion charging through focus group discussions. Firstly, unsuccessful efforts on congestion and air pollution alleviation have engendered considerable controversy about whether such problems can be alleviated via some particular policies and provoked people to question the government's capability of coping with these problems. Secondly, more than half the participants remained doubtful about the transferability of policies implemented in Western countries, such as congestion charging. Third, some participants believed traffic congestion can never be alleviated by implementing pricing schemes, since the fundamental cause of congestion is Beijing's urban planning. Fourth, the uniqueness of Beijing, such as its population size and its attractiveness to migrants, was perceived as an important contributor to traffic congestion; therefore, traffic demand management can hardly be effective in Beijing.

It is clear that neither the information provided by the information sheet nor the knowledge about congestion charging previously obtained from other sources was considered as the basis for the formation of perceived effectiveness of congestion charging. Therefore, it is at least questionable that access to information influences people's perceptions of the effectiveness of congestion charging in this case.

The government, instead of the congestion charging policy itself, was repeatedly talked about when the participants were discussing the effectiveness of congestion charging. The four factors influencing perceived effectiveness of congestion charging, especially the first two, were firmly connected to participants' perceptions of governance and more generally, their trust in government, which is presented in the next section.

5.5 Trust Issues

As expected, participants' attitudes towards the government dominated the discussions in every group. Trust issues, including trust in government and trust towards experts, were the fundamental causes that underlie all the other issues relating to acceptability. This section describes the direct and indirect impacts of trust issues on the acceptability of congestion charging.

5.5.1 Trust in Government

5.5.1.1 Attitude Towards the Government in General

Some 70 of 73 participants expressed negative attitudes towards the government with varied degrees of dissatisfaction, disappointment and distrust. Although three bus/taxi drivers were supportive of congestion charging, they also complained about the government. There are three types of negative attitudes towards the government with their particular corresponding ways of expressing opinions in group discussions: (a) direct complaints about the government in general, expressing radical views; (b) metaphor and sarcasm, which implied distrust in government and (c) indifference about the problems of governance, including dereliction of duty, unsuccessful policies and the oppression of lay citizens.

Criticisms of congestion charging, which were usually directly linked to criticisms of the government in general, were represented in a fairly straightforward way. For example:

> They think we are something like their livestock; they have a stranglehold on us, on everything. So, when they think they need to use our

> money, they [obscenities] think they can take it. That's the logic of this policy (congestion charge), these different kinds of [obscenities] policies. So someday when they think they need your lives, they will take them, no doubt. (Male, younger than 45, new migrant, outer Beijing)

Some participants expressed their distrust in government in a more metaphorical and sarcastic way. They used ancient poems and fable stories to declare dissatisfaction with the regime. For example:

> "I saw them build the courtesan's quarters, saw them feast and make merry. But I saw, too, how the building collapsed."[2] It's so normal to us, especially Beijing people. (Male, younger than 45, Pekingese, inner Beijing)

As a response to another participant's complaints about how the government rides over lay citizens during mega events, this poem was quoted from a historical drama that depicts political corruption, political disappointment and political struggle in the late Ming dynasty (e.g., Lu, 2001), implying a disappointment with the political system.

Sarcasm about public policies also revealed distrust in government. "China's actual condition" was frequently mentioned in a sarcastic way, suggesting that the term is merely an excuse for the ineffectiveness of policies.

> When they are going to implement a policy, they talk about successful experiences in Western countries, but after the implementation, they always talk about the actual condition of China. [...] Western experience or actual condition, they always can pick one. [...] So from that perspective, the policy can never be unsuccessful, [...] because that depends on how they explain it. According to them, of course, the policy is effective; if it's not effective enough, it's just another reason for them to have another charge. Same old tricks. (Male, younger than 45, new migrant, inner Beijing)

A few participants appeared indifferent about the policy. However, it was clear that this indifference emanated from an accumulated disappointment

[2] This is from the historical drama "Taohua Shan" (translated as "The Peach Blossom Fan") which was completed in the early Qing Dynasty. The drama sketches the collapse of the Ming Dynasty (see Kong et al., 2015; for interpretation of the drama, see also Struve, 1980; Li, 1995b).

in the policies that have been implemented and a generalised distrust in the Party. It was not a lack of intention to engage in public affairs, which was regarded as a cultural attribute of Chinese people by some official interviewees (see Sects. 4.3.4 and 4.4.3).

> I think, for me, if the policy coincidently mitigates the problem, that's fine, that's [obscenities] good. But if the policy is not effective, like we paid but we get nothing because of the policy, I believe in most cases it's just like this. [...] Don't bother, don't feel angry, don't feel upset. Because that's exactly the way they treat us. (Male, younger than 45, Pekingese, outer Beijing)

A strong sense of helplessness was embodied in this quote. It can reflect several important contextual aspects in the Chinese context, including obedience to authority, servitude and the relationship between the ruler and the ruled (see Sect. 2.3.1.3). On the one hand, the participant implied that he was well aware that cadres, as representatives of the government, have been oppressing lay citizens; on the other hand, he expressed a feeling of the smallness of individuals against the state apparatus. This group of participants was arguably the most disappointed with the current system. Not only did they distrust the idea that the government serves the people, but also they gave up expecting a less inequitable and corrupt society than those who directly or indirectly complained about the system. It is noteworthy that these participants were relatively older than their group mates, and they talked apparently less than the others.

In fact, all the group discussions were flooded with this sense of helplessness in regard to the perception that lay citizens are excluded from the whole policy process. According to most of the participants, living with whatever was delivered is the only reaction open to lay citizens, because other reactions were not only deemed risky by almost all participants, but also, as some participants suggested, they could bring about worse consequences.

> If the congestion problem is not solved, then it's because the charge is too low, if the smog problem is not solved, then again it's because the charge is too low. That's why I say it is really cunning. So [...] in the future, if you (the government) ask me "do you think the traffic is bad, the congestion problem is serious?" I must tell you "No, there is no congestion here." If you ask me "do you think the smog problem is serious? Do

> you think the city is not liveable anymore?" I must tell you, "No our air is very clean, there is no smog here. The air quality is as good as Tibet [...]." it is because of you, actually, because you complain about congestion, you complain about smog, then they implemented the traffic restrictions, they implemented the license plate lottery, and now they are going to implement road pricing. [...] Because they will not suffer, and the only ones who will suffer from our own complaints are ourselves. (Male, older than 45, Pekingese, outer Beijing)

Overall, the participants showed distrust in government during group discussions. Sections 5.5.1.2 to 5.5.1.6 describe the five main underlying causes and specific embodiments of distrust in government in this context, and Sect. 5.5.3 discusses how distrust in government may influence public acceptability of congestion charging via other determinants.

5.5.1.2 "Measures with China's Characteristics"

Although congestion charging policies have been implemented in many cities in developed countries, most of the participants considered the Beijing congestion charge as a typical "measure with China's characteristics". Measures, solutions and policies with China's characteristics were intensively discussed in four groups. The term "with China's characteristics" is derived from the theoretical system of socialism with Chinese characteristics (Deng, 1984; Hu, 2012; Jiang, 1997; Xi, 2017) which is officially identified as political theories representing Marxism-Leninism adapted to China's actual conditions in certain periods of time. However, the notion of measures with China's characteristics was mocked by all of those who mentioned it. It was considered an abrupt way of solving problems, dereliction of duty or government prevarication.

For many participants, it is an abrupt way to solve a problem by implementing a charge, whatever its purpose is, but nonetheless, this is pervasive in local-level administration, for example:

> I think the policy is really stupid [...] but it's normal. I think for the government, they think nothing cannot be solved by imposing taxes. If one tax doesn't work, just impose another tax. (Male, younger than 45, new migrant, Outer Beijing)

Since it was regarded as an oversimplified measure for coping with congestion and smog problems, participants also believed that implementing such a policy is an embodiment of local cadres' dereliction of duty, thereby engendering the low perceived effectiveness of congestion charging.

> I actually don't really care how much this policy could alleviate the congestion and smog problem. I just feel that the way they propose this policy, and of course all of the previous policies, is not good. As you said, they (local cadres) are not performing their duties. (Female, younger than 45, Pekingese, outer Beijing)

Contrary to public policies, which influence people's everyday life, participants in these groups indicated that the government is highly capable of solving traffic congestion and air pollution during mega events.

> Dust storms remained a serious problem for years. It was solved because of the Beijing Olympic Games. Also, APEC Blue happened because of the Asia-Pacific Economic Cooperation meeting. During the meeting our sky was blue. (Male, younger than 45, Pekingese, inner Beijing)

However, the APEC Blue[3] was a result of a clean-up campaign directly led by the top leaders of the party. Some participants complained that Beijing residents' everyday lives were significantly influenced by a series of strict measures carried out before and during the APEC summit, for example:

> If you look at what they did to reduce emission, that's [obscenities]. Some 10,000 factories were forced to suspend production during the APEC meeting. Many industrial plants, [...] construction sites, even petrol stations were inspected. Many, many vehicles, millions of private vehicles were kept off the roads. [...] We want good air quality, we want that APEC Blue, but in this way? (Female, younger than 45, Pekingese, inner Beijing)

As factories restarted production and private cars returned to the streets after the APEC summit, the effect of the pollution control campaign faded rapidly (see BBC, 2014a; China Current, 2014). This campaign was also regarded as a typical measure with China's characteristics by these participants. They expressed a strong discontent towards the abrupt way to mitigate traffic congestion and air pollution in short-term, despite the

[3] This was the top Beijing environmental keyword for 2014 (China Daily, 2014).

fact that the effect of the clean-up campaign was highly praised by Chinese experts (e.g., Lin et al., 2017; Wang et al., 2016; Zhang et al., 2016).

Similar temporary air pollution control measures have been carried out during international mega events in China, such as the Beijing Olympic Games (e.g., Chen et al., 2013), the 2010 Guangzhou Asian Games (e.g., Tao et al., 2015) and the 2016 Hangzhou G20 summit (Wang et al., 2018). The impacts of these mega events on people's everyday lives were also mentioned as evidence of measures with China's characteristics during group discussions. Notwithstanding the officially praised and self-witnessed air quality improvements during these events, these participants did not perceive these measures favourably. Instead, they showed a strong antipathy to these abrupt but effective measures.

Furthermore, some participants questioned the purpose of alleviating congestion and air pollution, since these problems have always been temporarily solved during mega events.

> Beijing is the face of our country; that's all they care about. All these temporarily or maybe permanently solved problems are not because of us, they are solved because foreigners were coming. They just don't want to lose face in front of foreigners. They do it for foreigners. (Male, older than 45, Pekingese, inner Beijing)

This represented a feeling that policies are not made for lay citizens. Although only a few participants directly spoke up about this, the purpose of implementing congestion charging was extensively discussed by over half the participants which, in turn, implied they held this attitude.

5.5.1.3 The Purpose of Implementing Congestion Charging

The perceived motivations for implementing congestion charging significantly influenced participants' attitudes towards congestion charging—those who believed congestion and smog alleviation is one of the purposes of implementing this policy were apparently more supportive, whereas most of the participants questioned the motivation.

Many people gave credence to the notion that implementing congestion charging is merely a new way to collect money from the public. They vehemently criticised the policy as "wheedling money out of lay-citizens", "grabbing money from the public", "robbery" or "deprivation", for example:

> Exactly, all the resources are firmly clenched in the government's hands. So there is no doubt that this kind of policy is a robbery. Absolutely. (Male, younger than 45, new migrant, inner Beijing)

Since the participants perceived that the purpose of the policy was to collect money from the public, its effectiveness on congestion and smog alleviation was disregarded. These participants believed that alleviating congestion and smog was a paperwork gimmick instead of the real purpose; hence, there was no point in expecting the policy to alleviate congestion and smog.

> I feel that it's just an excuse to implement the policy: the real purpose is to collect money. So they just need to have an explanation. Of course, congestion is a very good excuse, but recently smog is even a better one, as that problem is far more serious than congestion. So I think of course if you look at the congestion and smog problem, the policy might have some impact, but it doesn't matter. [...] They (the government) don't really need to solve the problem; they don't tell us how much the problem will be alleviated. Because that's not important, the important thing is they get the money. (Male, older than 45, new migrant, outer Beijing)

A few participants implied that they thought the purpose of implementing the policy was to collect money because of the non-transparent revenue allocation when they were asked to talk about revenue allocation.

> Robbing the rich to help the poor, you are a hero; robbing the rich but not helping the poor, then you are just a bandit. (Female, younger than 45, Pekingese, outer Beijing)

Some participants thought that congestion and smog alleviation was one of the purposes of implementing congestion charging, but nonetheless, they suggested that collecting money might be more important. Even so, they were less discontented with the policy than those who believed the real purpose of this policy was to collect money.

> The government has to do something to solve the problem. [...] Even though I know a large amount of money I pay will be in corrupt cadres' pockets, I think they should do this. [...] I think, it's better than nothing, at least. [...] It can't be totally ineffective. (Male, younger than 45, Pekingese, inner Beijing)

This seems to imply that this participant had a higher perceived effectiveness of congestion charging. However, there was no clue that this perceived effectiveness related to congestion charging. These participants never mentioned what might make congestion charging an effective policy in Beijing or how the policy might be effective. They thought the policy could be effective because they believed the government wanted to mitigate the problem. In other words, the perceived effectiveness of a policy largely depends on the extent to which the individual perceived the government's willingness to take action.

Two participants in one group argued that collecting money is not the purpose of implementing the policy.

> For example Shanghai could collect about 8 billion CNY per year with a license plate auction. [...] A large amount of money, for us. But for them (the government), it's nothing. [...] The tax revenue in Beijing is about one trillion per year, so 8 billion is just a drop in their bucket. [...] I don't think the government needs to do this to collect money, in fact, because it has a lot of ways, other ways to collect money, more surreptitious ways. (Male, younger than 45, Pekingese, outer Beijing)

However, this does not imply that these participants had a higher level of trust in government. On the contrary, they thought that Beijing does not need to collect money via a transport policy because of its political importance. They also suggested that collecting money from the public is a common purpose of implementing policies, which represented a lack of trust in government in general.

The participants did not explicitly clarify why congestion charging raised such discontent; nevertheless, three main issues constantly referred to by the participants may directly contribute to the sense that congestion charging is robbery or exploitation. Firstly, the charge will increase the living cost in Beijing, which is already extremely high for new migrants (see also Zhang et al., 2007; Zheng et al., 2009). Secondly, participants questioned the purpose of implementing a charge, because they never expected a transparent revenue allocation. Abundant evidence in the literature indicates the importance of transparency in revenue management (e.g., Grisolía et al., 2015; King et al., 2007; Santos & Rojey, 2004). However, revenue allocation was wrapped in mist to the participants, and this is discussed in Sect. 5.1.4. Thirdly, this discontent emanated from a perception that the revenue will end up in corrupt cadres' pockets. This fits into a wider perception of political corruption, which is discussed in Sect. 5.1.5.

Besides, there is another ideological root of this perception that the purpose of implementing a charge is to collect money from the public in the Chinese context. As discussed in Chapter 2, the political system throughout Chinese history could be regarded as "outside Confucianism inside Legalism". According to the most famous Legalist theoreticians, as well as the policies Legalist practitioners introduced, the ruler should debilitate the public to strengthen the regime (see Han, 1964; Shang, 1928; see also Goldin, 2013; Pines, 2014). Policies had been implemented for this purpose since the Qin dynasty.[4] For example, during the Discourses on Salt and Iron (simplified Chinese: 盐铁论)[5] in the Han dynasty,[6] Sang Hongyang expressly stated that taxes should never be levied for delivering public service and that the ruler should extort taxes for his own ends (Kuan, 1967). He further explained that poor people are either sluggards or inebriates; hence, it is the most asinine idea for the ruler to help the poor. Although their opponents, the Confucianist Literati under the honorary titles *xianliang* (virtue), and *wenxue* (culture), fiercely argued against the Legalist policies implemented by Emperor Wu, they claimed that local aristocrats should have the power to tax the public instead of the emperor. In other words, the Confucianist and Legalist ideas had a high consistency in terms of the administrative logic that the ruling classes have the right to levy taxes for their own interests (see also Han Fei's interpretation of public interests; Goldin, 2001). It is worth keeping in mind that Sang Hongyang and his ideas were widely endorsed and propagated during the China's Great Cultural Revolution (e.g., Luo, 1974[7]).

[4] 221–206 BC.

[5] This was a debate held in 81 BC. It happened because Confucianists disagreed with a large variety of state interventions imposed by the previous Emperor Wu, who was considered a great emperor in the Han dynasty. These policies included monopolies on China's salt and iron enterprises, price stabilization schemes and taxes on capital. The debate was between two opposing factions: Legalist ministers, such as Sang Hongyang, and Confucianist Literati. Therefore, it was usually regarded as a great debate between Confucianism and Legalism.

[6] 202 BC–220 AD.

[7] This is an article originally published in the *Red Flag*, which was a theoretical political journal of the CCP, one of the "Two Newspapers and One Magazine" during the 1960s and 1970s. This article was repeatedly edited by Zhang Chunqiao and Yao Wenyuan,

Due to the perpetual practice of tax imposition for the interests of the ruling class, it is not surprising that the participants deemed a tax or a charge as a measure that "grabs money from the public for the ruling class". This is of vital importance to understand the participants' resentment towards congestion charging.

5.5.1.4 *Transparency in Revenue Reallocation*

Revenue allocation plays a crucial role in public acceptability of congestion pricing, which has been intensively discussed in the literature (e.g., Hensher & Puckett, 2005; Leape, 2006; Rouwendal & Verhoef, 2006; Santos, 2004; Santos & Bhakar, 2006; Small, 1992; Verhoef et al., 1997; see also Newbery & Santos, 1999). Also, revenue allocation and the equity issue, which is another determinant of public acceptability of congestion charging, are inseparable in the Western context (e.g., Eliasson & Mattsson, 2006; Levine & Garb, 2002; Litman, 1996; Rajé, 2003). However, this is not the case in this context.

Revenue allocation was not a concern for the participants. Only two participants in one group referred to revenue allocation before they were directly asked to talk about it, while other participants were very confused about this issue. They were unacquainted with this term, and most of them indicated that they had never thought about this issue.

> I think it (revenue allocation) is too far away from our life actually. So it's kind of irrelevant, to be honest. (Male, younger than 45, Pekingese, inner Beijing)

> Yeah, we don't care how it (revenue) could be used, because we never know how they (the government) use the money. (Female, younger than 45, new migrant, outer Beijing)

The participants suggested a variety of options to use the revenue after they were compelled to discuss this issue. Fewer than 20 participants mentioned that the revenue could be used for transport investments and smog mitigation, including public transport subsidies, electric vehicle subsidies, environmental protection, reforestation, new subway lines, new highways, the high-speed rail system and new technology in the

who were the most important members of the Central Cultural Revolution Group and the notorious Gang of Four.

transport field. However, participants suggested many more irrelevant options, including investment in scientific research, healthcare in both urban and rural areas, new kindergartens, higher education, tourism, heating systems, public security, national defence, counter-terrorism and food safety governance. This shows that most of the participants merely thought about how the money could be used by the government instead of regarding revenue allocation as an equitable redistribution of resources. Therefore, revenue allocation was considered an irrelevant issue to congestion charging.

It was considered irrelevant because many participants thought there would be different government organs to collect and use the revenue; hence, it was pointless to consider how another government organ might use the money.

> How they are going to use the money is totally a different thing. You know the one who collects money and the one who uses the money are not in the same department. [...] So the one who collects money cannot decide how the money will be used. And the one who uses the money doesn't care how the money was collected. (Male, older than 45, Pekingese, outer Beijing)

Some participants directly stated that it is not important to let the public know how the revenue is going to be used because lay citizens do not have the knowledge to think about this issue.

> We have no idea how the government should use our money; we have no idea about it. So it will not make the policy more acceptable if you tell me how you are going to use it. Because I don't know if it's right or wrong. You know, I don't have this experience. (Female, older than 45, Pekingese, outer Beijing)

The way the government uses the revenue was regarded as much less important than the transparency of using the revenue.

> I think if they let us know how they use that money, I think I will be more pleased to accept that. But you know, China. I think the problem is not how they use that money, the problem is whether they let us know how they are going to use that money, and whether it is real. (Female, older than 45, Pekingese, inner Beijing)

However, none of the participants thought the revenue allocation for congestion charging could be transparent in China. Most of the participants indicated that it is still not trustworthy even if the government promises to make the revenue allocation public.

> Anything related to transparency is [obscenities]. Anything that requires transparency is meaningless. [...] We really don't know how our money is going to be used. So I may believe you if you tell me the money will be used for stability maintenance, for families (of corrupt cadres) living abroad, for (corrupt cadres) keeping concubines, for bribing foreign companies. I don't know, the more ridiculous it sounds, the easier it is for me to believe. Because they are always way beyond my imagination. (Male, younger than 45, new migrant, outer Beijing)

This depicted a low level of trust in government. Moreover, it revealed a strong interconnection between low transparency and corruption. The participants believed the government (or its cadres) are corrupt because of lack of transparency and, indubitably, a lack of transparency, in turn, breeds corruption (see Brunetti & Weder, 2003; Ohashi, 2009). Therefore, it was difficult for the participants to trust the government because of their perception of corrupt cadres and a lack of transparency, even if the government attempts to make the information public.

As presented in Sect. 5.5.1.3, the participants regarded the charge as a measure that the government would apply to collect money from the public, while in this section, the results showed that the participants did not expect any benefit from the taxation. Together, they engendered a premonition that the charge will let the public "pay for nothing" and finally resulted in a low level of public acceptability of congestion charging.

5.5.1.5 Cadres

Cadres, especially grassroots or low-level cadres, were the main target of participants' criticisms. One criticism was directly related to congestion charging, which was perceived as a social inequity issue of "granting a new privilege to cadres" (presented in Sect. 5.5.1.6). However, more participants focused on talking about corrupt cadres as a whole and political corruption in general, which significantly undermined their trust in government.

Most of the participants believed that the ultimate outcome of implementing congestion charging would be citizens' money in corrupt cadres' pockets, whatever the original purpose or motivation of implementing the policy was.

> Maybe the purpose is not that, [...] but the results are always like this. So it doesn't matter, what they want to achieve (before the implementation) actually, whatever they want to reach will end up with corruption. So, well maybe they really wanted to improve the air quality when they first proposed this policy, I don't know, but I think the result is quite clear, we just pay extra money to make those corrupt ones richer. (Male, younger than 45, Pekingese, inner Beijing)

Moreover, for around half of the participants, less corruption was the only expectation for the implementation of the policy. It is evident that the participants would easily find the revenue allocation favourable if they were convinced that the money would not be taken by corrupt cadres.

> I think, ideally, no corruption. I don't want the money they collected to go to some corrupt cadres' pockets. I hope the money will not be used to buy luxury houses, luxury bags, luxury cars. I hope the money will not be used to flatter those cadres' mistresses. (Female, older than 45, new migrants, inner Beijing)

On the one hand, this shows the participants lacked taxpayers' awareness of their rights and obligations, since their notion of the link between tax payments and redistribution was distorted (see Al-Maghrebi et al., 2016; Csontos et al., 1998; Kallbekken & Sælen, 2011); on the other hand, their cordial abhorrence of corruption was revealed.

There were four types of participant perceptions of corrupt cadres, which may influence the implementation of congestion charging. Firstly, participants thought that cadres are not likely to alleviate congestion and smog because of their own interests.

> Nobody actually wants to solve the problem, because those cadres get tons of benefits from those heavy industries, but what can they get from environmental protection? Nothing. (Male, older than 45, new migrants, inner Beijing)

Secondly, many cadres were regarded as "poorly educated" people who never followed a reasonable policymaking process. This shows that some participants were doubtful about cadres' ability to make good policies. Also, this is related to participants' perceptions of the abrupt way of solving problems, which was presented in Sect. 5.5.1.2.

> You know it's (Western countries) not like in China, a stupid cadre, maybe one who does not even have a bachelor's degree, heard about a policy and then he can decide whether he want to implement this policy. (Male, younger than 45, new migrant, inner Beijing)

Thirdly, many participants believed that cadres were shortsighted and that they pursued short-term achievements. Therefore, traffic congestion and smog were regarded as inevitable outcomes of the GDP-oriented development, which has been massively criticised by different sectors of society (e.g., Hu, 2017; Lu & Lo, 2007; Ngok & Huang, 2014; Wang et al., 2015; Yin et al., 2014). Meanwhile, these participants also suggested that congestion and smog alleviation would never been a concern of cadres, since alleviating them is not a short-term achievement. This agreed with the results of interviews as presented in Sect. 4.3.3.

> They (cadres) will move to another city because of these short-term achievements, so they will not be affected by the policy they implemented after they left the city. So I think that's the reason why they never have a long-term strategy for the development of a city. […] To speak bluntly, the purpose of implementing different kinds of policies is not to solve a problem or to achieve a more effective administration or whatever, it's political opportunism. (Male, younger than 45, Pekingese, outer Beijing)

Fourthly, participants considered congestion and smog as results of cadres' dereliction of duty.

> All of these (heavy pollution industry, illegal emission factories) should be avoided, but none of them was. […] They know exactly what should be done but they never take any action. (Male, older than 45, new migrant, outer Beijing)

Consequently, participants argued whether lay citizens should be responsible for traffic congestion and smog in Beijing, and this is presented in the next section.

In summary, none of the participants expressed positive attitudes towards cadres who were involved in specific public policymaking. Moreover, participants always resonated with other participants' perceptions of corrupt cadres. Many of them, especially those who did not actively participate in group discussions, appeared to be much more willing to talk about corruption and corrupt cadres' behaviours. In addition, none of the participants argued that cadres who would be involved in policymaking of this policy might be honest, including those who clearly stated that they trust the Central Committee of the CCP. Apparently, it was a shared understanding that corruption is pervasive, and it was highly likely that the policymakers for congestion charging would be corrupt cadres. With this perception, a high public acceptability of congestion charging was unattainable.

5.5.1.6 *Congestion and Smog Alleviation: Whose Responsibility?*

Since it was postulated that congestion and smog were results of cadres' dereliction of duty, many participants regarded implementing congestion charging as evading responsibility. Participants in all nine groups had lengthy discussions about who should be responsible for mitigating smog, while congestion was rarely mentioned in these debates, which implied the indisputable responsibility of private car users for traffic congestion. However, as congestion charging was introduced as part of the smog alleviation plan, the participants expressed their discontents towards the policy.

According to most of the participants, the government should be responsible for smog alleviation.

> This (smog) is also from the government's mistakes. They made mistakes. We are victims, we are all [obscenities] victims here. Is it reasonable to let victims pay for what the [obscenities] assailants do? (Male, older than 45, new migrants, inner Beijing)

Heavily polluting industries were regarded as much bigger contributors to the nationwide smog, whereas most of the participants thought the government failed to regulate these heavily polluting factories.

> This policy just restricts us, but those heavily polluting industries, those companies should also do something to solve the problem. I mean, they did much more than us. We ordinary people, just drive our cars maybe

> one or two hours a day, but they are polluting our air every second. […] I don't think this (congestion charging) will improve our air quality because those heavily polluting factories will still be there. (Female, older than 45, Pekingese, outer Beijing)

It was presumed that the government did not make enough effort to regulate polluting industries because of cadres chasing fast GDP growth while lay citizens were as lambs to the slaughter. After experiencing decades of ineffective industrial pollution control (e.g., Andrews-Speed et al., 2003; Tilt, 2007; Zheng & Shi, 2017), the participants were unwilling to pay for a transport policy that was partly proposed to alleviate air pollution.

There were intense disagreements between different age groups. In general, older participants thought private car users are responsible to alleviate smog, while younger participants repudiated the idea.

> I told my son to think about his daughter, my granddaughter. I asked him, was there smog when you are a child? He was born in Beijing, and he said no. […] I think the problem is not only caused by the government: every car user should be responsible for that consequence. (Male, older than 45, new migrant, outer Beijing)

Similar dialogue between older participants and their children was mentioned simultaneously in different groups, which implied different ideas about drivers' responsibility for smog alleviation between older and younger people. It also revealed that their perception of drivers' responsibility was not merely derived from the fact that many of them, as non-car users, would be less affected by the policy. This notion of responsibility, on the one hand, emerged from Confucianist family values (see Sect. 5.2); on the other hand, it was inseparable from the socialist ideology and the prevalent practice of planned economy in the Mao Era (e.g., Dernberger, 1999; Kirkby, 2018). Since public ownership, dedication and sometimes self-sacrifice have been highly praised and propagated since the early stage of China's Communist revolution[8] (e.g., Ahn, 1975; Brugger, 2018b;

[8] For example, the People's Commune was highly praised as "large in size and collective in nature (simplified Chinese: 一大二公)", and "working without remuneration" has been praised as a communist spirit. It is worth nothing that this is still an officially praised spirit, but it is usually mentioned as a special trait of members of the CCP, instead of a requirement of every individual in the Mao Era. As another example, Mao highly praised

Lin, 1990; Zhong et al., 2001), many older participants expressed a moral approbation to the collective interests which their group mates could hardly refute.

Mao's legacy played a vitally important role in older participants' discussions about trust and inequity issues; however, it has been rarely regarded as a factor influencing older people's ideas about policies and social issues in the transport domain. Admittedly, Mao's legacy was also ignored by observers in other fields, but they have been increasingly aware of the continuity between the Mao Era and the post-Mao Era (e.g., Heilmann & Perry, 2011; Rene, 2013; Wei, 2011).

Younger participants argued that car users, or car users in Beijing, should not pay the charge because they are not the only contributors to air pollution. There was no distinct disagreement between younger car owners and non-car owners in regard to this issue.

> So my point is, we contribute to this serious problem, we are aware of this, but we are not the only ones who contribute to this. Why should we pay for this while all the others don't? (Male, younger than 45, new migrant, outer Beijing)

Although a few participants reckoned that all Beijing residents should be responsible for smog alleviation, they did not regard congestion charging as a way to shoulder the responsibility.

> I do know everyone who lives in this city has some kind of responsibility to make it better. We want to take our responsibility, and I think we are taking this responsibility, but not by this kind of policy. (Male, younger than 45, Pekingese, outer Beijing)

The above-mentioned evidence shows that congestion charging as one part of the smog alleviation plan was criticised by the participants. Although the participants mostly laid the blame for air pollution on polluting industries and rural factories, the government was always spear-headed due to participants' perceptions that the government is incapable

a spirit "fearing neither hardship not death (simplified Chinese: 一不怕苦二不怕死)" in April 1969. The grassroots cadre Yang Shuicai was also praised for his dedication and self-sacrifice spirit: "as long as the wheeler does not fall down, I will just keep on pushing (simplified Chinese: 小车不倒只管推)". Similar slogans met the eye everywhere in the Mao Era.

of monitoring, regulating or overseeing these sources of pollution. The proposition of congestion charging, therefore, aroused a feeling that the government was evading its responsibilities.

5.5.1.7 Summary

As presented in Sect. 5.5.1.1, the overwhelming majority of participants distrusted the government, which is a pernicious barrier to implementing congestion charging in Beijing. Five key factors that generated this distrust in government were identified: (a) the perception of abrupt implementation of policies, (b) the perception of the purpose of implementing the policy, (c) a lack of transparency in revenue management, (d) the perception of corrupt cadres and (e) the government's responsibility for smog alleviation. They are both the underlying causes and the embodiments of people's low levels of trust in government. Since the notion of trust in government is rather intractable because of its vagueness, these five key factors offer policymakers a more practical agenda for re-establishing people's trust in government, on which the implementation of congestion charging heavily relies.

5.5.2 Trust Towards Experts

Compared to the government, experts were even less trusted. Experts (simplified Chinese: 专家, pinyin: *zhuanjia*) have been labelled as "bricksperts" (砖家, *zhuanjia*) and professors (simplified Chinese: 教授, pinyin: *jiaoshou*) have been labelled as "screaming beasts" (叫兽, jiaoshou) by Chinese netizens since 2013 (China Digital Times, 2013; Han, 2018; Shei, 2014). Both neologisms describe so-called intellectuals who speak under the orders of officials or dishonest businessmen in a sarcastic and humiliating way. In this study, experts were excessively rebuked and humiliated in all the nine groups.

The overwhelming majority of the participants directly linked experts with talking nonsense. For example:

> I have seen a guy who said that the policy in our country is "encouraging car ownership but not encouraging car use". [obscenities] shameless. [...] "China's car ownership is not high enough, it's still much lower than a developed country. And automobile manufacturing is an important industry in China, almost the biggest industry in China. [...] So we should encourage people to buy cars and not allow them to use cars." Have you

> ever heard about such a [obscenities] nonsense? I don't know where this theory come from, I'm poorly educated, I'm totally a [obscenities]. I really cannot understand. (Male, younger than 45, Pekingese, outer Beijing)

Other expert opinions were criticised and satirised in group discussions, including (a) bike use increases traffic congestion, and people should stop using bikes (China Youth Daily, 2003), (b) kitchen fumes are a major cause of Beijing's smog (Quartz, 2016), (c) smog is the best defence against U.S. laser weapons (BBC, 2014), (d) petitioners are suffering from paranoid personality disorder (Sina, 2009) and (e) widening China's rich-poor gap promotes social development[9] (Global Times, 2012; see also Wu, 2009). Such expert opinions have been extensively reported in the past 20 years, and consequently, the reputation of experts and scholars has been ruined. Many participants were very emotional when they talked about bricksperts. Obscene language was repeatedly used when they mentioned scholars and experts.

The participants, on the one hand, directly stated that they "can never trust those experts"; on the other hand, they expressed their disdain for bricksperts, and sometimes intellectuals in general.

This disdain for intellectuals was embodied in three of the group discussions in which an analyst who had economic background, a researcher who worked in a state-owned think tank, and an urban planner were respectively encircled and suppressed in their own groups when they tried to explain the rationale for implementing congestion charging from their knowledge.

For example, the analyst who had an economic background talked about congestion as a negative externality of urban transport system. However she was satirised by other participants due to the "uselessness and absurdity of economic theories", for example:

> Hee hee, I don't know what you are talking about, but it sounds quite professional. I know nothing about those externalities, those price mechanisms. I don't know and I don't [obscenities] care about this [obscenities] nonsense. (Male, younger than 45, new migrant, inner Beijing)

[9] This economist had many other eye-catching theories, such as "(the government) must sacrifice one generation of workers (30 million people) to carry out economic reform" and "(the government) should abolish the national pension to make people work harder". These quotes were not mentioned by the participants.

As this quote shows, participants' attitudes towards experts were arguably worse than their distrust and discontent towards bricksperts. It was verging on anti-intellectualism.

This anti-intellectualist tendency has three main roots in this context. Traditionally, it was originated from a theory of *shixue* (simplified Chinese: 实学, genuine talent or real learning) in the late Ming Dynasty[10] (see Huang & de Bary, 1993; Ng & Wang, 2005; Struve, 1988). Politically, before the economic reform in 1978, a lack of knowledge was highly praised and intellectuals were humiliated and purged in a series of political movements after Mao's rise to power in the early '40s (e.g., Gao, 2000; Liang, 2003; Thurston, 1988; Vladimirov, 1975; Wang, 2004; see also Goldman, 2009). It was not only in Mao's China that anti-intellectualism was widely applied to repress dissent in totalitarian regimes (see Courtois et al., 1999; Kiernan, 2002). Lately, intellectuals' role has changed after Mao (e.g., Chen, 2002; Mok, 1998); however, intellectuals have turned themselves into another corrupt group in the post-Tiananmen Era—there is academic corruption in almost all sectors of higher education (e.g., Chen & Chow, 2010; Ren, 2012; Yang, 2005).

According to the focus group participants' criticism, as well as netizens'[11] comments, it is evident that lay citizens are aware of the degeneration of Chinese intellectuals. Since the scholar-bureaucrat[12] has always been deemed as the conscience of the society (e.g., McDermott, 2006; Roddy, 1998), the degeneration of intellectuals has undoubtedly aroused a sense of betrayal by lay citizens. Together with Mao's inculcation of the "reactionary nature of intellectuals", it is not surprising that experts and scholars were excessively rebuked in group discussions.

There were two main underlying causes for participants to regard experts as bricksperts. Firstly, most of the participants thought those experts were merely government mouthpieces, using professional knowledge to varnish over cadres' arbitrary policymaking.

[10] This school opposed the Cheng-zhu school, which is also referred to as the Rationalist school, and the Lu-wang school. The basic idea is "to use knowledge for practical purposes", which is to some extent similar to pragmatism.

[11] Netizen is a portmanteau of the words Internet and citizen as in "citizen of the net". It refers to a person who is actively involved in online communities.

[12] Scholar-bureaucrats, also known as Literati, were politicians and government officials appointed by the emperor of China to perform day-to-day political duties from the Han dynasty to the end of the Qing dynasty in 1912.

> They say all the good words, and let us pay: the same old trick. [...] They just find some so-called experts to praise the [obscenities] policy, to praise those [obscenities] policymakers, to lick the stinky feet of those corrupt cadres. And then the only thing we need to do is to pay. (Male, older than 45, new migrant, inner Beijing)

These participants repeatedly called experts "pets of the government", for example:

> These experts are government's pets. They are loyal dogs of the government. (Male, younger than 45, Pekingese, inner Beijing)

Secondly, some participants disliked experts because experts always use jargon to confuse lay citizens, and thereby showing their arrogance.

> In China, you know, what they (experts) usually do is to make something that everyone can understand into a strange word which only a few people know. So yes, I think the way they talk about the issue is very stupid. (Female, younger than 45, Pekingese, outer Beijing)

The above-mentioned evidence shows that experts and scholars were highly distrusted by the participants. However, this distrust was not only derived from experts' arrogance and degeneration, but also from their role as servants of the government. In this sense, trust towards experts was directly linked with trust in government. The reason why experts received much more criticism might be that the participants, who self-identified as lay citizens, expected experts to speak on behalf of the public, whereas their expectation had been shattered by the indissoluble alliance between the government and academics in the post-Tiananmen Era.

5.5.3 *The Impact of Trust on Other Determinants of Public Acceptability*

Trust in government and trust towards experts are the fundamental causes of three other determinants of public acceptability of congestion charging.

Firstly, perceived access to information depends on trust in government and trust towards experts. However, most of the participants stated that government-owned media are unreliable.

> And I think if it's (information) from government-owned media, I think it's even more unreliable. They are good at making stories. (Female, older than 45, Pekingese, inner Beijing)

Some participants even stated that "the government is the main source of fake news" (Male, older than 45, new migrant, outer Beijing). Most of the participants, especially younger people, thought state-owned news can hardly be regarded as an information source, as it is merely a propaganda tool. Due to the absence of trust in government, information from official sources was perceived as a whitewash to deceive the public instead of providing information for the public. Experts' endorsements were repeatedly referred to as "flattering the government" and successful experience from the West introduced by government-owned media was perceived as dogmatic preaching. The overwhelming majority of the participants agreed that they needed only two pieces of information from official sources: (a) when the policy is going to be implemented, and (b) how much the charge is. This corroborates participants' distrust in state-owned media.

Also, some participants complained about 50-Cent Party, which was hired by the CCP in an attempt to manipulate public opinion on the internet[13] (see Fang & Repnikova, 2018; Han, 2015a; King et al., 2017; Repnikova, 2017; see also Han, 2015b). They thought their voices could not be heard because of the 50-Cent Party, resulting in their distrust towards favourable opinions on the internet.

> I don't even comment on news related to that, because they hire many 50-Cent Party members to praise the government, so if I say something, I will be under siege. So it really doesn't matter how I feel. I can do nothing: I can't even say anything. (Male, younger than 45, new migrant, outer Beijing)

Secondly, the perceived effectiveness of congestion charging was significantly influenced by trust in government and trust towards experts. As discussed in Sect. 5.4, the perceived effectiveness of previous policies has

[13] This issue itself is very interesting. However, I cannot expand it further due to word limitations. It is interesting that most of the participants did not mention the 50-Cent Party on the internet, because according to their perceptions of congestion charging, it is clear they got a lot of information from official sources. It is highly likely that they got this information via the 50-Cent Party's comments.

a direct impact on participants' perceptions of congestion charging. It is evident that the participants learnt from experience that different local authorities used all kinds of tricks to make the outcome of policies seemingly effective. Many migrant participants introduced a variety of tricks to make up PM 2.5 data, for example:

> For example last November, in Shijiazhuang, they set a lot of roadblocks around the Xuefu road. Only two cars could pass on the road, and trucks were not allowed to pass. There were many sprinklers around that place; the road was always wet. They were assigned by the local environmental protection bureau. They did this because there was an air sampler next to the road, in the campus. They did this to make the data look better. (Male, younger than 45, new migrant, outer Beijing)

Many participants satirised that "the environmental protection bureau's duty is not to protect the environment, but to protect the air sampler". Due to this kind of activities, the participants were dubious about the effectiveness of previous policies and congestion charging, because whatever the policy was effective or not, the government, with experts' help, would always find a way to make it appear statistically effective. However, according to their perceptions of congestion and smog problem presented in Sect. 5.2, none of the participants mentioned that these problems had been alleviated by any previously implemented policy, whose effectiveness and public acceptance had been highly praised by the government and experts. Therefore, the participants did not perceive congestion charging as an effective measure because of the absence of trust.

Thirdly, perceived social inequity was related to trust in government since many participants considered social inequity a result of public policies, including transport policies. They suggested that congestion charging cannot be acceptable in China because they believe the government only focuses on collecting money.

> I think [...] we usually take the capitalist part of the policy, but all of the other things are thrown away, for example how they deal with vulnerable groups [...], how they guarantee people's rights, how they balance winners and losers. [...] However, our government doesn't do that. (Male, older than 45, new migrant, outer Beijing)

Since these participants believed that the government would not consider social equity issues, they tended to think that whatever policy the government implemented would exacerbate social inequity, including congestion charging.

This section has comprehensively described the trust issue and its fundamental role in forming people's acceptability of congestion charging. Sections 5.5.1 and 5.5.2 have introduced its direct impacts on public acceptability and Sect. 5.5.3 has explained how it indirectly influences public acceptability via other determinants. It is clear that understanding the relationship between lay citizens and the government is at the core of investigating public acceptability in the Chinese context.

5.6 Perceived Social Inequity Issues

Although the research was designed and conducted for a study of the public acceptability of the proposed congestion charge policy in Beijing, social equity issues became overwhelmingly important in the interviews with policymakers, and even more so in the focus group discussions with lay citizens. It was totally unexpected for the researcher that most participants identified social inequities as one of the major concerns of the policy. This is unexpected because Chinese society has increasingly been described as materialistic since the Economic Reform in 1978 (e.g., Podoshen et al., 2011); the Chinese government has placed great emphasis on material well-being while social equity has always been subordinated to a loftier goal—revolution in the Mao era and economic growth in the post-Mao era. Most participants seemed to think that the congestion policy is unacceptable because they believe it will be in some way unfair, and/or it may worsen current social inequity problems in the city.

This section presents four types of perceived inequities relating to congestion charging identified in focus group discussions: inequities between the government and the public, inequities between the rich and the poor, inequities between residents of Beijing and residents of other cities and inequities between the Pekingese and new migrants. The influence of Chinese egalitarianism (see Sects. 2.3.1 and 2.3.2) was represented in these aspects of perceived inequities. This helps us to understand equity issues in the Chinese context properly and it instructs the questionnaire design. The results of the survey are in Sects. 6.2.2.4 and 6.3.2.4. Perceived social inequity was also extensively discussed in group discussions. A concise discussion on the relationship between

Chinese egalitarianism and the way participants perceived social inequity issues related to the introduction of congestion charging is presented in a journal paper (Liu et al., 2019, for my recent studies on transport inequities during the Covid-19 pandemic, see also Liu, 2021; Liu et al., 2021a, b); what is presented here is the key findings and their connections to public acceptability.

5.6.1 *Inequity: Government and the Public*

Government car users, mostly perceived as corrupt cadres, were perceived as the biggest and probably the only winners from the policy. None of the participants believed that government car users themselves will need to pay the charge; thus, there will be no charge and less congestion for these privileged classes to continue to drive in. In this way, other car users will sacrifice their personal interests to deliver a better service for cadres.

> There are still a lot of government cars, especially in Beijing. If, ideally, they could be scrupulous in separating public from private interests, in other words, they don't charge government cars, it is absolutely unfair. However, if they also charge government cars, then who pays for that? Of course, the government, that is to say, taxpayers pay for that. So, in other words, we pay for them. That is a little unreasonable. (Female, younger than 45, Pekingese, outer Beijing)

However, on the other hand, most of the participants were inclined to accept the fact that cadres could have the privilege although they apparently felt unsatisfied with the situation. In their opinion, social inequity is about inequalities of treatment between different groups of lay citizens, while inequalities between cadres and lay citizens were considered as irresistible and inevitable (see also Liu et al., 2019, 2020, 2021a, b). This is fundamentally caused by the traditional (originally Legalist) relationship between the ruler and the ruled (see Sect. 2.3.1.3).

5.6.2 *Inequity: The Rich and the Poor*

The great disparity in income equality before and after the Economic Reform has arguably exaggerated public perceptions of the polarization between the rich and poor. Many Chinese people, especially those who experienced a series of socialist movements in the '50s and '60s, exude nostalgia for the egalitarian past when they are thinking about the rich-poor gap at present.

> Back in the '80s, or '90s we didn't have such serious, such intense social contradictions. Not like nowadays, we blame each other. I think it's because society is becoming more and more unequal, and that's what makes us feel nervous. [...] I don't have a car. I also want to have a car, but I can't afford it. So, because of this [congestion charge] policy, I know it's more unlikely for me to own a car now. But on the other side, I become glad secretly that some people who are just a little richer than me cannot use their cars. So, they will not laugh at me, because you know those who have a similar economic status to you would laugh at you most. (Male, older than 45, new migrant, outer Beijing)

A notion of egalitarianism is clearly embodied in this quote. On the one hand, the participant worried about the situation that people around him have something that he does not have, rather than car use itself. On the other hand, depriving other people of that car is regarded as favourable and equal, even though he cannot himself derive any benefit from the deprival.

Poorer people and richer people hold relatively different views on this issue. Poorer people suspected that driving would become another privilege of the rich again.

> I think the policy makes public owned urban roads a scarce commodity, which means rich people can use them, but poor people cannot use them. (Female, younger than 45, Pekingese, outer Beijing)

While a few richer people think it is logical to make driving a privilege. It is an inevitable trend, because roads, as one kind of limited resources, should not be free of charge.

> We are born to be unequal. So, I don't think the policy is something that oppresses people. More and more people come into this city, and obviously the city cannot allow everyone to come in. So, I think they have to find a way to filter the people who can live in this city. Rich people can drive not because they are rich, but because they pay for it. If they don't pay, they also cannot drive. I don't think it's something unfair. I have paid for that service, right? When resources are limited, then of course some people

> cannot use it. So, in this case, those who pay can drive. (Male, younger than 45, new migrant, inner Beijing)

It is interesting to find out from the group discussion that an absolutely equal charge seems inadequate for the public. Most of the participants suggested that richer people should pay more than poorer car users to avoid the privilege of the rich. Because of egalitarianism, solving congestion or smog is low on their list of priorities. However, it is also doubtful that an absolutely equal distribution is exactly what people desire. It could be more accurate to describe the so-called egalitarian distribution as equally not to have something rather than equally to have something. People with egalitarian thoughts urge policymakers to take more from the rich, but they don't really ask for anything the rich have. In other words, what participants were expecting was not an egalitarian charge but an absolutely equally lower opportunity for richer people to use cars.

5.6.3 *Inequity: Residents of Beijing and Residents of Other Cities*

Most participants, including new migrants originally from the area surrounding Beijing, considered it inequitable that only residents in Beijing need to pay.

> I think the policy could be implemented in other cities as well, at least cities around Beijing, for example Tianjin, Shijiazhuang. [...] It's more equal for us because the smog problem is a nationwide problem; it's not only our problem. We are responsible for that, and they should be responsible for that too. So, I think they should pay too. (Male, older than 45, Pekingese, outer Beijing)

Since the authority has announced that a pilot congestion charge will be studied after the red alert of air pollution, the policy is widely regarded as a solution to the smog problem. Accordingly, it seems unequal that only Beijing residents need to pay extra money for this. However, most participants are dubious about the real purpose of the policy and its effectiveness in alleviating the smog problem.

> But I just don't know if this policy could be effective. Or maybe I will say, I don't believe this policy could solve the problem. [...] I think now the problem is they have implemented a lot of policies that make us pay more

> and more to drive our cars, but we never see any improvements. (Male, younger than 45, Pekingese, inner Beijing)

These participants did not trust that the policy could be effective; therefore, they do not want to be the only victims of a policy aimed at alleviating the nationwide smog problem. Thus, Beijing residents thought it would be more equitable if the policy was not only implemented in Beijing. This is clearly influenced by egalitarianism, in that participants expect to take something away from others to achieve an egalitarian distribution.

5.6.4 Inequity: Pekingese and New Migrants

Pekingese and new migrants hold different views on equity issues when discussing the introduction of a congestion charging scheme in Beijing. It is interesting that these two groups of participants blamed each other for different causes, most of which are not related to the congestion charging scheme itself.

On the one hand, some Pekingese blamed new migrants for air pollution and other social problems. Therefore, they thought implementing the policy may be necessary to regulate migrants.

> Because you know the problem in Beijing is mainly caused by them. Of course, we contribute to these problems as well, but you know it's different. For example, I think the policy could be good because I think we need such a policy to regulate those new migrants. Maybe not all of them, but the newly rich. Of course, they are rich, they can go wherever they want, but I think they are parasites of this city. (Male, younger than 45, Pekingese, outer Beijing)

On the other hand, new migrants expressed strong discontent with the policy. They believed that as newcomers to this city, they have already been unfairly treated in every aspect before and after they came to the city. Moreover, the policy itself is unequal, not to speak of leading to greater social inequities.

> At the end of autumn, farmers burn their straw and there is very heavy smoke everywhere. [...] We have had that experience for 20 years. So now, I think it is just because there is the same problem in cities now, big cities like Beijing. So, they now think it is a problem, it should be solved.

> We have had that experience for 20 years. Who cares about those farmers? Well not only farmers, people who live in those areas actually, like me. And now we come to Beijing, and we need to use our money to improve their air quality? (Male, younger than 45, new migrant, outer Beijing)

This participant is originally from a rural area. He thought that smog has attracted attention because urban residents are now suffering from this problem too. However, people like him have already suffered smog for a much longer time. Thus, the participant found it inequitable that rural and urban residents are treated differently. It is a result of the urban–rural dual structure in China. The urban–rural dual structure includes a variety of disparities such as household registration systems, political rights and land administrative systems. Consequences relating to transport can be divided into (a) urbanization, because of people's inclination to live in cities (Henderson et al., 2009) and (b) virulent hostility between people who live inside and outside cities (Wong et al., 2007). Because of the internal population migration, the demographic transition leads to a confrontation between people originally from urban and rural areas.

It is indubitable that Beijing, as the capital city of China, is one of the main beneficiaries of these policies and it has the most intense social contradictions hidden behind a harmonious appearance. For example, participants indicated that Beijing plunders many resources from the rest of the country, especially provinces around Beijing such as Hebei.

> I feel that Beijing has bled my hometown, the whole province. It is almost the worst province in this country. Bad economy, worst environment, very bad. The only reason is, it's near Beijing, the capital city. [...] I realize our young people have already contributed to this city, but they (Pekingese) are grabbing everything from our hometown. I can't feel happy. I know it's not related to this policy, but I just think it's ridiculous to let those contributors pay this money: you know many of them don't have a Beijing hukou. They get no benefit from staying here. (Male, older than 45, new migrant, inner Beijing)

New migrants think the Pekingese are born with privileges. The Pekingese may not even notice that they are sharing resources that new migrants may need decades of hard work to gain access to.

> I know this policy has been implemented in many foreign cities, but you know their societies are quite equal. You know, they don't have that privilege of the Beijing hukou. You know when we moved to here, my child was not allowed to register in a normal secondary high school in Beijing because we don't have a Beijing hukou. So our children can only study in schools for migrant workers. The educational resources are extremely poor. You know, teachers, campus. It's like they intentionally segregate us from them. It's like apartheid. (Female, older than 45, new migrant, outer Beijing)

Hukous remain one of the legacies of the planned economic system, obstructing urbanization and labour mobility (Liang, 2003). Even if new migrants could find productive employment, they will be treated as second-class citizens without a Beijing *hukou*. New migrants do not have equal access to a series of social resources, such as social security, housing subsidies and education in public schools (Tao & Xu, 2007). Thus, obtaining a Beijing *hukou* is one of the highest priority tasks for most new migrants.

Despite the fact that the congestion charge has no direct relationship with the *hukou* system, most new migrant participants spontaneously categorised the policy as a benefit for the Pekingese and exploitation of migrant workers. For new migrants, the policy seems to be another privilege of Beijing *hukou* holders, because they, as outsiders, pay for the Pekingese quality of life. It is evident that new migrant participants do not regard Beijing as their home. Therefore, they always have a sense of alienation from Beijing. Although new migrants may get the same benefits from the policy as the Pekingese do (less congestion, better air quality), they still felt they are unfairly treated. This sense of inequity is derived from a variety of privileges that the Beijing *hukou* grants, as well as from the great disparity between the development of Beijing and their hometowns.

5.6.5 *Resentment Towards the Privileged*

Privilege has featured at the centre of discourses of social inequities. The privileged group was recognised as another symbolic effect of the market-oriented economic reform. Some particular groups of people who have reaped the benefits of the reform, such as the rich and Pekingese, were identified as the privileged, while others have had a strong feeling of being oppressed and exploited. Since the congestion charge was expected to reduce car use, poorer car users indicated that the policy would exacerbate social contradictions between the privileged class and others.

> I think this policy will make prejudice between people more visible. For example, those who are still using cars every day may regard themselves as head and shoulders above others, because they can still use cars. (Female, younger than 45, Pekingese, inner Beijing)

The feeling of being oppressed causes the resentment against the rich, which has been a widespread social phenomenon in China for decades. This is mainly represented as a simmering resentment. It is derived from the negative emotions of relatively disadvantaged groups when they actively or passively compare themselves to richer people. People tend to take irrational actions to express their resentment against richer people.

> I don't have a private place for parking, so I park my car outdoors. My car got punctures for more than four times, and it was scratched many times: I cannot even remember. […] They did it intentionally. […] I'm not a rich man, alright? I haven't even bought a place to park my car because it's too expensive. These people just hate whoever is richer than themselves. And they don't think about how to work harder, how to make money by their own hands: they just hate you because they think you are richer. (Male, older than 45, new migrant, inner Beijing)

Public acceptability of congestion charging was significantly influenced by this resentment, inasmuch as car users were regarded as relatively richer people. Due to egalitarianism, the charge was regarded as a proper way to alleviate the differences between car users and non-car users by some participants who, to some extent, support the implementation of the policy.

> They (supporters of the policy) don't really care about whether this policy meets their expectation; they don't care. They just find that this is a good way to let rich people pay more. I heard someone said "great, you bought a car then you think you are rich? You need to pay for the charge now." Many people support this policy because of this. (Male, older than 45, Pekingese, inner Beijing)

The rich, especially the newly rich, were considered absolutely connected with corruption. Most lay citizens have an intimate knowledge of how violent and dishonest the primitive capital accumulation was during the early stage of the Economic Reform (e.g., Ngai, 2005; Tanner & Feder, 1993). Thus, the inappropriate behaviours of the rich morally justify lay-citizens' resentment. Although some people are merely indignant at dishonest ways to be rich, the resentment against the rich has been notably generalised and extremised (e.g., Holmstrom & Smith, 2000; Yan, 2009). According to the participants, it is likely that people would have emotional and violent reactions to richer people. Under such circumstances, those who became a little richer than others by their ability and hard work would be victims of the resentment. It is likely that their hard-earned quality of life may be crushed by a group of emotional people with a resentment against the rich (e.g., Huang, 2002; Moise, 2017).

Due to the feeling of being oppressed by the generalised "privileged group", Chinese egalitarianism leads to an expectation of privilege deprivation. However, Chinese egalitarianism focuses on denial rather than redistribution. Thus, it can never prompt lay citizens to consider revenue management, which is identified as a key determinant of public acceptability in the Western context.

5.7 Cultural Factors

Various cultural factors were touched on in group discussions, including obedience to authority, conformity to social norms in an authoritarian and patriarchal society, indifference about public affairs, the bystander attitude, a lack of civic awareness, self-censorship, self-deception, and a feeling that lay citizens are inferior to officials. Since many of them did not have clear relevance to public acceptability, only obedience to authority and conformity to social norms are presented in this section.

Most participants were generally obedient to authority although they complained and criticised the government. This obedience was not merely a form of reaction, because it is extremely risky to take part in protest activities, but also a way of thinking deeply rooted in Chinese people's minds.

> Their decision is unchangeable. We could only bargain for some little benefits: not benefits, I should say less sacrifice in most cases. So we could care

> about 30 or 50 CNY per day (the charge), we could discuss it. But questions like "is it good or bad", "is it suitable or not", or "will it be effective or not" are not something we should consider. (Female, older than 45, Pekingese, inner Beijing)

It is clear that this participant believed that a policy proposed by the government had to be accepted, whether it is favourable or not. Even if lay citizens need to sacrifice their own benefits, they should just obey the authority and carry on. More obedient participants, to some extent, were more likely to find the policy less unacceptable. They were also inclined to convince other participants who criticised the government and experts to accept whatever policy the government would implement.

The obedience to authority has long been identified as China's national character due to the Confucianist-Legalist hierarchical system. Evidence has been found in many different domains (e.g., Alston, 1989; Cheng et al., 2017; Chien, 2016; Farh & Cheng, 2000; Shafer & Simmons, 2011; Snell, 1999; Torres & Qin, 2017; Zhai, 2017); however, to my knowledge, this has rarely been considered as a factor influencing people's attitude towards transport policies in the Chinese context.

Conformity is another kind of social influence that may change people's attitudes or behaviour because of the views of others. Participants in four groups, mostly older people, discussed how the interactions between family members formed their perceptions of congestion charging. For example:

> I'm kind of authoritative in my family so [...] I don't know if he agrees or disagrees. But I could see that he uses public transport more; he even bought a bike, and he sometimes uses the bike. (Male, older than 45, new migrant, outer Beijing)

Some participants stated that Chinese people's attitude and behaviour are also significantly influenced by strangers.

> We are more confident about ourselves; we don't care about what other people think about us. Many young people, those who originally come from rural areas, small towns, they feel themselves inferior to others. So they are very sensitive about how other people judge them. (Male, older than 45, new migrant, inner Beijing)

The role of social conformity has recently been revealed in research on travel behaviour (e.g., Cherchi, 2017; Goetzke et al., 2015; Kim et al., 2014; Maness et al., 2015; Zhang et al., 2016); however, conformity to social norms was not identified as a main determinant of public acceptability. Nevertheless, at least in the Chinese context, the evidence shows that the participants' acceptability of congestion charging was highly likely to be influenced by others' opinions. This is probably because social conformity plays a much more crucial role in China, a collectivist country, than in individualist countries in the West (e.g., Cialdini et al., 1999; Hong et al., 2016; Takano & Sogon, 2008). Group pressures and how other people perceive opinions from their social surroundings in China greatly differ from other countries (see Chen, 2000; Huang & Harris, 1973; Zhou et al., 2009), but nonetheless, this is worth further exploration in other contexts.

5.8 General Discussion and Conclusion

This chapter has presented key findings from focus group discussions. It is clear that most of the determinants of the public acceptability of congestion charging identified in the Western context can hardly be used to understand and investigate public acceptability in the Chinese context.

Although some of them might be similar in appearance, the mechanisms of public acceptability were different in essence. Information is important in the Western context because policymakers need to convince the public via an understandable explanation of the aims of the policy and the implementation of the measure (e.g., Bonsall & Lythgoe, 2009; Rye et al., 2008). However, there is a lack of access to information and mistrust of information from official sources in the Chinese context.

Consequently, people's perceived effectiveness of the proposed scheme are relatively emotional reactions based on their attitudes towards previous policies and the government in general. Congestion charging, as the subject of discussion, played a dispensable role in group discussions even when they talked about the effectiveness of congestion charging. It was the government that was repeatedly mentioned instead of congestion charging itself when participants discussed its effectiveness. Evidence from the West highlighted the impact of perceived effectiveness on public acceptability of the proposed scheme (e.g., Gärling & Schuitema, 2007; Kallbekken & Sælen, 2011); however, there was no clear connection between perceived effectiveness and acceptability in the group discussions.

Perceived (in)equity appeared to be an important factor influencing the public acceptability of congestion charging. This is seemingly consistent with evidence from Western countries (e.g., Börjesson et al., 2015; Hysing, 2015; Weinstein & Sciara, 2006), but there was a conflict between perceived effectiveness and perceived equity in this case. As congestion charging was considered as conferring another privilege on the privileged class, an ineffective policy was expected by many of those who were more concerned about social inequity issues.

Trust issues, which consist of trust in government and trust towards experts, significantly influenced people's acceptability of congestion charging. Those who had less negative attitudes towards the government were apparently less hostile to congestion charging. Most of the criticisms of implementing congestion charging related to the lack of trust in government, including (a) the abrupt ways policies were implemented, (b) the purpose of implementing a charging policy, (c) transparency in revenue management, (d) corrupt cadres and (e) the government's responsibility for solving problems.

Trust was also at the core of these three determinants of public acceptability. Firstly, information from official sources was distrusted due to the absence of trust in government; therefore, people can never feel they have access to reliable information even if the government is willing to provide that information. Secondly, government's capacity to cope with congestion and air pollution was questioned due to the prevalence of unsuccessful attempts to mitigate such problems. Moreover, the effectiveness of the policy cannot be trusted because the participants despised experts who resort to any conceivable means to endorse the government. Thirdly, the policy was automatically related to social inequity and the privileged class, because the participants believed corruption would definitely intertwine with such a charging policy, which is indubitably a result of the breakdown of trust in government.

Furthermore, some determinants in the Western context were found inappropriate to investigate public acceptability in the Chinese context, including personal freedom, privacy concerns, revenue allocation and transparency. Personal freedom and privacy concerns were never mentioned by any participant, which indicates that these factors were not concerns of the participants. This is consistent with the literature on personal freedom and privacy concerns in collectivist cultures (e.g., Cecere et al., 2015; Maynard & Taylor, 1996; Miltgen & Peyrat-Guillard, 2014). Revenue allocation was only spontaneously intimated by two participants in one group, suggesting it plays an insignificant role in the Chinese context. Although the participants frequently mentioned transparency, it is an inseparable component of trust in government instead of an independent factor influencing public acceptability, since it always popped out as an explanation of their distrust in government.

To sum up, people's acceptability can hardly be deemed part of rational decision-making in the Chinese context. However, it is not as emotional as it seems to be. Because of the strong central power and limited political freedoms in an authoritarian regime (e.g., Levitsky & Way, 2010; Shorten, 2012; see also Lee & Zhang, 2013; Teets, 2013), individuals are subordinate to the country and personal interests are discouraged. In such a polity, public acceptability of a policy reflects an overall attitude towards the government rather than a perception of the particular policy. Therefore, Western context-based frameworks for assessing public acceptability (e.g., Eliasson & Jonsson, 2011; Eriksson et al., 2008; Kim et al., 2013; Schade & Schlag, 2000) are not applicable in this context.

Figure 5.2 shows the mechanism of the public acceptability of congestion charging. This framework depicts the public acceptability issue as an embodiment of trust in government. It might be useful for investigations of public acceptability in an authoritarian regime.

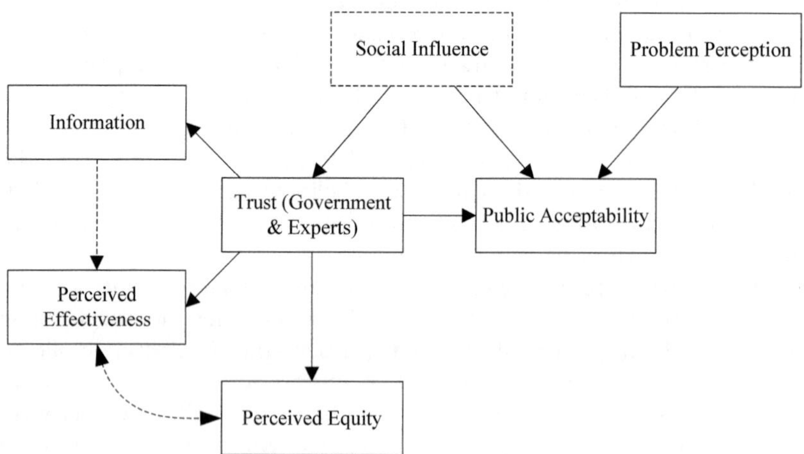

Fig. 5.2 Framework for public acceptability of congestion charging in the Chinese context

References

Afridi, F., Li, S. X., & Ren, Y. (2015). Social identity and inequality: The impact of China's hukou system. *Journal of Public Economics, 123*, 17–29.

Ahn, B. J. (1975). The political economy of the people's commune in China: Changes and continuities. *The Journal of Asian Studies, 34*(3), 631–658.

Al-Maghrebi, M. S., Ahmad, R., & Palil, M. R. (2016). Budget transparency and tax awareness towards tax compliance: A conceptual approach. *South East Asia Journal of Contemporary Business, Economics and Law, 10*(1), 95–101.

Alston, J. P. (1989). Wa, guanxi, and inhwa: Managerial principles in Japan, China, and Korea. *Business Horizons, 32*(2), 26–32.

Andrews-Speed, P., Yang, M., Shen, L., & Cao, S. (2003). The regulation of China's township and village coal mines: A study of complexity and ineffectiveness. *Journal of Cleaner Production, 11*(2), 185–196.

Bartley, B. (1995). Mobility impacts, reactions and opinions: Traffic demand management options in Europe, the MIRO project. *Traffic Engineering & Control, 36*, 596–603.

BBC. (2014a). *Daily life comes to stand-still in Beijing during APEC*. [Online]. https://www.bbc.co.uk/news/blogs-china-blog-29983799. Accessed 27 July 2019.

BBC. (2014b). *China: General says smog 'best defence' against US lasers*. [Online]. https://www.bbc.co.uk/news/blogs-news-from-elsewhere-26322868. Accessed 27 July 2019.

BBC. (2015). *Beijing subway fare hike weighs on commuters*. [Online]. https://www.bbc.co.uk/news/world-asia-30595286. Accessed 27 July 2019.

Björklund, E. M. (1986). The Danwei: Socio-spatial characteristics of work units in China's urban society. *Economic Geography, 62*(1), 19–29.

Bonsall, P., & Lythgoe, B. (2009). Factors affecting the amount of effort expended in responding to questions in behavioural choice experiments. *Journal of Choice Modelling, 2*(2), 216–236.

Börjesson, M., Eliasson, J., Hugosson, M. B., & Brundell-Freij, K. (2012). The Stockholm congestion charges—5 years on. Effects, acceptability and lessons learnt. *Transport Policy, 20*, 1–12.

Börjesson, M., Hamilton, C. J., Näsman, P., & Papaix, C. (2015). Factors driving public support for road congestion reduction policies: Congestion charging, free public transport and more roads in Stockholm, Helsinki and Lyon. *Transportation Research Part A: Policy and Practice, 78*, 452–462.

Bosker, M., Brakman, S., Garretsen, H., & Schramm, M. (2012). Relaxing Hukou: Increased labor mobility and China's economic geography. *Journal of Urban Economics, 72*(2–3), 252–266.

Bray, D. (2005). *Social space and governance in urban China: The danwei system from origins to reform*. Stanford University Press.

Bröcker, J., Korzhenevych, A., & Schürmann, C. (2010). Assessing spatial equity and efficiency impacts of transport infrastructure projects. *Transportation Research Part B: Methodological, 44*(7), 795–811.

Brugger, B. (2018a). *Chinese Marxism in Flux 1978–84: Essays on Epistemology*. Routledge.

Brugger, B. (2018b). *China: Liberation and transformation 1942–1962*. Routledge.

Brunetti, A., & Weder, B. (2003). A free press is bad news for corruption. *Journal of Public Economics, 87*(7), 1801–1824.

Cai, Y. (2002). The resistance of Chinese laid-off workers in the reform period. *The China Quarterly, 170*, 327–344.

Cecere, G., Le Guel, F., & Soulié, N. (2015). Perceived internet privacy concerns on social networks in Europe. *Technological Forecasting and Social Change, 96*, 277–287.

Chang, J. (2013). *Empress Dowager Cixi: The concubine who launched modern China*. Random House.

Chen, N. (2012). Branding national images: The 2008 Beijing summer Olympics, 2010 Shanghai World Expo, and 2010 Guangzhou Asian games. *Public Relations Review, 38*(5), 731–745.

Chen, S., & Chow, C. Y. (2010). China's science prowess questioned. *South China Morning Post, 29*, A6.

Chen, X. (2000). Growing up in a collectivist culture: Socialization and socioemotional development in Chinese children. In A. L. Comunian & U. P. Gielen (Eds.), *International perspectives on human development* (pp. 331–353). Pabst Science.

Chen, X. (2002). *Occidentalism: A theory of counter-discourse in post-Mao China*. Rowman & Littlefield.

Chen, X. (2009). Review of China's agricultural and rural development: Policy changes and current issues. *China Agricultural Economic Review, 1*(2), 121–135.

Chen, Y., Jin, G. Z., Kumar, N., & Shi, G. (2013). The promise of Beijing: Evaluating the impact of the 2008 Olympic Games on air quality. *Journal of Environmental Economics and Management, 66*(3), 424–443.

Cheng, L., Broome, M. E., Feng, S., & Hu, Y. (2017). Factors influencing the implementation of evidence in Chinese nursing practice. *Journal of Clinical Nursing, 26*(23–24), 5103–5112.

Cherchi, E. (2017). A stated choice experiment to measure the effect of informational and normative conformity in the preference for electric vehicles. *Transportation Research Part A: Policy and Practice, 100*, 88–104.

Chien, C. L. (2016). Beyond authoritarian personality: The culture-inclusive theory of Chinese authoritarian orientation. *Frontiers in Psychology, 7*, 924.

China Current. (2014). *APEC Blue: Looking Behind the Blue Sky*. [Online]. http://en.cncurrent.com/apec-blue-the-self-awareness-anxiety-and-discomforts-hidden-under-the-blue-sky/. Accessed 11 December 2018.

China Daily. (2013). *Today the chance of getting a license plate is 1%, why the traffic congestion index has not decreased three years after the license plate lottery?* [Online]. http://www.chinadaily.com.cn/dfpd/2013-12/26/content_17198387.htm. Accessed 27 July 2019 (in Chinese).

China Daily. (2014). *'APEC blue' tops Beijing environmental key words for 2014*. [Online]. http://www.chinadaily.com.cn/china/2014-12/24/content_19155697.htm. Accessed 27 July 2019.

China Digital Times. (2013). *Word of the Week: Brickspert*. [Online]. https://chinadigitaltimes.net/2013/08/word-of-the-week-brickspert/. Accessed 27 July 2019.

China Youth Daily. (2003). *The Fundamental Cause of Traffic Congestion: Bikes*. [Online]. http://www.china.com.cn/chinese/OP-c/421883.htm. Accessed 27 July 2019 (in Chinese).

China Youth Daily. (2010). *New policy announced: To get a Beijing license via the lottery system*. [Online]. http://zqb.cyol.com/content/2010-12/24/content_3468671.htm. Accessed 27 July 2019 (in Chinese).

Cialdini, R. B., Wosinska, W.,Barrett, D. W., & Butner, J. (1999). Compliance with a request in two cultures: The differential influence of social proof and commitment/consistency on collectivists and individualists. *Personality and Social Psychology Bulletin, 25*(10), 1242–1253.

Clee, A. (2007). *Driving away the traffic: What lessons can New York learn from London and Stockholm's experiences with congestion charging*. Tufts University.

CNTV. (2012). *Chained interests of the license plate lottery exposed: 200 thousand to get a Beijing a license plate*. [Online]. http://news.cntv.cn/china/20121213/100676.shtml. Accessed 22 November 2018 (in Chinese).

Courtois, S., Werth, N., Paczkowski, A., Bartosek, K., & Margolin, J.-L. (1999). *The black book of communism: Crimes, terror, repression*. Harvard University Press.

Csontos, L., Kornai, J., & Tóth, I. G. (1998). Tax awareness and reform of the welfare state: Hungarian survey results. *Economics of Transition, 6*(2), 287–312.

Davis, L. W. (2008). The effect of driving restrictions on air quality in Mexico City. *Journal of Political Economy, 116*(1), 38–81.

De Fond, M. L., Wong, T. J., & Li, S. (1999). The impact of improved auditor independence on audit market concentration in China. *Journal of Accounting and Economics, 28*(3), 269–305.

Deng, X. (1984). Building a socialism with a specifically Chinese character. *People's Daily*, 30.

Dernberger, R. F. (1999). The People's Republic of China at 50: The economy. *The China Quarterly, 159*, 606–615.

Eliasson, J., & Jonsson, L. (2011). The unexpected "yes": Explanatory factors behind the positive attitudes to congestion charges in Stockholm. *Transport Policy, 18*(4), 636–647.

Eliasson, J., & Mattsson, L. G. (2006). Equity effects of congestion pricing: Quantitative methodology and a case study for Stockholm. *Transportation Research Part A: Policy and Practice, 40*(7), 602–620.

Eriksson, L., Garvill, J., & Nordlund, A. M. (2008). Acceptability of single and combined transport policy measures: The importance of environmental and policy specific beliefs. *Transportation Research Part A: Policy and Practice, 42*(8), 1117–1128.

Fan, C. C. (2007). *China on the Move: Migration, the State, and the Household*. Routledge.

Fang, K., & Repnikova, M. 2018. Demystifying "Little Pink": The creation and evolution of a gendered label for nationalistic activists in China. *New Media & Society, 20*(6), 2162–2185.

Farh, J. L., & Cheng, B. S. (2000). A cultural analysis of paternalistic leadership in Chinese organizations. *Management and organizations in the Chinese context* (pp. 84–127). Palgrave Macmillan.

Farrell, S., & Saleh, W. (2005). Road-user charging and the modelling of revenue allocation. *Transport Policy, 12*(5), 431–442.

Fewsmith, J. (2016). *Dilemmas of reform in China: Political conflict and economic debate: Political conflict and economic debate*. Routledge.

Finlay, C. J., & Xin, X. (2010). Public diplomacy games: A comparative study of American and Japanese responses to the interplay of nationalism, ideology and Chinese soft power strategies around the 2008 Beijing Olympics. *Sport in Society, 13*(5), 876–900.

Francke, A., & Kaniok, D. (2013). Responses to differentiated road pricing schemes. *Transportation Research Part A: Policy and Practice, 48*, 25–30.

Fu, Y., & Gabriel, S. A. (2012). Labor migration, human capital agglomeration and regional development in China. *Regional Science and Urban Economics, 42*(3), 473–484.

Fujii, S., Gärling, T., Jakobsson, C., & Jou, R. C. (2004). A cross-country study of fairness and infringement on freedom as determinants of car owners' acceptance of road pricing. *Transportation, 31*(3), 285–295.

Gadenne, D. L., Kennedy, J., & McKeiver, C. (2009). An empirical study of environmental awareness and practices in SMEs. *Journal of Business Ethics, 84*(1), 45–63.

Gao, H. (2000). *How Did the Sun Rise over Yan'an?* The Chinese University of Hong Kong Press. (In Chinese).

Gao, H. (2012, April 16). Rumor, lies, and Weibo: How social media is changing the nature of truth in China. *The Atlantic*.

Gärling, T. (2007). Effectiveness, public acceptance, and political feasibility of coercive measures for reducing car traffic. In *Threats from car traffic to the quality of urban life*. Emerald Group Publishing Limited.

Gärling, T., & Schuitema, G. (2007). Travel demand management targeting reduced private car use: Effectiveness, public acceptability and political feasibility. *Journal of Social Issues, 63*(1), 139–153.

Gärling, T., Jakobsson, C., Loukopoulos, P., Fujii, S. (2008). Acceptability of road pricing. In E. Verhoef, E. Bliemer, L. Steg, & B. Van Wee (Eds.), *Pricing in Road Transport: Multidisciplinary Perspectives*. Edward Elgar.

Gaunt, M., Rye, T., & Allen, S. (2007). Public acceptability of road user charging: The case of Edinburgh and the 2005 referendum. *Transport Reviews, 27*(1), 85–102.

Global Times. (2012). *Shocking quotes from Chinese economists*. [Online]. http://opinion.huanqiu.com/1152/2012-08/3066125.html]. Accessed 22 December 2018 (in Chinese).

Global Times. (2013). *Chinese Singaporeans: well done China's license plate lottery policy and housing price adjustment*. [Online]. http://world.huanqiu.com/exclusive/2013-03/3706374.html. Accessed 22 November 2018 (in Chinese).

Goetzke, F., Gerike, R., Páez, A., & Dugundji, E. (2015). Social interactions in transportation: Analyzing groups and spatial networks. *Transportation, 42*(5), 723–731.

Goldin, P. R. (2001). Han Fei's doctrine of self-interest. *Asian Philosophy, 11*(3), 151–159.

Goldin, P. R. (2013). *Dao companion to the philosophy of Han Fei*. Springer.

Goldman, M. (2009). Repression of China's public intellectuals in the post-Mao era. *Social Research: An International Quarterly, 76*(2), 659–686.

Goldstein, A., & Guo, S. (1992). Temporary migration in Shanghai and Beijing. *Studies in Comparative International Development, 27*(2), 39–56.

Grisolía, J. M., López, F., & de Dios Ortúzar, J. (2015). Increasing the acceptability of a congestion charging scheme. *Transport Policy, 39*, 37–47.

Han, F. (1964). *Han Fei Tzu: Basic Writings* (B. Watson, Trans.). Columbia University Press.

Han, R. (2015a). Manufacturing consent in cyberspace: China's 'fifty-cent army.' *Journal of Current Chinese Affairs, 44*(2), 105–134.

Han, R. (2015b). Defending the authoritarian regime online: China's "voluntary fifty-cent army." *The China Quarterly, 224*, 1006–1025.

Han, R. (2018). *Contesting cyberspace in China*. Columbia University Press.

Hartmann, P., & Apaolaza-Ibáñez, V. (2012). Consumer attitude and purchase intention toward green energy brands: The roles of psychological benefits and environmental concern. *Journal of Business Research, 65*(9), 1254–1263.

Hatton, C. (2015). *Under the Dome: The smog film taking China by storm*. BBC China Blog. BBC.

Hau, T. D. (1990). Electronic road pricing: Developments in Hong Kong 1983–1989. *Journal of Transport Economics and Policy, 24*(2), 203–214.

Haven-Tang, C., Jones, E., & Webb, C. (2007). Critical success factors for business tourism destinations: Exploiting Cardiff s national capital city status and shaping its business tourism offer. *Journal of Travel & Tourism Marketing, 22*(3–4), 109–120.

Heilmann, S., & Perry, E. J. (Eds.). (2011). *Mao's invisible hand: The political foundations of adaptive governance in China*. Harvard University Asia Center.

Henderson J V, Quigley J, Lim E. 2009. *Urbanization in China: Policy issues and options*. Unpublished manuscript, Brown University.

Hensher, D. A., & Puckett, S. M. (2005). Road user charging: The global relevance of recent developments in the United Kingdom. *Transport Policy, 12*(5), 377–383.

Hensher, D. A., & Puckett, S. M. (2007). Congestion and variable user charging as an effective travel demand management instrument. *Transportation Research Part a: Policy and Practice, 41*(7), 615–626.

Holmstrom, N., & Smith, R. (2000). The necessity of gangster capitalism: Primitive accumulation in Russia and China. *Monthly Review, 51*(9), 1.

Hong, Y., Huang, N., Burtch, G., & Li, C. (2016). Culture, conformity and emotional suppression in online reviews. *Journal of the Association for Information Systems,* Forthcoming, Fox School of Business Research Paper, (16–020).

Hu, J. (2012, November 8). *Firmly March on the Path of Socialism with Chinese Characteristics and Strive to Complete the Building of a Moderately Prosperous Society in all Respects*. Political report delivered at the 18th national party congress, Beijing.

Hu, X. (2017). From coal mining to coal chemicals? Unpacking new path creation in an old industrial region of transitional China. *Growth and Change, 48*(2), 233–245.

Huan Kuan. (1967). *Discourses on Salt and Iron: A Debate on State Control of Commerce and Industry in Ancient China, Chapters I–XIX* (E. M. Gale, Trans.). Ch'engwen, Taipei.

Huang, L. C., & Harris, M. B. (1973). Conformity in Chinese and Americans: A field experiment. *Journal of Cross-Cultural Psychology., 4*(4), 427–434.

Huang, Y. (2002). Approaching "Pareto optimality"?—A critical analysis of media-orchestrated Chinese nationalism. *Intercultural Communication Studies, 11*(2), 69–88.

Huang, Z., & de Bary, W. T. (1993). *Waiting for the Dawn: A Plan for the Prince*. Columbia University Press.

Hughes, C. (2006). *Chinese nationalism in the global era*. Routledge.

Hysing, E. (2015). Citizen participation or representative government–Building legitimacy for the Gothenburg congestion tax. *Transport Policy, 39*, 1–8.

Hyun, K. D., & Kim, J. (2015). The role of new media in sustaining the status quo: Online political expression, nationalism, and system support in China. *Information, Communication & Society, 18*(7), 766–781.

Ison, S. (2000). Local authority and academic attitudes to urban road pricing: A UK perspective. *Transport Policy, 7*(4), 269–277.

Jaensirisak, S., Wardman, M., & May, A. D. (2005). Explaining variations in public acceptability of road pricing schemes. *Journal of Transport Economics and Policy, 39*(2), 127–153.

Jakobsson, C., Fujii, S., & Gärling, T. (2000). Determinants of private car users' acceptance of road pricing. *Transport Policy, 7*(2), 153–158.

Jiang, Z. (1997, October 6–12). Hold high the great banner of Deng Xiaoping Theory for an all round advancement of the cause of building socialism with Chinese characteristics into the 21st century. *Beijing Review*, 10–33.

Jiang, J., Xie, D., Ye, B., Shen, B., & Chen, Z. (2016). Research on China's cap-and-trade carbon emission trading scheme: Overview and outlook. *Applied Energy, 178*, 902–917.

Johnston, A. I. (2017). Is Chinese Nationalism Rising? *Evidence from Beijing. International Security, 41*(3), 7–43.

Jones, P. (1998). Urban Road Pricing: Public Acceptability and Barriers to Implementation. In: Button K.J., Verhoef, E.T. (Eds.). *Road Pricing, Traffic Congestion and the Environment*. Edward Elgar Publishing.

JRJ. (2018). *Only one out of 2000 people can get a license, some people did fake marriage for license plates.* [Online]. http://finance.jrj.com.cn/2018/02/28065724164610.shtml. Accessed 22 November 2018 (in Chinese).

Kallbekken, S., & Sælen, H. (2011). Public acceptance for environmental taxes: Self-interest, environmental and distributional concerns. *Energy Policy, 39*(5), 2966–2973.

Kiernan, B. (2002). *The Pol Pot regime: Race, power, and genocide in Cambodia under the Khmer Rouge, 1975–79*. Yale University Press.

Kim, J., Rasouli, S., & Timmermans, H. (2014). Expanding scope of hybrid choice models allowing for mixture of social influences and latent attitudes: Application to intended purchase of electric cars. *Transportation Research Part A: Policy and Practice, 69*, 71–85.

Kim, J., Schmöcker, J. D., Fujii, S., & Noland, R. B. (2013). Attitudes towards road pricing and environmental taxation among US and UK students. *Transportation Research Part A: Policy and Practice, 48*, 50–62.

King, D., Manville, M., & Shoup, D. (2007). The political calculus of congestion pricing. *Transport Policy, 14*(2), 111–123.

King, G., Pan, J., & Roberts, M. E. (2017). How the Chinese government fabricates social media posts for strategic distraction, not engaged argument. *American Political Science Review, 111*(3), 484–501.

Kirkby, R. J. (2018). *Urbanization in China: Town and country in a developing economy 1949–2000 AD*. Routledge.

Kong, S., Chen, S.-H., Acton, H., & Birch, C. (2015). *The Peach Blossom Fan*. University of California Press.

Koop, G., & Tole, L. (2001). Deforestation, distribution and development. *Global Environmental Change, 11*(3), 193–202.

Krätke, S. (2004). City of talents? Berlin's regional economy, socio-spatial fabric and "worst practice" urban governance. *International Journal of Urban and Regional Research, 28*(3), 511–529.

Kwong, J. (2011). Education and identity: The marginalisation of migrant youths in Beijing. *Journal of Youth Studies, 14*(8), 871–883.

Leape, J. (2006). The London congestion charge. *Journal of Economic Perspectives, 20*(4), 157–176.

Lee, C. K., & Zhang, Y. (2013). The power of instability: Unraveling the microfoundations of bargained authoritarianism in China. *American Journal of Sociology, 118*(6), 1475–1508.

Levine, J., & Garb, Y. (2002). Congestion pricing's conditional promise: Promotion of accessibility or mobility? *Transport Policy, 9*(3), 179–188.

Levitsky, S., & Way, L. A. (2010). *Competitive authoritarianism: Hybrid regimes after the Cold War*. Cambridge University Press.

Li, H., Bao, W., Xiu, C., Zhang, Y., & Xu, H. (2010). Energy conservation and circular economy in China's process industries. *Energy, 35*(11), 4273–4281.

Li, G. (1995a). *A glossary of political terms of the People's Republic of China*. Chinese University Press.

Li, W. Y. (1995b). The representation of history in the Peach Blossom Fan. *Journal of the American Oriental Society*, 421–433.

Li, X., Stanton, B., Fang, X., & Lin, D. (2006). Social stigma and mental health among rural-to-urban migrants in China: A conceptual framework and future research needs. *World Health & Population, 8*(3), 14–31.

Li, X., Zhou, W., & Ouyang, Z. (2013). Forty years of urban expansion in Beijing: What is the relative importance of physical, socioeconomic, and neighborhood factors? *Applied Geography, 38*, 1–10.

Liang, K. (2003). The Rise of Mao and his cultural legacy: The Yan'an rectification movement. *Journal of Contemporary China, 12*(34), 225–228.

Liao, T. F., & Wang, C. (2018). Permanent emergency: Inequality in access to hospitalisation among urban elderly Chinese. *Global Public Health, 13*(8), 1098–1113.

Lin, H., Liu, T., Fang, F., Xiao, J., Zeng, W., Li, X., & Qian, Z. (2017). Mortality benefits of vigorous air quality improvement interventions during the periods of APEC Blue and Parade Blue in Beijing, China. *Environmental Pollution, 220*, 222–227.

Lin, J. Y. (1990). Collectivization and China's agricultural crisis in 1959–1961. *Journal of Political Economy, 98*(6), 1228–1252.

Litman, T. (1996). Using road pricing revenue: Economic efficiency and equity considerations. *Transportation Research Record: Journal of the Transportation Research Board, 1558*, 24–28.

Litman, T. (2004). *London Congestion Pricing. Implications for Other Cities.* Victoria Transport Policy Institute

Liu, Q. (2021). Immobility: Surviving the COVID-19 outbreak. In C. Zhang (Eds.), *Human Security in China - A Post-Pandemic State*, Palgrave, 150–171

Liu, A. A., Linn, J., Qin, P., & Yang, J. (2018). Vehicle ownership restrictions and fertility in Beijing. *Journal of Development Economics, 135*, 85–96.

Liu, Q., An, Z., Liu, Y., Ying, W., & Zhao, P. (2021a). Smartphone-based services, perceived accessibility, and transport inequity during the COVID-19 pandemic: A cross-lagged panel study. *Transportation Research Part D: Transport and Environment, 97*, 102941.

Liu, Q., Liu, Y., Zhang, C., An, Z., & Zhao, P. (2021b). Elderly mobility during the COVID-19 pandemic: A qualitative exploration in Kunming, China. *Journal of Transport Geography, 96*, 103176.

Liu, Q., Lucas, K., & Marsden, G. (2019). Public acceptability of congestion charging in Beijing, China: How transferrable are Western ideas of public acceptability? *International Journal of Sustainable Transportation*, 1–14.

Liu, Q., Lucas, K., & Marsden, G. (2020). Public acceptability of congestion charging in Beijing, China: How transferrable are Western ideas of public acceptability? *International Journal of Sustainable Transportation, 15*(2), 97–110.

Liu, Q., Lucas, K., Marsden, G., & Liu, Y. (2019). Egalitarianism and public perception of social inequities: A case study of Beijing congestion charge. *Transport Policy, 74*, 47–62.

Liu, T., Qi, Y., Cao, G., & Liu, H. (2015). Spatial patterns, driving forces, and urbanization effects of China's internal migration: County-level analysis based on the 2000 and 2010 censuses. *Journal of Geographical Sciences, 25*(2), 236–256.

Lorenzoni, I., Nicholson-Cole, S., & Whitmarsh, L. (2007). Barriers perceived to engaging with climate change among the UK public and their policy implications. *Global Environmental Change, 17*(3–4), 445–459.

Lu, T. (2001). *Persons, Roles, and Minds: Identity in Peony Pavilion and Peach Blossom Fan*. Stanford University Press.

Lu, W. M., & Lo, S. F. (2007). A closer look at the economic-environmental disparities for regional development in China. *European Journal of Operational Research, 183*(2), 882–894.

Lü, X., & Perry, E. J. (Eds.). (1997). *Danwei: The changing Chinese workplace in historical and comparative perspective*. Me Sharpe.

Luo, S. (1974). Class Conflict in Qin-Han Dynasty. *Red Flag*, 8. [Online]. https://ccradb.appspot.com/post/3749. Accessed 15 December 2018 (in Chinese).

Ma, L. (2015). The Beijing Smog: Between Media Frames and Public Perceptions. *China Media Research, 11*(4), 6–15.

Mahendra, A. (2008). Vehicle restrictions in four Latin American cities: Is congestion pricing possible? *Transport Reviews, 28*(1), 105–133.

Maness, M., Cirillo, C., & Dugundji, E. R. (2015). Generalized behavioral framework for choice models of social influence: Behavioral and data concerns in travel behavior. *Journal of Transport Geography, 46*, 137–150.

Maynard, M. L., & Taylor, C. R. (1996). A comparative analysis of Japanese and US attitudes toward direct marketing. *Journal of Direct Marketing, 10*(1), 34–44.

McDermott, J. P. (2006). *A social history of the Chinese book: books and literati culture in late imperial China*. Hong Kong University Press.

McQuaid, R., & Grieco, M. (2005). Edinburgh and the politics of congestion charging: Negotiating road user charging with affected publics. *Transport Policy, 12*(5), 475–476.

Miao, P. (2003). Deserted streets in a jammed town: The gated community in Chinese cities and its solution. *Journal of Urban Design, 8*(1), 45–66.

Miltgen, C. L., & Peyrat-Guillard, D. (2014). Cultural and generational influences on privacy concerns: A qualitative study in seven European countries. *European Journal of Information Systems, 23*(2), 103–125.

Moise, E. E. (2017). *Land reform in China and North Vietnam: Consolidating the revolution at the village level*. UNC Press Books.

Mok, K. H. (1998). *Intellectuals and the State in Post-Mao China*. Springer.

Navarria, G. (2016). To censor or not to censor: Roots, current trends and the long-term consequences of the Chinese Communist Party's fear of the internet. *Communication, Politics & Culture, 49*(2), 82–110.

Newbery, D. M., & Santos, G. (1999). Road taxes, road user charges and earmarking. *Fiscal Studies, 20*(2), 103–132.

Ngai, P. (2005). Global production, company codes of conduct, and labor conditions in China: A case study of two factories. *The China Journal*, (54), 101–113.

Ngok, K. L., & Huang, G. (2014). Policy paradigm shift and the changing role of the state: The development of social policy in China since 2003. *Social Policy and Society, 13*(2), 251–261.

Ng, O. C., & Wang, Q. E. (2005). *Mirroring the past: The writing and use of history in Imperial China*. University of Hawaii Press.

Ohashi, H. (2009). Effects of transparency in procurement practices on government expenditure: A case study of municipal public works. *Review of Industrial Organization, 34*(3), 267–285.

People's Daily. (2010). *Interpretation of current events: Beijing License Plate Lottery from the next year*. [Online]. Available from: http://cpc.people.com.cn/GB/64093/82429/83083/13568812.html. Accessed 22 November 2018 (in Chinese).

Pines, Y. (2014). *Legalism in Chinese Philosophy* (Winter 2014 Edition, E. N. Zalta, Eds.). The Stanford Encyclopedia of Philosophy. http://plato.stanford.edu/archives/win2014/entries/chinese-legalism/. Accessed 27 July 2019.

Podoshen, J. S., Li, L., & Zhang, J. (2011). Materialism and conspicuous consumption in China: A cross-cultural examination. *International Journal of Consumer Studies, 35*(1), 17–25.

Poell, T., De Kloet, J., & Zeng, G. (2014). Will the real Weibo please stand up? Chinese online contention and actor-network theory. *Chinese Journal of Communication, 7*(1), 1–18.

Postiglione, G. A. 2015. *Education and social change in China: Inequality in a market economy*. Routledge.

Pow, C. P. (2009). *Gated communities in China: Class, privilege and the moral politics of the good life*. Routledge.

Powers, D. S. (2016). 'Under the Dome' on Chinese air pollution, a documentary by Chai Jing. *Journal of Public Health Policy, 37*(1), 98–106.

Quartz. (2016). *Chinese state media is blaming its apocalyptic smog problem on kitchen fumes*. [Online] [Accessed 27 July 2019]. Available from: https://qz.com/872685/chinese-state-media-is-blaming-its-apocalyptic-smog-problem-on-kitchen-fumes/

Rajé, F. (2003). The impact of transport on social exclusion processes with specific emphasis on road user charging. *Transport Policy, 10*(4), 321–338.

Raux, C., & Souche, S. (2004). The acceptability of urban road pricing: A theoretical analysis applied to experience in Lyon. *Journal of Transport Economics and Policy, 38*(2), 191–215.

Ren, K. (2012). Fighting against academic corruption: A critique of recent policy developments in China. *Higher Education Policy, 25*(1), 19–38.

Rene, H. K. (2013). *China's Sent-down Generation: Public Administration and the Legacies of Mao's Rustication Program*. Georgetown University Press.

Repnikova, M. (2017). Media Openings and Political Transitions: Glasnost versus Yulun Jiandu. *Problems of Post-Communism, 64*(3–4), 141–151.

Rößger, L., Schade, J., Obst, D., Gehlert, T., Schlag, B., Bonsall, P., & Lythgoe, B. (2008). *Psychological constraints of user reactions towards differentiated charging*.

Roddy, S. (1998). *Literati Identity and Its Fictional Representations in Late Imperial China*. Stanford University Press.

Rouwendal, J., & Verhoef, E. T. (2006). Basic economic principles of road pricing: From theory to applications. *Transport Policy, 13*(2), 106–114.

Rye, T., Gaunt, M., & Ison, S. (2008). Edinburgh's congestion charging plans: An analysis of reasons for non-implementation. *Transportation Planning and Technology, 31*(6), 641–661.

Santos, G. (2004). Urban congestion charging: A second-best alternative. *Journal of Transport Economics and Policy, 38*(3), 345–369.

Santos, G., & Bhakar, J. (2006). The impact of the London congestion charging scheme on the generalised cost of car commuters to the city of London from a value of travel time savings perspective. *Transport Policy, 13*(1), 22–33.

Santos, G., & Rojey, L. (2004). Distributional impacts of road pricing: The truth behind the myth. *Transportation, 31*(1), 21–42.

Schade J., &Schlag, B. (2000). *Acceptability of urban transport pricing*. Valtion Taloudellinen Tutkimus.

Schade, J., & Schlag, B. (2003). Acceptability of urban transport pricing strategies. *Transportation Research Part f: Traffic Psychology and Behaviour, 6*(1), 45–61.

Shafer, W. E., & Simmons, R. S. (2011). Effects of organizational ethical culture on the ethical decisions of tax practitioners in mainland China. *Accounting, Auditing & Accountability Journal, 24*(5), 647–668.

Shang Yang. (1928). *The book of Lord Shang. A classic of the Chinese School of Law* (Duyvendak, Trans.). Arthur Probsthain.

Shei, C. (2014). *Understanding the Chinese Language: A Comprehensive Linguistic Introduction*. Routledge.

Shen, J. (2013). Increasing internal migration in China from 1985 to 2005: Institutional versus economic drivers. *Habitat International, 39*, 1–7.

Shorten, R. (2012). *Modernism and totalitarianism: Rethinking the intellectual sources of Nazism and Stalinism, 1945 to the present*. Springer.

Sina. (2009). *A Peking University professor: 99% of petitioners suffer from mental illnesses*. [Online]. http://news.sina.com.cn/c/2009-04-04/040815416940s.shtml. Accessed 27 July 2019 (in Chinese).

Small, K. A. (1992). Using the revenues from congestion pricing. *Transportation, 19*(4), 359–381.

Snell, R. S. (1999). Obedience to authority and ethical dilemmas in Hong Kong companies. *Business Ethics Quarterly, 9*(3), 507–526.

Steinfeld, E. S. (1999). *Forging reform in China: The fate of state-owned industry*. Cambridge University Press.

Struve, L. A. (1980). History and The Peach Blossom Fan. *Chinese Literature: Essays, Articles, Reviews., 2*(1), 55–72.

Struve, L. A. (1988). Huang Zongxi in context: A reappraisal of his major writings. *The Journal of Asian Studies, 47*(3), 474–502.

Su, D., & Fleisher, B. M. (1999). An empirical investigation of underpricing in Chinese IPOs. *Pacific-Basin Finance Journal, 7*(2), 173–202.

Sun, C., Yuan, X., & Xu, M. (2016). The public perceptions and willingness to pay: from the perspective of the smog crisis in China. *Journal of cleaner production, 112*, 1635–1644.

Sun, Y. (1995). *The Chinese Reassessment of Socialism, 1976–1992*. Princeton University Press.

Takano, Y., & Sogon, S. (2008). Are Japanese more collectivistic than Americans? Examining conformity in in-groups and the reference-group effect. *Journal of Cross-Cultural Psychology, 39*(3), 237–250.

Tang, J., Folmer, H., & Xue, J. (2013). Estimation of awareness and perception of water scarcity among farmers in the Guanzhong Plain, China, by means of a structural equation model. *Journal of Environmental Management, 126*, 55–62.

Tao, R., & Xu, Z. (2007). Urbanization, rural land system and social security for migrants in China. *The Journal of Development Studies, 43*(7), 1301–1320.

Tao, J., Zhang, L., Zhang, Z., Huang, R., Wu, Y., Zhang, R., & Zhang, Y. (2015). Control of $PM_{2.5}$ in Guangzhou during the 16th Asian Games period: Implication for hazy weather prevention. *Science of the Total Environment, 508*, 57–66.

Taylor, B., & Kalauskas, R. (2010). Addressing equity in political debates over road pricing: Lessons from recent projects. *Transportation Research Record: Journal of the Transportation Research Board, 2187*, 44–52.

Teets, J. C. (2013). Let many civil societies bloom: The rise of consultative authoritarianism in China. *The China Quarterly, 213*, 19–38.

Thorpe, N., Hills, P., & Jaensirisak, S. (2000). Public attitudes to TDM measures: A comparative study. *Transport Policy, 7*(4), 243–257.

Thurston, A. F. (1988). *Enemies of the people: The ordeal of the intellectuals in China's great Cultural Revolution*. Harvard University Press.

Tilt, B. (2007). The political ecology of pollution enforcement in China: A case from Sichuan's rural industrial sector. *The China Quarterly, 192*, 915–932.

Torres, M. S., & Qin, L. (2017). Chinese high school students' perceptions of freedom of expression: Implications for researching emerging civil liberties in global educational contexts. *Asia Pacific Education Review, 18*(1), 53–64.

Verhoef, E. T., Nijkamp, P., & Rietveld, P. (1997). The social feasibility of road pricing: A case study for the Randstad area. *Journal of Transport Economics and Policy, 31*, 255–276.

Vladimirov, P. P. (1975). *The Vladimirov Diaries: Yenan, China, 1942–1945*. Doubleday.

Waldron, A. (1995). Scholarship and patriotic education: The Great Wall Conference, 1994. *The China Quarterly, 143*, 844–850.

Waley, P. (2007). Tokyo-as-world-city: Reassessing the role of capital and the state in urban restructuring. *Urban Studies, 44*(8), 1465–1490.

Wang. (2004). *50 Years of the CCP*, Orient Press. (in Chinese)

Wang, D., & Chai, Y. (2009). The jobs–housing relationship and commuting in Beijing, China: The legacy of Danwei. *Journal of Transport Geography, 17*(1), 30–38.

Wang, L., Xu, J., & Qin, P. (2014). Will a driving restriction policy reduce car trips?—The case study of Beijing, China. *Transportation Research Part A: Policy and Practice, 67*, 279–290.

Wang, M. W., Chen, J., & Cai, R. (2018). Air quality and acute myocardial infarction in adults during the 2016 Hangzhou G20 summit. *Environmental Science and Pollution Research, 25*(10), 9949–9956.

Wang, S., Paul, M. J., & Dredze, M. (2015). Social media as a sensor of air quality and public response in China. *Journal of Medical Internet Research, 17*(3), e22.

Wang, Y. (2015). Politically connected polluters under smog. *Business and Politics, 17*(1), 97–123.

Wang, Y., Sun, M., Yang, X., & Yuan, X. (2016). Public awareness and willingness to pay for tackling smog pollution in China: A case study. *Journal of Cleaner Production, 112*, 1627–1634.

Wang, Y. P., Wang, Y., & Bramley, G. (2005). Chinese housing reform in state-owned enterprises and its impacts on different social groups. *Urban Studies, 42*(10), 1859–1878.

Wang, Z. (2008). National humiliation, history education, and the politics of historical memory: Patriotic education campaign in China. *International Studies Quarterly, 52*(4), 783–806.

Warner, M. (2012). *The Dragon Empress: Life and Times of Tz'u-hsi 1835–1908 Empress Dowager of China*. Random House.

Wei, C. G. (2011). Mao's Legacy Revisited: Its Lasting Impact on China and Post-Mao Era Reform. *Asian Politics & Policy, 3*(1), 3–27.

Wei, Z., Wang, B., Chen, T., & Lin, Y. (2016). Community development in urban Guangzhou since 1980: A social sustainability perspective. *International Review for Spatial Planning and Sustainable Development, 4*(4), 58–68.

Weinstein, A., & Sciara, G. C. (2006). Unraveling equity in HOT lane planning: A view from practice. *Journal of Planning Education and Research, 26*(2), 174–184.

Winslott-Hiselius, L., Brundell-Freij, K., Vagland, Å., & Byström, C. (2009). The development of public attitudes towards the Stockholm congestion trial. *Transportation Research Part a: Policy and Practice, 43*(3), 269–282.

Wong, K., Fu, D., Li, C. Y., & Song, H. X. (2007). Rural migrant workers in urban China: Living a marginalised life. *International Journal of Social Welfare, 16*(1), 32–40.

Wong, K. K. (2003). The environmental awareness of university students in Beijing. *China. Journal of Contemporary China, 12*(36), 519–536.

Wu, F., & Webber, K. (2004). The rise of "foreign gated communities" in Beijing: Between economic globalization and local institutions. *Cities, 21*(3), 203–213.

Wu, X. (2009). Income inequality and distributive justice: A comparative analysis of mainland China and Hong Kong. *The China Quarterly, 200*, 1033–1052.

Xi, J. (2017, October 18). *Secure a Decisive Victory in Building a Moderately Prosperous Society in All Respects and Strive for the Great Success of Socialism with Chinese Characteristics for a New Era*, delivered at the 19th National Congress of the Communist Party of China. [Online]. http://language.chinadaily.com.cn/19thcpcnationalcongress/2017-11/06/content_34188086_6.htm. Accessed 27 July 2019.

Xie, Y., & Costa, F. J. (1993). Urban planning in socialist China: Theory and practice. *Cities, 10*(2), 103–114.

Xinhua. (2008). *Beijing will implement the road space rationing policy during the Olympic Games*. [Online]. http://www.gov.cn/jrzg/2008-06/20/content_1022742.htm. Accessed 27 July 2019 (in Chinese).

Yan, Y. (2009). The Good Samaritan's new trouble: A study of the changing moral landscape in contemporary China 1. *Social Anthropology, 17*(1), 9–24.

Yang, J. Z., & Huang, J. (2017). Seeking for your own sake: Chinese citizens' motivations for information seeking about air pollution. *Environmental Communication*, 1–14.

Yang, J., Liu, Y., Qin, P., & Liu, A. A. (2014). A review of Beijing's vehicle registration lottery: Short-term effects on vehicle growth and fuel consumption. *Energy Policy, 75*, 157–166.

Yang, R. (2005). Corruption in china's higher education: A malignant tumor. *International Higher Education, 39*, 18–20.

Yeh, A. G. O., & Wu, F. (1999). The transformation of the urban planning system in China from a centrally-planned to transitional economy. *Progress in Planning, 51*(3), 167–252.

Yin, K., Wang, R., An, Q., Yao, L., & Liang, J. (2014). Using eco-efficiency as an indicator for sustainable urban development: A case study of Chinese provincial capital cities. *Ecological Indicators, 36*, 665–671.

Zhang, H., Wang, S., Hao, J., Wang, X., Wang, S., Chai, F., & Li, M. (2016). Air pollution and control action in Beijing. *Journal of Cleaner Production, 112*, 1519–1527.

Zhang, J., Yan, X., An, M., & Sun, L. (2017). The impact of Beijing subway's new fare policy on riders' attitude, travel pattern and demand. *Sustainability, 9*(5), 689.

Zhai, Y. (2017). Values of Deference to Authority in Japan and China. *International Journal of Comparative Sociology, 58*(2), 120–139.

Zhang, Z. Q., Zhou, Y., Lu, S. X., & Chen, Y. H. (2007). Return migration of rural laborer from western China: Causes and strategies. *Stat Res, 24*, 9–15.

Zhao, S. (2000). Chinese nationalism and its international orientations. *Political Science Quarterly, 115*(1), 1–33.

Zhao, S. (2004). *A nation-state by construction: Dynamics of modern Chinese nationalism*. Stanford University Press.

Zhao, Y. (1999). Leaving the countryside: Rural-to-urban migration decisions in China. *American Economic Review, 89*(2), 281–286.

Zhao, Z. (2009). *Prisoner of the State: The Secret Journal of Premier Zhao Ziyang*. Simon and Schuster.

Zheng, D., & Shi, M. (2017). Multiple environmental policies and pollution haven hypothesis: Evidence from China's polluting industries. *Journal of Cleaner Production, 141*, 295–304.

Zheng, S., Long, F., Fan, C. C., & Gu, Y. (2009). Urban villages in China: A 2008 survey of migrant settlements in Beijing. *Eurasian Geography and Economics, 50*(4), 425–446.

Zheng, Y. (1999). *Discovering Chinese nationalism in China: Modernization, identity, and international relations*. Cambridge University Press.

Zhong, X., Wang, Z., & Di, B. (Eds.). 2001. *Some of us: Chinese women growing up in the Mao era*. Rutgers University Press.

Zhou, H. (2000). Working with a dying ideology: Dissonance and its reduction in Chinese journalism. *Journalism Studies, 1*(4), 599–616.

Zhou, R., Horrey, W. J., & Yu, R. (2009). The effect of conformity tendency on pedestrians' road-crossing intentions in China: An application of the theory of planned behavior. *Accident Analysis & Prevention, 41*(3), 491–497.

Zhou, Y., & Ap, J. (2009). Residents' perceptions towards the impacts of the Beijing 2008 Olympic Games. *Journal of Travel Research, 48*(1), 78–91.

Zhu, N. (2002). The impacts of income gaps on migration decisions in China. *China Economic Review, 13*(2–3), 213–230.

CHAPTER 6

Results of the Quantitative Analysis

6.1 Introduction

This chapter presents the results of the public acceptability of the Beijing congestion charge survey, which was conducted on the streets in November 2017. It first gives the descriptive results of the survey and then the results of the SEM. It tests the insights and topic areas developed through the qualitative interviews and focus groups and therefore assesses the conceptual framework proposed in Chapter 5. This addresses the fourth objective of this research.

The first section of this chapter gives the descriptive results of the survey, which provide an overview of how acceptable the congestion charge is to residents in Beijing and respondents' attitudes towards other important elements of acceptability. In the second section, the SEM is applied to explore the relationships between different influencing factors further. It helps to identify key factors of public acceptability in the Chinese context.

6.2 Descriptive Results

6.2.1 Socio-Demographic Information of the Sample

This section introduces the socio-demographic information of the sample (Table 6.1). The sample is compared to the Beijing population in general. However, since I have no access to most of the statistics, only a few

Q. Liu, *Public Acceptability of Congestion Charging in China*,
https://doi.org/10.1007/978-981-19-0236-9_6

Table 6.1 Socio-demographic information of the sample

		Frequency	*Percentage*	*Beijing*
Heard about the CC	Yes	1060	96.0	
	No	44	4.0	
Age	18–30	342	31.0	24.6
	31–45	336	30.4	26.4
	46–60	285	25.8	21.8
	Above 60	141	12.8	14
Gender	Male	552	50.0	51.6
	Female	552	50.0	48.4
Annual household income (CNY)	<120 k	430	38.9	
	120 k–1 m	531	48.1	
	>1 m	143	13.0	
Pekingese/migrants	Pekingese	468	42.4	
	Migrants	636	57.6	
Residential area	Six inner-city districts (inside the third ring road)	373	33.8	18.8
	Six inner-city districts (outside the third ring road)	467	42.3	30.2
	Other districts	264	23.9	51
Car ownership	Car owner	755	68.4	
	Non-car owner	349	31.6	

items are compared. The Beijing data come from the Beijing Statistical Yearbook (Beijing Municipal Bureau of Statistics, 2017).

Given that people under 18 years old account for 13.2% of the Beijing population, the age distribution of the sample is about the same as the wider Beijing population. The proportion of older people is lower than that of the wider Beijing population, but this is reasonable since people over 70 years of age are banned from driving in China.

Since the Beijing Statistical Yearbook used other indices to measure the income level (per capita household income, household disposable income, per capita total expenditure and per capita expenditure on different purposes such as housing, education, health care and food), it is difficult to compare the sample accurately with the wider Beijing population. However, it is evident that the sample contains more high-income people. According to the Beijing Statistical Yearbook, the per capita annual disposable income is 53,829 CNY (Table 6.2) in the medium 20% of

Table 6.2 Basic data on urban households (by income level) (2016)

Item	*Average*	*Low income 20%*	*Medium–low income 20%*	*Medium income 20%*	*Medium–high income 20%*	*High income 20%*
Permanent population per household (persons)	2.7	3.1	2.9	2.6	2.6	2.3
Average employees per household (persons)	1.3	1.6	1.5	1.2	1.2	1.2
Dependents per employee (persons)	1.6	1.9	1.6	1.5	1.4	1.3
Per capita disposable income (yuan)	52,530	20,204	36,277	49,342	65,555	105,425
Per capita annual consumption expenditures (yuan)	35,416	16,848	26,223	33,181	43,944	64,717

Source Beijing Statistical Yearbook 2017

households in urban areas (permanent population per household: 2.6), so I calculate the average disposable income of medium-income households as 139,955 CNY, which is similar to the first threshold of the sample. This means that around 40–60% of urban residents fall into the category <120 k in the wider Beijing population. Similarly, the average disposable income of the richest 20% of households is 251,686, which is much less than the threshold of 1 m. I can only assume that people in above 1 million households make up less than 20% of the population; however, there is no other accessible official source showing the actual proportion of these households.

Although some data are open to the public, it is hard to tell to what extent the official data represent the actual situation. For instance, the total number of residents is underestimated because there are a large number of unregistered residents. The official statistics cover the permanent population and the permanent migrant population from 1978 to 2016, but they only cover changes in the registered population from 2015 to 2016. Since migrants who acquired a Beijing *hukou* are not counted as migrants, it is necessary to know the number of non-agricultural *hukou* holders who moved in and out to estimate the number of migrants. The purpose of the question is to ask whether the respondent is originally from Beijing, but the word originally was not used in the Chinese questionnaire because it would be considered geographical discrimination in the Chinese context. Therefore, some migrants who acquired a Beijing *hukou* and identified themselves as Pekingese also ticked off as Pekingese. Also, the yearbook shows that the number of migrants who acquired a Beijing *hukou* in 2015 and 2016 were 160,739 and 167,506, respectively, while the natural increases in the registered population were 116,219 and 49,366, respectively. Therefore, I assume that the actual proportion of migrants is greater than 57.6%.

People residing outside the fifth ring road make up a much larger proportion of the population (51%) than the sample (23.9%), while the sample has more people who live within the third ring road (33.8%) and between the third and fifth ring roads (42.3%) than the Beijing population (18.8 and 30.2%, respectively). The sample might contain more Pekingese and more richer people than the wider Beijing population because (a) housing prices inside the third ring road are very high, (b) 51.6% of the permanent migrant population resides outside the fifth ring road (People's Daily, 2015) and (c) only a few people who are originally from Beijing live outside the fifth ring road, so permanent residents outside the fifth ring road are highly likely to be migrants who have acquired a Beijing *hukou*.

Since car ownership is more of a household issue, it is more accurate to use the number of households instead of the permanent non-agricultural population (18.796 million) to calculate car ownership (vehicles per capita: 30.4%). However, the Beijing Statistical Yearbook only contains Beijing *hukou*-holder households (5.382 million households, 13.629 million people), I use the same household/resident ratio to estimate the number of households in the whole permanent population. The total number of civil motor vehicles is 5.717 million and the estimated number of households is 8.581 million, so the vehicles per household rate is 66.6%, which is about the same as the sample.

In general, people residing outside the fifth ring road (51%) are underrepresented in the sample (23.9%), while the sample has more people living within the third ring road (33.8%) and between the third and fifth ring roads (42.3%) than the Beijing population (18.8% and 30.2 respectively). For a city the size of Beijing, it is difficult to obtain representative population samples, but the sample may contain more native Pekingese and richer people than are represented in the Beijing-wide population, because the housing prices inside the third ring road are higher and 51.6% of the permanent migrant population resides outside the fifth ring road (People's Daily, 2015). The underrepresentation of people residing outside the fifth ring road may have influenced the impact of perceived *hukou*-related inequity. As the focus of this study is on understanding the significance of different acceptability constructs rather than on determining a representative pan-Beijing response to the charge, this slight bias should not be too problematic for the analysis or require weighting of the sample.

6.2.2 Descriptive Results of Key Issues

This section presents two main quantitative results: (a) descriptive results of each key element of the acceptability issue and (b) whether different population groups show different attitudes towards these issues. A normality test was first conducted to check whether the data are normally distributed because several statistical tests (e.g., ANOVA, *t* test) require this assumption. Since none of the data are likely to follow a normal distribution, non-parametric tests were conducted to determine the differences between population groups.

The Mood's median test was not adopted because of its relatively low statistical explanatory power for large samples (Freidlin & Gastwirth, 2000). The frequently used alternatives, the Mann-Whitney *U* test and the Kruskal-Wallis test, were used in this study. Specifically, the Mann-Whitney *U* test was used to test gender, Pekingese/migrants and car ownership; while the Kruskal-Wallis test was used to test age, income and residential area. The Mann-Whitney *U* test, the non-parametric alternative to the independent samples *t* test, is often used to compare two independent groups that are not normally distributed (Mann & Whitney, 1947; Nachar, 2008). The Kruskal-Wallis test extends the Mann-Whitney *U* test to compare more than two independent samples (Kruskal & Wallis, 1952). Dunn's (1964) test was used as a post hoc pairwise multiple comparisons procedure following the rejection of a Kruskal-Wallis test. It tested whether there are differences between each pair of the population group following the rejection of an ANOVA null hypothesis. Since the Kruskal-Wallis test and its post hoc tests are only used to inform subgroup SEM analyses by identifying groups that potentially have different attitudes towards congestion charging, detailed results of these tests are not included in this book (see Appendix 9 for the results in brief).

As Table 6.3 shows, the overwhelming majority of respondents had high levels of problem perception. Approximately three quarters of respondents thought they did not have enough information about the policy. Also, the congestion charge was perceived as more effective than previous transport policies such as traffic restrictions based on the last digit of the licence plate and the licence plate lottery.

More than three quarters of respondents felt the policy is unfair to poorer people, but fewer people thought the policy is inequitable to those who do not have Beijing *hukous*. Government car use was perceived as a serious problem. Further, the surveyed sample had a very low level of trust in government and trust towards experts. Moreover, the results show a relatively high level of obedience to authority and conformity to social norms.

More than three quarters of respondents did not want the congestion charge implemented. Just 31.8% of the respondents thought the policy is favourable to the society as a whole, while only 16.5% of respondents indicated that the policy is favourable to individuals.

6.2.2.1 Problem Perceptions

This section shows how respondents perceive traffic congestion and smog, which are the official reasons for implementing the congestion charge. Although only a few focus group participants regarded congestion or smog alleviation as one of the main reasons to implement the congestion charge, these two problems were discussed in every group. Problem perception is the first key element in many frameworks for public acceptability of road pricing in the Western context (e.g., Schade & Schlag, 2003; Schlag & Teubel, 1997). Therefore, it is taken as a start point to understand the acceptability of the Beijing congestion charge.

As Fig. 6.1 shows, most respondents had a high awareness of both these problems. Respondents who moderately or strongly agreed

Table 6.3 Indicators of determinants of public acceptability (6-point Likert-type scale)

Construct	*Item*	*Disagree (%)*	*Agree (%)*	*Mean*
Perception of congestion (Cronbach's alpha = 0.566)	PC1—Congestion is a serious problem in Beijing	0.1	99.9	5.59
	PC2—Traffic congestion has a great effect on my daily life	0.6	99.4	5.05
	PC3—I am always delayed by bad traffic on the road	10.1	89.9	4.58
Perception of smog (Cronbach's alpha = 0.587)	PS1—Smog is a serious problem in Beijing	0.6	99.4	5.86
	PS2—Smog is harmful to my health	5.9	94.1	5.02
	PS3—I pay a lot of attention to the smog problem	1.4	98.6	5.48
Information about congestion charge (Cronbach's alpha = 0.854)	AI1—I know when the policy is going to be implemented	87.8	12.2	1.98
	AI2—I know how much I need to pay	72.7	27.3	2.68
	AI3—The government is introducing experience from foreign cities	76.0	24.0	2.60
Social media (Cronbach's alpha = 0.902)	SM1—I can find useful information about the congestion charge on social media	53.2	46.8	3.21
	SM2—My opinion of the congestion charge is mainly based on information from social media	56.2	43.8	3.14
	SM3—Articles on social media help me to understand the congestion charge better	33.2	66.8	4.00
Perceived effectiveness of previous transport policies (Cronbach's alpha = 0.906)	EP1—Traffic restrictions based on the last digit of the licence plate have effectively alleviate traffic congestion	75.7	24.3	2.67
	EP2—The licence plate lottery has effectively alleviated traffic congestion	77.9	22.1	2.58

(continued)

Table 6.3 (continued)

Construct	*Item*	*Disagree (%)*	*Agree (%)*	*Mean*
	EP3—Previous policies can reach policymakers' expectations	82.8	17.2	2.47
Perceived effectiveness of congestion charge (Cronbach's alpha = 0.889)	EC1—A policy that has been successfully implemented in foreign countries could be effective in China	68.0	32.0	2.97
	EC2—The congestion charge could effectively alleviate the congestion problem in Beijing	43.1	56.9	3.65
	EC3—The congestion charge could effectively alleviate the smog problem in Beijing	74.2	25.8	2.62
	EC4—People will use cars less because of the congestion charge	28.1	71.9	3.94
Perceived income inequalities (Cronbach's alpha = 0.942)	EI1—The policy is inequitable to poorer car users	21.7	78.3	4.61
	EI2—The policy will cause more social inequalities	22.6	77.4	4.58
	EI3—The policy will make driving another privilege of the rich	22.6	77.4	4.56
Perceived *hukou*-related inequities (Cronbach's alpha = 0.937)	EH1—The policy is inequitable to new migrants	46.8	53.2	3.66
	EH2—People who don't have a Beijing *hukou* should not pay this charge	70.8	29.2	2.56
	EH3—The Pekingese are the main beneficiaries of the policy	57.7	42.3	3.21
Perceived government car use (Cronbach's alpha = 0.853)	EG1—The policy will place constraints on government car use	88.1	11.9	2.02
	EG2—Government car users themselves will pay the charge	84.4	15.6	2.16
	EG3—Government car use for private purposes is very rare	94.9	5.1	1.54

(continued)

Table 6.3 (continued)

Construct	*Item*	*Disagree (%)*	*Agree (%)*	*Mean*
Trust in government (Cronbach's alpha = 0.932)	TG1—The government wants to implement this policy to collect money from the people	25.5	74.5	4.34
	TG2—Other social problems caused by this policy are not policymakers' concern	25.5	74.5	4.30
	TG3—The policy cannot reach my expectation because of political corruption	18.0	82.0	4.75
	TG4—The revenue allocation will not be transparent	4.7	95.3	5.31
Trust towards experts (Cronbach's alpha = 0.911)	TE1—The congestion charge is not as good as experts say	22.2	77.8	4.54
	TE2—Experts are flattering cadres	18.7	81.3	4.68
Obedience to authority (Cronbach's alpha = 0.888)	CO1—I will not express my dissatisfaction publicly	26.5	73.5	4.25
	CO2—Even if I am not happy with it, I will do what the government requires me to do	24.9	75.1	4.35
	CO3—Cadres could make the right decision for me	62.0	38.0	2.93
Conformity to social norms (Cronbach's alpha = 0.925)	CS1—I will find it more acceptable if people around me think it is acceptable	37.6	62.4	3.89
	CS2—I will find it more unacceptable if people around me complain about it	36.7	63.3	3.90
Public acceptability (Cronbach's alpha = 0.958)	PA1—In general, I hope the policy will be implemented	77.1	22.9	2.48
	PA2—I think the policy is favourable to me as an individual	83.5	16.5	2.07
	PA3—I think the policy is favourable to society as a whole	68.2	31.8	2.95

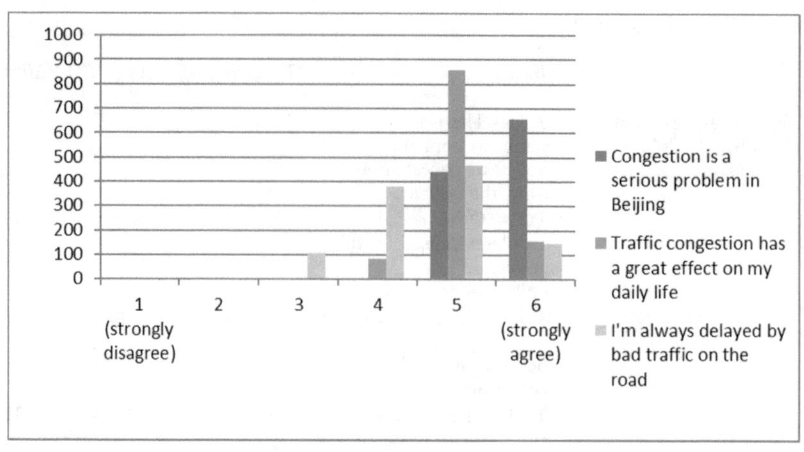

(a) Problem Perception: Congestion

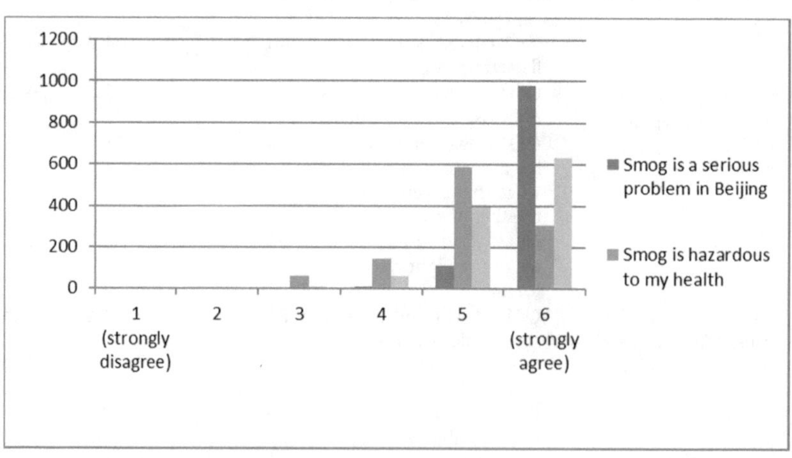

(b) Problem Perception: Smog

Fig. 6.1 Distribution of problem perception (The Y axis in these charts and all later charts in this chapter shows the count of respondents strongly disagreeing to strongly agreeing)

that congestion is a serious problem in Beijing (median: 6, IQR[1]: 1) accounted for 39.9 and 59.5%, respectively. Some 77.9% of respondents moderately agreed that congestion influences their daily life (median: 6, IQR: 0). Fewer people had a strong feeling that they are always delayed because of bad traffic (median: 5, IQR: 1) and 34.4% of respondents slightly agreed with the statement. In addition, 88.6% of respondents strongly agreed that smog is a serious problem in Beijing (median: 6, IQR: 0) and 92.9% of respondents paid a lot of attention to the smog problem (median: 6, IQR: 1). However, 5.5% of people somewhat disagreed that smog is hazardous to their health (median: 5, IQR: 1). Also, many fewer people (27.8%) had a strong feeling that smog is harmful to their health.

The results of Mann-Whitney *U* tests and Kruskal-Wallis tests showed that different age, income and residential area groups have different perceptions of the smog problem—older and higher-income people perceived the problem as worse, and the problem is perceived to be at its worst closest to the city centre. However, other statistically significant differences only exist in single problem perception items, which implies that there are few intergroup differences. It is worth noting that problem perception items were not related to whether the respondents are originally from Beijing or whether they own a car.

6.2.2.2 Access to Information

Information is another important factor influencing public acceptability in the Western literature. Two main themes about information were mentioned in interviews and discussed in focus groups: (a) a lack of top-down information channels and (b) social media as an information channel. Therefore, this section quantifies the extent to which respondents thought they have access to information about the congestion charge and whether people can get information about the congestion charge from social media.

As Fig. 6.2 shows, 12.2% of people thought they know when the policy will be implemented (median: 2, IQR: 2). More people (27.3%) thought they somewhat know how much they need to pay (median: 2, IQR: 2). Three quarters of respondents also thought they did not get information about road pricing schemes that have been implemented in

[1] Interquartile range: the first quartile subtracted from the third quartile.

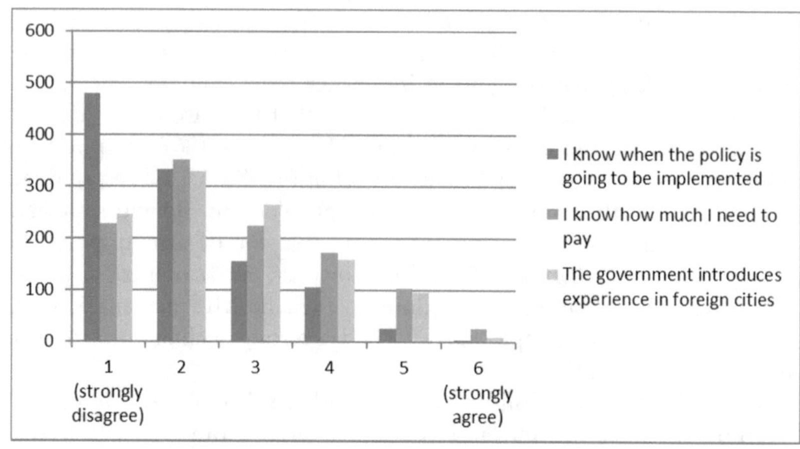

(a) Information: Access to Information

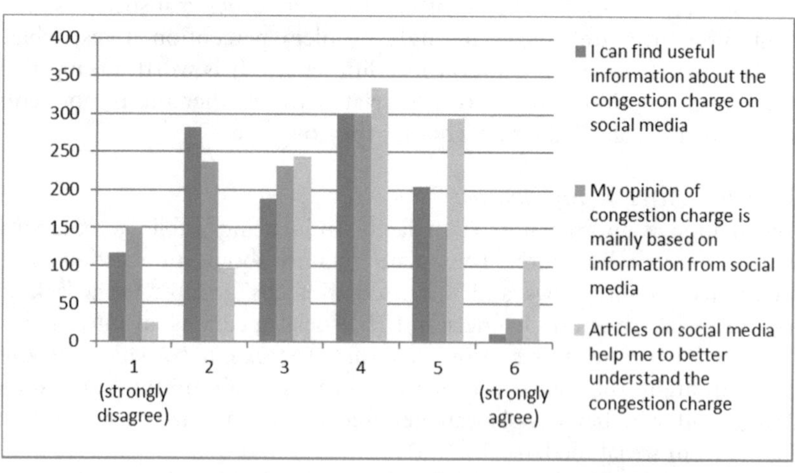

(b) Information: Social Media

Fig. 6.2 Distribution of information

foreign cities from the authority (median: 2, IQR: 1) and only 24% of respondents thought they somewhat noticed such information provided by the authority. Thus, the results verify focus group participants' idea that top-down channels cannot provide enough useful information about the congestion charge.

However, social media, even though some interviewees and many focus group participants considered them an alternative and much more effective information channel, may not play such an important role as they suggested. Although 66.8% of the respondents thought that articles on social media helped them to understand the policy better (median: 4, IQR: 2), less than half the respondents found useful information about the congestion charge on social media and 58.3% of them only slightly agreed with the statement "I can find useful information about the congestion charge on social media" (median: 3, IQR: 2). Although there is no official proposal yet, respondents who strongly and moderately disagreed with the statement accounted for 10.5 and 25.5%, respectively. Likewise, 56.2% of respondents somewhat disagreed that information obtained from social media influenced their opinions about the congestion charge (median: 3, IQR: 2). Even so, social media still seemed to provide more information to the public than official sources.

Kruskal-Wallis tests and Dunn's tests found that young people, the middle-income group and those who lived inside inner-city districts were better informed from social media. There was no statistically significant difference between different age, gender groups, Pekingese/migrants and car-owner/car free households regarding access to information and perception of social media.

6.2.2.3 *Perceived Effectiveness*

Section 2.1 showed that perceived effectiveness influences public acceptability of a pricing scheme in the Western literature. Besides, as the results of interviews and focus groups showed, the effectiveness of previously implemented policies is also expected to have a great impact on the perceived effectiveness of the newly proposed scheme in the Chinese context. Therefore, the perceived effectiveness section includes two parts: the perceived effectiveness of previous policies and the perceived effectiveness of the congestion charge.

As Fig. 6.3 shows, the respondents declared their dissatisfaction with previously implemented transport policies. Those who were dissatisfied with the traffic restriction based on the last digit of the licence (median:

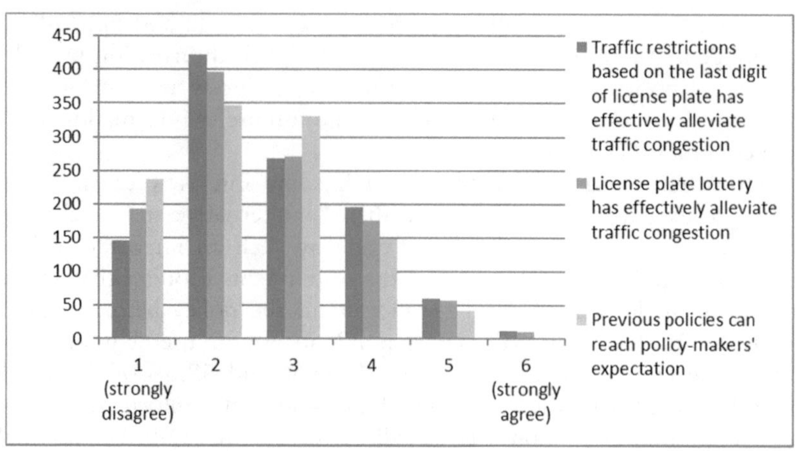

(a) Perceived Effectiveness of Previous Policies

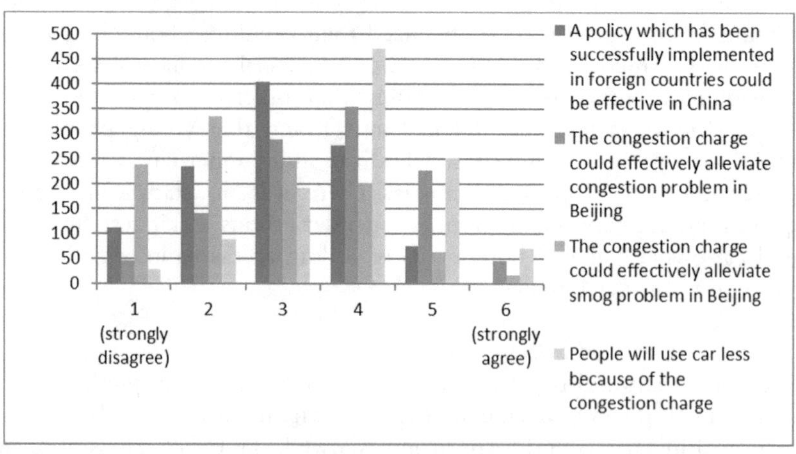

(b) Perceived Effectiveness of the Congestion Charge

Fig. 6.3 Distribution of perceived effectiveness

2, IQR: 1) accounted for 75.5% of participants, while 77.9% of respondents thought the licence plate lottery was ineffective (median: 2, IQR: 1). Some 82.8% of the respondents thought previous policies had not reached policymakers' expectations (median: 2, IQR: 1).

People felt more confident about the congestion charge than previous transport policies. Just 32% of the respondents thought that a policy could be effective in China if it had been successfully practised in foreign countries (median: 3, IQR: 2). The respondents considered congestion charge an effective way to alleviate congestion, but not to alleviate smog. Some 56.9% of people somewhat believed the congestion charge could effectively alleviate traffic congestion in Beijing (median: 4, IQR: 1) and 71.9% of them thought the congestion charge would make people use cars less (median: 4, IQR: 2). However, only 25.8% of the respondents believed the policy could alleviate the smog problem (median: 2, IQR: 2).

Respondents in low-income households were more sceptical about whether policies borrowed from the West can be effective in China, but they were more optimistic about congestion charging's effectiveness on smog alleviation. The Pekingese tended to believe in the effectiveness of policies that have been successfully implemented in the West. Those who live outside the inner-city districts were less dissatisfied with the effectiveness of previous transport policies in Beijing.

6.2.2.4 Perceived Equity

This section presents the extent to which respondents perceived the congestion charge as an equitable policy. It was unexpected that equity was the most frequently mentioned issue in focus group discussions as set out in Sect. 5.6. The participants mainly discussed three different types of inequities: (a) income inequality (privileges of the rich), (b) *hukou*-related inequity (privileges of the Pekingese) and (c) inequity between officials and lay citizens (privileges of cadres), especially government car use in this case. It appeared that equity was one of the main reasons why focus group participants were hostile to the congestion charge. Therefore, this section presents the results from a wider population to see if the focus group participants exaggerated inequities relating to the congestion charge.

Items reflecting income and *hukou*-related inequities had a different structure from other questions, in that these questions asked participants to agree or disagree with inequalities in treatment, for example, "People who don't have a Beijing *hukou* should pay this charge". Therefore, the values of these items were reverse scored in the analysis.

As Fig. 6.4 shows, in general, most of the respondents thought the congestion charge would cause social inequities. Some 78.3% of them thought the policy is inequitable to poor car users (median: 2, IQR: 2). In addition, 77.4% of the sample perceived the congestion charge as a cause of more social inequities (median: 2, IQR: 2) and another privilege of the rich (median: 2, IQR: 2). Meanwhile, 10% of the respondents moderately or strongly agreed with income equality items, suggesting that this group of people perceived that the congestion charge is equitable to all citizens.

There were divergent perceptions of *hukou*-related inequities, as 53.2% of the respondents somewhat agreed with the statement that "the policy is inequitable to new migrants" (median: 3, IQR: 3). Only 29.3% of the respondents thought that people who do not have a Beijing *hukou* should not pay this charge (median: 5, IQR: 3). Those who moderately and strongly disagreed with this statement accounted for 24.3 and 35.4% of the sample respectively. Most of the respondents (57.7%) did not think the Pekingese are the main beneficiaries (median: 4, IQR: 3), but 30.4% of individuals still moderately or strongly agreed that the Pekingese are the main beneficiaries. As 56.7% of the respondents identified themselves as migrants, it seems that a considerable number of migrants did not consider the policy particularly unfair to migrants, unlike many migrant focus groups participants.

Figure 6.4c presents issues relating to government car use and the congestion charge. These results show the extent to which the respondents perceived government car use as a problem and the extent to which they perceived that government and private cars would be treated equally. Some 88.1% of people did not think the congestion charge would constrain government car use (median: 2, IQR: 1), while 84.4% of people believed that government car users would not pay the charge themselves (median: 2, IQR: 1). In addition, 94.9% of the respondents thought it is common to use government cars for private purposes (median: 1, IQR: 1). The results showed a high public awareness of the privileges of government car users.

People aged 31–45 had different views on inequity issues relating to congestion charging. They perceived congestion charging as less inequitable to poorer people and they had less negative attitudes towards government car use. Females were more sympathetic to poorer people

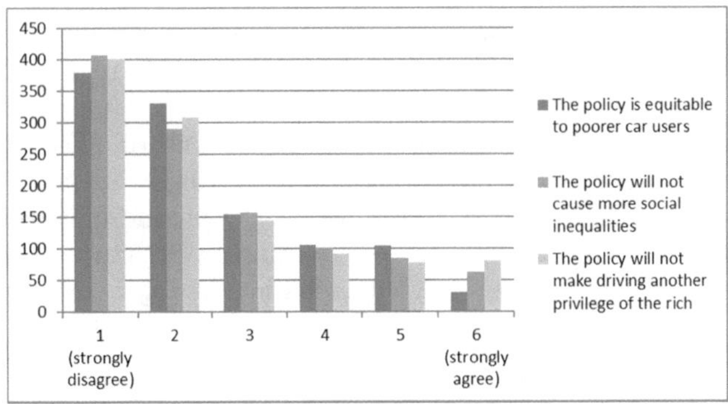

(a) Perceived Income Inequalities

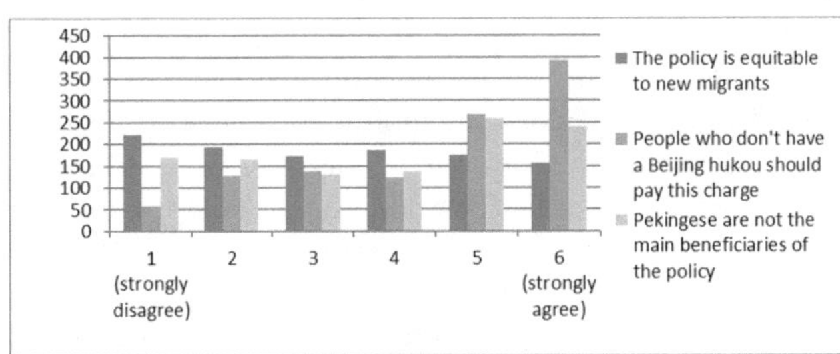

(b) Perceived *Hukou*-Related Inequities

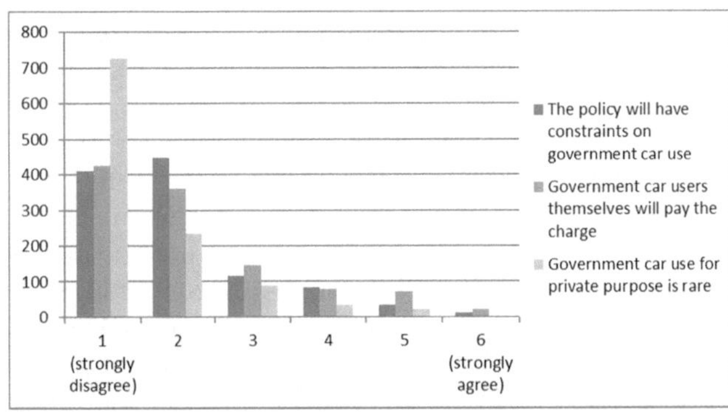

(c) Perceived Government Car Use

Fig. 6.4 Distribution of perceived equity

and they were less discontented with government car use. The high-income group perceived the policy as less inequitable to migrants, but they perceived government car use as a more serious problem. The Pekingese were less likely to think that congestion charging is inequitable to migrants. Residents living inside the third ring road perceived the policy as less inequitable to the poor, but they were more worried about government car use. Those who live outside the six inner-city districts felt there were more *hukou*-related inequities in regard to congestion charging.

6.2.2.5 Trust

Trust was identified as a key issue from the literature in Sect. 2.1. For instance, trust in government was highlighted as the most significant factor influencing the public acceptability of environmental taxation (Kim et al., 2013). Many topics relating to China's political system were discussed in focus groups, including the relationship between the government and people, a Communist way to solve problems, political and economic corruption, transparency, the cadre appointment system, GDP supremacy, etc. (see Sect. 5.5 for full details). All these topics reflected a low government credibility and a lack of public trust in government. Additionally, many participants indicated that they do not trust academics/experts. Therefore, this section presents the results of the two issues relating to trust. These items were also structured like the questions on income and *hukou*-related inequities and reverse scored for the analysis, as they would have been cumbersome and confusing if they had been structured like the earlier questions.

Figure 6.5a shows a low level of trust in government. Some 74.5% of the respondents believed that the purpose of implementing the congestion charge was to collect money from the public (median: 2, IQR: 2). Similarly, 74.5% of the respondents thought policymakers were not concerned about other social problems arising from the congestion charge (median: 2, IQR: 2). Furthermore, 82% of people agreed with the statement that the congestion charge cannot reach their expectations because of political corruption (median: 2, IQR: 2). Only 0.05% of respondents somewhat thought the government would let the public know how it used the money collected from the congestion charge, while the majority of people (95.3%) believed that the revenue allocation would not be transparent (median: 1, IQR: 1). About half the respondents (56.8%) strongly agreed that the revenue allocation would not be transparent.

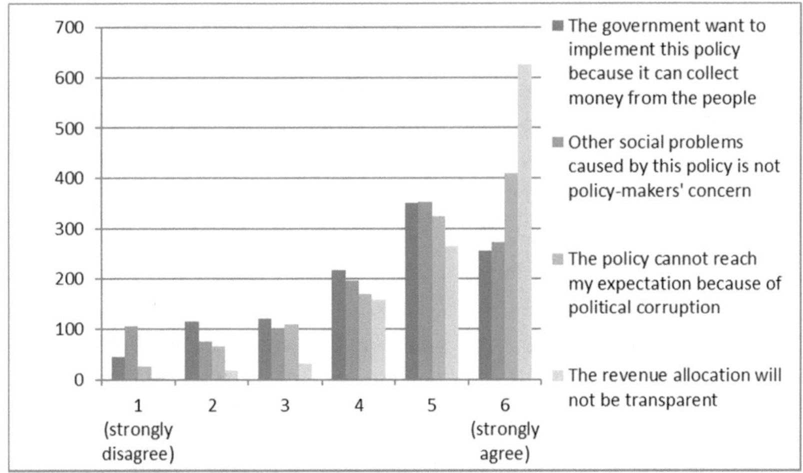

(a) Trust in Government

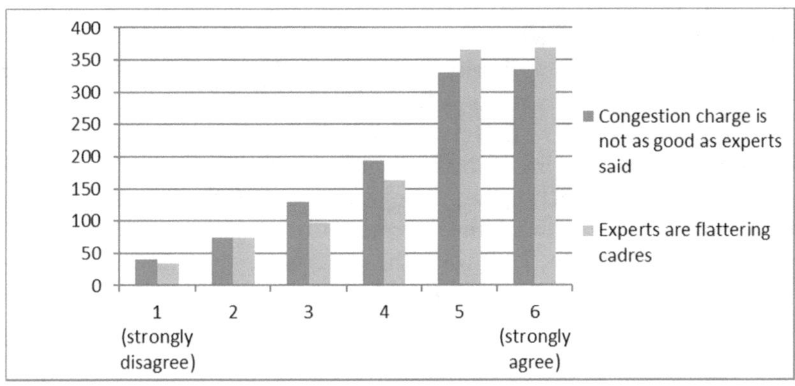

(b) Trust Towards Experts

Fig. 6.5 Trust issues

As Fig. 6.5b shows, most of the respondents had a low level of trust in experts. Some 77.8% of the respondents thought the congestion charge was not as good as experts said (median: 2, IQR: 2), while 81.3% of the respondents thought that scholars and experts were flattering cadres (median: 2, IQR: 2).

The Kruskal-Wallis tests indicated some statistically significant differences between subgroups (age, income, and residential area), but these pairwise differences were difficult to interpret by merely looking at the descriptive results. The overwhelming position is a lack of trust. The role of trust towards government and academics is further discussed in Sects. 6.3.2 and 6.3.3.

6.2.2.6 Cultural Factors

Many cultural factors that are rarely investigated in the Western literature were discussed in focus groups, such as obedience to authority, indifference to others, a wide gap between the rulers and the ruled, low civic awareness, social pressure and traditional family culture. Since some of these factors were only mentioned by a few participants and some are difficult to quantify, obedience to authority and social pressure were selected to analyse how cultural factors influence public acceptability in the Chinese context. Given that the public will finally accept whatever policies are implemented, it is of most importance to explore to what extent obedience and social pressure actually influence public acceptability or whether these factors merely influence their acceptance.

Figure 6.6a shows the extent to which the respondents were obedient to authority. Some 73.5% of the respondents suggested that they will not express their dissatisfaction in public (median: 4, IQR: 2) and 75.1% of the respondents agreed with the statement that even if they are not happy with the policy, they will do what the government requires them to do (median: 5, IQR: 2). However, many fewer people (38%) thought cadres could make the right decision for the public (median: 3, IQR: 2).

Figure 6.6b shows the extent to which the respondents thought they were influenced by people around them. Some 62.4% of the respondents would find the congestion charge more acceptable if people around them thought the policy was acceptable, while 63.3% of people would find it more unacceptable if people around them complained about the policy.

Kruskal-Wallis tests suggested that the elderly, high-income people and residents living inside the third ring road were less obedient and less likely to be influenced by others.

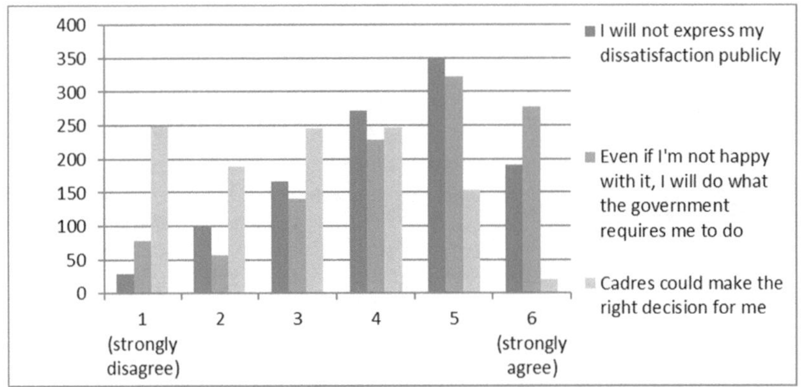

(a) Obedience

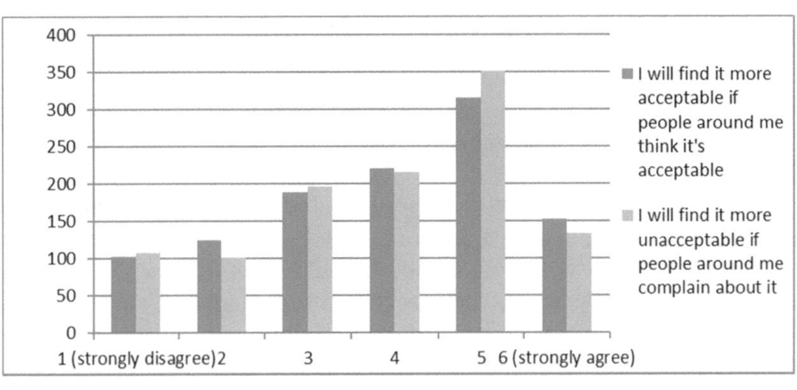

(b) Social Norms

Fig. 6.6 Cultural influences

6.2.2.7 Acceptability

As Fig. 6.7 shows, most of the respondents had negative attitudes towards congestion charging. Some 77.1% of the respondents did not wish the policy to be implemented (median: 2, IQR: 2). However, 83.5% of the respondents agreed that the policy is favourable to themselves as individuals (median: 2, IQR: 2). Those who strongly disagreed with the statement that the policy is favourable to individuals made up 49% of the

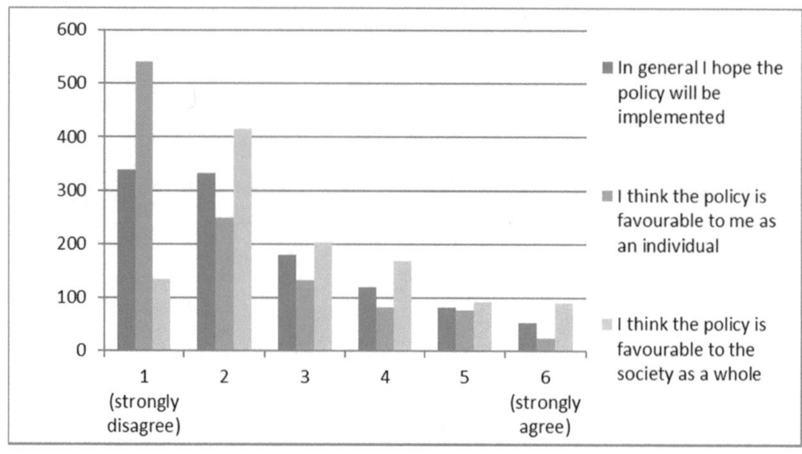

Fig. 6.7 Public acceptability of the congestion charge

whole sample. Just 31.8% of the respondents somewhat agreed that the congestion charge is favourable to society as a whole (median: 3, IQR: 2).

The public acceptability of congestion charging varied depending on age, income, residential area and household car ownership. Congestion charging was perceived less acceptable to older people. The 18–30 group had more negative attitudes towards congestion charging than the 31–45 group. Residents in high-income households and people living inside the third ring road were more discontent with congestion charging than other subgroups. Also, respondents in car-owning households were slightly less likely to agree that congestion charging is favourable to individuals, but there was no significant association between car ownership and other acceptability items.

6.2.2.8 Differences Between Subgroups

There were a few occasions where particular subgroups disagreed. Therefore, these differences were explored further after developing a more general structure equation model to understand the determinants and their relationships with acceptability.

Young people were more likely to think that information from social media helped them to understand congestion charging better. People aged 31–45 perceived congestion charging as less inequitable to poorer people, and they had less negative attitudes towards government car use. Older people were less obedient to authority and less likely to be influenced by others. The policy was perceived as more unacceptable by young people and older people.

There were no significant gender differences except for perceived social inequities—females were more sympathetic towards poorer people, but they were less discontented with government car use.

There are some interesting differences between different income groups. Firstly, low-income people had more negative attitudes towards policies borrowed from the West. This is probably because of state-led nationalism (Zhao, 1998), which had a greater impact on low-income people (Hoffmann & Larner, 2013). Secondly, the middle-income group was better informed from social media. Thirdly, the high-income group thought the policy was less inequitable to migrants, but they perceived government car use as a more serious problem. Also, the high-income group was less obedient and less likely to be influenced by other people. It is reasonable to assume that low-income people's acceptability is likely to be influenced by their level of trust, level of obedience and social conformity. This is further discussed in Sect. 6.3.3.3.

The Pekingese had more positive views on policies borrowed from the West, and they were less likely to think that the policy is inequitable to new migrants.

Residents living outside the inner-city districts were less informed from social media, and they were less dissatisfied with previous transport policies in Beijing. Also, since most of them were new migrants, they felt more *hukou*-related inequities. Residents living inside the third ring road, usually deemed as the privileged by others, perceived the policy as less inequitable to the poor, but they were more worried about government car use. They were less obedient to authority and less likely to conform to social norms. They were also more discontent with congestion charging than other groups of people.

6.2.2.9 Summary

In general, the descriptive results showed that although the surveyed sample had a high level of problem awareness, the respondents were very unhappy with the idea of congestion charging. They believed they have poor access to information about the policy, but social media may help them to get some useful information about the policy. They were dissatisfied with previous transport policies and doubted the effectiveness of congestion charging. Also, this policy was deemed inequitable to lay-citizens, especially lower-income people, and *hukou*-related inequities were less of a problem than income inequities. The surveyed sample had a very low level of trust in government and an even lower level of trust towards experts. Meanwhile, they were obedient to authority and likely to conform to social norms.

6.3 Structural Equation Modelling Results

SEM was applied to analyse the relationship between public acceptability and its determinants (see Sect. 3.5.3). It has been widely used in psychology and the social sciences because these confirmatory methods can provide a comprehensive means for assessing and modifying theoretical models and thereby offering the potential for further theory development. It fits well with the research objective—to explore the role of contextual factors in forming public acceptability in the Chinese context.

According to Koufteros (1999), Koufteros et al. (2001) and Golob (2003), the analytical approach should include an exploratory factor analysis (EFA), a confirmatory factor analysis (CFA) and the testing of the structural model (Fig. 6.8).

6.3.1 Exploratory Measurement Results

6.3.1.1 Corrected Item-Total Correlations

Item-total correlation is the correlation of the item with the composite score of all the items forming the same construct. The corrected item-total correlation refers to the correlation of an item with the summated score of the remaining items (Howard & Forehand, 1962). The higher the item-total correlations are, the more semantically similar the items are. Hence the item should be deleted if there is another item with an item-total correlation greater than 0.9 (e.g. Kriston et al., 2010; Mattick & Clarke, 1998). The commonly adopted bound of acceptable corrected item-related correlation is 0.35 (e.g. Beck et al., 1996; Saxe & Weitz, 1982), whereas some scholars argued that 0.20 is a satisfactory result (e.g., Bagby et al., 1994). Corrected item-total correlation tests were performed for each construct. As Table 6.4 shows, the corrected item-total correlations ranged from 0.382 to 0.890.

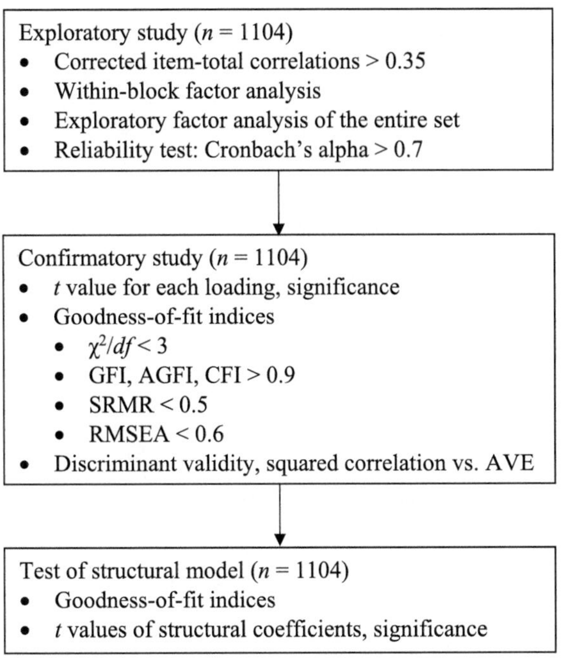

Fig. 6.8 General analytical approach

An EFA was used to uncover the underlying relationships between measured variables and to extract the main factors (Norris & Lecavalier, 2010). Principal component analysis (PCA) and principal axis factoring (PAF) are two widely used methods for factor extraction. PCA can reproduce the total variable variance, creating variables that are linear combinations of the original variables. However, there have been criticisms that researchers treated PCA and EFA as synonymous techniques (e.g. Fabrigar et al., 1999; Floyd & Widaman, 1995; Khodadady & Hashemi, 2010; Suhr, 2005). In this research, I conducted a factor analysis assuming that latent constructs or a causal model exists; however, PCA is merely a variable reduction technique (e.g. Bentler & Kano, 1990; Kambhatla & Leen, 1997). Unlike PCA, which focuses on both common and unique variance, PAF only seeks the least number of factors that account for the common variance of the set of measured variables. Thus, it is commonly used when the focus is to identify latent variables that

Table 6.4 Corrected item-total correlations

Variable		*Item*	*Corrected Item-Total Correlation*
Problem perception	Perception of congestion	PC1	0.404
		PC2	0.382
		PC3	0.427
	Perception of smog	PS1	0.427
		PS2	0.400
		PS3	0.447
Information	Access to information	AI1	0.736
		AI2	0.712
		AI3	0.749
	Social media	SM1	0.818
		SM2	0.804
		SM3	0.806
Perceived effectiveness	Perceived effectiveness of previous policies	EP1	0.850
		EP2	0.829
		EP3	0.764
	Perceived effectiveness of congestion charge	EC1	0.749
		EC2	0.800
		EC3	0.712
		EC4	0.776
Perceived equity	Perceived income inequalities	EI1	0.877
		EI2	0.890
		EI3	0.874
	Perceived *hukou*-related inequities	EH1	0.851
		EH2	0.861
		EH3	0.890
	Perceived inequities between cadres and lay-citizens	EG1	0.766
		EG2	0.746
		EG3	0.708
Trust	Trust in government	TG1	0.859
		TG2	0.865
		TG3	0.876
		TG4	0.846
	Trust towards experts	TE1	0.837
		TE2	0.837
Cultural influences	Obedience	CO1	0.795
		CO2	0.799
		CO3	0.754
	Social norms	CS1	0.861
		CS2	0.861

contribute to the common variance (e.g. Kline, 1998; Widaman, 1993). Although Gorsuch (1997) argued that PCA and PAF will give the same results when the correlations of items are high or a large number of variables load on the factors, it is adequate to use PAF to extract the factors in this study.

Two types of rotations which can be used to identify factors are orthogonal rotation and oblique rotation (Churchill & Iacobucci, 2006). Orthogonal rotations assume that the factors are not correlated, while oblique rotations assume there are correlations between factors (Jolliffe, 1986). The choices that researchers make between orthogonal and oblique rotations vary depending on the particular needs of the research goal. Many experts indicated that achieving a simple structure is essential to factor analysis and that choosing a particular type of rotation should depend on the reason for conducting factor analysis (e.g. Kline, 2014; Thurstone, 1947). Kim and Mueller (1978) thought that employing an orthogonal rotation may be preferable to oblique rotation because the former is simpler to understand and interpret. However, Costello and Osborne (2005) argued that although orthogonal rotation produces more easily interpretable results, it may neglect the interconnectedness between different factors that is usually expected in the social sciences. Hair et al. (1995) recommended using orthogonal rotation if the goal is to reduce the number of original variables; however, an oblique rotation is appropriate if a factor analysis is conducted to obtain theoretically meaningful factors. Therefore, an oblique rotation was chosen for this study.

Moreover, a within-block factor analysis was conducted before subjecting all items to checking for within-block dimensionality. There are some widely used techniques for testing unidimensionality, such as EFA (e.g. Conway & Huffcutt, 2003; Hickman et al., 2012), CFA (e.g. Houston, 2004; Schlegel et al., 2012), and Item Response Technique (IRT; e.g., Stout, 2002). Ziegler and Hagemann (2015) argued that EFA could only be considered as a starting point for testing dimensionality since it is a hypothesis-generating approach instead of a test. Therefore, CFA was employed to test the within-block dimensionality in this study. As Table 6.5 shows, there is a single factor with relatively high factor loadings in each block. The loadings of problem perception items are relatively lower (ranging from 0.722 to 0.766 and from 0.722 to 0.786 in Blocks 1 and 2, respectively) than items in other blocks. Therefore, I conclude that

Table 6.5 Within-block CFA

Block 1		*Block 2*		*Block 3*		*Block 4*		*Block 5*		*Block 6*		*Block 7*	
Item	*Factor*	*Item*	*Factor*	*Item*	*Factor*	*Item*	*Factor*	*Item*	*Factor*	*Item*	*Factor*	*Item*	*Factor*
PC1	0.742	PS1	0.757	AI1	0.885	SM1	0.921	EP1	0.936	EC1	0.862	EI1	0.945
PC2	0.722	PS2	0.722	AI2	0.871	SM2	0.913	EP1	0.926	EC2	0.895	EI2	0.952
PC3	0.766	PS3	0.786	AI3	0.894	SM3	0.914	EP1	0.891	EC3	0.835	EI3	0.944
										EC4	0.880		
Block 8		Block 9		Block 10		Block 11		Block 12		Block 13			
Item	Factor	Item	Factor	Item	Factor	Item	Factor	Item	Factor	Item	Factor		
EH1	0.932	EG1	0.900	TG1	0.923	TE1	0.958	CO1	0.911	CS1	0.965		
EH2	0.938	EG2	0.888	TG2	0.924	TE2	0.958	CO2	0.914	CS2	0.965		
EH3	0.957	EG3	0.869	TG3	0.932			CO3	0.889				
				TG4	0.915								

there is sufficient evidence of unidimensionality. The results from within-block factor analysis indicate that a given block of items is not represented by more than one factor. However, tests for unidimensionality may not be able to represent the relationships between items within one block and items within other blocks (Koufteros, 1999).

An EFA of the entire set of variables was then conducted. Since some of the factors are sub-constructs under more general constructs, correlations between these sub-constructs were expected. Also, according to the literature, there might be strong correlations between different constructs; for example, trust and perceived equity could be closely related. Due to this, the oblique rotation method with *oblimin*[2] was employed in this study. The results of EFA are in Table 6.6.

Both pattern matrix and structure matrix are presented in Table 6.6, although scholars usually focus on interpreting one of the matrices. The factor pattern matrix, which holds the factor loadings, contains standardised coefficients to reproduce the measures from the factors, while the factor structure matrix represents the correlations between factors and measured variables. Although factors are not orthogonal with oblique rotation, experts still prefer to interpret a factor as an isolated entity from other factors. A pattern matrix is usually preferred as the main tool for interpretation because it contains regression coefficients and therefore is relatively easier to interpret. However, since the coefficients in the pattern matrix take into account correlations among the factors when using oblique rotation, Maruyama (1997) suggested interpreting the factor structure matrix as well.

Factor loadings that represent the strength of the relationship between the item and the factor were used as indicators to interpret the role each item plays in a factor. Kim and Mueller (1978) suggested using 0.3 as a cut-off point for deciding whether the item makes a significant contribution to the corresponding factor. However, Hair et al. (1995) had a stricter criterion for the cut-off point for significance, suggesting that items could be retained if the factor loading values were greater than 0.6.

As shown in Table 6.6a, the percentages of variance explained of the eight factors were 28.737, 10.722, 10.236, 6.039, 5.333, 4.268, 3.830 and 2.839 respectively. The eight factors explained 72.004% of the variance in total.

[2] *Oblimin* rotation is a general form for obtaining oblique rotations. Oblique rotations include orthogonal rotation, allowing for factors that are correlated with one another.

Table 6.6 Exploratory factor analysis results

Item	*Factor 1*	*Factor 2*	*Factor 3*	*Factor 4*	*Factor 5*	*Factor 6*	*Factor 7*	*Factor 8*
(a) *Pattern matrix*								
PC1	0.047	−0.062	0.079	0.023	0.505[3]	−0.012	0.034	−0.024
PC2	0.016	0.007	−0.005	0.074	0.553	0.081	−0.051	−0.107
PC3	−0.026	0.033	0.201	−0.042	0.501	0.028	−0.095	−0.038
PS1	−0.066	−0.071	−0.172	0.006	0.592	−0.088	0.051	0.127
PS2	−0.078	0.116	−0.078	−0.067	0.572	−0.016	−0.026	0.037
PS3	0.051	−0.036	0.153	−0.044	0.506	−0.089	0.103	0.105
AI1	0.059	**0.658**	0.084	−0.018	−0.083	−0.115	−0.061	0.024
AI2	0.229	**0.602**	0.215	0.017	−0.039	−0.146	−0.013	0.094
AI3	0.091	**0.648**	0.074	−0.035	−0.071	−0.121	−0.119	0.039
SM1	−0.094	**0.846**	−0.140	0.022	0.005	0.000	−0.024	−0.058
SM2	−0.051	**0.806**	−0.132	−0.005	0.043	0.122	0.002	−0.084
SM3	−0.065	**0.811**	−0.106	−0.039	0.084	0.007	0.040	−0.017
EP1	−0.028	−0.038	−0.006	−0.012	0.005	−0.001	**−0.944**	0.019
EP2	0.055	−0.028	0.034	−0.011	0.041	0.006	**−0.893**	0.036
EP3	−0.021	0.079	−0.079	−0.013	−0.039	−0.089	**−0.749**	0.029
EC1	−0.060	0.058	−0.061	0.012	−0.015	**−0.759**	−0.043	−0.031
EC2	0.064	−0.043	0.066	0.009	0.009	**−0.889**	0.005	0.007
EC3	−0.024	0.080	−0.054	−0.015	0.019	**−0.682**	−0.083	−0.052
EC4	−0.018	−0.031	−0.029	−0.024	0.028	**−0.857**	0.010	−0.025
EI1	0.080	0.002	−0.020	−0.125	−0.028	−0.053	0.042	**−0.793**
EI2	0.097	0.015	−0.023	−0.060	−0.044	−0.071	−0.005	**−0.821**
EI3	0.073	0.048	0.060	−0.159	0.005	−0.048	0.015	**−0.773**

[3] Problem perception items loaded in Factor 5 but their loadings are lower than the cut-off (0.6).

Item	*Factor 1*	*Factor 2*	*Factor 3*	*Factor 4*	*Factor 5*	*Factor 6*	*Factor 7*	*Factor 8*
EH1	−0.018	0.010	0.003	**−0.817**	0.005	0.003	−0.013	−0.175
EH2	0.010	−0.014	−0.012	**−0.905**	0.025	−0.022	0.000	0.013
EH3	0.037	0.004	0.023	**−0.954**	−0.041	0.028	−0.018	0.027
EG1	0.492	−0.029	−0.106	0.035	0.026	−0.075	−0.087	−0.284
EG2	0.396	0.007	0.001	−0.009	0.062	−0.040	−0.116	−0.350
EG3	0.434	0.006	−0.025	0.001	0.031	−0.064	−0.139	−0.258
TG1	**0.717**	0.032	−0.169	−0.064	−0.023	−0.016	−0.029	−0.104
TG2	**0.864**	−0.012	−0.112	−0.095	0.005	0.039	−0.016	0.061
TG3	**0.832**	−0.003	−0.070	−0.054	−0.037	−0.017	−0.022	0.011
TG4	**0.790**	0.031	−0.034	0.028	−0.120	0.025	−0.002	−0.066
TE1	**0.820**	0.006	−0.084	0.008	0.006	−0.024	0.026	−0.040
TE2	**0.836**	0.031	0.092	−0.022	0.049	−0.016	−0.035	−0.016
CO1	0.016	0.084	**−0.758**	0.040	−0.042	−0.049	−0.049	0.018
CO2	0.020	0.065	**−0.784**	0.036	−0.035	−0.074	0.009	−0.097
CO3	0.121	0.052	**−0.686**	0.010	−0.052	−0.103	−0.107	−0.084
CS1	0.147	−0.020	**−0.801**	−0.023	−0.032	0.040	−0.009	0.080
CS2	0.076	−0.001	**−0.811**	−0.003	0.011	0.040	0.003	0.025
Eigenvalue	11.207	4.182	3.992	2.355	2.080	1.665	1.494	1.107
Percentage of variance	28.737	10.722	10.236	6.039	5.333	4.268	3.830	2.839
(b) *Structure matrix*								
PC1	−0.078	−0.117	0.181	−0.015	0.516	−0.016	0.057	0.018
PC2	−0.047	−0.039	0.077	0.012	0.532	0.016	−0.030	−0.054
PC3	−0.104	−0.011	0.289	−0.102	0.539	−0.050	−0.058	−0.003
PS1	−0.207	−0.099	0.001	0.065	0.590	−0.049	0.089	0.193
PS2	−0.131	0.096	0.043	−0.073	0.567	−0.095	−0.045	0.057
PS3	−0.149	−0.111	0.280	−0.048	0.548	−0.066	0.120	0.134
AI1	0.208	**0.724**	−0.090	−0.163	−0.119	−0.395	−0.367	−0.134
AI2	0.268	**0.644**	0.029	−0.152	−0.069	−0.415	−0.330	−0.111

(continued)

Table 6.6 (continued)

Item	*Factor 1*	*Factor 2*	*Factor 3*	*Factor 4*	*Factor 5*	*Factor 6*	*Factor 7*	*Factor 8*
AI3	0.259	**0.745**	−0.109	−0.191	−0.113	−0.433	−0.436	−0.159
SM1	0.116	**0.871**	−0.295	−0.098	−0.077	−0.310	−0.344	−0.140
SM2	0.119	**0.787**	−0.273	−0.116	−0.050	−0.187	−0.279	−0.167
SM3	0.083	**0.805**	−0.223	−0.142	0.013	−0.283	−0.266	−0.107
EP1	0.319	0.318	−0.135	−0.129	−0.011	−0.362	**−0.917**	−0.207
EP2	0.355	0.307	−0.102	−0.143	0.020	−0.361	**−0.887**	−0.217
EP3	0.319	0.412	−0.215	−0.127	−0.068	−0.417	**−0.816**	−0.194
EC1	0.226	0.365	−0.113	−0.140	0.024	**−0.785**	−0.367	−0.127
EC2	0.295	0.283	0.013	−0.177	0.072	**−0.884**	−0.351	−0.134
EC3	0.270	0.383	−0.116	−0.182	0.045	**−0.753**	−0.406	−0.179
EC4	0.253	0.295	−0.058	−0.187	0.082	**−0.848**	−0.333	−0.140
EI1	0.578	0.155	−0.145	−0.457	−0.089	−0.195	−0.237	**−0.889**
EI2	**0.621**	0.191	−0.176	−0.419	−0.114	−0.232	−0.301	**−0.919**
EI3	0.557	0.192	−0.063	−0.499	−0.041	−0.217	−0.263	**−0.877**
EH1	0.315	0.162	0.050	**−0.883**	0.031	−0.184	−0.173	−0.485
EH2	0.259	0.136	0.072	**−0.904**	0.063	−0.196	−0.138	−0.344
EH3	0.290	0.150	0.088	**−0.952**	−0.004	−0.169	−0.153	−0.365
EG1	**0.718**	0.165	−0.286	−0.228	−0.101	−0.286	−0.378	−0.593
EG2	**0.643**	0.176	−0.162	−0.284	−0.033	−0.262	−0.375	**−0.611**
EG3	**0.655**	0.192	−0.197	−0.254	−0.071	−0.292	−0.402	−0.552
TG1	**0.864**	0.225	−0.385	−0.303	−0.195	−0.288	−0.384	−0.577
TG2	**0.878**	0.148	−0.323	−0.298	−0.170	−0.238	−0.341	−0.481
TG3	**0.879**	0.170	−0.297	−0.281	−0.200	−0.284	−0.362	−0.503
TG4	**0.849**	0.172	−0.286	−0.212	−0.281	−0.222	−0.326	−0.520
TE1	**0.860**	0.158	−0.306	−0.232	−0.162	−0.269	−0.320	−0.513
TE2	**0.841**	0.171	−0.134	−0.285	−0.087	−0.297	−0.364	−0.500
CO1	0.251	0.268	**−0.798**	0.079	−0.205	−0.133	−0.218	−0.116

Item	*Factor 1*	*Factor 2*	*Factor 3*	*Factor 4*	*Factor 5*	*Factor 6*	*Factor 7*	*Factor 8*
CO2	0.310	0.258	**−0.828**	0.038	−0.207	−0.147	−0.198	−0.224
CO3	0.438	0.301	**−0.774**	−0.040	−0.220	−0.246	−0.345	−0.298
CS1	0.315	0.145	**−0.829**	0.045	−0.218	−0.035	−0.152	−0.122
CS2	0.263	0.152	**−0.823**	0.063	−0.169	−0.023	−0.132	−0.126
(c) *Factor correlation matrix*								
1	1.000	0.162	−0.266	−0.280	−0.183	−0.299	−0.381	−0.570
2	0.162	1.000	−0.197	−0.156	−0.077	−0.375	−0.382	−0.140
3	−0.266	−0.197	1.000	−0.085	0.205	0.054	0.158	0.141
4	−0.280	−0.156	−0.085	1.000	−0.042	0.194	0.147	0.388
5	−0.183	−0.077	0.205	−0.042	1.000	−0.064	0.025	0.066
6	−0.299	−0.375	0.054	0.194	−0.064	1.000	0.406	0.140
7	−0.381	−0.382	0.158	0.147	0.025	0.406	1.000	0.257
8	−0.570	−0.140	0.141	0.388	0.066	0.140	0.257	1.000

Table 6.6a, b together give an interpretable result that shows how observed items reflect latent constructs. After the elimination of items whose factor loadings were below 0.60, the loadings for the first factor ranged from 0.717 to 0.864. Also, Worthington and Whittaker (2006) indicated that a factor should only be retained if it could be interpreted in a meaningful way no matter how solid the empirical evidence for its retention. Hence, it is not only important to check whether the factor loadings are high enough to reach the cut-off point for significance, but also to examine whether these factors represent meaningful constructs.

The pattern matrix shows that the first factor represented trust issues, including trust in government and trust towards experts. However, the structure matrix shows there were significant correlations between the first factor and items about government car use, while items relating to income inequalities were borderline.

The loadings for the second factor, ranging from 0.644 to 0.871, represented access to information, including information acquired from official sources and social media. The loadings for the third factor (cultural influences including obedience and social pressure) ranged from 0.686 to 0.811, the fourth factor (*hukou*-related inequities) ranged from 0.817 to 0.954, the sixth factor (perceived effectiveness of the congestion charge) ranged from 0.682 to 0.889, the seventh factor (perceived effectiveness of previous policies) ranged from 0.749 to 0.944, and the eighth factor (perceived income inequalities) ranged from 0.773 to 0.821.

The loadings for Factor 5 were below the minimum acceptable value, but the loadings of problem perceptions are relatively higher than other items (ranging from 0.501 to 0.592, while the loadings of other items were below 0.2). Similar results were obtained from the structure matrix. Thus, Factor 5 represented problem perceptions including perceptions of congestion and smog.

Factor loadings of items relating to inequities between cadres and lay citizens for all factors were below 0.5. The loadings for Factors 1 and 8 were higher than other factors, ranging from 0.396 to 0.492 for Factor 1 and from 0.258 to 0.350 for Factor 8. However, the structure matrix showed that Factor 1 was also significantly correlated with the three items about inequities between cadres and lay citizens. Therefore, these three items were not eliminated at this stage.

It is of vital importance to check whether there are sizeable cross-loadings. Items that significantly load on multiple factors should be removed even though they may be critical to measure the factor sometimes. This is because (a) items with significant cross-loadings are difficult to interpret and (b) cross-loadings might be attributable to statistical artefacts (Yoo & Donthu, 2001). Some scholars indicated that there should be at least a difference of 0.20 between loadings on the two components (e.g., Speckens et al., 1996). Others argued that it is acceptable if item loadings in the main factor are higher than that in other factors (e.g., Gow et al., 2005).

As Table 6.6c shows, there was no significant cross-loading of items. Most of the items only strongly loaded on the intended factors, except items about inequities between cadres and lay citizens. Still, none of these three items had cross-loadings greater than 0.40. Besides, the cross-loaded factor (the eighth factor) did not account for even 25% of the variance in the item (Podsakoff et al., 1997). Therefore, no item was removed because of high cross-loading.

The factor correlation matrix indicated that Factor 1 (trust) had relatively high correlations with Factor 8 (perceived income inequalities) and Factor 7 (perceived effectiveness of previous policies). Factor 2 (access to information) was correlated with Factor 6 (perceived effectiveness of the congestion charge) and Factor 7. The two factors about equity issues (*hukou*-related inequities and perceived income inequalities) were also closely related. There were relatively weak correlations between the third factor (cultural influences) and other factors, ranging from 0.054 to 0.266. The fifth factor (problem perception) only had weak correlations with the first (0.183) and third factors (0.205); the correlations between the fifth factor and other factors were below 0.1. Since the eight factors made sense of the latent constructs, the factor correlation matrix could provide an initial understanding of how these factors are correlated.

6.3.1.2 *Coefficient Alpha and Reliability*

Cronbach's alpha is widely used for testing reliability (Koufteros, 1999). The Cronbach's alpha values for each construct are in Table 6.7. The loadings for the fifth factor were lower than the cut-off point, but items about problem perceptions were not removed because their loadings were borderline. Nevertheless, the Cronbach's alpha value of the fifth factor was lower than the satisfactory reliability value recommended by experts (0.75) (e.g., Churchill & Iacobucci, 2006; Litwin & Fink, 1995). The Cronbach's alpha values of other constructs were well above the satisfactory value of 0.75, ranging from 0.853 to 0.958. Cronbach's alpha has

Table 6.7 Cronbach's Alpha values for each construct

Construct	*Cronbach's Alpha*
Trust issues (TG1, TG2, TG3, TG4, TE1, TE2)	0.945
Access to information (AI1, AI2, AI3, SM1, SM2, SM3)	0.891
Cultural influences (CO1, CO2, CO3, CS1, CS2)	0.911
Hukou-related inequities (EH1, EH2, EH3)	0.937
Problem perceptions (PC1, PC2, PC3, PS1, PS2, PS3)	0.697
Perceived effectiveness of the congestion charge (EC1, EC2, EC3, EC4)	0.889
Perceived effectiveness of previous policies (EP1, EP2, EP3)	0.906
Perceived income inequalities (EI1, EI2, EI3)	0.942
Inequities between cadres and lay-citizens (EG1, EG2, EG3)	0.853
Public acceptability (PA1, PA2, PA3)	0.958

disadvantages: (a) it can be inflated if the scale has a large number of items and (b) it is based on the assumption that all the measured items are equally reliable (Gerbing & Anderson, 1988).

6.3.2 Structural Equation Modelling

6.3.2.1 Confirmatory Factor Analysis

The EFAs are usually considered preliminary analyses because unidimensionality cannot be directly assessed. Therefore, experts suggested that CFA should be employed to test whether the data confirm the generated model (e.g. Garver & Mentzer, 1999; Lu et al., 2007).

The path diagram in Fig. 6.9 presents the measurement model of this study. There are nine latent variables made up of their corresponding indicators. AMOS 20 was used to conduct the analysis. In the diagram, indicators (observed variables) are represented by squares, while constructs (latent variables) are represented by oval-shaped circles (Arbuckle, 2010). Variables e1–e36, represented by small circles, are errors in observed variables. Unidirectional arrows pointing towards observed variables indicate the effect of the latent variable on the observed variable. Latent variables are connected with each other by curved arrows, representing the correlations between the latent variables. To standardise the indicators of a construct, one of the loadings in each construct is manually set to a value of 1.0 (Jöreskog & Sörbom, 1993; Koufteros, 1999).

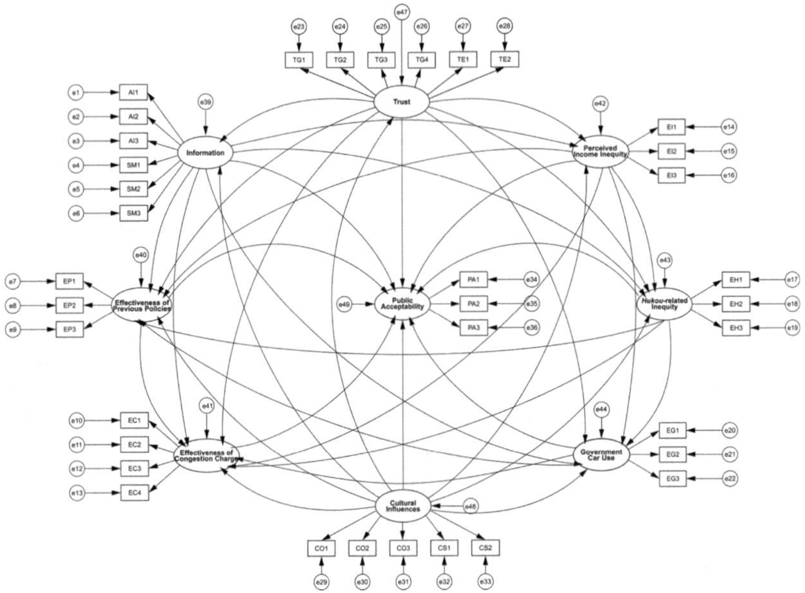

Fig. 6.9 Measurement model

6.3.2.2 Convergence Validity and Item Reliability

Convergence validity is usually assessed by *t* values, which represent the parameter estimate divided by its standard error (e.g., Dunn et al., 1994). The *t* value is shown as a critical ratio (CR) in the AMOS outputs. An absolute value of the CR greater than 1.96 indicates statistical significance (Byrne, 2016).

Factor loadings represent the relationships between latent variables and their corresponding observed variables. A larger value of factor loading provides stronger evidence that the latent and observed variables are correlated.

Item reliability is estimated by R^2 values. R^2 values greater than 0.50 imply acceptable reliability (Bollen, 1989). The R^2 values are shown as squared multiple correlations in AMOS outputs.

Factor loadings, standardised factor loadings, standard errors, CR values and R^2 values are in Table 6.8. All the observed variables exceed the critical ratio at the 0.95 level of significance, indicating significant relationships between indicators and their respective constructs. The

Table 6.8 Parameter estimates, CR and R^2 for the model

Item	*Latent variable*	*Factor loading*	*Standardised factor loading*	*SE*[a]	*CR*[b]	R^2
SM2	Access to information	1.000	0.799	c		0.858
SM1		1.048	0.863	0.039	27.101	0.876
AI3		1.008	0.813	0.087	11.623	0.902
AI2		1.112	0.833	0.102	10.858	0.780
AI1		0.863	0.804	0.079	10.925	0.827
SM3		0.980	0.850	0.033	29.328	0.740
EP3	Perceived effectiveness of previous policies	1.000	0.808			0.824
EP2		1.261	0.911	0.046	27.327	0.811
EP1		1.245	0.915	0.044	28.556	0.830
EC2	Perceived effectiveness of the congestion charge	1.000	0.763			0.668
EC1		1.080	0.891	0.043	25.397	0.664
EC3		0.914	0.814	0.041	22.187	0.691
EC4		0.921	0.825	0.040	23.162	0.831
EI3	Perceived income inequalities	1.000	0.910			0.798
EI2		0.972	0.923	0.029	33.759	0.771
EI1		0.868	0.896	0.025	34.760	0.664
EH3	*Hukou*-related inequities	1.000	0.948			0.558
EH2		0.820	0.891	0.018	44.780	0.806
EH1		0.891	0.898	0.024	37.733	0.794
EG3	Inequities between cadres and lay-citizens	1.000	0.747			0.898
EG2		1.527	0.815	0.069	22.218	0.802
EG1		1.484	0.878	0.065	22.692	0.852
CS2	Cultural influences	1.000	0.893			0.828
CS1		1.070	0.911	0.028	37.972	0.681
CO3		0.870	0.832	0.070	12.359	0.663
CO2		0.863	0.815	0.068	12.678	0.795
CO1		0.787	0.817	0.066	11.847	0.583
TG1	Trust issues	1.000	0.911			0.837
TG2		1.120	0.901	0.032	34.813	0.829
TG3		0.945	0.908	0.029	33.112	0.653
TG4		0.615	0.860	0.018	34.171	0.722
TE1		0.930	0.909	0.043	21.835	0.646
TE2		0.841	0.883	0.044	19.017	0.694
PA1	Public acceptability of the congestion charge	1.000	0.950			0.662
PA2		0.925	0.936	0.017	53.359	0.744
PA3		0.988	0.926	0.020	50.653	0.639

[a]SE is an estimate of the standard error of the covariance

[b]CR is the critical ratio obtained by dividing the estimate of the covariance by its standard error. A value exceeding 1.96 represents a level of significance of 0.05

[c]Indicates a parameter fixed at 1.0 in the original solution

squared correlations ranged from 0.558 to 0.902, providing evidence of acceptable item reliability.

6.3.2.3 *Goodness of Fit and Discriminant Validity*

Table 6.9 presents multiple goodness-of-fit measures provided by AMOS. There are three groups of goodness-of-fit measures: absolute fit indices, relative fit indices and parsimony fit indices (McDonald & Ho, 2002). Absolute fit indices assess the extent to which the hypothetical model fits the observed data. Relative fit indices show the results of comparisons between a chi-square test for the tested model and that for a baseline model in which all measured variables are uncorrelated. Parsimony fit indices assess whether the theoretical model is unnecessarily complex by penalising models that are less parsimonious. All the indices recommended by Hooper et al. (2008) were presented, including normed chi-square, GFI, AGFI, SRMR, RMSEA, NFI and CFI.

The *p*-value of the chi-square (shown as CMIN in AMOS outputs, $\chi^2 = 1564.394$, $df = 558$) was 0.000, providing a significant result at the 0.05 threshold. According to Barrett (2007), a good model fit should

Table 6.9 Goodness-of-fit indices

Category	*Index*	*Model value*	*Recommended value*	*Acceptance*
Absolute fit indices	χ^2/df	2.803 ($\chi^2 =$ 1564.394, $df =$ 558)	<3 good fit; <5 reasonable fit	Good
	GFI	0.916	>0.9 good fit; >0.8 reasonable fit	Good
	AGFI	0.880	>0.9 good fit; >0.8 reasonable fit	Reasonable
	SRMR	0.0432	<0.05 good fit; <0.08 reasonable fit	Good
	RMSEA	0.058	<0.06 good fit; <0.10 reasonable fit	Good
Relative fit indices	NFI	0.911	Above 0.9	Good
	TLI	0.907	Above 0.9	Good
	IFI	0.949	Above 0.9	Good
	CFI	0.933	Above 0.9	Good
Parsimony fit indices	PGFI	0.766	Above 0.5	Good
	PNFI	0.511	Above 0.5	Good
	PCFI	0.557	Above 0.5	Good

provide a nonsignificant result; therefore, the statistically based measure suggests that the hypothesised model cannot represent the observed data. However, the chi-square statistic is very sensitive to sample size, as it always rejects the model when the sample size is large (Bentler & Bonett, 1980; Jöreskog & Sörbom, 1993). Tanaka (1993) and Maruyama (1997) indicated that almost all the chi-square statistics provide significant results when the sample size is larger than 200. On the other hand, the chi-square statistic may not discriminate between well-fitting and poor-fitting models when small samples are used (Kenny & McCoach, 2003). The chi-square statistic is therefore not relied on as evidence for acceptance or rejection (Scherrmelleh-Engel et al., 2003; Vandenberg, 2006). Wheaton et al. (1977) proposed the normed chi-square (χ^2/df) to minimise the impact of sample size. A ratio of 3 or less indicates a good model fit (Kline, 1998). Multiple indices were used to provide a holistic view of goodness-of-fit.

The goodness-of-fit statistic (GFI) was created to show how closely the model replicates the observed covariance matrix, while the AGFI is an adjusted GFI based on degrees of freedom (Tabachnick & Fidell, 2007). These statistics range from 0 to 1. Most experts suggest that values of 0.90 or greater indicate good model fit and values in the 0.80–0.89 range represent reasonable model fit (e.g. Bentler, 1982; Hu & Bentler, 1999). However, some scholars suggested a value lower than 0.9 as an acceptable cut-off of the GFI when the number of estimated parameters is relatively large (Doll et al., 1994). Similarly, MacCallum and Hong (1997) suggested a less rigorous criterion of the AGFI when the number of estimated parameters is relatively large. As Table 6.9 shows, the GFI and AGFI had values of 0.916 and 0.880. Due to a large number of parameters estimated, the results indicated a good model fit.

The values of the standardised root mean square residual (SRMR) range from 0 to 1. A value of 0.05 or lower indicates a good model fit (e.g., Jöreskog & Sörbom, 1993), while values no higher than 0.08 are considered as a reasonable model fit (e.g., Hu & Bentler, 1999). The result shows that the average residual correlation was 0.043, which provides evidence of good model fit.

The Root Mean Square Error of Approximation (RMSEA) is a more informative index than many other indices (e.g., Browne & Arminger, 1995; Marsh & Balla, 1994; Steiger, 1990). MacCallum et al. (1996) recommended that a value of 0.08 or lower shows a good model fit and an RMSEA value from 0.08 to 0.1 represents a reasonable fit. Cut-off values of 0.06 (Hu & Bentler, 1999) and 0.07 (Steiger, 2007) are also widely adopted in this field. The most rigorous cut-off is used in this study due to the good performance of the RMSEA index. The RMSEA value of the hypothetical model was 0.058, which provides evidence of good model fit.

There are four relative fit indices in Table 6.9. The normed fit index (NFI) was 0.911, the Tucker Lewis Index (TLI, also known as non-normed fit index NNFI) was 0.907, the incremental index (IFI) was 0.949 and the comparative fit index (CFI) was 0.933. Among them, the CFI is one of the most widely reported indices because it is not affected by sample size (Fan et al., 1999). All the relative fit indices exceeded the recommended threshold of 0.9 (Bentler & Bonett, 1980) which further supports acceptance of the model.

The parsimonious goodness-fit-index (PGFI) was 0.766, the parsimonious normed fit index (PNFI) was 0.511, and the parsimonious comparative-fit-index (PCFI) was 0.557. All of these are parsimony fit indices, and their values exceed the recommended level of 0.5 (Cheung & Rensvold, 2002; Mulaik et al., 1989; Williams & Holahan, 1994), confirming that the model is sufficiently parsimonious. In summary, these indices provided sufficient evidence that the observed data is represented by the hypothesised model.

Discriminant validity was tested by comparing the average variance extracted (AVE) with the squared correlation between constructs. Discriminant validity refers to the extent to which factors are uncorrelated. Constructs should relate more strongly to their own observed variables than other constructs (Fornell & Larcker, 1981). Therefore, the AVE for a construct should be higher than the value of squared correlation between the construct and other constructs. As Table 6.10 shows, all the squared correlations were lower than the AVEs, which provides evidence of discriminant validity for all the constructs.

6.3.2.4 Results of Structural Equation Modelling

Table 6.11 presents the standardised estimates of the model. The cultural influence construct, which consists of obedience to authority and social pressure, had a strong direct effect (0.534) on trust issues, but it did not have such a strong direct effect on access to information about the congestion charge (0.171), perceived *hukou*-related equity (−0.177), perceived government car use (0.077) or public acceptability of congestion charge (0.111). Its direct influence on other constructs, including

Table 6.10 Correlations and squared correlation between factors

Variable	*AVE*[a]	*PA*	*TR*	*CI*	*GC*	*HR*	*IE*	*EC*	*EP*	*IN*
Public acceptability	0.884	1.0								
Trust	0.802	0.874^{**}	1.0							
		(0.764)[b]								
Cultural influence	0.730	0.551^{**}	0.534^{**}	1.0						
		(0.304)	(0.285)							
Government car use	0.664	0.756^{**}	0.767^{**}	0.450^{**}	1.0					
		(0.572)	(0.588)	(0.203)						
Hukou-related equity	0.833	0.372^{**}	0.361^{**}	0.051	0.337^{**}	1.0				
		(0.138)	(0.130)	(0.003)	(0.114)					
Income equality	0.828	0.663^{**}	0.661^{**}	0.303^{**}	0.684^{**}	0.535^{**}	1.0			
		(0.440)	(0.440)	(0.092)	(0.468)	(0.286)				
Effectiveness of the congestion charge	0.680	0.295^{**}	0.259^{**}	0.196^{**}	0.261^{**}	0.126^{*}	0.174^{**}	1.0		
		(0.087)	(0.067)	(0.038)	(0.068)	(0.016)	(0.030)			
Effectiveness of previous policies	0.773	0.361^{**}	0.347^{**}	0.289^{**}	0.313^{**}	0.091	0.211^{**}	0.359^{**}	1.0	
		(0.130)	(0.120)	(0.084)	(0.098)	(0.008)	(0.045)	(0.129)		
Information	0.821	0.283^{**}	0.240^{**}	0.251^{**}	0.186^{**}	0.153^{**}	0.183^{**}	0.406^{**}	0.362^{**}	1.0
		(0.080)	(0.058)	(0.063)	(0.035)	(0.023)	(0.033)	(0.165)	(0.131)	

[a]Average variance extracted (AVE) = (sum of squared standardized loading)/[(sum of squared standardized loadings) + (sum of indicator measurement error)]
[b]Squared correlation
$^{*}p < 0.01$
$^{**}p < 0.001$

Table 6.11 Results of structural equation modelling

Variable			*Estimate*	*SE*[a]	*CR*[b]
Trust	←	Cultural influence	**0.534**	0.060	9.428
Information	←	Cultural influence	**0.171**	0.049	2.860
Information	←	Trust	**0.149**	0.036	3.170
Income equality	←	Trust	**0.693**	0.044	16.641
Income equality	←	Cultural influence	−0.076	0.046	–1.824
Income equality	←	Information	0.035	0.042	1.134
Hukou-related equity	←	Trust	0.100	0.069	1.939
Hukou-related equity	←	Income equality	**0.508**	0.059	11.016
Hukou-related equity	←	Information	**0.080**	0.058	2.440
Hukou-related equity	←	Cultural influence	**−0.177**	0.058	–4.309
Government car use	←	Trust	**0.516**	0.024	10.886
Government car use	←	Income equality	**0.340**	0.021	7.946
Government car use	←	*Hukou*-related equity	−0.033	0.012	–1.069
Government car use	←	Cultural influence	**0.077**	0.019	2.268
Government car use	←	Information	−0.015	0.019	–0.544
Effectiveness of previous policy	←	Information	**0.289**	0.039	6.472
Effectiveness of previous policy	←	Cultural influence	0.077	0.031	1.723
Effectiveness of previous policy	←	Trust	**0.186**	0.040	3.037
Effectiveness of previous policy	←	Government car use	**0.138**	0.082	2.141
Effectiveness of previous policy	←	Income equality	−0.063	0.036	–1.096
Effectiveness of previous policy	←	*Hukou*-related equity	−0.037	0.019	–0.941
Effectiveness of the congestion charge	←	Trust	0.034	0.047	0.544
Effectiveness of the congestion charge	←	Government car use	**0.153**	0.097	2.286
Effectiveness of the congestion charge	←	Income equality	−0.067	0.041	–1.161
Effectiveness of the congestion charge	←	Information	**0.306**	0.046	6.428

(continued)

Table 6.11 (continued)

Variable			*Estimate*	*SE*[a]	*CR*[b]
Effectiveness of the congestion charge	←	Cultural influence	−0.007	0.035	– 0.168
Effectiveness of the congestion charge	←	Effectiveness of previous policy	**0.202**	0.042	5.494
Effectiveness of the congestion charge	←	*Hukou*-related equity	0.034	0.022	0.849
Public acceptability	←	Cultural influence	**0.111**	0.027	4.640
Public acceptability	←	Trust	**0.600**	0.038	16.689
Public acceptability	←	Information	0.037	0.030	1.727
Public acceptability	←	Effectiveness of previous policy	0.026	0.032	1.279
Public acceptability	←	Effectiveness of the congestion charge	0.034	0.029	1.677
Public acceptability	←	income equality	**0.094**	0.032	3.011
Public acceptability	←	*Hukou*-related equity	0.038	0.017	1.783
Public acceptability	←	Government car use	**0.145**	0.075	4.002

[a]SE is an estimate of the standard error of the covariance

[b]CR is the critical ratio obtained by dividing the estimate of the covariance by its standard error. A value exceeding 1.96 represents a level of significance of 0.05.

the perceived effectiveness of previous policies and the congestion charge, and perceived income equality, were not statistically significant.

Trust issues, which consist of trust in government and trust towards experts, have impacts on many factors. The effect of trust on public acceptability (0.600) was remarkable: respondents with higher levels of trust had higher levels of acceptance of the congestion charge. This was the highest direct effect on public acceptability. Also, trust significantly influenced how respondents perceived income equality (0.693) and government car use (0.516). In other words, the more the respondents trusted the government and experts, the less likely they perceived congestion charge as a cause of income inequality. Similarly, the higher the level of trust, the less likely respondents perceived government car use as a serious problem in China. Besides, respondents with higher levels of trust were more likely to think they have access to information about the congestion charge (0.149). Trust also directly affects the perceived effectiveness of previous policies (0.186), but not the perceived effectiveness of the congestion charge.

The effects of information on the perceived effectiveness of previous policies (0.289) and the congestion charge (0.306) were relatively high. However, the information did not have a direct effect on public acceptability, which implied that obtaining more information about the policy did not make it more acceptable. Information had a rather marginal effect on perceived *hukou*-related equity (0.080), but its effects on the other two constructs on equity issues were not statistically significant.

Respondents who perceived previous policies as more effective were more likely to perceive the congestion charge as an effective policy (0.202). Nevertheless, neither the perceived effectiveness of previous policies nor the perceived effectiveness of the congestion charge had statistically significant effects on public acceptability.

Equity issues were correlated with each other. Perceived income equality had direct effects on perceived *hukou*-related equity (0.508) and perceived government car use (0.340), but there was a lack of support for a positive relationship between perceived *hukou*-related equity and perceived government car use. Moreover, perceived government car use had a direct effect on the perceived effectiveness of previous policies (0.138) and the congestion charge (0.153), but perceived effectiveness was not influenced by other equity issues.

Perceived income equality and perceived government car use had significant direct effects on the level of public acceptability (0.094 and 0.145, respectively). Respondents who perceived less income inequality found the congestion charge more acceptable. Likewise, the less seriously the respondent perceived government car use as a problem, the higher his or her acceptability of the congestion charge.

However, only examining direct effects can lead to misunderstandings. Since constructs are interconnected, indirect effects can sometimes be strong. As Table 6.12 shows, the indirect effect of cultural influence on public acceptability (0.440) was much larger than its direct effect (0.111). Trust also had a relatively large indirect effect on the public acceptability of the congestion charge (0.210). The total effect of one construct on another is the sum of the direct effect and all indirect effects from the first construct acting through all intermediate constructs on the second construct.

Figure 6.10 presents the causal model of public acceptability. The arrows in Fig. 6.10 symbolise the direct effect between two constructs. Paths that do not have significant direct effects on public acceptability are not presented because although sometimes the indirect effect of a

Table 6.12 Standardised total effects

	Public acceptability of the congestion charge		
	Direct effect	*Indirect effect*	*Total effect*
Cultural influence	0.111	**0.440**	**0.551**
Trust	**0.600**	0.210	**0.811**
Information	0.037	0.026	0.063
Income equality	0.094	0.065	**0.159**
Hukou-related equity	0.038	−0.005	0.033
Government car use	0.145	0.010	**0.154**
Effectiveness of previous policy	0.026	0.007	0.033
Effectiveness of the congestion charge	0.034	–	0.034

– no relationship defined

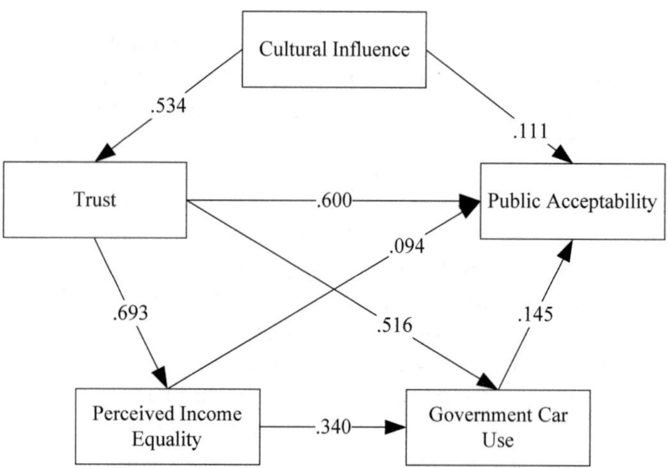

Fig. 6.10 Standardised estimates of factors influencing public acceptability

construct could be substantially larger than its direct effect, the total effects of the four other constructs are still lower than 0.1. Therefore, it is inappropriate to consider them (information, perceived effectiveness of previous policies and the congestion charge, and perceived hukou related equity) as factors influencing public acceptability.

In sum, the tests of the structural model offer some insightful results. Firstly, the result points to trust as the dominant factor influencing the public acceptability of the congestion charge. Although trust in government is also identified as one of the key determinants of public acceptability in the literature, it is not at the core of the acceptability issue in the West. Secondly, although cultural influence does not have a strong direct effect on public acceptability, its indirect effect is noteworthy. This is an important finding because if cultural factors come out as significant factors in the Chinese context, they are likely to be different in different places. However, this has not been part of the picture before. Hence, other studies might be missing something important. It remains to be explored whether this result can go beyond China, but neither does this allow other researchers to assume it does not matter. Thirdly, equity issues such as income equality and government car use to influence public acceptability. Fourthly, there is a lack of evidence that public acceptability of congestion charge in Beijing is affected by some factors that have been identified as important in the Western context, such as access to information and the perceived effectiveness of the policy.

6.3.3 Differences Between Subgroups

This section presents the differences between subgroups. The original structural equation model was used to calculate the estimation results of subgroups. If the goodness-of-fit indices indicated that the specified model did not fit the empirical data, the same analytical approach was applied to analyse the data.

Since the sample sizes of the older and high-income groups were rather small, the sample size requirements for SEM must be considered. Although investigators found it difficult to develop guidelines for sample size requirements (e.g. MacCallum et al., 1999; Tanaka, 1987), some rules of thumb have been applied: (a) 10 cases per variable (Nunnally, 1967), (b) 100 as the minimum sample size (Boomsma, 1985) and (c) five observations per estimated parameter (Bentler & Chou, 1987).

Both the older and high-income groups meet the minimum SEM sample size requirement, but I found that the sample size requirement of the elderly group should be higher than that of the high-income group and it is not proper to model the older group separately. This is because 11 indicators needed to be eliminated because of low factor loadings, thereby decreasing the number of indicators of several factors. According to Wolf et al. (2013), sample size requirements increase if the number of indicators of a factor decreases. Moreover, in the older group model, some factors only have one corresponding indicator, which is unacceptable. Therefore, people aged 45–60 and people older than 60 were merged into one group.

6.3.3.1 *Age*

The analytical approach was applied to analyse Age Group 1 (18–30). Social media and information about the congestion charge were separated into two factors in the exploratory study, while items relating to government car use were eliminated due to their low factor loadings. The estimation results of different age groups are in Fig. 6.11.

For young people (18–30), the level of trust had a weaker effect on their perceived income inequality; however, this was the only group that perceived that income equality directly influenced the acceptability of the congestion charge. This may be due to the increasing living costs and life stress of young people in big cities in China (see Liang et al., 2016; Zhang et al., 2011). In addition, information from social media significantly influences young people's acceptability of the policy. This is probably because young people were better informed from social media (see Sect. 6.2.2.8). It is also interesting that young people's attitudes towards information from social media influenced the way they perceived income inequities.

Perception of government car use did not influence the 18–30 group's acceptability of the congestion charge, but its impact on older people's acceptability was significant. Perceived effectiveness of the congestion charge significantly influenced middle-aged (31–45) respondents' acceptability, while the perceived effectiveness of previous policies influenced older people's (older than 45) acceptability. Although attitude towards previous policies did not directly influence middle-aged people's acceptability, it significantly influenced their perceived effectiveness of congestion charging. This may reflect greater life experience and cynicism about the promised policy impacts.

It is clear that the modelled relationships were more complex for the over-30s—there were more factors influencing their attitudes. For the 31–45 group, it is interesting to observe that both access to information and perceived effectiveness played a role, which implies that, to some extent, this group of people was making rational decisions based on costs and benefits.

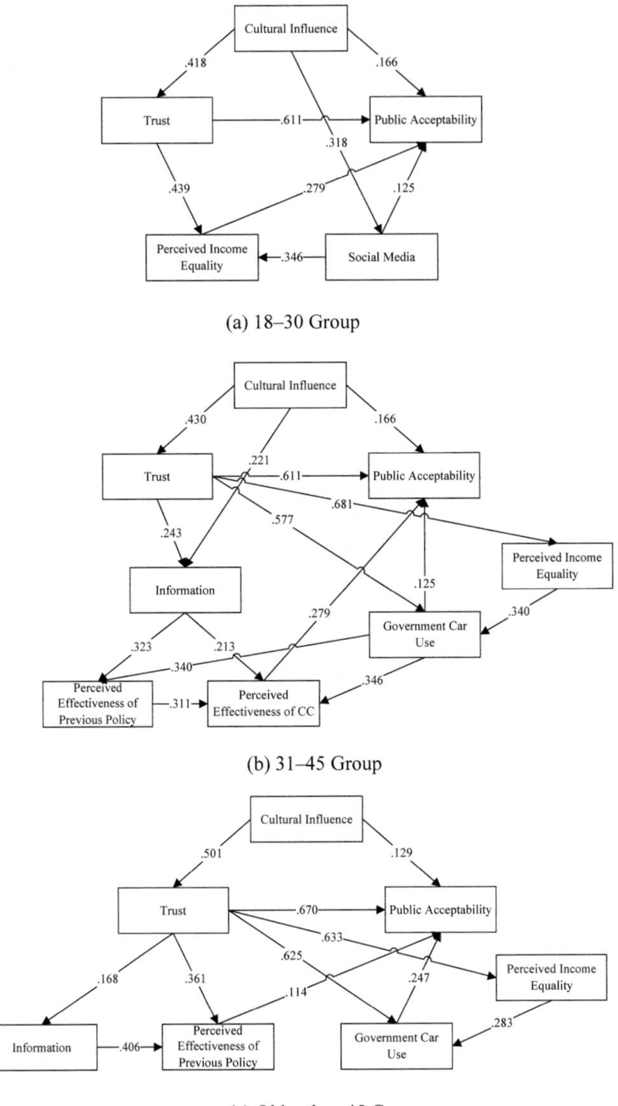

Fig. 6.11 Estimation results of different age groups

6.3.3.2 *Gender*

The analytical approach was applied to analyse Gender Group 2 (Female). Items AI2, CO1, CO2 and CO3 were eliminated because of low factor loadings. The estimation results of different gender groups are in Fig. 6.12.

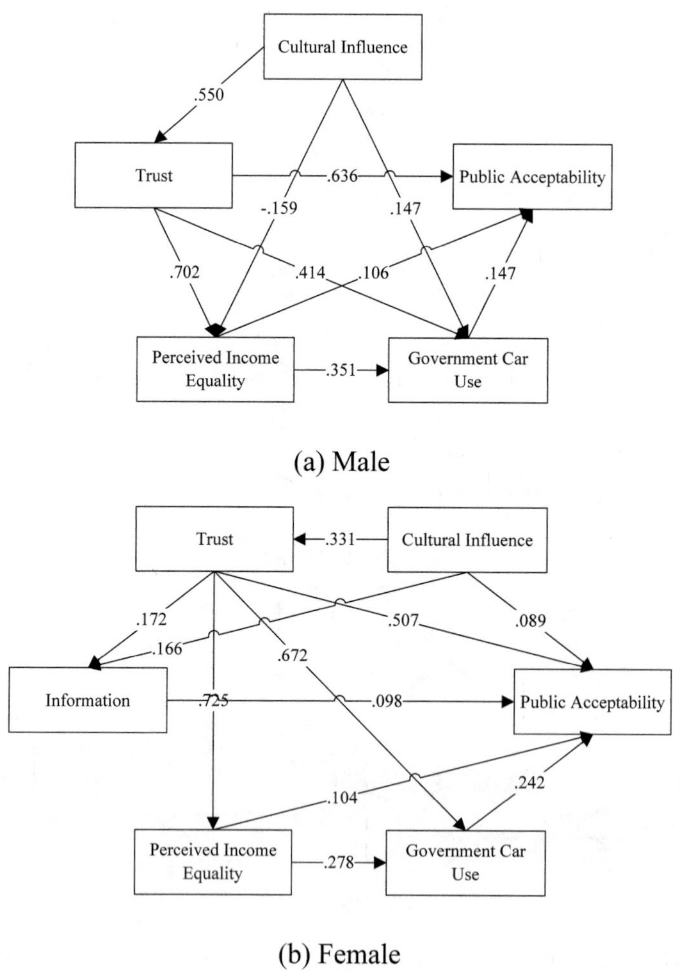

Fig. 6.12 Estimation results of different gender groups

Although the level of conformity did not have a direct effect on males' attitudes towards congestion charging, its total effect was greater than that of females. This indicates that males who conform to social norms were more likely to trust the government than females. It is interesting that the higher level of conformity males had, the more likely they perceived congestion charging as another symbol of social inequity. Besides, government car use had a greater impact on females' acceptability. Also, access to information had a small but significant influence on females' acceptability but its impact on males' acceptability was not significant.

6.3.3.3 Income

Due to the small sample size of rich people (household income higher than 1 m CNY), the original model did not fit the empirical data. Therefore, the analytical approach was applied to analyse Income Group 3 (above 1 m CNY). Items about trust in government and items about access to information about the congestion charge had low factor loadings, but they were still included as separate factors since they were considered important factors influencing public acceptability. However, their effects on public acceptability were not statistically significant. Moreover, the model fit indices were reduced by retaining trust in government and access to information about the congestion charge as separated factors. Hence, these items were eliminated. The estimation results of different income groups are in Fig. 6.13.

As expected (see Sect. 6.2.2.8), obedience and social conformity had stronger impacts on low-income respondents' acceptability of the congestion charge. Compared to other groups, obedient low-income people were more likely to accept the policy. By contrast, cultural factors did not have a significant impact on rich people's acceptability. Its indirect effect on acceptability was even smaller than for lower-income groups. Likewise, the level of trust had a stronger effect on low-income people's acceptability of the congestion charge, while its effect on high-income people's acceptability was much lower.

Unlike the other income groups, perceived income equality did not have a significant effect on low-income people's acceptability of the congestion charge. Instead, the policy was less unacceptable to low-income people if they perceived the policy as more equitable to migrants. However, perceived income equality played the most significant role for high-income people's acceptability. The results indicated that, for richer

Fig. 6.13 Estimation results of different income groups

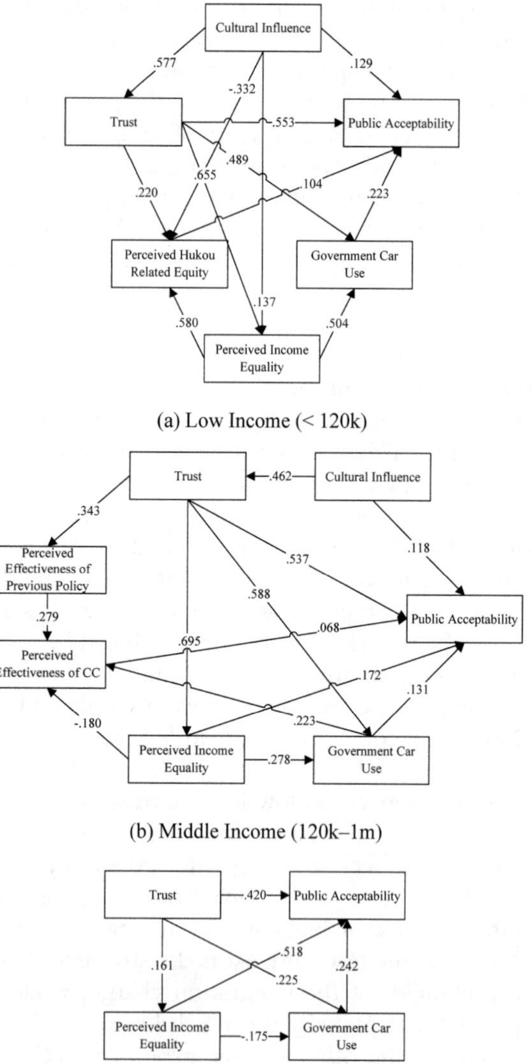

people, the more equitable they perceived the congestion charge, the higher their acceptability of it.

Perceived effectiveness of the congestion charge had a significant effect on middle-income people's acceptability. Although the effect was relatively weak compared to other factors, it suggested that some middle-income people consider the introduction of congestion charging from a costs-and-benefits perspective.

The simplicity of the model for high-income people is noteworthy—their acceptability boils down to perceived equity, trust and government car use. Moreover, these determinants were much less correlated with each other than in other groups.

6.3.3.4 Pekingese/Migrants

The estimation results for the Pekingese and migrants are in Fig. 6.14. For the Pekingese, cultural factors had a negative effect on perceived income equality, indicating that those who are more obedient to authority and more likely to conform to social norms were less likely to perceive the congestion charge as equitable. Also, the perceived effectiveness of previous transport policies had a significant effect on the Pekingese's acceptability of the congestion charge. However, the perceived effectiveness of previous policies featured for long-standing Pekingese residents but not for migrants, who were more likely to be influenced by this policy. Trust had a stronger effect on migrants' acceptability, which was not directly influenced by perceived income equity.

It was unexpected that *hukou*-related equity did not have a significant impact on migrants' acceptability of the congestion charge. This is basically because (a) some migrants who had lived in Beijing for a long time still identified themselves as migrants, (b) many migrants who had obtained a Beijing *hukou* still identified themselves as migrants and (c) migrants themselves are a diverse group, so the extent to which they connected social inequities with the *hukou* system varied depending on their socioeconomic status and political inclinations. It might be better to consider residents living outside the fifth ring road as the relatively marginalised new migrants who are unfairly treated because of the *hukou* system (see Sect. 6.3.3.5).

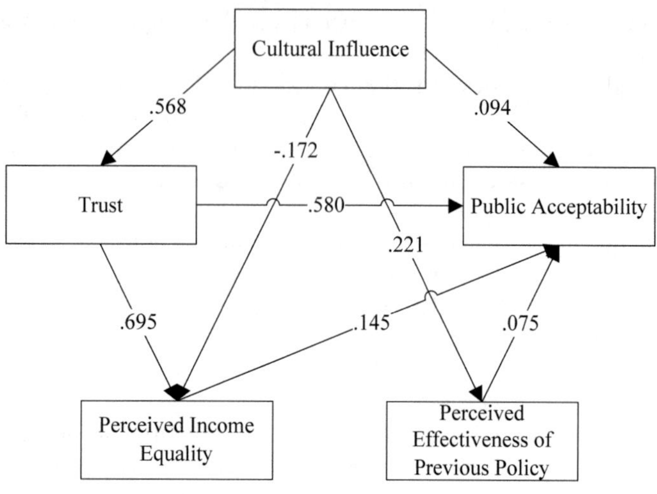

(a) Pekingese

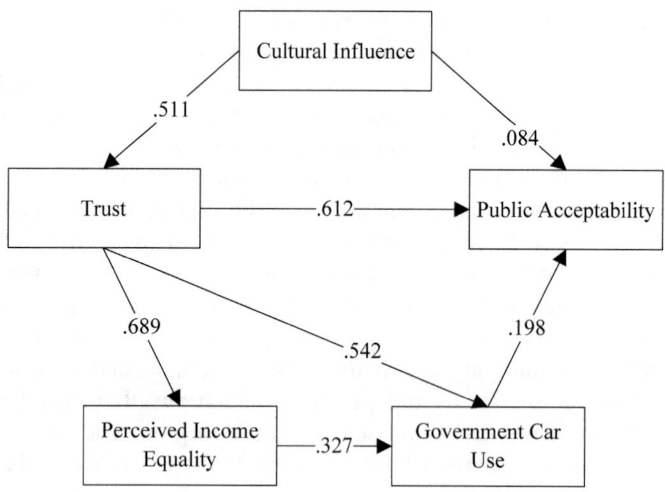

(b) Migrants

Fig. 6.14 Estimation results of Pekingese and migrants

6.3.3.5 Residential Areas

The analytical approach was applied to Residential Area Group 3 (outside the fifth ring road). Items AI2, CO1, CO2 and CO3 were eliminated because of low factor loadings. The estimation results of different residential area groups are in Fig. 6.15.

For those who live inside the third ring road, the information had a significant effect on their acceptability of the congestion charge. This is probably because people living inside the third ring road (or their family members and relatives) were highly likely to be in cadres and employees of public institutions, so they had better access to information. They were less obedient to authority and less likely to be influenced by other people (see Sect. 6.2.2.8), and their level of obedience and conformity did not directly influence their acceptability of the congestion charge.

Equity issues played important roles for those who live between the third and the fifth ring road, as their acceptability was significantly influenced by perceived income equality, perceived *hukou*-related equity and government car use.

For those who live outside the fifth ring road, cultural factors did not have a significant direct effect on acceptability of the congestion charge, but its indirect effect was strong. The effect of perceived income equality was not significant, while perceived *hukou*-related equity and social media significantly influenced their acceptability. This is because the vast majority of people in this group were new migrants, usually known as "Beijing drifters", who went to Beijing to seek a livelihood. They usually work in Beijing with no fixed abode, no Beijing *hukou* and no sense of belonging (e.g. Dong & Blommaert, 2009; Li, 2013).

6.4 Conclusion

This chapter answers the third research question of the study: what factors influenced the public acceptability of congestion charging in the Chinese context? In general, trust in government and trust towards academics is at the core of public acceptability of congestion charging in this study. Respondents who had lower levels of trust were less likely to support the policy. Those who had lower levels of obedience to authority and conformity to social norms were less likely to trust the government and academics and therefore tended to find congestion charging more unacceptable. The level of trust also significantly influenced perceived income inequity and attitudes towards government car use, which are

Fig. 6.15 Estimation results of residents of different areas

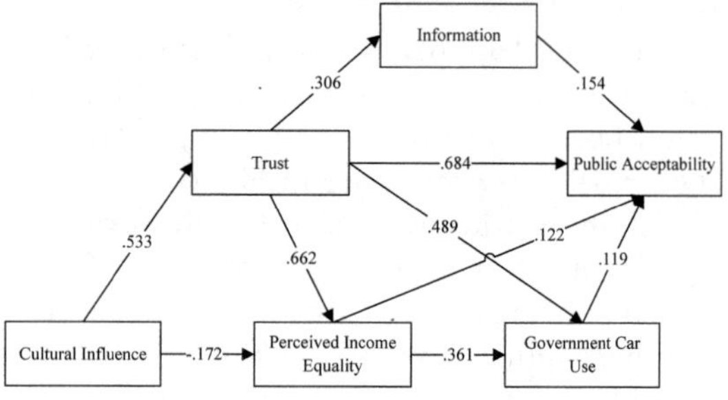

(a) Inside the Third Ring Road

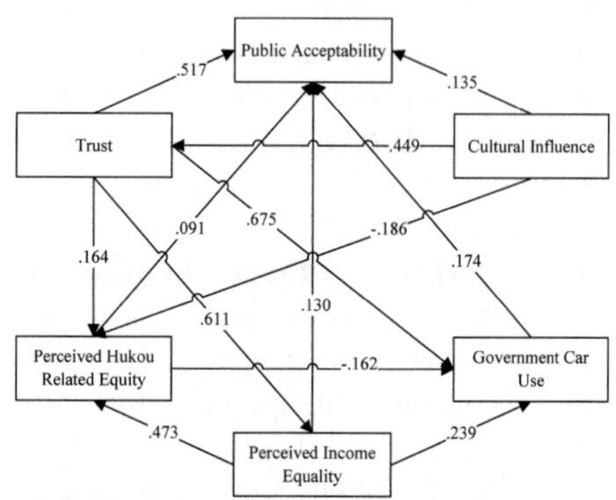

(b) The Third–the Fifth Ring Road

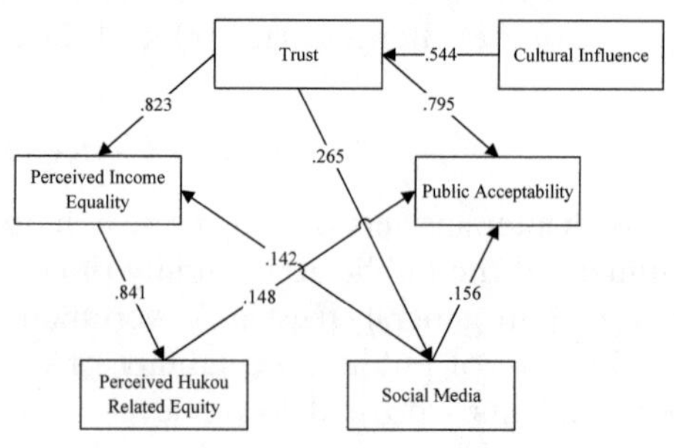

(c) Outside the Fifth Ring Road

another two determinants of public acceptability of congestion charging in the Chinese context. Other Western context-based determinants are not supported in the Chinese context, such as access to information and the perceived effectiveness of the proposed scheme, but it is noteworthy that the perceived effectiveness of previous transport policies is significantly correlated with the perceived effectiveness of congestion charging. These findings indicate that Western frameworks cannot be directly used to assess public acceptability in the Chinese context.

Subgroup comparisons revealed some interesting differences between population groups, even though they were sometimes difficult to interpret. Perceived income inequity had a stronger impact on young people's acceptability of congestion charging. The perceived effectiveness of congestion charging played a notable role in middle-aged people's acceptability while older people paid more attention to the effectiveness of previous policies. Low-income people were more likely to be influenced by the level of obedience, social conformity and trust in government and academics, while whether the government and academics are trustworthy or not had much less impact on high-income people's acceptability—their attitudes towards the policy mainly depended on to the extent to which they perceived the policy as equitable.

References

Arbuckle, J. L. (2010). *IBM SPSS Amos 19 user's guide* (p. 635). Amos Development Corporation.

Bagby, R. M., Parker, J. D., & Taylor, G. J. (1994). The twenty-item Toronto Alexithymia Scale—I. Item selection and cross-validation of the factor structure. *Journal of Psychosomatic Research, 38*(1), 23–32.

Barrett, P. (2007). Structural equation modelling: Adjudging model fit. *Personality and Individual Differences, 42*(5), 815–824.

Beck, A. T., Steer, R. A., & Brown, G. K. (1996). Beck depression inventory-II. *San Antonio, 78*(2), 490–498.

Beijing Municipal Bureau of Statistics. (2017). *Beijing Statistical Yearbook.* [Online] http://tjj.beijing.gov.cn/nj/main/2017-tjnj/zk/indexch.htm. Accessed 27 July 2019 (in Chinese).

Bentler, P. M. (1982). Confirmatory factor analysis via noniterative estimation: A fast, inexpensive method. *Journal of Marketing Research, 19*, 417–424.

Bentler, P. M., & Bonett, D. G. (1980). Significance tests and goodness of fit in the analysis of covariance structures. *Psychological Bulletin, 88*(3), 588–606.

Bentler, P. M., & Chou, C. P. (1987). Practical issues in structural modeling. *Sociological Methods & Research, 16*(1), 78–117.

Bentler, P. M., & Kano, Y. (1990). On the equivalence of factors and components. *Multivariate Behavioral Research, 25*(1), 67–74.

Bollen, K. A. (1989). *Structural equations with latent variables.* Wiley-Interscience Publication.

Boomsma, A. (1985). Nonconvergence, improper solutions, and starting values in LISREL maximum likelihood estimation. *Psychometrika, 50*(2), 229–242.

Browne, M. W., & Arminger, G. (1995). Specification and estimation of mean- and covariance-structure models. In *Handbook of statistical modeling for the social and behavioral sciences* (pp. 185–249). Springer.

Byrne, B. M. (2016). *Structural equation modeling with AMOS: Basic concepts, applications, and programming*. Routledge.

Cheung, G. W., & Rensvold, R. B. (2002). Evaluating goodness-of-fit indexes for testing measurement invariance. *Structural Equation Modeling, 9*(2), 233–255.

Churchill, G. A., & Iacobucci, D. (2006). *Marketing research: Methodological foundations*. Dryden Press.

Conway, J. M., & Huffcutt, A. I. (2003). A review and evaluation of exploratory factor analysis practices in organizational research. *Organizational Research Methods, 6*(2), 147–168.

Costello, A. B., & Osborne, J. W. (2005). Best practices in exploratory factor analysis: Four recommendations for getting the most from your analysis. *Practical Assessment, Research & Evaluation, 10*(7), 1–9.

Doll, W. J., Xia, W., & Torkzadeh, G. (1994). A confirmatory factor analysis of the end-user computing satisfaction instrument. *MIS Quarterly, 18*(4), 453–461.

Dong, J., & Blommaert, J. (2009). Space, scale and accents: Constructing migrant identity in Beijing. In J. Collins, S. Slembrouck, & M. Baynham (Eds.), *Globalization and language in contact* (pp. 42–61). Continuum.

Dunn, O. J. (1964). Multiple comparisons using rank sums. *Technometrics, 6*(3), 241–252.

Dunn, S. C., Seaker, R. F., & Waller, M. A. (1994). Latent variables in business logistics research: Scale development and validation. *Journal of Business Logistics, 15*(2), 145.

Fabrigar, L. R., Wegener, D. T., MacCallum, R. C., & Strahan, E. J. (1999). Evaluating the use of exploratory factor analysis in psychological research. *Psychological Methods, 4*(3), 272.

Fan, X., Thompson, B., & Wang, L. (1999). Effects of sample size, estimation methods, and model specification on structural equation modeling fit indexes. *Structural Equation Modeling: A Multidisciplinary Journal, 6*(1), 56–83.

Floyd, F. J., & Widaman, K. F. (1995). Factor analysis in the development and refinement of clinical assessment instruments. *Psychological Assessment, 7*(3), 286.

Fornell, C., & Larcker, D. F. (1981). Structural equation models with unobservable variables and measurement error: Algebra and statistics. *Journal of Marketing Research, 18*, 382–388.

Freidlin, B., & Gastwirth, J. L. (2000). Should the median test be retired from general use? *The American Statistician, 54*(3), 161–164.

Garver, M. S., & Mentzer, J. T. (1999). Logistics research methods: Employing structural equation modeling to test for construct validity. *Journal of Business Logistics, 20*(1), 33–57.

Gerbing, D. W., & Anderson, J. C. (1988). An updated paradigm for scale development incorporating unidimensionality and its assessment. *Journal of Marketing Research, 25*(2), 186–192.

Golob, T. F. (2003). Structural equation modeling for travel behavior research. *Transportation Research Part B: Methodological, 37*(1), 1–25.

Gorsuch, R. L. (1997). Exploratory factor analysis: Its role in item analysis. *Journal of Personality Assessment, 68*(3), 532–560.

Gow, A. J., Whiteman, M. C., Pattie, A., & Deary, I. J. (2005). Goldberg's 'IPIP' Big-Five factor markers: Internal consistency and concurrent validation in Scotland. *Personality and Individual Differences, 39*(2), 317–329.

Hair, J., Anderson, R., Tatham, R., & Black, W. (1995). *Multivariate data analysis with readings* (4th ed.). Prentice Hall International.

Hickman, R. L., Jr., Pinto, M. D., Lee, E., & Daly, B. J. (2012). Exploratory and confirmatory factor analysis of the decision regret scale in recipients of internal cardioverter defibrillators. *Journal of Nursing Measurement, 20*(1), 21–34.

Hoffmann, R., & Larner, J. (2013). The demography of Chinese nationalism: A field-experimental approach. *The China Quarterly, 213*, 189–204.

Hooper, D., Coughlan, J., & Mullen, M. (2008). Structural equation modelling: Guidelines for determining model fit. *Electronic Journal of Business Research Methods, 6*(1), 53–60.

Houston, M. B. (2004). Assessing the validity of secondary data proxies for marketing constructs. *Journal of Business Research, 57*(2), 154–161.

Howard, K. I., & Forehand, G. A. (1962). A method for correcting item-total correlations for the effect of relevant item inclusion. *Educational and Psychological Measurement, 22*(4), 731–735.

Hu, L., & Bentler, P. M. (1999). Cutoff criteria for fit indexes in covariance structure analysis: Conventional criteria versus new alternatives. *Structural Equation Modeling, 6*(1), 1–55.

Jolliffe, I. T. (1986). Principal component analysis and factor analysis. In *Principal component analysis*. Springer.

Jöreskog, K. G., & Sörbom, D. (1993). *LISREL 8: Structural equation modeling with the SIMPLIS command language*. Scientific Software International.

Kambhatla, N., & Leen, T. K. (1997). Dimension reduction by local principal component analysis. *Neural Computation, 9*(7), 1493–1516.

Kenny, D. A., & McCoach, D. B. (2003). Effect of the number of variables on measures of fit in structural equation modeling. *Structural Equation Modeling, 10*(3), 333–351.

Khodadady, E., & Hashemi, M. R. (2010). Construct validity of beliefs about language learning: Componential or factorial. *Ferdowsi Review, 1*(1), 3–20.

Kim, J. O., & Mueller, C. W. (1978). *Introduction to factor analysis: What it is and how to do it* (No. 13). Sage.

Kim, J., Schmöcker, J. D., Fujii, S., & Noland, R. B. (2013). Attitudes towards road pricing and environmental taxation among US and UK students. *Transportation Research Part A: Policy and Practice, 48*, 50–62.

Kline, P. (2014). *An easy guide to factor analysis*. Routledge.

Kline, R. B. (1998). *Principles and practice of structural equation modeling*. Guilford Press.

Koufteros, X. A. (1999). Testing a model of pull production: A paradigm for manufacturing research using structural equation modeling. *Journal of Operations Management, 17*(4), 467–488.

Koufteros, X., Vonderembse, M., & Doll, W. (2001). Concurrent engineering and its consequences. *Journal of Operations Management, 19*(1), 97–115.

Kriston, L., Scholl, I., Hölzel, L., Simon, D., Loh, A., & Härter, M. (2010). The 9-item Shared Decision Making Questionnaire (SDM-Q-9). Development and psychometric properties in a primary care sample. *Patient education and counseling, 80*(1), 94–99.

Kruskal, W. H., & Wallis, W. A. (1952). Use of ranks in one-criterion variance analysis. *Journal of the American Statistical Association, 47*(260), 583–621.

Li, W. (2013). "Hukou" status, place affiliation and identity formation: The case of migrant workers in Metropolitan Beijing. *Procedia Environmental Sciences, 17*, 842–851.

Liang, W., Lu, M., & Zhang, H. (2016). Housing prices raise wages: Estimating the unexpected effects of land supply regulation in China. *Journal of Housing Economics, 33*, 70–81.

Litwin, M. S., & Fink, A. (1995). *How to measure survey reliability and validity* (Vol. 7). Sage.

Lu, C. S., Lai, K. H., & Cheng, T. E. (2007). Application of structural equation modeling to evaluate the intention of shippers to use Internet services in liner shipping. *European Journal of Operational Research, 180*(2), 845–867.

MacCallum, R. C., & Hong, S. (1997). Power analysis in covariance structure modeling using GFI and AGFI. *Multivariate Behavioral Research, 32*(2), 193–210.

MacCallum, R. C., Browne, M. W., & Sugawara, H. M. (1996). Power analysis and determination of sample size for covariance structure modeling. *Psychological Methods, 1*(2), 130.

MacCallum, R. C., Widaman, K. F., Zhang, S., & Hong, S. (1999). Sample size in factor analysis. *Psychological Methods, 4*(1), 84.

Mann, H. B., & Whitney, D. R. (1947). On a test of whether one of two random variables is stochastically larger than the other. *The Annals of Mathematical Statistics*, 50–60.

Marsh, H. W., & Balla, J. (1994). Goodness of fit in confirmatory factor analysis: The effects of sample size and model parsimony. *Quality and Quantity, 28*(2), 185–217.

Maruyama, G. (1997). *Basics of structural equation modeling*. Sage.

Mattick, R. P., & Clarke, J. C. (1998). Development and validation of measures of social phobia scrutiny fear and social interaction anxiety. *Behaviour Research and Therapy, 36*(4), 455–470.

McDonald, R. P., & Ho, M. H. R. (2002). Principles and practice in reporting structural equation analyses. *Psychological Methods, 7*(1), 64–82.

Mulaik, S. A., James, L. R., Van Alstine, J., Bennett, N., Lind, S., & Stilwell, C. D. (1989). Evaluation of goodness-of-fit indices for structural equation models. *Psychological Bulletin, 105*(3), 430.

Nachar, N. (2008). The Mann-Whitney U: A test for assessing whether two independent samples come from the same distribution. *Tutorials in Quantitative Methods for Psychology, 4*(1), 13–20.

Norris, M., & Lecavalier, L. (2010). Evaluating the use of exploratory factor analysis in developmental disability psychological research. *Journal of Autism and Developmental Disorders, 40*(1), 8–20.

Nunnally, J. C. (1967). *Psychometric theory*. McGraw-Hill.

People's Daily. (2015). *Beijing authority reveal the population distribution of Beijing for the first time*. Available online: http://politics.people.com.cn/n/2015/0522/c1001-27039783.html. Accessed 27 July 2019 (in Chinese).

Podsakoff, P. M., Ahearne, M., & MacKenzie, S. B. (1997). Organizational citizenship behavior and the quantity and quality of work group performance. *Journal of Applied Psychology, 82*(2), 262–270.

Saxe, R., & Weitz, B. A. (1982). The SOCO scale: A measure of the customer orientation of salespeople. *Journal of Marketing Research, 19*(3), 343–351.

Schade, J., & Schlag, B. (2003). Acceptability of urban transport pricing strategies. *Transportation Research Part F: Traffic Psychology and Behaviour, 6*(1), 45–61.

Schermelleh-Engel, K., Moosbrugger, H., & Müller, H. (2003). Evaluating the fit of structural equation models: Tests of significance and descriptive goodness-of-fit measures. *Methods of Psychological Research Online, 8*(2), 23–74.

Schlag, B., & Teubel, U. (1997). Public acceptability of transport pricing. *IATSS Research, 21*, 134–142.

Schlegel, K., Grandjean, D., & Scherer, K. R. (2012). Emotion recognition: Unidimensional ability or a set of modality-and emotion-specific skills? *Personality and Individual Differences, 53*(1), 16–21.

Speckens, A. E., Spinhoven, P., Sloekers, P. P., Bolk, J. H., & van Hemert, A. M. (1996). A validation study of the Whitely Index, the Illness Attitude Scales, and the Somatosensory Amplification Scale in general medical and general practice patients. *Journal of Psychosomatic Research, 40*(1), 95–104.

Steiger, J. H. (1990). Structural model evaluation and modification: An interval estimation approach. *Multivariate Behavioral Research, 25*(2), 173–180.

Steiger, J. H. (2007). Understanding the limitations of global fit assessment in structural equation modeling. *Personality and Individual Differences, 42*(5), 893–898.

Stout, W. (2002). Psychometrics: From practice to theory and back. *Psychometrika, 67*(4), 485–518.

Suhr, D. D. (2005). Principal component analysis vs. exploratory factor analysis. *SUGI 30 Proceedings, 203*, 230.

Tabachnick, B. G., & Fidell, L. S. (2007). *Using multivariate statistics*. Allyn & Bacon/Pearson Education.

Tanaka, J. S. (1987). "How big is big enough?": Sample size and goodness of fit in structural equation models with latent variables. *Child Development, 58*(1), 134–146.

Tanaka, J. S. (1993). Multifaceted conceptions of fit in structure equation models. In K. A. Bollen & J. S. Long (Eds.), *Testing structural equation models* (pp. 136–162). Sage.

Thurstone, L. L. (1947). *Multiple-factor analysis: A development and expansion of the vectors of mind*. University of Chicago Press.

Vandenberg, R. J. (2006). Statistical and methodological myths and urban legends: Where, pray tell, did they get this idea? *Organizational Research Methods, 9*, 194–201.

Wheaton, B., Muthen, B., Alwin, D. F., & Summers, G. F. (1977). Assessing reliability and stability in panel models. *Sociological Methodology, 8*, 84–136.

Widaman, K. F. (1993). Common factor analysis versus principal component analysis: Differential bias in representing model parameters? *Multivariate Behavioral Research, 28*(3), 263–311.

Williams, L. J., & Holahan, P. J. (1994). Parsimony-based fit indices for multiple-indicator models: Do they work? *Structural Equation Modeling: A Multidisciplinary Journal, 1*(2), 161–189.

Wolf, E. J., Harrington, K. M., Clark, S. L., & Miller, M. W. (2013). Sample size requirements for structural equation models: An evaluation of power, bias, and solution propriety. *Educational and Psychological Measurement, 73*(6), 913–934.

Worthington, R. L., & Whittaker, T. A. (2006). Scale development research: A content analysis and recommendations for best practices. *The Counseling Psychologist, 34*(6), 806–838.

Yoo, B., & Donthu, N. (2001). Developing a scale to measure the perceived quality of an Internet shopping site (SITEQUAL). *Quarterly Journal of Electronic Commerce, 2*(1), 31–45.

Zhang, J., Wieczorek, W. F., Conwell, Y., & Tu, X. M. (2011). Psychological strains and youth suicide in rural China. *Social Science & Medicine, 72*(12), 2003–2010.

Zhao, S. (1998). A state-led nationalism: The patriotic education campaign in post-Tiananmen China. *Communist and Post-Communist Studies, 31*(3), 287–302.

Ziegler, M., & Hagemann, D. (2015). Testing the unidimensionality of items: Pitfalls and Loopholes. *European Journal of Psychological Assessment, 31*, 231–237.

CHAPTER 7

Discussion: Authoritarian Public Accessibility

This chapter discusses the appropriateness of Western frameworks for assessing the public acceptability of congestion charging in the Chinese context by comparing the framework established in this study and Western context-based frameworks in the literature. This comparison can help to explain existing similarities and the uniqueness of public acceptability between China and the West.

Figure 7.1 presents public acceptability and its determinants in the Chinese context. Compared to Western context-based frameworks (e.g., Eriksson et al., 2006, 2008; Schlag & Teubel, 1997), this is a very simple framework in which public acceptability is only influenced by four factors: cultural factors (obedience and conformity), trust, perceived income equity and government car use.

Ironically, determinants directly related to the policy in Western context-based frameworks are missing from this framework, including understandable information about the policy, the perceived effectiveness and efficiency of the policy and the allocation of revenue generated by this policy. These factors are important in the West because practically, the rationale for studying public acceptability is to identify sources of public support (e.g., Gaunt et al., 2006; Hårsman & Quigley, 2010), which is important for policymaking in democracies (e.g., Dalton et al., 2001; Zittel & Fuchs, 2007). To generate public support, people need understandable information to consider whether the charge can effectively

Q. Liu, *Public Acceptability of Congestion Charging in China*,
https://doi.org/10.1007/978-981-19-0236-9_7

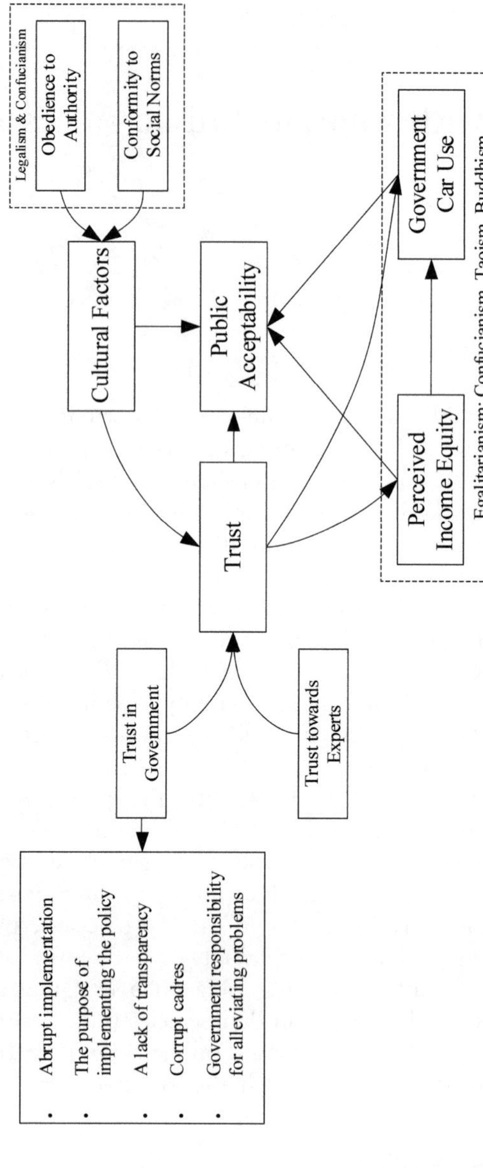

Fig. 7.1 Public acceptability in the Chinese context

alleviate the problem, whether it is the best available option and whether the revenue allocation is equitable.

However, as discussed in Chapter 4, the motivations for Chinese policymakers to consider public acceptability can hardly be generating public support for the policy—theoretically, they need to consider this because of the official ideology of the CCP "to serve the people"; pragmatically, they have to avoid trouble because on occasion, this type of policy may result in mass incidents, which will ruin the cadres' political careers. Although cadres always say that "the interests of the people come before all else" (simplified Chinese: 人民的利益高于一切),[1] cadres have never been obligated to consider the extent to which lay people feel satisfied with a policy before and after its implementation. Because the power of Chinese politicians is granted by their superiors instead of the public, they do not have to convince the public of the benefits of the policy. Therefore, the issue of public acceptability in the Chinese context is fundamentally different from that in democracies.

Due to the traditional Chinese (especially Legalist) relationship between the state and the people (Sect. 2.3.1.3) and the current political system (e.g., Wu, 2015a, b), there is no sufficient way for lay people to participate in policymaking. Therefore, naturally, there is no need for lay citizens to pay attention to information about a policy that is not yet implemented because they have never been allowed to think about how the government can improve the policy.

The perceived effectiveness of the proposed scheme is related to public acceptability in the Western context (e.g., Gärling & Schuitema, 2007; Jaensirisak et al., 2005). Since the policy will be implemented no matter how effective it is if the government (usually via a few high-level cadres) decides to do so, whether lay citizens perceive it as an effective policy before its implementation is irrelevant to their acceptance of the policy. Moreover, almost all policies implemented by all levels of government are propagated as effective, successful policies that meet the compelling needs of the people (see also Brady, 2009; Landsberger, 2001; Zhang, 2011). Thinking about the effectiveness of the proposed scheme is therefore a futile effort.

Furthermore, revenue allocation plays an important role in the West (e.g., Bristow et al., 2010; Gehlert et al., 2011; Jaensirisak et al., 2005;

[1] From the Constitution of the Communist Party of China. The original sentence is "the interests of the Party and the people come before all else".

Schuitema & Steg, 2008), but it should not be considered as a determinant of public acceptability in the Chinese context. Because of the traditional Legalist-Confucianist values (Sect. 2.3.1), it is more accurate to deem what the government delivers to the public as bestowing gifts on lay citizens, which can be accepted but cannot be expected. Thus, revenue management can never be a concern for Chinese lay citizens. Therefore, although some population groups (e.g., public transport users) may get benefits from certain means of revenue allocation, spontaneously thinking about how the government should allocate the money is completely out of the question in the Chinese context.

As discussed in Sect. 5.6, although perceived income equity is seemingly the same as one of the key determinants in the West, perceived equity, it has to be interpreted in a different way. Firstly, the Chinese interpretation of equity showed a strong egalitarian tendency with Chinese features (Sect. 2.3.2.1), which is different from the Western interpretation of egalitarianism (e.g., Bowles et al., 1998; Fogel, 2000). In this case, a Chinese egalitarian expectation would be to reduce the chance of car use equally for all lay citizens (see Sect. 5.6; Liu et al., 2019). Secondly, although inequities between the rich and the poor are closely related to accessibility opportunities, focus group participants paid less attention to whether they themselves have access to jobs, goods and services. Due to Chinese egalitarianism, people focused more on whether other population groups have a more convenient access to those opportunities. Thirdly, government car use was rarely discussed in the literature on the public acceptability of congestion charging, but it was one of the key determinants in the Chinese context. This is because government car users were perceived as the biggest, and probably the only winners from the policy—even if government cars are not free from the charge, taxpayers need to cover their cost. However, government cars are always linked to corruption. Private use of government cars has been widely reported (e.g., Li, 1998; Zhang & Chan, 2013) and the vast majority of survey respondents perceived this as a very serious problem (see Sect. 6.2.2.4). Fourthly, *hukou*-related inequity was identified as one of the main concerns in focus group discussions (see Sect. 5.6.3); however, the structure model did not support this finding. There are several possible reasons for this: (a) participants in migrant groups discussed a variety of *hukou*-related inequities; however, these inequities may not be perceived as issues related to congestion charging; (b) due to the stimulator strategy (see Sect. 3.4.3), focus group participants may somehow express more radical views, which may exaggerate negative attitudes towards the *hukou* system and (c) these determinants were most important for residents living outside the inner city districts, who are mostly new, poorer and marginalised migrants (see Sect. 6.3.3.5), which suggests that *hukou*-related issues are only concerns of some groups of people. Finally, the two determinants relating to social equity (perceived income inequities and government car use) are closely related to level of trust in the Chinese context.

Trust in government and trust towards experts predominantly influenced the public acceptability of congestion charging in the Chinese context (see Sect. 6.3). This corroborates previous research (e.g., Kim et al., 2013) that trust in government has the strongest effect on the public acceptability of congestion charge. This is distinct from the Western context because it seems to relate, drawing on the focus groups (see Sect. 5.5.1), to belief in whether the government is fully acting for the citizens when there is no alternative political choice available. In this case, trust in government can be reflected in the following aspects. Firstly, people perceived implementing a charge as a typically abrupt way to solve problems and a sign of local cadres' dereliction of duty. Secondly, the purpose of implementing a charging policy is usually perceived as collecting money from the public in the Chinese context. Thirdly, although focus group participants did not expect particular ways to reallocate revenue generated from the policy, it is a shared understanding that the revenue management cannot be transparent. Fourthly, evidence from focus groups and the survey indicated that most people perceived corruption as a pervasive phenomenon in contemporary China. Fifthly, this policy was regarded as shirking government's responsibility for alleviating problems by placing responsibility with lay citizens. These five aspects have fuelled a clear narrative about how corrupt cadres (who represent the CCP) attempt to use the congestion charging policy as a tool to grab money from lay citizens.

Academics and experts were extremely disliked by both focus group participants and survey respondents. This is because the government only consults with alleged experts instead of seeking the opinions of the public (Zhao, 2005). However, the effectiveness of previous policies that were widely endorsed by experts have often not met citizens' expectations; therefore, academics and experts were perceived as the "running dogs" (simplified Chinese: 走狗, 狗腿子) of the privileged class (see Sect. 5.5.2 and Sect. 6.2.2.5).

The findings of this study also verify the hypothesis that obedience to authority and conformity to social norms have a significant impact on public acceptability in the Chinese context. This sort of contextual factor has not been taken into consideration in previous policy acceptability literature.

Because of the strong central power and the limited political freedoms in an authoritarian regime like China, lay citizens are subordinate to the state, the government and the Party. Therefore, the public acceptability of a policy reflects an overall attitude towards the government rather than a perception of the particular policy. In the framework in Fig. 7.1, all the other determinants are closely related to trust in government—external experts are the mouthpiece of the government, social inequities are caused by improper policies implemented by the government, and government cars are used for private purposes because the Government has connived with corrupt cadres. Fundamentally, the difference between public acceptability in the Chinese and Western contexts is the difference between authoritarian and democratic regimes. As Marx (1843, pp. 88–89) stated:

> In all states distinct from democracy the state, the law, the constitution is dominant without really governing, that is, materially permeating the content of the remaining non-political spheres. In democracy the constitution, the law, the state, so far as it is political constitution, is itself only a self-determination of the people, and a determinate content of the people.

References

Brady, A. M. (2009). *Marketing dictatorship: Propaganda and thought work in contemporary China*. Rowman & Littlefield Publishers.

Bristow, A. L., Wardman, M., Zanni, A. M., & Chintakayala, P. K. (2010). Public acceptability of personal carbon trading and carbon tax. *Ecological Economics, 69*(9), 1824–1837.

Bowles, S., Gintis, H., & Brighouse, H. (1998). *Recasting egalitarianism: New rules for communities, states and markets*. Verso.

Dalton, R. J., Burklin, W. P., & Drummond, A. (2001). Public opinion and direct democracy. *Journal of Democracy, 12*(4), 141–153.

Eriksson, L., Garvill, J., & Nordlund, A. M. (2006). Acceptability of travel demand management measures: The importance of problem awareness, personal norm, freedom, and fairness. *Journal of Environmental Psychology, 26*(1), 15–26.

Eriksson, L., Garvill, J., & Nordlund, A. M. (2008). Acceptability of single and combined transport policy measures: The importance of environmental and policy specific beliefs. *Transportation Research Part A: Policy and Practice, 42*(8), 1117–1128.

Fogel, R. W. (2000). *The fourth great awakening and the future of egalitarianism.* University of Chicago Press.

Gärling, T., & Schuitema, G. (2007). Travel demand management targeting reduced private car use: Effectiveness, public acceptability and political feasibility. *Journal of Social Issues, 63*(1), 139–153.

Gaunt, M., Rye, T., & Ison, S. (2006). Gaining public support for congestion charging: Lessons from referendum in Edinburgh Scotland. *Transportation Research Record, 1960*(1), 87–93.

Gehlert, T., Kramer, C., Nielsen, O. A., & Schlag, B. (2011). Socioeconomic differences in public acceptability and car use adaptation towards urban road pricing. *Transport Policy, 18*(5), 685–694.

Hårsman, B., & Quigley, J. M. (2010). Political and public acceptability of congestion pricing: Ideology and self-interest. *Journal of Policy Analysis and Management, 29*(4), 854–874.

Jaensirisak, S., Wardman, M., & May, A. D. (2005). Explaining variations in public acceptability of road pricing schemes. *Journal of Transport Economics and Policy, 39*(2), 127–153.

Kim, J., Schmöcker, J. D., Fujii, S., & Noland, R. B. (2013). Attitudes towards road pricing and environmental taxation among US and UK students. *Transportation Research Part A: Policy and Practice, 48*, 50–62.

Landsberger, S. R. (2001). Learning by what example? Educational propaganda in twenty-first-century China. *Critical Asian Studies, 33*(4), 541–571.

Liu, Q., Lucas, K., & Marsden, G. (2020). Public acceptability of congestion charging in Beijing, China: How transferrable are Western ideas of public acceptability? *International Journal of Sustainable Transportation, 15*(2), 97–110.

Liu, Q., Lucas, K., Marsden, G., & Liu, Y. (2019). Egalitarianism and public perception of social inequities: A case study of Beijing congestion charge. *Transport Policy, 74*, 47–62.

Marx, K. (1843 [1977]). *Critique of Hegel's "Philosophy of Right"* (J. O'Malley, Ed.). Cambridge University Press.

Schlag, B., & Teubel, U. (1997). Public acceptability of transport pricing. *IATSS Research, 21*, 134–142.

Schuitema, G., & Steg, L. (2008). The role of revenue use in the acceptability of transport pricing policies. *Transportation Research Part F: Traffic Psychology and Behaviour, 11*(3), 221–231.

Wu, G. (2015a). *China's Party Congress: Power, legitimacy, and institutional manipulation.* Cambridge University Press.

Wu, G. (2015b). *Paradoxes of China's Prosperity: Political Dilemmas and Global Implications*. World Scientific.

Zhang, Q., & Chan, J. L. (2013). New development: Fiscal transparency in China—Government policy and the role of social media. *Public Money & Management, 33*(1), 71–75.

Zhang, X. (2011). *The transformation of political communication in China: From propaganda to hegemony*. World Scientific.

Zhao, D. (2015). *The Confucian-Legalist State: A new theory of Chinese history*. Oxford University Press.

Zittel, T., & Fuchs, D. (Eds.). (2007). *Participatory democracy and political participation: Can participatory engineering bring citizens back in?* Routledge.

CHAPTER 8

Conclusion and Recommendations

This final chapter of this book synthesises its research findings and clarifies its implications for further research and policymaking. It presents the key determinants of the public acceptability of congestion charging in the city of Beijing and discusses the extent to which Western notions of public acceptability are transferable to a different context. The chapter starts with the research questions the thesis answers. Next, a number of policy implications derived from the key findings are provided. The key findings that address the gaps in the literature are outlined. Then the empirical, methodological and theoretical contributions of the research to knowledge are outlined. The limitations of the study are then introduced. Finally, it discusses the implications for future studies.

8.1 Research Questions

8.1.1 Do Policymakers Consider Public Acceptability, and Why?

There is no simple answer to this question—professional stakeholders had different opinions about whether public acceptability has been and should be a concern of policymakers. Even so, most of the interviewees stated or implied that high-level cadres, especially party leaders, attach great importance to this issue, whereas public opinions are conventionally ignored by lower-level cadres, especially grassroots cadres.

Q. Liu, *Public Acceptability of Congestion Charging in China*,
https://doi.org/10.1007/978-981-19-0236-9_8

People who may potentially play a role in the policymaking in this context were identified prior to investigating policymakers' opinions. The results show that academics and planners were not considered policymakers, although some academics may be consulted about the policy (see also Almén, 2016; Wang & Guo, 2015). Nonetheless, they acted as observers who interpreted the motivation for implementing public policies and cadres' behaviours. Despite the complexity of the power relations, cadres were able to answer questions about public acceptability and surprisingly, they had a shared view on its role in the policymaking.

According to the interviewees, there are two drivers that motivate high-level cadres to consider public acceptability. First, theoretically, considering public acceptability is derived from the governing idea of the CCP "to serve the people"; hence, high-level cadres were deemed self-motivated to consider this issue by most of the interviewees due to their higher level of self-cultivation and theoretical understanding of Chinese Marxism-Leninism. More practically, high-level cadres have to think about citizens' attitudes towards proposed policies because unfavourable policies have increasingly caused mass incidents, which may considerably undermine China's authoritarian rules (see also Chen & Reese, 2015; Lee & Zhang, 2013; Yang, 2009; Zheng, 2009).

However, due to a series of barriers, public opinions may not be a major concern for low-level cadres who are more directly involved in the policymaking for specific policies. Firstly, socialist ideology is no longer the main reason for being a member of the Party (see also Dynon, 2008; Holbig, 2013; Kwong, 1994; Sun, 2017); consequently, it is difficult to carry out theoretical governing ideas at the grassroots level. Secondly, compared to a variety of shortcuts to pursue cadres' political careers, such as vanity projects and bribery (e.g., Wang, 2016; Ye et al., 2014), the public acceptability of proposed policies is usually not one of the criteria for cadres' assessment; therefore, public opinions are more likely to be deemed an encumbrance on the path to their career advancement. Thirdly, public discontent with the scheme can be more effectively alleviated via media control (see also Buekens & Boudry, 2015). Fourthly, lay citizens further discourage cadres from thinking about the public acceptability of proposed schemes because of several culture-specific characteristics of the Chinese people, which were repeatedly mentioned by participants in both stakeholder interviews and focus groups, such as obedience to authority, the supremacy of rulers and the unwillingness to express opinions. It is a shared understanding by interviewees and focus group participants that ignoring public acceptability in local-level policymaking is prevalent.

Although the answer to this question remains unclear—different, sometimes contradictory, explanations and interpretations have been given by different interviewees—recent evidence shows that public opinion has become increasingly important for local policymaking (e.g., Cai & Zhou, 2019; Esarey, 2015; Heberer & Trappel, 2013; Liu et al., 2017; Wu et al., 2018). However, none of the interviewees mentioned gaining public support as a motivation for considering public acceptability. The political pressure that urges local cadres to consider public acceptability comes from their superiors instead of the public. Therefore, the core concern of public acceptability in this context is to avoid troubles and risks instead of obtaining public support. It further influences citizens' interpretations of what the government should deliver and their expectations from the implementation of the policy.

8.1.2 *To What Extent Are Western Notions of Public Acceptability Transferrable to the Chinese Context?*

Since acceptability and acceptance are the same word in Chinese language (see Sect. 4.2"), interviewees and focus group participants mostly did not differentiate between citizens' attitudes towards the policy and their reactions to the policy after its implementation. A proposed scheme is therefore inevitably deemed acceptable to the public whatsoever because the public has to follow the rules once the policy is implemented, even if many citizens dislike it. Hence, to understand what the Western notion of public acceptability means in this context, we must focus on people's attitudes towards a policy and their approvals, complaints, criticism and jokes instead of their anticipated reactions, which are normally substituted by passive and sometimes reluctant obedience to authority.

Most of the themes that emerged from focus group discussions with citizens are different from Western context-based determinants of the public acceptability of congestion charging. Although these factors might be conceptualised using the same words as in Western frameworks, they must be interpreted differently.

Information plays an important role in the Western context because policymakers have to inform the public about the aims and measures of the policy to secure public support (e.g., Gärling & Schuitema, 2007; Rye et al., 2008). Hence the complexity and understandable details of the proposed scheme have been considered as factors influencing public acceptability in the Western context (e.g., Clee, 2007; Francke & Kaniok, 2013). In this study, however, the theme information refers to a lack of access to information about the proposed scheme before the implementation and mistrust of information from official sources. Although many participants believed that lay citizens can acquire more information nowadays via social media, there is no evidence that their attitudes towards the policy are influenced by social media.

Due to the lack of information about the proposed scheme, the perceived effectiveness of congestion charging was rarely based on cost–benefit considerations. Instead, the perceived effectiveness of the proposed scheme greatly depends on their attitudes towards previous policies (not only transport policies, but also all public policies) and the government in general. Perceived effectiveness has been highlighted as one of the most important determinants of the public acceptability of congestion charging (e.g., Gärling & Schuitema, 2007; Kallbekken & Sælen, 2011); however, no clear connection between perceived effectiveness and acceptability emerged from the group discussions.

Perceived inequity significantly influences people's attitudes towards congestion charging in the group discussions, which is consistent with evidence from the West (e.g., Börjesson et al., 2015; Hysing, 2015; Weinstein & Sciara, 2006). Moreover, the results revealed that perceived inequity is correlated with perceived effectiveness in this context—those who believed the policy can effectively alleviate congestion and smog problems were also inclined to anticipate that the policy may cause further social inequities. Since congestion charging was deemed a new privilege to the privileged class, an ineffective policy was expected by those who were more concerned about social inequities.

Numerous studies identified trust in government as a key determinant of public acceptability (e.g., Kim et al., 2013). The results from focus group discussions suggest that trust is strongly correlated with other determinants of public acceptability, namely access to information, perceived effectiveness and perceived inequities. In this study, trust towards both government and experts significantly influenced participants' attitudes towards the proposed scheme. Experts and academics, who have been repeatedly referred to as lackeys of the party, received even more criticism than the government. Those who had less negative attitudes towards the government were apparently less hostile to congestion charging. Most of the criticisms of implementing congestion charging related to the absence of trust in government, including (a) the abrupt way of implementing policies, (b) the purpose of implementing a charging policy—to collect money from the public, (c) a lack of transparency in revenue management, (d) pervasive corruption and (e) the government's responsibility to solve problems.

Some determinants identified in the Western context were found inappropriate to investigate public acceptability in the Chinese context. As expected, personal freedom and privacy were not concerns of the participants, which is in line with the literature on collectivist cultures (e.g., Maynard & Taylor, 1996; Miltgen & Peyrat-Guillard, 2014). Revenue allocation, although it was mentioned by some participants, should be deemed an inseparable component of the construct trust in government instead of an independent factor influencing public acceptability.

To conclude, the answer to RQ2 is that due to the strong central power and limited political freedoms in an authoritarian regime (e.g., Levitsky & Way, 2010; Shorten, 2012), individuals are subordinate to the country and considering personal interests is discouraged. Public acceptability of a policy, therefore, reflects an overall attitude towards the government rather than a perception of the particular policy.

8.1.3 *What Factors Influence the Public Acceptability of Congestion Charging in the Chinese Context?*

The SEM analysis of the public survey results shows that trust in government and trust towards experts play a dominant role in respondents' support or lack of support for congestion charging. This corroborates previous research (Kim et al., 2013) that trust has the strongest effect on the public acceptability of congestion charging. This is distinct from the Western context because it seems to relate, drawing on the focus groups, to belief in whether government is fully acting for the citizens when there is no alternative in prospect. The results verify the hypothesis that obedience to authority and social norms have a significant impact on public acceptability in the Chinese context. The results are in line with the Western literature that public acceptability is influenced by perceived fairness (e.g., Jakobsson et al., 2000) but this extends to perceptions of government car use (see also Chen & Zhao, 2013).

Some other determinants that have previously been important in the Western context are not supported in the Chinese context, such as access to information and the perceived effectiveness of the proposed scheme. In agreement with the result from Nanjing (Sun et al., 2016), I concluded that perceived effectiveness does not affect public acceptability in the Chinese context. Together, the dominant influence of trust, perceived inequity and obedience, as well as a lack of consideration of the effectiveness of the plan, can manifest the main differences between public acceptability in the Western and Chinese contexts.

China's policymaking process (Lieberthal & Oksenberg, 1990; Wu, 2015a, b) may lead to the key differences in public acceptability. Chinese people are assumed to be indifferent concerning detailed information about policies that are still at the planning stage; hence, access to information is regarded as unnecessary to acquire public support in China. This assumption has ineluctably led to a pervasive expert-cult phenomenon (e.g., Zhang & Chen, 2004) that the government only consults with experts instead of seeking the opinions of the public (Zhao, 2005). Citizens, therefore, do not have experiences of personally evaluating the effectiveness of a proposed scheme. Consequently, public acceptability depends largely on people's attitudes towards the government and experts, but is not very much affected by citizens' perceptions of the effectiveness of the policies that might be under scrutiny. However, the effectiveness of previous policies that were widely endorsed by experts have often not met citizens' expectations. This could explain respondents' hostility to experts and the lack of importance of information.

To sum up, many of the constructs in Western acceptability studies are either inappropriate or subject to quite different interpretations, and therefore the Western notion of public acceptability cannot easily be transferred to an authoritarian context such as China.

8.2 Policy Implications

The messages to policymakers are straightforward—simply adopting Western ideas of policy acceptability and directly using Western context-based methods cannot adequately accommodate citizens' attitudes to inform public policymaking.

Marsden and Stead (2011) found that policy transfers between similar contexts are pervasive in the transport domain while policies and practices that attract Chinese policymakers are mostly adopted from Western contexts (Wang, 2010). However, the findings of this study suggest that such activities may lead to undesirable and most probably negative consequences. For example, since an effective congestion charge was perceived as conferring another privilege on an already privileged group (especially cadres) by many of those who are concerned about social inequities while perceived effectiveness does not influence public acceptability, stubbornly emphasising the effectiveness of congestion charging in problem alleviation may not just be a futile attempt, but also a decision that provokes citizens' hostility to the privileged and ultimately, the government. Due to the absence of citizens' engagement in the policymaking process and countless unsuccessful policies endorsed by experts and academics, professional advocacy may not help to convince citizens of the benefits of the policy. These lessons cannot easily be drawn from the Western literature. Policymakers and practitioners should therefore build their understanding upon field investigations into the cultural and political contexts when considering policy transfers.

The findings also suggest that most of measures to generate public support in the Western context may not have the same outcomes in China because the public acceptability of congestion charging in the Chinese context is dominantly influenced by people's attitudes towards the CCP, and many important determinants in the Western context do not have significant impacts. As discussed in Chapters 5 and "6", the fundamental cause of these differences is the strong central power and the limited political freedoms. Although theoretically, the people are the masters of the country, findings from focus group discussions clearly manifested a shared perception that lay citizens are belittled and inferior. This implies that the institution of "the position of the people as masters of the country" is at least not sufficiently implemented at the level of grassroots administration.

In the Chinese context, there are many shortcuts to increase public support for congestion charging in the short term. Firstly, the government can launch propaganda campaigns to improve people's general attitudes towards the Party. The government could create a narrative that, on the one hand, introduces a few successful congestion charging policies in the West to indicate that the policy is not merely a money grab tool, and on the other hand, satirises unimplemented plans because of the Western democratic process. This can be used to influence suggestible citizens that thinking about personal gains and losses is morally wrong and that self-sacrifice is for the greater good of the society. Further, this enhances the official discourse that China's model is better than Western democracy and therefore promotes public trust in government. Secondly, because conformity to social norms is a key determinant and because of the traditional Confucian culture, the government could focus on convincing older people of the aim of the policy (alleviating smog), which is important for their descendants. Thirdly, efforts could be made to convince different groups of people that other population groups will sacrifice more because of the proposed scheme. This can be especially useful to convince lower income people and new migrants because they are more likely to expect an egalitarian policy outcome—the Government does not necessarily guarantee them a more equitable redistribution, but the chance that richer people will no longer be able to use their cars may effectively win their hearts. Fourthly, anti-corruption campaigns that focus on private use of government cars may be helpful to generate public support for this policy. However, these measures cannot have positive long-term effects, and some may have negative effects in the longer term.

To cope with the low acceptability of this policy and other policies in the longer term, some fundamental changes in the relationship between the government and the people are necessary. Although in China's official ideology, the dictatorship of the proletariat is the nature of Socialist states, working-class people, lay citizens, do not have a chance to exercise their political power. The results showed that the public was indifferent about public affairs. Therefore, efforts should be made to encourage lay citizens to participate in policymaking by providing access to information and secured channels to gather public opinions. Since lay citizens are discontented with the CCP's abrupt way of solving problems, incorporating citizens' satisfaction levels into the cadres' performance assessment may restrict local cadres. To eliminate the preconceived idea that the purpose of implementing a charging policy is to collect money from the public, the government should attempt to consult with lay citizens about revenue management, and the revenue allocation should be transparent. Making cadres' assets (including assets overseas) public could be the silver bullet for tackling corruption. However, all these measures require institutional changes that are highly unlikely to happen in the next 10 years. This is because of the traditional Legalist-Confucian state-people relationship in which the ruled are deemed trivial things owned by the ruler. The nature of public acceptability in the Chinese context will not change if the state-people relationship keeps the status quo. *When a policy must be treated as infinite royal graciousness that can only be bestowed, lay citizens can never really think about whether they want to accept it or not.*

It is worth noting that such a relationship is against Marxist theory. In Marx's *Critique of the Gotha Program* (1875, p. 94), he attacked the programme because it fundamentally misunderstood the state–society relationship:

> It is by no means the aim of the workers, who have got rid of the narrow mentality of humble subjects, to set the state free. In the German Empire, the "state" is almost as "free" as in Russia. Freedom consists in converting the state from an organ superimposed upon society into one completely subordinate to it; and today, too, the forms of state are more free or less free to the extent that they restrict the "freedom of the state".
>
> The German Workers' party—at least if it adopts the program—shows that its socialist ideas are not even skin-deep; in that, instead of treating existing society (and this holds good for any future one) as the basis of the existing state (or of the future state in the case of future society), it treats the state rather as an independent entity that possesses its own intellectual, ethical, and libertarian bases.

The China model, including the political and economic policies of the P.R. China after Mao's death in 1976, has recently been thought of as an alternative for developing countries. This is partly because the Government is able to "concentrate on accomplishing major tasks" (simplified Chinese: 集中力量办大事). Policies and mega projects have been approved and implemented speedily. However, this seemingly effective and efficient approach may result in increasingly serious problems. The core of this model is a leading role of an authoritarian Party, an absence of political liberalisation, and belittled lay citizens who have to sacrifice their own rights and benefits for the "greater good of the society". As the research findings revealed, lay citizens are discontent with the proposed scheme and previous policies, dissatisfied with current social inequity, and ultimately, disappointed in the government and its cadres. It is questionable how this model can alleviate these accumulated problems, because in such circumstances, policymakers are unable to hear the (real) voice of the people even if they want to, and therefore they cannot find a proper way to "serve the people".

8.3 Contribution to Knowledge

This section discusses the empirical, methodological and theoretical contribution of the research to knowledge.

8.3.1 *Empirical Contribution to Knowledge*

One of the gaps in the literature was a lack of investigation into the public acceptability of congestion charging in authoritarian regimes. Interpretation of how lay citizens in an authoritarian state perceive a policy as acceptable and which key elements may influence public acceptability were also less developed.

During this research, people's attitudes towards the idea of congestion charging were explored in the context of Beijing. This challenged not only a shared understanding among high-level cadres that Chinese lay citizens are more likely to perceive congestion charging as acceptable than people in democratic states, but also previous studies, which usually directly adopted Western context-based frameworks and determinants to define and study public acceptability in the Chinese context.

This research has shown that public acceptability is a relatively less complex issue in the Chinese context than in Western frameworks. Many previously identified factors influencing public acceptability are missing from public acceptability in the Chinese context, such as access to information, the perceived effectiveness of the proposed scheme and revenue allocation. However, trust towards government and experts predominantly influences people's support for congestion charging. Also, obedience to authority and conformity to social norms significantly influence public acceptability in the Chinese context.

By scrutinising the relationship between public acceptability and its key determinants in the Chinese context, this research suggests that the government is unlikely to obtain public support for a particular policy by advocating it as an effective way to alleviate the problems. Rebuilding public trust in government can fundamentally change people's attitudes towards proposed schemes.

8.3.2 *Methodological Contribution to Knowledge*

The methodological approach enabled an opportunity to understand the complex nature of public acceptability in the Chinese context instead of relying on existing Western context-based frameworks and statistically motivated models to conduct analysis.

Qualitative approaches were rarely used to study transport policies in the Chinese context. Most researchers directly adopted Western context-based frameworks to obtain some evidence from China without thinking about the differences between the contexts. Previous studies on the public acceptability/acceptance of Chinese transport policies, therefore, can only add some contextually unique determinants into the existing frameworks based on the subjective feelings of the authors. These newly added factors were usually fragmented; hence, it was difficult to interpret the results and to use these factors in future studies.

The abductive approach used to conduct stakeholder interviews is especially useful to explore policy-related issues in an authoritarian context because the policymaking cannot be transparent, and sometimes it is difficult to identify the true policymakers. This approach was used to generate an interpretation of cadres' (as the representatives of the CCP) motivation for considering public opinion, which could be compared with the presumption of public acceptability in democracies, where citizens can exercise their political power. This helped me to understand the fundamental differences between public acceptability in the Chinese and Western contexts.

Focus groups were rarely used in the transport field in China, probably because it is time consuming and Chinese people are assumed unwilling to participate in such a discussion with strangers. The stimulator tactic used in this study can be used to encourage people to participate actively in group discussions.

Based on the methodological approach, results from stakeholder interviews and focus group discussions were used to inform the questionnaire design. All the items were selected from key themes formed in the qualitative analysis and were quoted from focus group discussions. This ensured that the quantitative survey could include all the relevant elements that might influence public acceptability and scrutinise the relationship between these factors, which is important for using SEM. The quantitative survey then tested the hypotheses developed from qualitative studies. In summary, using a mixed approach enabled me to capture the messiness of public opinions on congestion charging in the Chinese context.

8.3.3 Theoretical Contribution to Knowledge

Reviewing the traditional Chinese schools of thoughts and current political system challenged the existing Western context-based interpretation of public acceptability. The public acceptability of a policy should be interpreted in a different way in an authoritarian context where the public is subordinated to those who have the power to make a policy. In such circumstances, public acceptability should be treated as the willingness to obey the authority rather than a supportive attitude towards the proposed scheme. Consequently, the general attitudes towards the authority play a more important role in forming public acceptability than in democracies, and the acceptability of a particular policy could also be used to reflect public attitudes towards the government.

Despite the fact that a variety of policies have been transferred to China from the West since the economic reform, few have studied the transferability of Western ideas or policy to an authoritarian context. This study revealed how the notion of public acceptability deviated from its democratic underpinnings. Due to the vagueness of the Chinese language, the fact that the people have to obey an implemented policy was used to claim a high acceptance of the policy, which further generated an official narrative showing the support, approval, satisfaction and consent of the people.

The results showed that the two contextual factors, obedience to authority and conformity to social norms, significantly influence public acceptability in the Chinese context, which suggested that contextual factors are more important than has been previously considered within public acceptability studies.

8.4 Limitations

This section discusses the limitations of each part of the study.

Since the sample of stakeholder interviews was not big enough and the participants were selected via personal connections, the results, inevitably, are subject to the selection of participants, which may exclude those who play important roles in policymaking but regard public acceptability as less relevant. Moreover, the selection of interviewees was based on a presumption that only high-level cadres matter in the policymaking, whereas the role of low-level cadres, especially grassroots cadres, was discussed by many interviewees. Their opinions, however, were not reflected in this study. This sample, therefore, does not represent the full range of opinion on this matter. Furthermore, although the abductive research strategy generated rich and in-depth data to interpret policymakers' opinions about public acceptability and their motivations to consider it, it is difficult to verify the interpretation directly. Nonetheless, I attempted to understand the decision-making context, which is one of the underlying causes of the non-transferability of the Western notion of public acceptability.

The policy used for focus group discussions had to be hypothetical because there was no proposed scheme at hand when the discussions took place. Due to the sampling technique, the focus group participants may have been more sensitive to the congestion charging policy, which may have exaggerated the problems. Despite the fact that the stimulator tactic has successfully encouraged participants who might initially be unwilling to share their ideas with strangers to participate actively in group discussions, it is likely that moderate opinions were difficult to find. This may further exaggerate the problems, since those with extreme views, to some extent, dominated the debates. Also, most of the poor migrants were inclined to go along with others; thus, it is doubtful whether their own opinions have been reflected. Although this qualitative study cannot represent all the views of lay citizens, it helps to develop a deep understanding of different ways in which different population groups might respond to a congestion charging scheme and to conduct a quantitative survey to explore key determinants of the public acceptability of congestion charging in the Chinese context.

The quantitative survey has following limitations. First, a number of culture-specific factors identified in focus group discussions were not examined. Although they might be potentially important in shaping people's attitudes towards the proposed scheme, they are either difficult to quantify or have unclarified relations with other factors. Second, this is a small sample in Beijing terms, and therefore it still cannot be representative. Third, problem perceptions, including perceptions of congestion and smog, were excluded from the analysis due to low internal consistency. Nevertheless, this is unlikely to have significant impacts on the modelling results because most of the respondents were well aware of both of the problems and the problem perceptions. They influenced public acceptability via information and perceived effectiveness, neither of which were significant in the public acceptability of congestion charging. Fourth, the results can only reflect people's attitudes towards the general concept of congestion charging instead of a concrete proposed scheme, which is, to some extent, different from public acceptability studies in the Western context. Nonetheless, the results are sufficiently clear to suggest that Western ideas of policy acceptability cannot be directly transferred to analyse attitudes in the Chinese context.

8.5 Future Research Implications

The public acceptability of road pricing schemes has been extensively studied in the past; however, most of the studies were carried out in democracies, which share similar policymaking processes. Therefore, it is questionable whether Western context-based frameworks for analysing public acceptability and previous empirical findings are transferrable to different contexts such as China, which is distinct from the West culturally, socially and politically. As China has increasingly engaged in international affairs (e.g., Harnisch et al., 2015; Tull, 2006) and the China model has received attention in various domains and been introduced in developing countries (e.g., Bell, 2016; Teets, 2014), the case of China can provide valuable insights from a different standpoint into how public acceptability is viewed and what factors influence public attitudes towards a proposed scheme.

This research helps to fill in the gap between public acceptability studies in the Western context and their transferability to non-Western contexts. This research presents an attempt to understand the role of public acceptability in the policymaking and to explore factors influencing the public acceptability of transport policies in an authoritarian context.

Stakeholder interviews provided an opportunity to get a glimpse into how policymakers consider the public acceptability issue in this context and to interpret their motivations to address it thereafter. Although interpretations generated via the abductive research strategy cannot easily be verified, this research is an initial attempt to scrutinise the role of public acceptability in the policymaking of a transport policy. Due to the limited number of studies in the Chinese context, this interpretation requires further evidence to verify it. While this research was intended to sort out the roles that cadres from different organs might play, the mechanism of power during policymaking remains obscure; it further raised the question of how different levels of cadres consider public acceptability and exercise their power. This deserves further exploration to understand the policymaking process and to identify key decision-makers who should be targeted for more in-depth understanding of this issue. Moreover, since the abductive research strategy can yield the most likely conjecture based on observation, it can be widely applied in future investigations into issues relating to the policymaking, which is an elusive process in almost every authoritarian regime.

Focus group discussions were undertaken to explore how lay citizens respond to the introduction of congestion charging and further, to identify potential determinants of public acceptability in the Chinese context. The results highlighted several culture-specific issues that were raised in group conversations on congestion charging. I set out to explore determinants of public acceptability in an authoritarian regime. However, this attempt was limited by the sample, the hypothetical scheme and the fact that most Chinese citizens are inexperienced in focus group discussions. Consequently, I piloted the stimulator tactic in this study. More evidence is necessary to support and diversify the findings from this study. Since the results suggest that the public acceptability of a policy largely depends on the general attitudes towards the government instead of the perception of the particular policy, the findings of this study can be generalised to other public policies in this context and be verified by different evidence bases. Most of the potential determinants identified in this study are well worth further investigation, such as access to information, perceived inequities and trust in government. The stimulator tactic, even though it is clearly an imperfect method that may silence moderate voices, is practical to encourage active opinion expressions. Unwillingness to express opinions is partly the reason why group discussions are rarely adopted to study Chinese context-based objectives; this tactic can therefore be applied in future observations on issues participants are not confident enough to discuss.

A more representative sample should be obtained to assess the public acceptability of congestion charging in the city of Beijing. Future research should be conducted to see if the acceptability of a concrete scheme is distinct from that of a general concept of congestion charging. Moreover, citizens' responses to details of the proposed scheme before and after the implementation deserve further investigation. Given the differences between cities, evidence from other sites can definitely enrich our understanding of the public acceptability of policies in the Chinese context. Most importantly, the findings of this study indicate that contextual cultural factors might be more important than has been previously considered within public acceptability studies. The role of context and cultural values should be considered in future studies.

Policy transfer (e.g., Dolowitz & Marsh, 2000; Evans, 2017; James & Lodge, 2003), policy diffusion (e.g., Berry, 1994; Boushey, 2010; Simmons & Elkins, 2004) and policy convergence (e.g., Bennett, 1991; Busch & Jörgens, 2005; Drezner, 2001) have been extensively studied since the '80s. Policy transfer and diffusion have played a significant part in China's economic and social development and governance practices since the economic reform. There are two seemingly contradictory phenomena in this process: on the one hand, in official discourses, which are also endorsed by the majority of Chinese academics, China must uphold its fundamental political system (the unity of the leadership of the Party, the position of the people as masters of the country and law-based governance[1]) and must never adopt a Western political structure, such as the separation of powers (QsTheory,[2] 2017); on the other hand, a wide range of economic and public policies have been directly copied from the West (e.g., Clifton & Díaz-Fuentes, 2014; Liu et al., 2014). There are clearly gaps in the literature on policy transfer and policy diffusion where authoritarian policy transfer, as well as policy transfer between democratic and authoritarian contexts, remains to be explored (see Hall & Ambrosio, 2017). Given the significant differences in cultural, political and institutional conditions between China and the West, policy transfer and diffusion in the Chinese context are probably distinct from Western contexts (see Foster, 2016). The high frequency and intensity of policy transfer and diffusion activities in post-reform China provide a strong and valuable evidence base to elucidate their mechanism in authoritarian regimes. Therefore, there is a compelling need for more effort in this research area.

References

Almén, O. (2016). Information for autocrats: Representation in Chinese local congresses. MELANIE MANION. Cambridge University Press, 2015. xii+ 189 pp.£ 59.99; $89.99. ISBN 978-1-107-63703-0. *The China Quarterly, 227*, 812–813.

Bell, D. A. (2016). *The China model*. Princeton University Press.

[1] It is noteworthy that leadership of the Party is above all. As three generations of the CCP leadership (Jiang, Hu and Xi) repeatedly stated in reports at Party Congress, "Leadership of the Party is the fundamental guarantee that the people are the masters of the country and that the country is ruled by law (党的领导是人民当家作主和依法治国的根本保证)" (Hu, 2012; Jiang, 1997; Xi, 2017).

[2] QsTheory (求是) is a political theory periodical published by the Central Party School and the Central Committee of the CCP. It is the Communist Party's main theoretical journal.

Bennett, C. J. (1991). What is policy convergence and what causes it? *British Journal of Political Science, 21*(2), 215–233.

Berry, F. S. (1994). Innovation in public management: The adoption of strategic planning. *Public Administration Review*, 322–330.

Börjesson, M., Hamilton, C. J., Näsman, P., & Papaix, C. (2015). Factors driving public support for road congestion reduction policies: Congestion charging, free public transport and more roads in Stockholm, Helsinki and Lyon. *Transportation Research Part A: Policy and Practice, 78*, 452–462.

Boushey, G. (2010). *Policy diffusion dynamics in America*. Cambridge University Press.

Buekens, F., & Boudry, M. (2015). The dark side of the loon: Explaining the Temptations of Obscurantism. *Theoria, 81*(2), 126–142.

Busch, P. O., & Jörgens, H. (2005). The international sources of policy convergence: Explaining the spread of environmental policy innovations. *Journal of European Public Policy, 12*(5), 860–884.

Cai, Y., & Zhou, T. (2019). Online political participation in China: Local government and differentiated response. *The China Quarterly, 238*, 331–352.

Chen, W., & Reese, S. D. (Eds.). (2015). *Networked China: Global dynamics of digital media and civic engagement*. Routledge.

Chen, X., & Zhao, J. (2013). Bidding to drive: Car license auction policy in Shanghai and its public acceptance. *Transport Policy, 27*, 39–52.

Clee, A. (2007). *Driving away the traffic: What lessons can New York learn from London and Stockholm's experiences with congestion charging*. Tufts University.

Clifton, J., & Díaz-Fuentes, D. (2014). Is the organisation for economic co-operation and development ready for China? *Emerging Markets Finance and Trade, 50*(sup6), 21–36.

Dolowitz, D. P., & Marsh, D. (2000). Learning from abroad: The role of policy transfer in contemporary policy-making. *Governance, 13*(1), 5–23.

Drezner, D. W. (2001). Globalization and policy convergence. *International Studies Review, 3*(1), 53–78.

Dynon, N. (2008). "Four Civilizations" and the evolution of post-Mao Chinese socialist ideology. *The China Journal*, (60), 83–109.

Esarey, A. (2015). Winning hearts and minds? Cadres as microbloggers in China. *Journal of Current Chinese Affairs, 44*(2), 69–103.

Evans, M. (Ed.). (2017). *Policy transfer in global perspective*. Taylor & Francis.

Foster, K. W. (2016). Chinese public policy innovation and the diffusion of innovations: An initial exploration. *Chinese Public Administration Review, 3*(1/2), 1–13.

Francke, A., & Kaniok, D. (2013). Responses to differentiated road pricing schemes. *Transportation Research Part A: Policy and Practice, 48*, 25–30.

Gärling, T., & Schuitema, G. (2007). Travel demand management targeting reduced private car use: Effectiveness, public acceptability and political feasibility. *Journal of Social Issues, 63*(1), 139–153.

Hall, S. G., & Ambrosio, T. (2017). Authoritarian learning: A conceptual overview. *East European Politics, 33*(2), 143–161.

Heberer, T., & Trappel, R. (2013). Evaluation processes, local cadres' behaviour and local development processes. *Journal of Contemporary China, 22*(84), 1048–1066.

Holbig, H. (2013). Ideology after the end of ideology. China and the quest for autocratic legitimation. *Democratization, 20*(1), 61–81.

Hu, J. (2012, November 8). *Firmly March on the Path of Socialism with Chinese Characteristics and Strive to Complete the Building of a Moderately Prosperous Society in all Respects*. Political report delivered at the 18th national party congress, Beijing.

Hysing, E. (2015). Citizen participation or representative government–Building legitimacy for the Gothenburg congestion tax. *Transport Policy, 39*, 1–8.

Jakobsson, C., Fujii, S., & Gärling, T. (2000). Determinants of private car users' acceptance of road pricing. *Transport Policy, 7*(2), 153–158.

James, O., & Lodge, M. (2003). The limitations of 'policy transfer'and 'lesson drawing'for public policy research. *Political Studies Review, 1*(2), 179–193.

Jiang, Z. (1997, October 6–12). Hold high the great banner of Deng Xiaoping Theory for an all round advancement of the cause of building socialism with Chinese characteristics into the 21st century. *Beijing Review*, 10–33.

Kallbekken, S., & Sælen, H. (2011). Public acceptance for environmental taxes: Self-interest, environmental and distributional concerns. *Energy Policy, 39*(5), 2966–2973.

Kim, J., Schmöcker, J. D., Fujii, S., & Noland, R. B. (2013). Attitudes towards road pricing and environmental taxation among US and UK students. *Transportation Research Part A: Policy and Practice, 48*, 50–62.

Kwong, J. (1994). Ideological crisis among China's youths: Values and official ideology. *British Journal of Sociology*, 247–264.

Lee, C. K., & Zhang, Y. (2013). The power of instability: Unraveling the microfoundations of bargained authoritarianism in China. *American Journal of Sociology, 118*(6), 1475–1508.

Levitsky, S., & Way, L. A. (2010). *Competitive authoritarianism: Hybrid regimes after the Cold War*. Cambridge University Press.

Lieberthal, K., & Oksenberg, M. (1990). *Policy making in China: Leaders, structures, and processes*. Princeton University Press.

Liu, Y., Martinez-Vazquez, J., & Qiao, B. (2014). *Falling short: Intergovernmental transfers in China*.

Liu, L., Wang, P., & Wu, T. (2017). The role of nongovernmental organizations in China's climate change governance. *Wiley Interdisciplinary Reviews: Climate Change, 8*(6), e483.

Marsden, G., & Stead, D. (2011). Policy transfer and learning in the field of transport: A review of concepts and evidence. *Transport Policy, 18*(3), 492–500.

Maynard, M. L., & Taylor, C. R. (1996). A comparative analysis of Japanese and US attitudes toward direct marketing. *Journal of Direct Marketing, 10*(1), 34–44.

Miltgen, C. L., & Peyrat-Guillard, D. (2014). Cultural and generational influences on privacy concerns: A qualitative study in seven European countries. *European Journal of Information Systems, 23*(2), 103–125.

Rye, T., Gaunt, M., & Ison, S. (2008). Edinburgh's congestion charging plans: An analysis of reasons for non-implementation. *Transportation Planning and Technology, 31*(6), 641–661.

Shorten, R. (2012). *Modernism and totalitarianism: Rethinking the intellectual sources of Nazism and Stalinism, 1945 to the present*. Springer.

Simmons, B. A., & Elkins, Z. (2004). The globalization of liberalization: Policy diffusion in the international political economy. *American Political Science Review, 98*(1), 171–189.

Sun, X., Feng, S., & Lu, J. (2016). Psychological factors influencing the public acceptability of congestion pricing in China. *Transportation Research Part F: Traffic Psychology and Behaviour, 41*, 104–112.

Sun, Y. (2017). The rise of Protestantism in post-Mao China: State and religion in historical perspective. *American Journal of Sociology, 122*(6), 1664–1725.

Teets, J. C. (2014). *Civil society under authoritarianism: The China model*. Cambridge University Press.

Wang, P. (2016). Military corruption in China: The role of *guanxi* in the buying and selling of military positions. *The China Quarterly, 228*, 970–991.

Wang, Q., & Guo, G. (2015). Yu Keping and Chinese intellectual discourse on good governance. *The China Quarterly, 224*, 985–1005.

Wang, R. (2010). Shaping urban transport policies in China: Will copying foreign policies work? *Transport Policy, 17*(3), 147–152.

Weinstein, A., & Sciara, G. C. (2006). Unraveling equity in HOT lane planning: A view from practice. *Journal of Planning Education and Research, 26*(2), 174–184.

Wu, G. (2015a). *China's Party Congress: Power, legitimacy, and institutional manipulation*. Cambridge University Press.

Wu, G. (2015b). *Paradoxes of China's Prosperity: Political Dilemmas and Global Implications*. World Scientific.

Wu, J., Xu, M., & Zhang, P. (2018). The impacts of governmental performance assessment policy and citizen participation on improving environmental performance across Chinese provinces. *Journal of Cleaner Production, 184*, 227–238.

Xi, J. (2017, October 18). *Secure a Decisive Victory in Building a Moderately Prosperous Society in All Respects and Strive for the Great Success of Socialism with Chinese Characteristics for a New Era*, delivered at the 19th National Congress of the Communist Party of China. [Online]. http://language.chinadaily.com.cn/19thcpcnationalcongress/2017-11/06/content_34188086_6.htm. Accessed 27 July 2019.

Yang, G. (2009). *The power of the internet in China: Citizen activism online*. Columbia University Press.

Ye, G., Jin, Z., Xia, B., & Skitmore, M. (2014). Analyzing causes for reworks in construction projects in China. *Journal of Management in Engineering, 31*(6), 04014097.

Zhang, H., & Chen, F. (2004). Studies in science of science. Public participation in technological decisionmaking process. *Studies in Science of Science, 22*, 476–481.

Zhao, J. (2005). Defects and improvement of public participation principle in Chinese environment law. *Environmental Science and Technology, 28*(2), 54–55.

Zheng, X. (2009). *The making of modern Chinese politics: Political culture, protest repertoires, and nationalism in the Sichuan Railway Protection Movement* (Doctoral dissertation). UC San Diego.

Appendix A: Participant Information Sheet and Consent Form for Interviews

Participant Information Sheet

The title of the research project
Analysing Public Acceptability of Sustainable Transport Policy in the Chinese Context: The Case of Congestion Charge in Beijing

You are being invited to take part in this research project. Before you decide it is important for you to understand why the research is being done and what it will involve. Please take time to read the following information carefully and discuss it with others if you wish. Ask me if there is anything that is not clear or if you would like more information. Take time to decide whether or not you wish to take part.

As we know Beijing's congestion charge will be implemented in the near future, this research aims at investigating the public acceptability of the proposed congestion charge scheme. Two main questions will be answered in this research: Can researchers use a Western context-based framework to study public acceptability in China and what measure can increase public acceptability of sustainable transport policies in China? The duration of the project is three years. You were chosen as a representative of politicians/scholars/political commentators/citizens helping us to understand why public acceptability should be decision-makers' concern; to explore differences in understanding of public acceptability between decision-makers and the public. You will be involved in the

Q. Liu, *Public Acceptability of Congestion Charging in China*,
https://doi.org/10.1007/978-981-19-0236-9

research for about one hour. You will be interviewed during the research. The questions are related to public acceptability of transport policies in the Chinese context. You are expected to frankly express your opinion about these questions and give your explanations in detail, and I guarantee that the data will be anonymized and kept confidentially. While there are no immediate benefits for those people participating in the project, it is hoped that this work will improve the effectiveness of Beijing's congestion charge.

It is up to you to decide whether or not to take part. If you do decide to take part you will be given this information sheet to keep (and be asked to sign a consent form) and you can still withdraw up until the result of the research is published without it affecting any benefits that you are entitled to in any way. You do not have to give a reason.

The China Scholarship Council is funding this research.

Contact information:
Qiyang Liu
tsql@leeds.ac.uk
+44 (0)7424740083

Prof. Karen Lucas PhD
K.Lucas@leeds.ac.uk
+44 (0)113 34 38086

Consent Form

Institute for Transport Studies

Consent to take part in Analyzing Public Acceptability of Sustainable Transport Policy in The Chinese Context: The Case of Congestion Charge in Beijing	Add your initials next to the statement if you agree
I confirm that I have read and understand the information sheet dated [insert date] explaining the above research project and I have had the opportunity to ask questions about the project.	
I understand that my participation is voluntary and that I am free to withdraw at any time without giving any reason and without there being any negative consequences. In addition, should I not wish to answer any particular question or questions, I am free to decline. Contact number: +44 (0)7424740083. Data already provided will be destroyed if I decide to withdraw.	
I give permission for members of the research team to have access to my anonymised responses. I understand that my name will not be linked with the research materials, and I will not be identified or identifiable in the report or reports that result from the research. I understand that my responses will be kept strictly confidential.	
I agree for the data collected from me to be stored and used in relevant future research in an anonymised form.	
I understand that other genuine researchers may use my words in publications, reports, web pages, and other research outputs, only if they agree to preserve the confidentiality of the information as requested in this form.	
I understand that relevant sections of the data collected during the study, may be looked at by individuals from the University of Leeds or from regulatory authorities where it is relevant to my taking part in this research. I give permission for these individuals to have access to my records.	
I agree to take part in the above research project and will inform the lead researcher should my contact details change.	

Name of participant	
Participant's signature	
Date	
Name of lead researcher	Qiyang Liu
Signature	Qiyang Liu
Date*	

*To be signed and dated in the presence of the participant.
Once this has been signed by all parties the participant should receive a copy of the signed and dated participant consent form, the letter/ pre-written script/ information sheet and any other written information provided to the participants. A copy of the signed and dated consent form should be kept with the project's main documents which must be kept in a secure location.

Project title Analyzing Public Acceptability of Sustainable Transport Policy in The Chinese Context: The Case of Congestion Charge in Beijing	*Document type*	*Version #*	*Date*
	Eg consent form for...		

Appendix B: Participant Information Sheet and Consent Form for Focus Groups

Participant Information Sheet

The title of the research project
Analysing Public Acceptability of Sustainable Transport Policy in the Chinese Context: The Case of Congestion Charge in Beijing

You are being invited to take part in this research project. Before you decide it is important for you to understand why the research is being done and what it will involve. Please take time to read the following information carefully and discuss it with others if you wish. Ask me if there is anything that is not clear or if you would like more information. Take time to decide whether or not you wish to take part.

As we know Beijing's congestion charge will be implemented in the near future, this research aims at investigating the public acceptability of the proposed congestion charge scheme. Two main questions will be answered in this research: Can researchers use a Western context-based framework to study public acceptability in China and what measure can increase public acceptability of sustainable transport policies in China? The duration of the project is three years. You were chosen as a representative of Chinese citizens helping us to gather ideas of factors influencing the public acceptability of road pricing and to what extent philosophical, cultural and political factors influence the public acceptability of transport policies. You will be involved in the research for about two hours. You will

Q. Liu, *Public Acceptability of Congestion Charging in China*,
https://doi.org/10.1007/978-981-19-0236-9

participate in focus groups during the research. The questions are related to public acceptability of transport policies in the Chinese context. You are expected to frankly express your opinion about these questions and give your explanations in detail, and I guarantee that the data will be anonymized and kept confidentially. While there are no immediate benefits for those people participating in the project, it is hoped that this work will improve the effectiveness of Beijing's congestion charge.

It is up to you to decide whether or not to take part. If you do decide to take part you will be given this information sheet to keep (and be asked to sign a consent form) and you can still withdraw up until the result of the research is published without it affecting any benefits that you are entitled to in any way. You do not have to give a reason.

The China Scholarship Council is funding this research.

Contact information:
Qiyang Liu
tsql@leeds.ac.uk
+44 (0)7424740083

Prof. Karen Lucas PhD
K.Lucas@leeds.ac.uk
+44 (0)113 34 38086

Consent Form

Institute for Transport Studies

Consent to take part in Analyzing Public Acceptability of Sustainable Transport Policy in The Chinese Context: The Case of Congestion Charge in Beijing	Add your initials next to the statement if you agree
I confirm that I have read and understand the information sheet dated [insert date] explaining the above research project and I have had the opportunity to ask questions about the project.	
I understand that my participation is voluntary and that I am free to withdraw at any time without giving any reason and without there being any negative consequences. In addition, should I not wish to answer any particular question or questions, I am free to decline. Contact number: +44 (0)7424740083. Data already provided will be destroyed if I decide to withdraw.	
I give permission for members of the research team to have access to my anonymised responses. I understand that my name will not be linked with the research materials, and I will not be identified or identifiable in the report or reports that result from the research. While the researcher will maintain confidentiality, other participants may not guarantee full confidentiality.	
I agree for the data collected from me to be stored and used in relevant future research in an anonymised form.	
I understand that other genuine researchers may use my words in publications, reports, web pages, and other research outputs, only if they agree to preserve the confidentiality of the information as requested in this form.	
I understand that relevant sections of the data collected during the study, may be looked at by individuals from the University of Leeds or from regulatory authorities where it is relevant to my taking part in this research. I give permission for these individuals to have access to my records.	
I agree to take part in the above research project and will inform the lead researcher should my contact details change.	

Name of participant	
Participant's signature	
Date	
Name of lead researcher	Qiyang Liu
Signature	......Qiyang Liu......
Date*	

*To be signed and dated in the presence of the participant.
Once this has been signed by all parties the participant should receive a copy of the signed and dated participant consent form, the letter/ pre-written script/ information sheet and any other written information provided to the participants. A copy of the signed and dated consent form should be kept with the project's main documents which must be kept in a secure location.

Project title Analyzing Public Acceptability of Sustainable Transport Policy in The Chinese Context: The Case of Congestion Charge in Beijing	*Document type*	*Version #*	*Date*
	consent form		

Appendix C: Ethical Approval

Qiyang Liu
ITS
University of Leeds
Leeds, LS2 9JT

ESSL, Environment and LUBS (AREA) Faculty Research Ethics Committee
University of Leeds
8th September 2016
Dear Qiyang

Title of study:	**Analysing Public Acceptability of Sustainable Transport Policy in The Chinese Context: The Case of Congestion Charge in Beijing**
Ethics reference:	**AREA 16-003**

I am pleased to inform you that the above research application has been reviewed by the ESSL, Environment and LUBS (AREA) Faculty Research Ethics Committee and following receipt of your response to the Committee's initial comments, I can confirm a favourable ethical opinion as of the date of this letter. The following documentation was considered:

Q. Liu, *Public Acceptability of Congestion Charging in China*,
https://doi.org/10.1007/978-981-19-0236-9

Document	*Version*	*Date*
AREA 16-003 Qiyang Liu_Ethical_review R3 with amendments.doc	1	26/08/16
AREA 16-003 Qiyang Liu_Ethical_review R3.doc	2	26/08/16
AREA 16-003 Qiyang Liu_Information Sheet (Focus group).docx	1	11/08/16
AREA 16-003 Qiyang Liu_participant_consent_form (Focus groups).doc	1	11/08/16
AREA 16-003 Qiyang Liu_Information Sheet (Interview).docx	1	11/08/16
AREA 16-003 Qiyang Liu_participant_consent_form (Interviews).doc	1	11/08/16
AREA 16-003 Qiyang Liu_Interview Questions.docx	1	11/08/16
AREA 16-003 Qiyang Liu_Fieldwork_Assessment_Form.docx	1	11/08/16

Please notify the committee if you intend to make any amendments to the information in your ethics application as submitted at the date of this approval as all changes must receive ethical approval prior to implementation. The amendment form is available at http://ris.leeds.ac.uk/Ethics Amendment.

Please note: You are expected to keep a record of all your approved documentation, as well as documents such as sample consent forms and other documents relating to the study. This should be kept in your study file, which should be readily available for audit purposes. You will be given a two week notice period if your project is to be audited. There is a checklist listing examples of documents to be kept which is available at http://ris.leeds.ac.uk/EthicsAudits.

We welcome feedback on your experience of the ethical review process and suggestions for improvement. Please email any comments to ResearchEthics@leeds.ac.uk.

Yours sincerely
Jennifer Blaikie
Senior Research Ethics Administrator, Research & Innovation Service
On behalf of Dr Kahryn Hughes, Chair, AREA Faculty Research Ethics Committee

CC: Student's supervisor(s)

Appendix D: Prepared List of Challenging Follow-Up Questions for Interviews

1. Why does the only ruling party need to consider public opinions?
2. Chinese people sometimes also say no to the government. For example, several months ago, the government proposed a new policy, 'the demolishing walls policy'. How could they do that if Chinese people are obedient?
3. In your opinion, how would citizens react to this policy?
4. I found many complaints about the policy online, from many different aspects, do you know this? Have you thought about these issues?
5. People's complaints: in your opinion are they really showing their dissatisfaction?
6. I believe most of the people will accept whatever the government proposed but what we can see is that they sometimes reacted in a very fierce way, very violent way. Why?
7. The government started thinking about this policy many years ago, why is it still not implemented?
8. Who first proposed this policy? The previous head of the municipal commission of transport?
9. Do you think those policies are not that acceptable?
10. Why don't Chinese people do something? They don't believe the government will listen to them or they are just indifferent?
11. If Chinese people will obey the government anyway, why the government still need to consider about them?

Q. Liu, *Public Acceptability of Congestion Charging in China*, https://doi.org/10.1007/978-981-19-0236-9

12. As far as I know, many low level cadres are very poorly educated and don't even know what does "the People" mean. How could they get promoted?
13. Any inside information about the policy? When will it be implemented?
14. The CPC propaganda is not just the CCTV news. It is a whole system. For example, the politics exam is also a propaganda. Chinese people have to go for politics classes until a PhD degree. Do you think it's still effective?
15. How many government cars in Beijing? Which department have the accurate number of government cars in Beijing?
16. Will a cadre be punished if they use government car for private use? How?
17. We cannot see local cadres pay much attention to the people. For example the new design and reconstruction project in the city centre, citizens are complaining, a lot. How could we say cadres are acting for the people?
18. Who will make the final decision?
19. Is the ministry of transport involved in the policymaking?
20. There are a lot of non-professional policymakers who know nothing about transport. How could they know whether the policy is going to be effective.
21. When and where has the CPC ever implemented the governing idea?
22. If the official governing idea is not implemented, how could we say it is actually the real governing idea?
23. In the past, in my childhood, I think people were always shocked by the news about corrupt cadres, but now I will find it incredible if you tell me there is a honest cadres. I think nowadays it's a very common understanding of our cadres. Will it influence public acceptability?
24. Do you believe what those experts say? (they have to be cooperative and they have to say what you want to listen).
25. When you consulted with an expert, what you really want to get from him? professional advices? or just a proper reason to legitimate your idea which maybe come from nowhere?
26. Why didn't the government give citizens some information about the new policy? This kind of information will not influence the ruling of the CPC.

27. Who will be violently against a transport policy? and why?
28. Do Chinese people trust the party?
29. Do they trust the central committee or local government?
30. Do you hate corruption?
31. Is corruption pervasive? Why?
32. Other questions about corruption, anti-corruption campaign: not listed because of ethical considerations.

Appendix E: Questionnaire

Chinese Version

问卷调查

这份问卷是关于北京市居民对拥堵费的态度的调查。这份调查是 PhD 论文的一部分，其结果将不会用于除研究以外的任何用途。请您花大约 10 分钟左右的时间完成这份问卷。谢谢。

1. 我听说过拥堵费。

1. 是 2. 否

多大程度上我同意一下说法，请从 1-6 中选择

1: 非常不同意, 2: 比较不同意, 3: 有一点不同意, 4: 有一点同意, 5: 比较同意 6: 非常同意

	非常不同意	比较不同意	有一点不同意	有一点同意	比较同意	非常同意
北京的交通拥堵是一个严重问题						
交通拥堵严重影响我的日常生活						
我时常因为交通拥堵被耽误						
北京的雾霾是一个严重的问题						
雾霾严重影响我的健康						
我对雾霾问题很关注						
我知道拥堵费将在何时实施						
我知道拥堵费如何收费						
政府曾介绍过别的国家实行的拥堵费						
我能从社交媒体上得到关于拥堵费的有用信息						
我对于拥堵费的看法主要基于社交媒体上的信息						
社交媒体上的文章能帮我更好地理解拥堵费						

Q. Liu, *Public Acceptability of Congestion Charging in China*, https://doi.org/10.1007/978-981-19-0236-9

尾号限行政策有效的缓解了交通拥堵						
车牌摇号政策有效的缓解了交通拥堵						
之前的交通政策总的来说达到了预期目标						
在国外成功实施的政策在中国也能成功实施						
拥堵费能有效地解决北京的拥堵问题						
拥堵费能有效地解决北京的雾霾问题						
因为拥堵费，人们将减少私家车的使用						
拥堵费对不富裕的小汽车使用者是不公平的						
拥堵费将进一步引起社会的不公平						
拥堵费将使小汽车使用成为另一富人的特权						
拥堵费对外地人是不公平的						
没有北京户口的人不应该付拥堵费						
北京人将是拥堵费的主要得益者						
拥堵费对公务车有约束力						
公务车使用者本人将付拥堵费						
公车私用这种情况很罕见						

政府想要实施拥堵费是因为想从老百姓那收钱						
政府不关系拥堵费导致的其他社会问题						
由于腐败问题，拥堵费不能满足我的预期						
政府收到的拥堵费如何使用是不透明的						
拥堵费不像专家说的那么好						
推崇拥堵费的专家是在迎合政府						
我不会公开表示我对这一政策的不满						
即便我对这一政策不满意，我也会照政府要求的做						
政府官员能帮我做正确的决定						
如果我周围的人认为这一政策可接受，我会觉得它更可接受						
如果我周围的人认为这一政策不可接受，我会觉得它更不可接受						
总的来说我希望这个政策能得以实施						
我认为拥堵费对我个人有好处						
我认为拥堵费对社会有好处						

您的年龄是：1. 18-30 岁, 2. 31-45 岁, 3. 46-60 岁, 4. 60 岁以上

您的性别是：1. 男, 2. 女

您的家庭年收入为 1. <12 万, 2. 12 万-100 万, 3. >100 万

您是：1. 北京人， 2. 外地人

您住在：1. 城六区 (三环内), 2. 城六区 (三环外), 3. 非城六区.

您拥有私家车吗. 1. 是, 2. 否

English Version

This questionnaire is about whether your attitude towards the congestion charge which is still at the planning stage. It is part of the PhD programme on Chinese people's acceptability of the congestion charge, and it will not be used for any other purpose. It will take you about 10 minutes to do this questionnaire. Thank you.

1. I have heard about the Beijing congestion charge before.
   1. Yes, 2. No

To what extent do you agree or disagree the following statements. Please choose from scale 1–6.

1: Strongly disagree, 2: Moderately disagree, 3: Slightly disagree, 4: Slightly agree, 5: Moderately agree 6: Strongly agree.

	1	*2*	*3*	*4*	*5*	*6*
Congestion is a serious problem in Beijing						
Traffic congestion has a great effect on my daily life						
I'm always delayed by bad traffic on the road						
Smog is a serious problem in Beijing						
Smog is hazardous to my health						
I pay much attention to the smog problem						
I know when the policy is going to be implemented						
I know how much I need to pay						
The government introduces experience in foreign cities						
I can find useful information about the congestion charge on social media						
My opinion of congestion charge is mainly based on information from social media						
Articles on social media help me to better understand the congestion charge						
Traffic restrictions based on the last digit of licence plate has effectively alleviate traffic congestion						
License plate lottery has effectively alleviated traffic congestion						
Previous policies can reach policymakers' expectation						
A policy which has been successfully implemented in foreign countries could be effective in China						
The congestion charge could effectively alleviate congestion problem in Beijing						
The congestion charge could effectively alleviate smog problem in Beijing						
People will use car less because of the congestion charge						
The policy is inequitable to poorer car users						
The policy will cause more social inequalities						
The policy makes driving another privilege of the rich						
The policy is inequitable to new migrants						

(continued)

(continued)

	1	*2*	*3*	*4*	*5*	*6*
People who don't have a Beijing hukou should not pay this charge						
Pekingese are the main beneficiaries of the policy						
The policy has constraints on government car use						
Government car users themselves will pay the charge						
Government car use for private purpose is very rare						
The government want to implement this policy because it can collect money from the people						
Other social problems caused by this policy is not policymakers' concern						
The policy cannot reach my expectation because of political corruption						
The revenue allocation will not be transparent						
Congestion charge is not as good as experts said						
Experts are flattering cadres						
I will not express my dissatisfaction publicly						
Even if I'm not happy with it, I will do what the government requires me to do						
Cadres could make the right decision for me						
I will find it more acceptable if people around me think it's acceptable						
I will find it more unacceptable if people around me complain about it						
In general I hope the policy will be implemented						
I think the policy is favourable to me as an individual						
I think the policy is favourable to the society as a whole						

44. Age: 1. 18–30, 2. 31–45, 3. 46–60, 4. above 60
45. Gender: 1. Male, 2. Female
46. Household Income: 1. <120k, 2. 120k-1m, 3. >1m
47. Pekingese 1. or migrants 2.
48. Which area you live in: 1. six inner-city districts (inside the 3rd ring road), 2. six inner-city districts (outside the 3rd ring road), 3. other districts
49. Do you own a car. 1. Yes, 2. No

Appendix F: Themes and Codes (Interviews)

Q. Liu, *Public Acceptability of Congestion Charging in China*,
https://doi.org/10.1007/978-981-19-0236-9

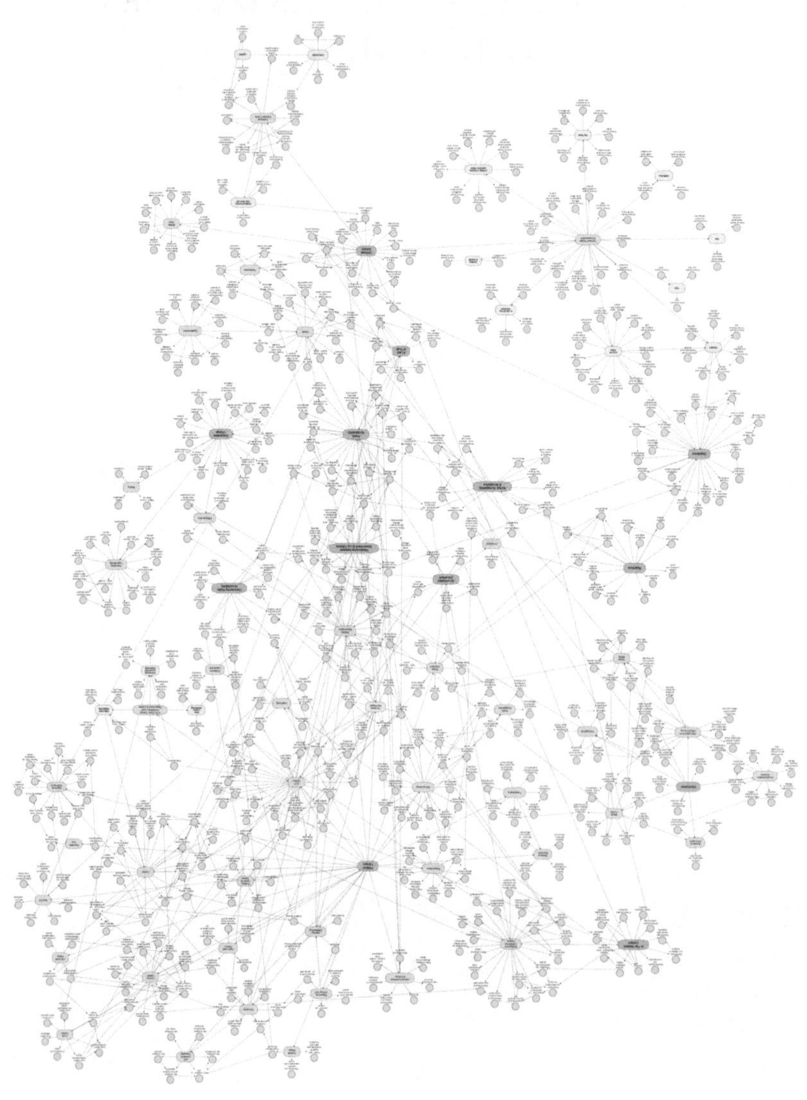

Appendix G: Themes and Codes (Focus Groups)

Q. Liu, *Public Acceptability of Congestion Charging in China*, https://doi.org/10.1007/978-981-19-0236-9

References

Aarts, H., & Dijksterhuis, A. (2003). The silence of the library: Environment, situational norm, and social behavior. *Journal of Personality and Social Psychology, 84*(1), 18.

Abrego, L. J. (2011). Legal consciousness of undocumented Latinos: Fear and stigma as barriers to claims-making for first- and 1.5-generation immigrants. *Law & Society Review, 45*(2), 337–370.

Advox. (2013). *China: Bloggers "Forced to Drink Tea" with Police*. [Online]. https://advox.globalvoices.org/2013/02/19/china-bloggers-forced-to-drink-tea-with-police/. Accessed 27 July 2019.

Afridi, F., Li, S. X., & Ren, Y. (2015). Social identity and inequality: The impact of China's hukou system. *Journal of Public Economics, 123*, 17–29.

Ahn, B. J. (1975). The political economy of the people's commune in China: Changes and continuities. *The Journal of Asian Studies, 34*(3), 631–658.

Ajzen, I. (1991). The theory of planned behavior. *Organizational Behavior and Human Decision Processes, 50*(2), 179–211.

Al-Maghrebi, M. S., Ahmad, R., & Palil, M. R. (2016). Budget transparency and tax awareness towards tax compliance: A conceptual approach. *South East Asia Journal of Contemporary Business, Economics and Law, 10*(1), 95–101.

Almén, O. (2016). Information for autocrats: Representation in Chinese local congresses. MELANIE MANION. Cambridge University Press, 2015. xii+ 189 pp.£ 59.99; $89.99. ISBN 978-1-107-63703-0. *The China Quarterly, 227*, 812–813.

Alston, J. P. (1989). Wa, guanxi, and inhwa: Managerial principles in Japan, China, and Korea. *Business Horizons, 32*(2), 26–32.

Q. Liu, *Public Acceptability of Congestion Charging in China*, https://doi.org/10.1007/978-981-19-0236-9

Andrews-Speed, P., Yang, M., Shen, L., & Cao, S. (2003). The regulation of China's township and village coal mines: A study of complexity and ineffectiveness. *Journal of Cleaner Production, 11*(2), 185–196.

Appleton, S., & Song, L. (2008). Life satisfaction in urban China: Components and determinants. *World Development, 36*(11), 2325–2340.

Arbuckle, J. L. (2010). *IBM SPSS Amos 19 user's guide* (p. 635). Amos Development Corporation.

Asparouhov, T., & Muthén, B. (2009). Exploratory structural equation modeling. *Structural Equation Modeling: A Multidisciplinary Journal, 16*(3), 397–438.

Bachman, D. (2006). *Bureaucracy, economy, and leadership in China: The institutional origins of the Great Leap Forward*. Cambridge University Press.

Bagby, R. M., Parker, J. D., & Taylor, G. J. (1994). The twenty-item Toronto Alexithymia Scale—I. Item selection and cross-validation of the factor structure. *Journal of Psychosomatic Research, 38*(1), 23–32.

Bardhan, P. (2002). Decentralization of governance and development. *Journal of Economic Perspectives, 16*(4), 185–205.

Barnouin, B., & Yu, C. (1993). *Ten years of turbulence: The Chinese cultural revolution*. Routledge.

Barrett, P. (2007). Structural equation modelling: Adjudging model fit. *Personality and Individual Differences, 42*(5), 815–824.

Bartley, B. (1995). Mobility impacts, reactions and opinions: Traffic demand management options in Europe, the MIRO project. *Traffic Engineering & Control, 36*, 596–603.

Baumgartner, H., & Homburg, C. (1996). Applications of structural equation modeling in marketing and consumer research: A review. *International Journal of Research in Marketing, 13*(2), 139–161.

BBC. (2013). *Tea? Reining in dissent the Chinese way*. [Online]. https://www.bbc.co.uk/news/world-asia-china-21027416. Accessed 27 July 2019.

BBC. (2014a). *Daily life comes to stand-still in Beijing during APEC*. [Online]. https://www.bbc.co.uk/news/blogs-china-blog-29983799. Accessed 27 July 2019.

BBC. (2014b). *China: General says smog 'best defence' against US lasers*. [Online]. https://www.bbc.co.uk/news/blogs-news-from-elsewhere-26322868. Accessed 27 July 2019.

BBC. (2015). *Beijing subway fare hike weighs on commuters*. [Online]. https://www.bbc.co.uk/news/world-asia-30595286. Accessed 27 July 2019.

BBC Trending. (2013). *China smog: as cities choke, the people joke*. [Online]. http://www.bbc.co.uk/news/blogs-trending-25413649. Accessed 27 July 2019.

Beck, A. T., Steer, R. A., & Brown, G. K. (1996). Beck Depression Inventory-II. *San Antonio, 78*(2), 490–498.

Beijing Municipal Bureau of Statistics. (2017a). *Beijing Statistical Yearbook*. [Online]. http://tjj.beijing.gov.cn/nj/main/2017-tjnj/zk/indexch.htm. Accessed 27 July 2019 (in Chinese).

Beijing Municipal Bureau of Statistics. (2017b). *Beijing Statistical Yearbook*. http://tjj.beijing.gov.cn/nj/main/2017-tjnj/zk/indexch.htm. Accessed 27 July 2019 (in Chinese).

Beijing Municipal Commission of Transport. (2011). *The comprehensive congestion-alleviation measures are effective*. [Online]. https://archive.is/20120729143830/http://www.bjjtw.gov.cn/gzdt/ywsds/201105/t20110523_36570.htm#selection-391.0-391.8. Accessed 27 July 2019 (in Chinese).

Beijing Municipal Environmental Protection Bureau. (2015). *Guo I old vehicles, banned to enter the city center from next year*. [Online]. http://www.bjepb.gov.cn/bjepb/323265/397983/424801/index.html. Accessed 27 July 2019 (in Chinese).

Beijing Transportation Research Centre. (2011). *Urban Road Traffic Performance Index* (DB11/T 785–2011). (in Chinese).

Bell, D. A. (2016). *The China model*. Princeton University Press.

Benedict, R. (1967). *The chrysanthemum and the sword: Patterns of Japanese culture*. Houghton Mifflin Harcourt.

Bentler, P. M. (1982). Confirmatory factor analysis via noniterative estimation: A fast, inexpensive method. *Journal of Marketing Research, 19*, 417–424.

Bentler, P. M., & Bonett, D. G. (1980). Significance tests and goodness of fit in the analysis of covariance structures. *Psychological Bulletin, 88*(3), 588–606.

Bentler, P. M., & Chou, C. P. (1987). Practical issues in structural modeling. *Sociological Methods & Research, 16*(1), 78–117.

Bentler, P. M., & Kano, Y. (1990). On the equivalence of factors and components. *Multivariate Behavioral Research, 25*(1), 67–74.

Berry, F. S. (1994). Innovation in public management: The adoption of strategic planning. *Public Administration Review*, 322–330.

Berthoff, R. (1982). Peasants and artisans, puritans and republicans: Personal liberty and communal equality in American history. *The Journal of American History, 69*(3), 579–598.

Bian, Y. (2002). Chinese social stratification and social mobility. *Annual Review of Sociology*, 91–116.

Bianco, L. (2001). *Peasants without the party: Grass-roots movements in twentieth-century China*. ME Sharpe.

Bicchieri, C. (2005). *The grammar of society: The nature and dynamics of social norms*. Cambridge University Press.

Bicchieri, C. (2010). Norms, preferences, and conditional behavior. *Politics, Philosophy & Economics, 9*(3), 297–313.

Billioud, S. (2007). Confucianism, "cultural tradition" and official discourses in China at the start of the new century. *China Perspectives, 2007*(3), 50–65.

Billioud, S., & Thoraval, J. (2007). Jiaohua: The Confucian revival in China as an educative project. *China Perspectives, 2007*(4), 4–20.

Bing. (2013). *“5 Surprising Benefits of Smog” Jokes CCTV, Chinese Reactions*. [Online]. http://www.chinasmack.com/2013/stories/5-surprising-benefits-of-smog-jokes-cctv-chinese-reactions.html. Accessed 27 July 2019.

Bird, J., & Morris, J. (2006). *Steering through change: Winning the debate on road pricing*. Institute for Public Policy Research.

Bird, J., & Vigor, A. (2006). *Charging forward-a review of public attitudes towards road pricing in the UK*.

Björklund, E. M. (1986). The Danwei: Socio-spatial characteristics of work units in China’s urban society. *Economic Geography, 62*(1), 19–29.

Blaikie, N. (2007). *Approaches to social enquiry: Advancing knowledge*. Polity.

Blaike, N. (2010). *Designing social research: The logic of anticipation* (2nd ed.). Oxford.

Bollen, K. A. (1989). *Structural Equations with Latent Variables*. Wiley-Interscience Publication.

Bonsall, P., & Lythgoe, B. (2009). Factors affecting the amount of effort expended in responding to questions in behavioural choice experiments. *Journal of Choice Modelling, 2*(2), 216–236.

Boomsma, A. (1985). Nonconvergence, improper solutions, and starting values in LISREL maximum likelihood estimation. *Psychometrika, 50*(2), 229–242.

Boone, H. N., & Boone, D. A. (2012). Analyzing Likert Data. *Journal of Extension, 50*(2), 1–5.

Boorman, H. L. (1963). How to be a Good Communist: The Political Ethics of Liu Shao-Ch’I. *Asian Survey*, 372–383.

Børdsgaard, K. E., & Chen, G. (2009a, December). *China’s attempt to professionalize its civil service* (EAI Background Brief No. 494).

Børdsgaard, K. E., & Chen, G. (2009b, December). *China’s civil service reform: An update* (EAI Background Brief No. 493).

Borins, S. F. (1988). Electronic road pricing: An idea whose time may never come. *Transportation Research Part A: General, 22*(1), 37–44.

Börjesson, M., Eliasson, J., Hugosson, M. B., & Brundell-Freij, K. (2012). The Stockholm congestion charges—5 years on. Effects, acceptability and lessons learnt. *Transport Policy, 20*, 1–12.

Börjesson, M., Hamilton, C. J., Näsman, P., & Papaix, C. (2015). Factors driving public support for road congestion reduction policies: Congestion charging, free public transport and more roads in Stockholm, Helsinki and Lyon. *Transportation Research Part A: Policy and Practice, 78*, 452–462.

Börjesson, M., & Kristoffersson, I. (2015). The Gothenburg congestion charge: Effects, design and politics. *Transportation Research Part A: Policy and Practice, 75*, 134–146.

Börjesson, M., & Kristoffersson, I. (2018). The Swedish congestion charges: Ten years on. *Transportation Research Part A: Policy and Practice, 107*, 35–51.

Bosker, M., Brakman, S., Garretsen, H., & Schramm, M. (2012). Relaxing Hukou: Increased labor mobility and China's economic geography. *Journal of Urban Economics, 72*(2–3), 252–266.

Bottelier, P. (2018). *Economic policy making in China (1949–2016): The role of economists*. Routledge.

Boushey, G. (2010). *Policy diffusion dynamics in America*. Cambridge University Press.

Bowles, S., Gintis, H., & Brighouse, H. (1998). *Recasting egalitarianism: New rules for communities, states and markets*. Verso.

Brady, A. M. (2009). *Marketing dictatorship: Propaganda and thought work in contemporary China*. Rowman & Littlefield Publishers.

Brady, A. M., & Wang, J. (2009). China's strengthened new order and the role of propaganda. *Journal of Contemporary China, 18*(62), 767–788.

Bray, D. (2005). *Social space and governance in urban China: The danwei system from origins to reform*. Stanford University Press.

Bristow, A. L., Wardman, M., Zanni, A. M., & Chintakayala, P. K. (2010). Public acceptability of personal carbon trading and carbon tax. *Ecological Economics, 69*(9), 1824–1837.

Bröcker, J., Korzhenevych, A., & Schürmann, C. (2010). Assessing spatial equity and efficiency impacts of transport infrastructure projects. *Transportation Research Part B: Methodological, 44*(7), 795–811.

Broadhurst, R., & Wang, P. (2014). After the Bo Xilai trial: Does corruption threaten China's future? *Survival, 56*(3), 157–178.

Brødsgaard, K. E. (2012). Politics and business group formation in China: The Party in control? *The China Quarterly, 211*, 624–648.

Brook, T., & Frolic, B. M. (2015). *Civil society in China*. Routledge.

Brown, B. E. (1991). *The Buddha nature: A study of the Tathāgatagarbha and Ālayavijñāna* (Vol. 11). Motilal Banarsidass Publ.

Brown, J. D. (2000). What issues affect Likert-scale questionnaire formats. *Shiken: JALT Testing & Evaluation SIG Newsletter, 4*(1), 27–33.

Browne, M. W., & Arminger, G. (1995). Specification and estimation of mean- and covariance-structure models. *Handbook of statistical modeling for the social and behavioral sciences* (pp. 185–249). Springer.

Brugger, B. (2018a). *Chinese Marxism in Flux 1978–84: Essays on Epistemology*. Routledge.

Brugger, B. (2018b). *China: Liberation and transformation 1942–1962*. Routledge.

Brunetti, A., & Weder, B. (2003). A free press is bad news for corruption. *Journal of Public Economics, 87*(7), 1801–1824.

Bryman, A. (2016). *Social research methods*. Oxford University Press.

Buekens, F., & Boudry, M. (2015). The dark side of the loon: Explaining the Temptations of Obscurantism. *Theoria, 81*(2), 126–142.

Burgess, R. G. (2002). *In the field: An introduction to field research*. Routledge.

Burnard, P. (1991). A method of analysing interview transcripts in qualitative research. *Nurse Education Today, 11*(6), 461–466.

Busch, P. O., & Jörgens, H. (2005). The international sources of policy convergence: Explaining the spread of environmental policy innovations. *Journal of European Public Policy, 12*(5), 860–884.

Butollo, F., & Ten Brink, T. (2012). Challenging the atomization of discontent: Patterns of migrant-worker protest in China during the series of strikes in 2010. *Critical Asian Studies, 44*(3), 419–440.

Byrne, B. M. (2016). *Structural equation modeling with AMOS: Basic concepts, applications, and programming*. Routledge.

Cai, Y. (2002). The resistance of Chinese laid-off workers in the reform period. *The China Quarterly, 170*, 327–344.

Cai, Y. (2003). Collective ownership or cadres' ownership? The non-agricultural use of farmland in China. *The China Quarterly, 175*, 662–680.

Cai, Y. (2008). Local governments and the suppression of popular resistance in China. *The China Quarterly, 193*, 24–42.

Cai, Y. (2010). *Collective resistance in China: Why popular protests succeed or fail*. Stanford University Press.

Cai, Y., & Zhou, T. (2019). Online political participation in China: Local government and differentiated response. *The China Quarterly, 238*, 331–352.

Cambridge English Dictionary. http://dictionary.cambridge.org/dictionary/english/culture?a=british. Accessed 27 July 2019.

Carifio, J., & Perla, R. J. (2007). Ten common misunderstandings, misconceptions, persistent myths and urban legends about Likert scales and Likert response formats and their antidotes. *Journal of Social Sciences, 3*(3), 106–116.

Castells, M. (2008). The new public sphere: Global civil society, communication networks, and global governance. *The ANNALS of the American Academy of Political and Social Science, 616*(1), 78–93.

Cecere, G., Le Guel, F., & Soulié, N. (2015). Perceived internet privacy concerns on social networks in Europe. *Technological Forecasting and Social Change, 96*, 277–287.

Cervero, R., & Day, J. (2008). Suburbanization and transit-oriented development in China. *Transport Policy, 15*(5), 315–323.

Chan, H. S. (2004). Cadre personnel management in China: The nomenklatura system, 1990–1998. *The China Quarterly, 179*, 703–734.

Chan, W. T. (2008). *A Source Book in Chinese Philosophy*. Princeton University Press.

Chang, C. (1963). Creativity and Taoism: A study of Chinese philosophy, art, and poetry. *Philosophy East and West, 13*(1), 74–77.

Chang, C. S. (2007). *The Rise of the Chinese Empire: Nation, state, & imperialism in early China, ca. 1600 BC–AD 8*. University of Michigan Press.

Chang, J. (2013). *Empress Dowager Cixi: The concubine who launched modern China*. Random House.

Charmaz, K. (2014). *Constructing grounded theory*. Sage.

Cheesman, N. (2015). *Opposing the rule of law*. Cambridge University Press.

Chen, C. C., & Lee, Y. T. (2008). *Leadership and management in China: Philosophies, theories, and practices*. Cambridge University Press.

Chen, H., Pu, X., Xiangzhao, F., & Fen, L. (2008). Public attitudes towards policy instruments for congestion mitigation in Shanghai. *Chinese Journal of Population Resources and Environment, 6*(3), 40–47.

Chen, F. (2000). Subsistence crises, managerial corruption and labour protests in China. *The China Journal, 44*, 41–63.

Chen, N. (2003). From propaganda to public relations: Evolutionary change in the Chinese government. *Asian Journal of Communication, 13*(2), 96–121.

Chen, N. (2012). Branding national images: The 2008 Beijing summer Olympics, 2010 Shanghai World Expo, and 2010 Guangzhou Asian games. *Public Relations Review, 38*(5), 731–745.

Chen, S., & Chow, C. Y. (2010). China's science prowess questioned. *South China Morning Post, 29*, A6.

Chen, W. (2012). The initial translation of "philosophy" and its development: Debates between "Tetsugaku" and "Rigaku." *Taiwan Journal of East Asian Studies, 9*(2), 1–43.

Chen, W., & Reese, S. D. (Eds.). (2015). *Networked China: Global dynamics of digital media and civic engagement*. Routledge.

Chen, X. (2000). Growing up in a collectivist culture: Socialization and socioemotional development in Chinese children. In A. L. Comunian & U. P. Gielen (Eds.), *International perspectives on human development* (pp. 331–353). Pabst Science.

Chen, X. (2002). *Occidentalism: A theory of counter-discourse in post-Mao China*. Rowman & Littlefield.

Chen, X. (2007). *From the May Fourth Movement to Communist Revolution*. SUNY Press.

Chen, X. (2009). Review of China's agricultural and rural development: Policy changes and current issues. *China Agricultural Economic Review, 1*(2), 121–135.

Chen, X. (2012). *Social protest and contentious authoritarianism in China*. Cambridge University Press.

Chen, X. (2013). The rising cost of stability. *Journal of Democracy, 24*(1), 57–64.

Chen, X., & Zhang, H. (2012, January). Evaluate the effects of car ownership policies in Chinese megacities: A contrastive study of Beijing and Shanghai. In *91st Annual Meeting. Transportation Research Board Conference* (pp. 22–26).

Chen, X., & Zhao, J. (2013a). Bidding to drive: Car license auction policy in Shanghai and its public acceptance. *Transport Policy, 27*, 39–52.

Chen, X., & Zhao, J. (2013b). *Car owners as a supporting constituency of car deterring policies: Preference variations in Shanghai's car licensing policy*. Transportation Research Board 92nd Annual Meeting (13-4374).

Chen, Y., Jin, G. Z., Kumar, N., & Shi, G. (2013). The promise of Beijing: Evaluating the impact of the 2008 Olympic Games on air quality. *Journal of Environmental Economics and Management, 66*(3), 424–443.

Chen, Y., & Zhou, L. A. (2007). The long-term health and economic consequences of the 1959–1961 famine in China. *Journal of Health Economics, 26*(4), 659–681.

Cheng, F., Zhang, X., & Shenggen, F. (2002). Emergence of urban poverty and inequality in China: Evidence from household survey. *China Economic Review, 13*(4), 430–443.

Cheng, J. Y. (2012). *China: A new stage of development for an emerging superpower*. City University of HK Press.

Cheng, L., Broome, M. E., Feng, S., & Hu, Y. (2017). Factors influencing the implementation of evidence in Chinese nursing practice. *Journal of Clinical Nursing, 26*(23–24), 5103–5112.

Cherchi, E. (2017). A stated choice experiment to measure the effect of informational and normative conformity in the preference for electric vehicles. *Transportation Research Part A: Policy and Practice, 100*, 88–104.

Cherry, C., & Cervero, R. (2007). Use characteristics and mode choice behavior of electric bike users in China. *Transport Policy, 14*(3), 247–257.

Cherry, C. R., Yang, H., Jones, L. R., & He, M. (2016). Dynamics of electric bike ownership and use in Kunming, China. *Transport Policy, 45*, 127–135.

Cheung, G. W., & Rensvold, R. B. (2002). Evaluating goodness-of-fit indexes for testing measurement invariance. *Structural Equation Modeling, 9*(2), 233–255.

Cheung, K. C. K. (2012). Away from socialism, towards Chinese characteristics: Confucianism and the futures of Chinese nationalism. *China Information, 26*(2), 205–218.

Cheung, M., & Liu, M. (2004). The self-concept of Chinese women and the indigenization of social work in China. *International Social Work, 47*(1), 109–127.

Chien, C. L. (2016). Beyond authoritarian personality: The culture-inclusive theory of Chinese authoritarian orientation. *Frontiers in Psychology, 7*, 924.

China Current. (2014). *APEC Blue: Looking Behind the Blue Sky*. [Online]. http://en.cncurrent.com/apec-blue-the-self-awareness-anxiety-and-discomforts-hidden-under-the-blue-sky/. Accessed 11 December 2018.

China Daily. (2013). *Today the chance of getting a license plate is 1%, why the traffic congestion index has not decreased three years after the license plate lottery?* [Online]. http://www.chinadaily.com.cn/dfpd/2013-12/26/content_17198387.htm. Accessed 27 July 2019 (in Chinese).

China Daily. (2014). *'APEC blue' tops Beijing environmental key words for 2014.* [Online]. http://www.chinadaily.com.cn/china/2014-12/24/content_19155697.htm. Accessed 27 July 2019.

China Digital Times. (2013). *Word of the Week: Brickspert.* [Online]. https://chinadigitaltimes.net/2013/08/word-of-the-week-brickspert/. Accessed 27 July 2019.

Chinanews. *Half of Beijing's population live far from downtown.* http://www.ecns.cn/cns-wire/2015/05-22/166429.shtml. Accessed 27 July 2019.

China News Service. (2015). *Beijing plan to pilot congestion charge, citizens: Not reasonable.* [Online]. http://news.sohu.com/20151205/n429872590.shtml. Accessed 27 July 2019 (in Chinese).

China Youth Daily. (2003). *The Fundamental Cause of Traffic Congestion: Bikes.* [Online]. http://www.china.com.cn/chinese/OP-c/421883.htm. Accessed 27 July 2019 (in Chinese).

China Youth Daily. (2010). *New policy announced: To get a Beijing license via the lottery system.* [Online]. http://zqb.cyol.com/content/2010-12/24/content_3468671.htm. Accessed 27 July 2019 (in Chinese).

Choi, Y. (2011). The evolution of "socialism with Chinese Characteristics": Its elliptical structure of socialist Principles and China's realities. *Pacific Focus, 26*(3), 385–404.

Chomeya, R. (2010). Quality of psychology test between Likert scale 5 and 6 points. *Journal of Social Sciences, 6*(3), 399–403.

Chow, T. T. (2013). *May Fourth Movement.* Harvard University Press.

Christiansen, F., & Rai, S. M. (2014). *Chinese politics and society: An introduction.* Routledge.

Chu, C. C., & Lee, R. D. (1994). Famine, revolt, and the dynastic cycle. *Journal of Population Economics, 7*(4), 351–378.

Chu, H., & Gardner, D. K. (1990). *Learning to Be a Sage: Selections from the "Conversations of Master Chu," Arranged Topically.* University of California Press.

Chuang-tzu, & Palmer, M. (2006). *The Book of Chuang Tzu.* Penguin UK.

Churchill, G. A., & Iacobucci, D. (2006). *Marketing research: Methodological foundations.* Dryden Press.

Cialdini, R. B., Wosinska, W.,Barrett, D. W., & Butner, J. (1999). Compliance with a request in two cultures: The differential influence of social proof and commitment/consistency on collectivists and individualists. *Personality and Social Psychology Bulletin, 25*(10), 1242–1253.

Clark, P. (2008). *The Chinese cultural revolution: A history.* Cambridge University Press.

Clark, P. (2012). *Youth culture in China: From red guards to netizens*. Cambridge University Press.

Clee, A. (2007). *Driving away the traffic: What lessons can New York learn from London and Stockholm's experiences with congestion charging*. Tufts University.

Clifton, J., & Díaz-Fuentes, D. (2014). Is the organisation for economic co-operation and development ready for China? *Emerging Markets Finance and Trade, 50*(sup6), 21–36.

Clinton, R. L. (1997). *God and man in the law: The foundations of Anglo-American constitutionalism*. University Press of Kansas.

CNTV. (2012). *Chained interests of the license plate lottery exposed: 200 thousand to get a Beijing a license plate*. [Online]. http://news.cntv.cn/china/20121213/100676.shtml. Accessed 22 November 2018 (in Chinese).

Cohen, M. L. (1991). Being Chinese: The peripheralization of traditional identity. *Daedalus*, 113–134.

Cohn, A., Maréchal, M. A., Tannenbaum, D., & Zünd, C. L. (2019). Civic honesty around the globe. *Science, 8712*(June), 1–9.

Cole, M., & Scribner, S. (1974). *Culture & thought: A psychological introduction*. Wiley.

Coleman, J. S. (1994). *Foundations of social theory*. Harvard University Press.

Conway, J. M., & Huffcutt, A. I. (2003). A review and evaluation of exploratory factor analysis practices in organizational research. *Organizational Research Methods, 6*(2), 147–168.

Corbett, R. (2009). The question of natural law in Aristotle. *History of Political Thought, 30*(2), 229–250.

Costello, A. B., & Osborne, J. W. (2005). Best practices in exploratory factor analysis: Four recommendations for getting the most from your analysis. *Practical Assessment, Research & Evaluation, 10*(7), 1–9.

Courtois, S., Werth, N., Paczkowski, A., Bartosek, K., & Margolin, J.-L. (1999). *The black book of communism: Crimes, terror, repression*. Harvard University Press.

Creemers, R. (2017). Cyber China: Upgrading propaganda, public opinion work and social management for the twenty-first century. *Journal of Contemporary China, 26*(103), 85–100.

Cresswel, J. W. (1994). *Research design: Qualitative and quantitative approaches*. Sage.

Creswell, J. W., & Miller, D. L. (2000). Determining validity in qualitative inquiry. *Theory into Practice, 39*(3), 124–130.

Csontos, L., Kornai, J., & Tóth, I. G. (1998). Tax awareness and reform of the welfare state: Hungarian survey results. *Economics of Transition, 6*(2), 287–312.

Cudeck, R., & MacCallum, R. C. (Eds.). (2012). *Factor analysis at 100: Historical developments and future directions*. Routledge.

Cullinane, S., & Cullinane, K. (2003). Car dependence in a public transport dominated city: Evidence from Hong Kong. *Transportation Research Part D: Transport and Environment, 8*(2), 129–138.

Cuttance, P., & Ecob, R. (Eds.). (2009). *Structural modeling by example: Applications in educational, sociological, and behavioral research*. Cambridge University Press.

Dahl, R. A. (1973). *Polyarchy: Participation and opposition*. Yale University Press.

Dahlberg, L., & McCaig, C. (Eds.). (2010). *Practical research and evaluation: A start-to-finish guide for practitioners*. Sage.

Dahlgren, J. (2002). High-occupancy/toll lanes: Where should they be implemented? *Transportation Research Part A: Policy and Practice, 36*(3), 239–255.

Dahlgren, P. (2018). Media, knowledge and trust: The deepening epistemic crisis of democracy. *Javnost—The Public, 25*(1–2), 20–27.

Dai, Z. (2018). Chairman Xi Jinping Animated Online Videos: Representation of Paternalistic Leadership in a Postmodern Age. *Chinese Studies, 7*(2), 183–196.

Dalton, R. J., Burklin, W. P., & Drummond, A. (2001). Public opinion and direct democracy. *Journal of Democracy, 12*(4), 141–153.

D'Amato, A. (2011). *On the connection between law and justice* (Faculty Working Papers No. 2). http://scholarlycommons.law.northwestern.edu/facultyworkingpapers/2

Danermark, B., Ekstrom, M., & Jakobsen, L. (2005). *Explaining society: An introduction to critical realism in the social sciences*. Routledge.

Davis, L. W. (2008). The effect of driving restrictions on air quality in Mexico City. *Journal of Political Economy, 116*(1), 38–81.

De Groot, J., & Schuitema, G. (2012). How to make the unpopular popular? Policy characteristics, social norms and the acceptability of environmental policies. *Environmental Science & Policy, 19*, 100–107.

De Groot, J., & Steg, L. (2006). Impact of transport pricing on quality of life, acceptability, and intentions to reduce car use: An exploratory study in five European countries. *Journal of Transport Geography, 14*(6), 463–470.

De Jong, M. (2012). The pros and cons of Confucian values in transport infrastructure development in China. *Policy and Society, 31*(1), 13–24.

De Jong, M., Mu, R., Stead, D., Ma, Y., & Xi, B. (2010). Introducing public–private partnerships for metropolitan subways in China: What is the evidence? *Journal of Transport Geography, 18*(2), 301–313.

De Fond, M. L., Wong, T. J., & Li, S. (1999). The impact of improved auditor independence on audit market concentration in China. *Journal of Accounting and Economics, 28*(3), 269–305.

Defoort, C. (2001). Is there such a thing as Chinese philosophy? Arguments of an implicit debate. *Philosophy East and West*, 393–413.

Deng, X. (1984). Building a socialism with a specifically Chinese character. *People's Daily*, 30.

Deng, Y., & O'Brien, K. J. (2013). Relational repression in China: Using social ties to demobilize protesters. *The China Quarterly, 215*, 533–552.

Denzin, N. K., & Lincoln, Y. S. (Eds.). (1998). *Collecting and interpreting qualitative materials*. Sage.

Dernberger, R. F. (1999). The People's Republic of China at 50: The economy. *The China Quarterly, 159*, 606–615.

Diamond, L., & Morlino, L. (Eds.). (2005). *Assessing the quality of democracy*. JHU Press.

Dickson, B. J. (2000). Cooptation and corporatism in China: The logic of party adaptation. *Political Science Quarterly, 115*(4), 517–540.

Diepeveen, S., Ling, T., Suhrcke, M., Roland, M., & Marteau, T. M. (2013). Public acceptability of government intervention to change health-related behaviours: A systematic review and narrative synthesis. *BMC Public Health, 13*(1), 756.

Dikötter, F. (2010). *Mao's great famine: The history of China's most devastating catastrophe, 1958–1962*. Bloomsbury Publishing USA.

Ding, X. L. (2000). The illicit asset stripping of Chinese state firms. *The China Journal, 43*, 1–28.

Dittmer, L. (1974). *Liu Shao-Chi and the Chinese cultural revolution: The politics of mass criticism* (No. 10). University of California Press.

Dittmer, L. (1981). Death and transfiguration: Liu Shaoqi's rehabilitation and contemporary Chinese politics. *The Journal of Asian Studies, 40*(3), 455–479.

Dittmer, L. (2015). *Liu Shaoqi and the Chinese cultural revolution*. Routledge.

Doll, W. J., Xia, W., & Torkzadeh, G. (1994). A confirmatory factor analysis of the end-user computing satisfaction instrument. *MIS Quarterly, 18*(4), 453–461.

Dolowitz, D. P., & Marsh, D. (2000). Learning from abroad: The role of policy transfer in contemporary policy-making. *Governance, 13*(1), 5–23.

Domes, J. (1982). New Policies in the Communes: Notes on Rural Societal Structures in China, 1976–1981. *The Journal of Asian Studies, 41*(02), 253–267.

Dong, J., & Blommaert, J. (2009). Space, scale and accents: Constructing migrant identity in Beijing. In J. Collins, S. Slembrouck, & M. Baynham (Eds.), *Globalization and language in contact* (pp. 42–61). Continuum.

Drezner, D. W. (2001). Globalization and policy convergence. *International Studies Review, 3*(1), 53–78.

Dubois, A., & Gadde, L. E. (2002). Systematic combining: An abductive approach to case research. *Journal of Business Research, 55*(7), 553–560.

Dunn, O. J. (1964). Multiple comparisons using rank sums. *Technometrics, 6*(3), 241–252.

Dunn, S. C., Seaker, R. F., & Waller, M. A. (1994). Latent variables in business logistics research: Scale development and validation. *Journal of Business Logistics, 15*(2), 145.

Dunne, C. (2011). The place of the literature review in grounded theory research. *International Journal of Social Research Methodology, 14*(2), 111–124.

Dunne, D. D., & Dougherty, D. (2016). Abductive reasoning: How innovators navigate in the labyrinth of complex product innovation. *Organization Studies, 37*(2), 131–159.

Dutton, M. R. (1992). *Policing and punishment in China: From patriarchy to "the people"* (Vol. 141). Cambridge University Press.

Duyvendak, J. J. L. (1928). *The Book of Lord Shang*. Probsthain.

Dyck, A. R. (2004). *A commentary on Cicero*. University of Michigan Press.

Dynon, N. (2008). "Four Civilizations" and the evolution of post-Mao Chinese socialist ideology. *The China Journal*, (60), 83–109.

Dyson, K., & Maes, I. (Eds.). (2017). *Architects of the Euro: Intellectuals in the Making of European Monetary Union*. Oxford University Press.

Eagleton, T. (1991). *Ideology: An introduction* (Vol. 9). Verso.

Edin, M. (2003). State capacity and local agent control in China: CCP cadre management from a township perspective. *The China Quarterly, 173*, 35–52.

Eliasson, J., & Jonsson, L. (2011). The unexpected "yes": Explanatory factors behind the positive attitudes to congestion charges in Stockholm. *Transport Policy, 18*(4), 636–647.

Eliasson, J., & Mattsson, L. G. (2006). Equity effects of congestion pricing: Quantitative methodology and a case study for Stockholm. *Transportation Research Part A: Policy and Practice, 40*(7), 602–620.

Ellickson, R. C. (2009). *Order without law: How neighbors settle disputes*. Harvard University Press.

Elster, J. (2011). Hard and soft obscurantism in the humanities and social sciences. *Diogenes, 58*(1–2), 159–170.

Englehart, N. A. (2000). Rights and culture in the Asian values argument: The rise and fall of Confucian ethics in Singapore. *Human Rights Quarterly, 22*(2), 548–568.

Epstein, W. (2017). *The masses are the ruling classes: Policy romanticism, democratic populism, and social welfare in America*. Oxford University Press.

Erie, M. S. (2012). Property rights, legal consciousness and the new media in China: The hard case of the 'toughest nail-house in history.' *China Information, 26*(1), 35–59.

Eriksson, L., Garvill, J., & Nordlund, A. M. (2006). Acceptability of travel demand management measures: The importance of problem awareness, personal norm, freedom, and fairness. *Journal of Environmental Psychology, 26*(1), 15–26.

Eriksson, L., Garvill, J., & Nordlund, A. M. (2008). Acceptability of single and combined transport policy measures: The importance of environmental and policy specific beliefs. *Transportation Research Part A: Policy and Practice, 42*(8), 1117–1128.

Esarey, A. (2015). Winning hearts and minds? Cadres as microbloggers in China. *Journal of Current Chinese Affairs, 44*(2), 69–103.

Esarey, A., & Xiao, Q. (2011). Digital communication and political change in China. *International Journal of Communication, 5*, 298–319.

Evans, M. (Ed.). (2017). *Policy transfer in global perspective*. Taylor & Francis.

Fabrigar, L. R., Wegener, D. T., MacCallum, R. C., & Strahan, E. J. (1999). Evaluating the use of exploratory factor analysis in psychological research. *Psychological Methods, 4*(3), 272.

Fan, C. C. (2007). *China on the move: Migration, the state, and the household*. Routledge.

Fan, C. S. (2016). *Culture, institution, and development in China: The economics of national character*. Routledge.

Fan, Y. (2000). A classification of Chinese culture. *Cross Cultural Management: An International Journal, 7*(2), 3–10.

Fan, X., Thompson, B., & Wang, L. (1999). Effects of sample size, estimation methods, and model specification on structural equation modeling fit indexes. *Structural Equation Modeling: A Multidisciplinary Journal, 6*(1), 56–83.

Fang, K., & Repnikova, M. (2018). Demystifying "Little Pink": The creation and evolution of a gendered label for nationalistic activists in China. *New Media & Society, 20*(6), 2162–2185.

Farh, J. L., & Cheng, B. S. (2000). A cultural analysis of paternalistic leadership in Chinese organizations. *Management and organizations in the Chinese context* (pp. 84–127). Palgrave Macmillan.

Farrell, S., & Saleh, W. (2005). Road-user charging and the modelling of revenue allocation. *Transport Policy, 12*(5), 431–442.

Fei, H. T. (1939). *Peasant life in China: A field study of country life in the Yangtze Valley*. Routledge & Dutton.

Fei, X., Fei, H. T., & Redfield, M. P. (1980). *China's gentry: Essays on rural-urban relations*. University of Chicago Press.

Fei, X., Hamilton, G. G., & Wang, Z. (1992). *From the soil, the foundations of Chinese society: A translation of Fei Xiaotong's Xiangtu Zhongguo, with an introduction and epilogue*. University of California Press.

Feng, J., Dijst, M., Wissink, B., & Prillwitz, J. (2017). Changing travel behaviour in urban China: Evidence from Nanjing 2008–2011. *Transport Policy, 53*, 1–10.

Feng, S., & Ma, Z. (2010). *Performance analysis on private vehicle plate auction in Shanghai*. 6th Advanced Forum on Transportation of China (AFTC 2010).

Feng, S. W., Li, Q., & Xu, D. (2012). *The private car license plate auction in Shanghai: Macro-effectiveness and micro-mechanisms*. COTA International Conference of Transportation Professionals, Beijing.

Feng, W., Gu, B., & Cai, Y. (2016). The end of China's one-child policy. *Studies in Family Planning, 47*(1), 83–86.

Feng, Y., & Bodde, D. (1983). *A history of Chinese philosophy* (Vol. 1). Princeton University Press.

Festinger, L. (1962). *A theory of cognitive dissonance* (Vol. 2). Stanford University Press.

Fewsmith, J. (2013). *The logic and limits of political reform in China*. Cambridge University Press.

Fewsmith, J. (2016). *Dilemmas of reform in China: Political conflict and economic debate*. Routledge.

Finlay, C. J., & Xin, X. (2010). Public diplomacy games: A comparative study of American and Japanese responses to the interplay of nationalism, ideology and Chinese soft power strategies around the 2008 Beijing Olympics. *Sport in Society, 13*(5), 876–900.

Finnis, J. (2011). *Natural law and natural rights*. Oxford University Press.

Flad, R. K. (2011). *Salt production and social hierarchy in ancient China: An archaeological investigation of specialization in China's Three Gorges*. Cambridge University Press.

Flick, U. (2018). *An introduction to qualitative research*. Sage.

Floyd, F. J., & Widaman, K. F. (1995). Factor analysis in the development and refinement of clinical assessment instruments. *Psychological Assessment, 7*(3), 286.

Fogel, R. W. (2000). *The fourth great awakening and the future of egalitarianism*. University of Chicago Press.

Foley, K., Wallace, J. L., & Weiss, J. C. (2018). The political and economic consequences of Nationalist Protest in China: The 2012 Anti-Japanese Demonstrations. *The China Quarterly, 236*, 1131–1153.

Fornell, C., & Larcker, D. F. (1981). Structural equation models with unobservable variables and measurement error: Algebra and statistics. *Journal of Marketing Research, 18*, 382–388.

Foster, K. W. (2016). Chinese public policy innovation and the diffusion of innovations: An initial exploration. *Chinese Public Administration Review, 3*(1/2), 1–13.

Franceschini, I., & Negro, G. (2014). The 'Jasmine Revolution' in China: The limits of the cyber-utopia. *Postcolonial Studies, 17*(1), 23–35.

Francke, A., & Kaniok, D. (2013). Responses to differentiated road pricing schemes. *Transportation Research Part A: Policy and Practice, 48*, 25–30.

Frederickson, H. G. (2002). Confucius and the moral basis of bureaucracy. *Administration & Society, 33*(6), 610–628.

Freedman, M. (1958). *Lineage organization in Southeastern China*. Athlone Press.

Freedman, M. (1966). *Chinese lineage and society: Fukien and Kwangtung* (No. 33). Athlone Press.

Freidlin, B., & Gastwirth, J. L. (2000). Should the median test be retired from general use? *The American Statistician, 54*(3), 161–164.

Friedman, E. (2016). *National identity and democratic prospects in socialist China*. Routledge.

Fromm, E., Suzuki, D. T., & De Martino, R. (1970). *Zen Buddhism and psychoanalysis*. HarperCollins.

Fu, K. W., Chan, C. H., & Chau, M. (2013). Assessing censorship on microblogs in China: Discriminatory keyword analysis and the real-name registration policy. *IEEE Internet Computing, 17*(3), 42–50.

Fu, Q. (2015). From the founding to the ruling party: The identity crisis of Mao Zedong and the Communist Party of China. *Fudan Journal of the Humanities and Social Sciences, 8*(3), 447–469.

Fu, V. K. (1998). Estimating generalized ordered logit models. *Stata Technical Bulletin, 44*(8), 27–30.

Fu, Y., & Gabriel, S. A. (2012). Labor migration, human capital agglomeration and regional development in China. *Regional Science and Urban Economics, 42*(3), 473–484.

Fu, Z. (1993). *Autocratic tradition and Chinese politics*. Cambridge University Press.

Fu, Z. (1996). *China's legalists: The earliest totalitarians and their art of ruling*. ME Sharpe.

Fujii, S., Gärling, T., Jakobsson, C., & Jou, R. C. (2004). A cross-country study of fairness and infringement on freedom as determinants of car owners' acceptance of road pricing. *Transportation, 31*(3), 285–295.

Fukuyama, F. (1989). The end of history? *The National Interest, 16*, 3–18.

Fukuyama, F. (1995). Confucianism and democracy. *Journal of Democracy, 6*(2), 20–33.

Fukuyama, F. (2012). The patterns of history. *Journal of Democracy, 23*(1), 14–26.

Fukuyama, F. (2015). Why is democracy performing so poorly? *Journal of Democracy, 26*(1), 11–20.

Gadenne, D. L., Kennedy, J., & McKeiver, C. (2009). An empirical study of environmental awareness and practices in SMEs. *Journal of Business Ethics, 84*(1), 45–63.

Gallagher, M. E. (2006). Mobilizing the law in China: "Informed disenchantment" and the development of legal consciousness. *Law & Society Review, 40*(4), 783–816.

Gan, H., & Ye, X. (2018). Will commute drivers switch to park-and-ride under the influence of multimodal traveler information? A stated preference investigation. *Transportation Research Part F: Traffic Psychology and Behaviour, 56*, 354–361.

Gao, H. (2000). *How did the Sun Rise over Yan'an?* The Chinese University of Hong Kong Press. (in Chinese).

Gao, H. (2012, April 16). Rumor, lies, and Weibo: How social media is changing the nature of truth in China. *The Atlantic.*

Garland, R. (1991). The mid-point on a rating scale: Is it desirable. *Marketing Bulletin, 2*(1), 66–70.

Gärling, T. (2007). Effectiveness, public acceptance, and political feasibility of coercive measures for reducing car traffic. In *Threats from car traffic to the quality of urban life*. Emerald Group Publishing Limited.

Gärling, T., Jakobsson, C., Loukopoulos, P., Fujii, S. (2008). Acceptability of road pricing. In E. Verhoef, E. Bliemer, L. Steg, & B. Van Wee (Eds.), *Pricing in Road Transport: Multidisciplinary Perspectives*. Edward Elgar.

Gärling, T., & Schuitema, G. (2007). Travel demand management targeting reduced private car use: Effectiveness, public acceptability and political feasibility. *Journal of Social Issues, 63*(1), 139–153.

Garver, M. S., & Mentzer, J. T. (1999). Logistics research methods: Employing structural equation modeling to test for construct validity. *Journal of Business Logistics, 20*(1), 33–57.

Gastil, J., Black, L., & Moscovitz, K. (2008). Ideology, attitude change, and deliberation in small face-to-face groups. *Political Communication, 25*(1), 23–46.

Gaunt, M., Rye, T., & Allen, S. (2007). Public acceptability of road user charging: The case of Edinburgh and the 2005 referendum. *Transport Reviews, 27*(1), 85–102.

Gaunt, M., Rye, T., & Ison, S. (2006). Gaining public support for congestion charging: Lessons from referendum in Edinburgh Scotland. *Transportation Research Record, 1960*(1), 87–93.

Gehlert, T., Kramer, C., Nielsen, O. A., & Schlag, B. (2011). Socioeconomic differences in public acceptability and car use adaptation towards urban road pricing. *Transport Policy, 18*(5), 685–694.

Geng, J., Long, R., & Chen, H. (2016). Impact of information intervention on travel mode choice of urban residents with different goal frames: A controlled trial in Xuzhou, China. *Transportation Research Part A: Policy and Practice, 91*, 134–147.

Gerbing, D. W., & Anderson, J. C. (1988). An updated paradigm for scale development incorporating unidimensionality and its assessment. *Journal of Marketing Research, 25*(2), 186–192.

Gerring, J. (2006). *Case study research: Principles and practices.* Cambridge University Press.

Gilley, B. (2008). Legitimacy and institutional change: The case of China. *Comparative Political Studies, 41*(3), 259–284.

Gilley, B. (2009). Is democracy possible? *Journal of Democracy, 20*(1), 113–127.

Giuliano, G. (1994). Equity and fairness considerations of congestion pricing. *Transportation Research Board Special Report*, 242.

Glaser, B. G., & Strauss, A. L. (1967). *Discovery of grounded theory: Strategies for qualitative research.* Wiedenfeld and Nicholson.

Global Times. (2012). *Shocking quotes from Chinese economists.* [Online]. http://opinion.huanqiu.com/1152/2012-08/3066125.html]. Accessed 22 December 2018 (in Chinese).

Global Times. (2013). *Chinese Singaporeans: well done China's license plate lottery policy and housing price adjustment*. [Online]. http://world.huanqiu.com/exclusive/2013-03/3706374.html. Accessed 22 November 2018 (in Chinese).

Goetzke, F., Gerike, R., Páez, A., & Dugundji, E. (2015). Social interactions in transportation: Analyzing groups and spatial networks. *Transportation, 42*(5), 723–731.

Golafshani, N. (2003). Understanding reliability and validity in qualitative research. *The Qualitative Report, 8*(4), 597–606.

Goldin, P. R. (2001). Han Fei's doctrine of self-interest. *Asian Philosophy, 11*(3), 151–159.

Goldin, P. R. (2011). Persistent Misconceptions about Chinese "Legalism." *Journal of Chinese Philosophy, 38*(1), 88–104.

Goldin, P. R. (2013). *Dao companion to the philosophy of Han Fei.* Springer.

Goldman, M. (1981). China's Intellectuals. *Index on Censorship, 10*(6), 85–89.

Goldman, M. (2009). Repression of China's public intellectuals in the post-Mao era. *Social Research: An International Quarterly, 76*(2), 659–686.

Goldstein, A., & Guo, S. (1992). Temporary migration in Shanghai and Beijing. *Studies in Comparative International Development, 27*(2), 39–56.

Golob, T. F. (2003). Structural equation modeling for travel behavior research. *Transportation Research Part B: Methodological, 37*(1), 1–25.

Good, K. (2003). Democracy and the control of elites. *Journal of Contemporary African Studies, 21*(2), 155–172.

Gorsuch, R. L. (1997). Exploratory factor analysis: Its role in item analysis. *Journal of Personality Assessment, 68*(3), 532–560.

Gow, A. J., Whiteman, M. C., Pattie, A., & Deary, I. J. (2005). Goldberg's 'IPIP' Big-Five factor markers: Internal consistency and concurrent validation in Scotland. *Personality and Individual Differences, 39*(2), 317–329.

Graham, A. C. (1989). *Disputes ofthe Tao: Philosophical arguments in ancient china.* Open Court.

Gray, D., & Begg, D. (2001). *Delivering congestion charging in the UK: What is required for its successful introduction?* Robert Gordon University.

Gregor, A. J., & Chang, M. H. (1979). Anti-Confucianism: Mao's last campaign. *Asian Survey, 19*(11), 1073–1092.

Grisolía, J. M., López, F., & de Dios Ortúzar, J. (2015). Increasing the acceptability of a congestion charging scheme. *Transport Policy, 39*, 37–47.

Guldin, G. E. (1994). From the Soil: The Foundations of Chinese Society, a Translation of Fei Xiaotong's Xiangtu Zhongguo (Introduction and Epilogue by Gary G. Hamilton and Wang Zheng, 169 p.) [University of California Press. Hard cover $35.00, ISBN 0-520-07795-4; paperback $11.00, ISBN 0-520-07796-2]. *The China Quarterly, 137*, 262–263.

Guo, G. (2009). China's local political budget cycles. *American Journal of Political Science, 53*(3), 621–632.

Guo, J. (2014). *Interpretation of the basic content of Core Socialist Values. People's Publishing House* (in Chinese).

Guo, S., & Guo, B. (Eds.). (2008). *China in search of a harmonious society.* Lexington Books.

Guo, Y. (2008). Corruption in transitional China: An empirical analysis. *The China Quarterly, 194*, 349–364.

Gustafsson, B. A., Shi, L., & Sicular, T. (Eds.). (2008). *Inequality and public policy in China.* Cambridge University Press.

Hair, J., Anderson, R., Tatham, R., & Black, W. (1995). *Multivariate data analysis with readings* (4th ed.). Prentice Hall International.

Hakim, C. (1987). *Research design: Strategies and choices in the design of social research.* Allen & Unwin.

Hall, S. G., & Ambrosio, T. (2017). Authoritarian learning: A conceptual overview. *East European Politics, 33*(2), 143–161.

Hamilton, G. G. (1990). Patriarchy, patrimonialism, and filial piety: A comparison of China and Western Europe. *British Journal of Sociology, 41*(1), 77–104.

Han, F. (1964). *Han Fei Tzu: Basic Writings* (B. Watson, Trans.). Columbia University Press.

Han, F., & Watson, B. (1964). *Han Fei Tzu.* Columbia University Press.

Han, R. (2015a). Manufacturing consent in cyberspace: China's 'fifty-cent army.' *Journal of Current Chinese Affairs, 44*(2), 105–134.

Han, R. (2015b). Defending the authoritarian regime online: China's "voluntary fifty-cent army." *The China Quarterly, 224*, 1006–1025.

Han, R. (2018a). *Contesting cyberspace in China: Online expression and authoritarian resilience.* Columbia University Press.

Han, R. (2018b). Withering gongzhi: Cyber criticism of Chinese public intellectuals. *International Journal of Communication, 12*, 1966–1987.

Han, R. (2018c). *Contesting cyberspace in China.* Columbia University Press.

Hancock, G. R. (2003). Fortune cookies, measurement error, and experimental design. *Journal of Modern Applied Statistical Methods, 2*(2), 293–305.

Hao, H., Wang, H., & Ouyang, M. (2011). Comparison of policies on vehicle ownership and use between Beijing and Shanghai and their impacts on fuel consumption by passenger vehicles. *Energy Policy, 39*(2), 1016–1021.

Hardin, G. (1968). The Tragedy of the Commons. *Science, 162*(3859), 1243–1248.

Harding, H. (1971). China: Toward revolutionary pragmatism. *Asian Survey, 11*(1), 51–67.

Hardoon, D. R., Szedmak, S., & Shawe-Taylor, J. (2004). Canonical correlation analysis: An overview with application to learning methods. *Neural Computation, 16*(12), 2639–2664.

Hårsman, B., & Quigley, J. M. (2010). Political and public acceptability of congestion pricing: Ideology and self-interest. *Journal of Policy Analysis and Management, 29*(4), 854–874.

Hartford, K., & Goldstein, S. M. (2016). *Single sparks: China's rural revolutions.* Routledge.

Hartmann, P., & Apaolaza-Ibáñez, V. (2012). Consumer attitude and purchase intention toward green energy brands: The roles of psychological benefits and environmental concern. *Journal of Business Research, 65*(9), 1254–1263.

Hassid, J. (2008). Controlling the Chinese media: An uncertain business. *Asian Survey, 48*(3), 414–430.

Hatemi, P. K., Alford, J. R., Hibbing, J. R., Martin, N. G., & Eaves, L. J. (2008). Is there a 'party' in your genes? *Political Research Quarterly, 62*, 584–600.

Hatton, C. (2015). *Under the Dome: The smog film taking China by storm*. BBC China Blog. BBC.

Hau, T. D. (1990). Electronic road pricing: Developments in Hong Kong 1983–1989. *Journal of Transport Economics and Policy, 24*(2), 203–214.

Haven-Tang, C., Jones, E., & Webb, C. (2007). Critical success factors for business tourism destinations: Exploiting Cardiffs national capital city status and shaping its business tourism offer. *Journal of Travel & Tourism Marketing, 22*(3–4), 109–120.

Hayek, F. A. (1960 [2014]). *The constitution of liberty*. Routledge.

He, K., Huo, H., Zhang, Q., & He, D. (2005). Oil consumption and CO_2 emissions in China's road transport: Current status, future trends, and policy implications. *Energy Policy, 33*(12), 1499–1507.

He, G., Mol, A. P., & Lu, Y. (2016). Public protests against the Beijing-Shenyang high-speed railway in China. *Transportation Research Part D: Transport and Environment, 43*, 1–16.

He, L. Y., & Qiu, L. Y. (2016). Transport demand, harmful emissions, environment and health co-benefits in China. *Energy Policy, 97*, 267–275.

Heberer, T., & Trappel, R. (2013). Evaluation processes, local cadres' behaviour and local development processes. *Journal of Contemporary China, 22*(84), 1048–1066.

Hechter, M., & Opp, K. D. (Eds.). (2001). *Social norms*. Russell Sage Foundation.

Hegel, G. W. F., & Brown, R. F. (2006). *Lectures on the history of philosophy: Greek philosophy* (Vol. 1). Oxford University Press.

Heilmann, S., & Perry, E. J. (Eds.). (2011). *Mao's invisible hand: The political foundations of adaptive governance in China*. Harvard University Asia Center.

Heinrich, A., & Pleines, H. (2018). The meaning of 'limited pluralism' in media reporting under authoritarian rule. *Politics and Governance, 6*(2), 103–111.

Hellman, J. S. (1998). Winners take all: The politics of partial reform in post communist transitions. *World Politics, 50*(02), 203–234.

Henderson, J. V., Quigley, J., & Lim, E. (2009). *Urbanization in China: Policy issues and options*. Unpublished manuscript, Brown University.

Heng, C. K. (1999). *Cities of aristocrats and bureaucrats: The development of medieval Chinese cityscapes*. University of Hawaii Press.

Hensher, D. A., & Puckett, S. M. (2005). Road user charging: The global relevance of recent developments in the United Kingdom. *Transport Policy, 12*(5), 377–383.

Hensher, D. A., & Puckett, S. M. (2007). Congestion and variable user charging as an effective travel demand management instrument. *Transportation Research Part A: Policy and Practice, 41*(7), 615–626.

Hickman, R. L., Jr., Pinto, M. D., Lee, E., & Daly, B. J. (2012). Exploratory and confirmatory factor analysis of the decision regret scale in recipients of internal cardioverter defibrillators. *Journal of Nursing Measurement, 20*(1), 21–34.

Hillman, B., & Tuttle, G. (Eds.). (2016). *Ethnic conflict and protest in Tibet and Xinjiang: Unrest in China's west*. Columbia University Press.

Ho Chi Minh. (1945, September 2). *Declaration of Independence of the Democratic Republic of Vietnam*. [Online]. http://www.chinhphu.vn/cttdtcp/en/about_vietnam01.html. Accessed 20 March 2019.

Hobbes, T. (1651 [2006]). *Leviathan*. A&C Black.

Hoffmann, R., & Larner, J. (2013). The demography of Chinese nationalism: A field-experimental approach. *The China Quarterly, 213*, 189–204.

Holbig, H. (2008). Ideological reform and political legitimacy in China: Challenges in the post-Jiang era. In *Regime legitimacy in contemporary China* (pp. 27–48). Routledge.

Holbig, H. (2009). Remaking the CCP's ideology: Determinants, progress, and limits under Hu Jintao. *Journal of Current Chinese Affairs, 38*(3), 35–61.

Holbig, H. (2013). Ideology after the end of ideology. China and the quest for autocratic legitimation. *Democratization, 20*(1), 61–81.

Holbig, H., & Gilley, B. (2010). Reclaiming legitimacy in China. *Politics & Policy, 38*(3), 395–422.

Holcombe, C. (2011). *A history of East Asia: From the origins of civilization to the twenty-first century*. Cambridge University Press.

Holloway Jr., R. L. (1969). Culture: A human domain. *Current Anthropology*, 395–412.

Holmstrom, N., & Smith, R. (2000). The necessity of gangster capitalism: Primitive accumulation in Russia and China. *Monthly Review, 51*(9), 1.

Hong, J., Chu, Z., & Wang, Q. (2011). Transport infrastructure and regional economic growth: Evidence from China. *Transportation, 38*(5), 737–752.

Hong, Y., Huang, N., Burtch, G., & Li, C. (2016). Culture, conformity and emotional suppression in online reviews. *Journal of the Association for Information Systems,* Forthcoming, Fox School of Business Research Paper, (16–020).

Hookham, S. K. (1991). *The Buddha within: Tathagatagarbha doctrine according to the Shentong interpretation of the Ratnagotravibhaga* (No. 104). SUNY Press.

Hooper, D., Coughlan, J., & Mullen, M. (2008). Structural equation modelling: Guidelines for determining model fit. *Electronic Journal of Business Research Methods, 6*(1), 53–60.

Hopf, T. (2012). *Reconstructing the Cold War: The early years, 1945–1958*. Oxford University Press.

Hoppe, H. H. (2018). *Democracy—The god that failed: The economics and politics of monarchy, democracy and natural order*. Routledge.

Hornby, A. S., & Wehmeier, S. (1995). *Oxford advanced learner's dictionary* (Vol. 1428). Oxford University Press.

Hou, Q., & Li, S. M. (2011). Transport infrastructure development and changing spatial accessibility in the Greater Pearl River Delta, China, 1990–2020. *Journal of Transport Geography, 19*(6), 1350–1360.

Houston, M. B. (2004). Assessing the validity of secondary data proxies for marketing constructs. *Journal of Business Research, 57*(2), 154–161.

Howard, K. I., & Forehand, G. A. (1962). A method for correcting item-total correlations for the effect of relevant item inclusion. *Educational and Psychological Measurement, 22*(4), 731–735.

Howell, J. (1993). *China opens its doors: The politics of economic transition.* Harvester Wheatsheaf.

Hsiao, K. C. (1976). Legalism and autocracy in traditional China. *Chinese Studies in History, 10*(1–2), 125–143.

Hsu, C. L. (2001). Political narratives and the production of legitimacy: The case of corruption in post-Mao China. *Qualitative Sociology, 24*(1), 25–54.

Hu, J. (2012, November 8). *Firmly March on the Path of Socialism with Chinese Characteristics and Strive to Complete the Building of a Moderately Prosperous*

Society in all Respects. Political report delivered at the 18th national party congress, Beijing.

Hu, L., & Bentler, P. M. (1999). Cutoff criteria for fit indexes in covariance structure analysis: Conventional criteria versus new alternatives. *Structural Equation Modeling, 6*(1), 1–55.

Hu, X. (2017). From coal mining to coal chemicals? Unpacking new path creation in an old industrial region of transitional China. *Growth and Change, 48*(2), 233–245.

Huan Kuan. (1967). *Discourses on Salt and Iron: A Debate on State Control of Commerce and Industry in Ancient China, Chapters I–XIX* (E. M. Gale, Trans.). Ch'engwen, Taipei.

Huang, L. C., & Harris, M. B. (1973). Conformity in Chinese and Americans: A field experiment. *Journal of Cross-Cultural Psychology, 4*(4), 427–434.

Huang, R. (2011). *Yellow River and Blue Mountains*. Linking Publishing.

Huang, S. C. (1999). *Essentials of neo-Confucianism: Eight major philosophers of the Song and Ming periods*. Greenwood Publishing Group.

Huang, Y. (2002). Approaching "Pareto optimality"?—A critical analysis of media-orchestrated Chinese nationalism. *Intercultural Communication Studies, 11*(2), 69–88.

Huang, Y. H. (2000). The personal influence model and Gao Guanxi in Taiwan Chinese public relations. *Public Relations Review, 26*(2), 219–236.

Huang, Z., & de Bary, W. T. (1993). *Waiting for the Dawn: A Plan for the Prince*. Columbia University Press.

Hughes, C. (2006). *Chinese nationalism in the global era*. Routledge.

Hurst, W., Liu, M., Liu, Y., & Tao, R. (2014). Reassessing collective petitioning in rural China: Civic engagement, extra-state violence, and regional variation. *Comparative Politics, 46*(4), 459–482.

Hysing, E. (2015). Citizen participation or representative government–Building legitimacy for the Gothenburg congestion tax. *Transport Policy, 39*, 1–8.

Hysing, E., Frändberg, L., & Vilhelmson, B. (2015). Compromising sustainable mobility? The case of the Gothenburg congestion tax. *Journal of Environmental Planning and Management, 58*(6), 1058–1075.

Hyun, K. D., & Kim, J. (2015). The role of new media in sustaining the status quo: Online political expression, nationalism, and system support in China. *Information, Communication & Society, 18*(7), 766–781.

Ieromonachou, P., Potter, S., & Warren, J. P. (2006). Norway's urban toll rings: Evolving towards congestion charging? *Transport Policy, 13*(5), 367–378.

Ikels, C. (1993). Chinese kinship and the state: Shaping of policy for the elderly. *Annual Review of Gerontology and Geriatrics, 13*(1), 123–146.

Ip, P. K. (2009). Is Confucianism good for business ethics in China? *Journal of Business Ethics, 88*(3), 463–476.

Ip, P. K. (2009). The challenge of developing a business ethics in China. *Journal of Business Ethics, 88*(1), 211–224.

Ison, S. (2000). Local authority and academic attitudes to urban road pricing: A UK perspective. *Transport Policy, 7*(4), 269–277.

Jacobs, L., Guopei, G., & Herbig, P. (1995). Confucian roots in China: A force for today's business. *Management Decision, 33*(10), 29–34.

Jaensirisak, S., Wardman, M., & May, A. D. (2005). Explaining variations in public acceptability of road pricing schemes. *Journal of Transport Economics and Policy, 39*(2), 127–153.

Jakobsson, C., Fujii, S., & Gärling, T. (2000). Determinants of private car users' acceptance of road pricing. *Transport Policy, 7*(2), 153–158.

Jakobsson, U. (2004). Statistical presentation and analysis of ordinal data in nursing research. *Scandinavian Journal of Caring Sciences, 18*(4), 437–440.

James, O., & Lodge, M. (2003). The limitations of 'policy transfer'and 'lesson drawing'for public policy research. *Political Studies Review, 1*(2), 179–193.

James, P. (2014). *Urban sustainability in theory and practice: Circles of sustainability*. Routledge.

James, P., & Steger, M. (2010). *Globalization and culture, Vol. 4: Ideologies of globalism*. Sage.

Jamieson, S. (2004). Likert scales: How to (ab) use them. *Medical Education, 38*(12), 1217–1218.

Jarvie, I. C., Milford, K., & Miller, D. W. (Eds.). (2006). *Karl Popper: A Centenary Assessment Volume I*. Ashgate Publishing Ltd.

Jeffreys, E. (2007). Debating the legal regulation of sex-related bribery and corruption in the People's Republic of China. In *Sex and sexuality in China* (pp. 167–186). Routledge.

Jensen, A. F., Cherchi, E., & Mabit, S. L. (2013). On the stability of preferences and attitudes before and after experiencing an electric vehicle. *Transportation Research Part D: Transport and Environment, 25*, 24–32.

Jia, G., Chen, Y., Xue, X., Chen, J., Cao, J., & Tang, K. (2011). Program management organization maturity integrated model for mega construction programs in China. *International Journal of Project Management, 29*(7), 834–845.

Jia, N., Zhang, Y., He, Z., & Li, G. (2017). Commuters' acceptance of and behavior reactions to license plate restriction policy: A case study of Tianjin, China. *Transportation Research Part D: Transport and Environment, 52*, 428–440.

Jiang, Z. (1997, October 6–12). Hold high the great banner of Deng Xiaoping Theory for an all round advancement of the cause of building socialism with Chinese characteristics into the 21st century. *Beijing Review*, 10–33.

Jiang, J., Xie, D., Ye, B., Shen, B., & Chen, Z. (2016). Research on China's cap-and-trade carbon emission trading scheme: Overview and outlook. *Applied Energy, 178*, 902–917.

Jiang, S. (2015). *5 things to know about China's 'Inconvenient Truth'*. http://edition.cnn.com/2015/03/02/asia/china-smog-documentary/. Accessed 27 July 2019.

Jin, G. (1993). Socialism and tradition: The formation and development of modern Chinese political culture. *The Journal of Contemporary China, 2*(3), 3–17.

Jin, Q. (1999). *The culture of power: The Lin Biao incident in the Cultural Revolution*. Stanford University Press.

Johansson, B., & Mattsson, L. G. (Eds.). (2012). *Road pricing: Theory, empirical assessment and policy*. Springer Science & Business Media.

Johnston, A. I. (2017). Is Chinese Nationalism Rising? Evidence from Beijing. *International Security, 41*(3), 7–43.

Joireman, J. A., Lasane, T. P., Bennett, J., Richards, D., & Solaimani, S. (2001). Integrating social value orientation and the consideration of future consequences within the extended norm activation model of proenvironmental behaviour. *British Journal of Social Psychology, 40*(1), 133–155.

Jolliffe, I. T. (1986). Principal component analysis and factor analysis. In *Principal component analysis*. Springer.

Jones, P. (1998). Urban road pricing: Public acceptability and barriers to implementation. In K. J. Button & E. T. Verhoef (Eds.), *Road pricing, traffic congestion and the environment*. Edward Elgar Publishing.

Jöreskog, K. G., & Sörbom, D. (1993). *LISREL 8: Structural equation modeling with the SIMPLIS command language*. Scientific Software International.

Josephson, J. R., & Josephson, S. G. (Eds.). (1996). *Abductive inference: Computation, philosophy, technology*. Cambridge University Press.

JRJ. (2018). *Only one out of 2000 people can get a license, some people did fake marriage for license plates*. [Online]. http://finance.jrj.com.cn/2018/02/28065724164610.shtml. Accessed 22 November 2018 (in Chinese).

Kallbekken, S., & Sælen, H. (2011). Public acceptance for environmental taxes: Self-interest, environmental and distributional concerns. *Energy Policy, 39*(5), 2966–2973.

Kambhatla, N., & Leen, T. K. (1997). Dimension reduction by local principal component analysis. *Neural Computation, 9*(7), 1493–1516.

Kaplan, D. (2008). *Structural equation modeling: Foundations and extensions*. Sage.

Kelman, H. C., & Hamilton, V. L. (1989). *Crimes of obedience: Toward a social psychology of authority and responsibility*. Yale University Press.

Kenny, D. A., & McCoach, D. B. (2003). Effect of the number of variables on measures of fit in structural equation modeling. *Structural Equation Modeling, 10*(3), 333–351.

Kenworthy, J., & Hu, G. (2002). Transport and urban form in Chinese cities: an international comparative and policy perspective with implications for sustainable urban transport in China. *disP-The Planning Review, 38*(151), 4–14.

Khodadady, E., & Hashemi, M. R. (2010). Construct validity of beliefs about language learning: Componential or factorial. *Ferdowsi Review, 1*(1), 3–20.

Kiernan, B. (2002). *The Pol Pot regime: Race, power, and genocide in Cambodia under the Khmer Rouge, 1975–79*. Yale University Press.

Kim, J., Rasouli, S., & Timmermans, H. (2014). Expanding scope of hybrid choice models allowing for mixture of social influences and latent attitudes: Application to intended purchase of electric cars. *Transportation Research Part A: Policy and Practice, 69*, 71–85.

Kim, J., Schmöcker, J. D., Bergstad, C. J., Fujii, S., & Gärling, T. (2014). The influence of personality on acceptability of sustainable transport policies. *Transportation, 41*(4), 855–872.

Kim, J., Schmöcker, J. D., Fujii, S., & Noland, R. B. (2013). Attitudes towards road pricing and environmental taxation among US and UK students. *Transportation Research Part A: Policy and Practice, 48*, 50–62.

Kim, J. O., & Mueller, C. W. (1978). *Introduction to factor analysis: What it is and how to do it* (No. 13). Sage.

King, D., Manville, M., & Shoup, D. (2007). The political calculus of congestion pricing. *Transport Policy, 14*(2), 111–123.

King, G., Pan, J., & Roberts, M. E. (2013). How censorship in China allows government criticism but silences collective expression. *American Political Science Review, 107*(2), 326–343.

King, G., Pan, J., & Roberts, M. E. (2017). How the Chinese government fabricates social media posts for strategic distraction, not engaged argument. *American Political Science Review, 111*(3), 484–501.

King, N. (1994). The qualitative research interview. In C. Cassell & G. Symon (Eds.), *Qualitative methods in organizational research: A practical guide* (pp. 14–36). Sage.

Kirkbride, P. S., Tang, S. F., & Westwood, R. I. (1991). Chinese conflict preferences and negotiating behaviour: Cultural and psychological influences. *Organization Studies, 12*(3), 365–386.

Kirkby, R. J. (2018). *Urbanization in China: Town and country in a developing economy 1949–2000 AD*. Routledge.

Kirkland, R. (2004). *Taoism: The enduring tradition*. Routledge.

Kitamura, R., Nakayama, S., & Yamamoto, T. (1999). Self-reinforcing motorization: Can travel demand management take us out of the social trap? *Transport Policy, 6*(3), 135–145.

Kitschelt, H. (1999). *Post-communist party systems: Competition, representation, and inter-party cooperation*. Cambridge University Press.

Kline, P. (2014). *An easy guide to factor analysis*. Routledge.

Kline, R. B. (1998). *Principles and practice of structural equation modeling*. Guilford Press.

Knoblock, J. (1994). *Xunzi: A translation and study of the complete works* (Vol. 3). Stanford University Press.

Kong, S., Chen, S.-H., Acton, H., & Birch, C. (2015). *The Peach Blossom Fan*. University of California Press.

Konsky, C., Eguchi, M., Blue, J., & Kapoor, S. (2000). Individualist-collectivist values: American, Indian and Japanese cross-cultural study. *Intercultural Communication Studies, 9*(1), 69–84.

Koop, G., & Tole, L. (2001). Deforestation, distribution and development. *Global Environmental Change, 11*(3), 193–202.

Kottenhoff, K., & Freij, K. B. (2009). The role of public transport for feasibility and acceptability of congestion charging—The case of Stockholm. *Transportation Research Part A: Policy and Practice, 43*(3), 297–305.

Kou, C. W., & Tsai, W. H. (2014). "Sprinting with small steps" towards promotion: Solutions for the age dilemma in the CCP cadre appointment system. *The China Journal, 71*, 153–171.

Koufteros, X. A. (1999). Testing a model of pull production: A paradigm for manufacturing research using structural equation modeling. *Journal of Operations Management, 17*(4), 467–488.

Koufteros, X., Vonderembse, M., & Doll, W. (2001). Concurrent engineering and its consequences. *Journal of Operations Management, 19*(1), 97–115.

Krätke, S. (2004). City of talents? Berlin's regional economy, socio-spatial fabric and 'worst practice' urban governance. *International Journal of Urban and Regional Research, 28*(3), 511–529.

Kraus, W. (1991). *Private business in China: Revival between ideology and pragmatism*. University of Hawaii Press.

Kriston, L., Scholl, I., Hölzel, L., Simon, D., Loh, A., & Härter, M. (2010). The 9-item Shared Decision Making Questionnaire (SDM-Q-9). Development and psychometric properties in a primary care sample. *Patient Education and Counseling, 80*(1), 94–99.

Kroeber, A. L., & Kluckhohn, C. (1952). *Culture: A critical review of concepts and definitions*. Harvard University.

Kruskal, W. H., & Wallis, W. A. (1952). Use of ranks in one-criterion variance analysis. *Journal of the American Statistical Association, 47*(260), 583–621.

Kuang-Chien, C. (1971). ON THE AMPHIBIAN NATURE OF THOUGHT. *Chinese Studies in Philosophy, 2*(4), 264–267.

Kuklick, B. (2013). *Blind oracles: Intellectuals and war from Kennan to Kissinger*. Princeton University Press.

Kung, J. K. S., & Lin, J. Y. (2003). The causes of China's Great Leap Famine, 1959–1961*. *Economic Development and Cultural Change, 52*(1), 51–73.

Kutcher, N. (2000). The fifth relationship: Dangerous friendships in the Confucian context. *The American Historical Review, 105*(5), 1615–1629.

Kuzon, W. M., Jr., Urbanchek, M. G., & McCabe, S. (1996). The seven deadly sins of statistical analysis. *Annals of Plastic Surgery, 37*(3), 265–272.

Kvale, S., & Brinkmann, S. (2008). *InterViews: Learning the craft of qualitative research interviewing*. Sage.

Kwong, J. (1994). Ideological crisis among China's youths: Values and official ideology. *British Journal of Sociology*, 247–264.

Kwong, J. (2011). Education and identity: The marginalisation of migrant youths in Beijing. *Journal of Youth Studies, 14*(8), 871–883.

Landsberger, S. R. (2001). Learning by what example? Educational propaganda in twenty-first-century China. *Critical Asian Studies, 33*(4), 541–571.

Laozi, Roig, J. V., & Little, S. (2007). *Tao te ching*. National Braille Press.

Larson, W. (2009). *From Ah Q to Lei Feng: Freud and revolutionary spirit in 20th century China*. Stanford University Press.

Leape, J. (2006). The London congestion charge. *Journal of Economic Perspectives, 20*(4), 157–176.

Lee, C. K., & Shen, Y. (2009). China: The paradox and possibility of a public sociology of labor. *Work and Occupations, 36*(2), 110–125.

Lee, C. K., & Zhang, Y. (2013). The power of instability: Unraveling the microfoundations of bargained authoritarianism in China. *American Journal of Sociology, 118*(6), 1475–1508.

Lee, H. Y. (1980). *The politics of the Chinese cultural revolution: A case study* (No. 17). University of California Press.

Lee, K. K. (1998). Confucian tradition in the contemporary Korean family. *Confucianism and the Family*, 249–266.

Lee, T. H. (2000). *Education in traditional China: A history* (Vol. 13). Brill.

Leese, D. (2011). *Mao Cult: Rhetoric and Ritual in China's Cultural Revolution*. Cambridge University Press.

Legge, J. (2009). *The Confucian analects, the great learning & the doctrine of the mean*. Cosimo Inc.

Lei, Y. W. (2013). The political consequences of the rise of the Internet: Political beliefs and practices of Chinese netizens. In *Political Communication in China* (pp. 37–68). Routledge.

Leibold, J. (2011). Blogging alone: China, the internet, and the democratic illusion? *The Journal of Asian Studies, 70*(4), 1023–1041.

Leites, N. (1953). Stalin as an intellectual. *World Politics, 6*(1), 45–66.
Leng, S. C. (1977). The role of law in the People's Republic of China as reflecting Mao Tse-Tung's influence. *Journal of Criminal Law and Criminology*, 356–373.
Levenson, J. R. (1968). *Confucian China and its modern fate: A trilogy*. University of California Press.
Levine, J., & Garb, Y. (2002). Congestion pricing's conditional promise: Promotion of accessibility or mobility? *Transport Policy, 9*(3), 179–188.
Levitsky, S., & Way, L. A. (2010). *Competitive authoritarianism: Hybrid regimes after the Cold War*. Cambridge University Press.
Lewis, M. E. (2009). *The early Chinese Empires: Qin and Han* (Vol. 1). Harvard University Press.
Lewis, N. C. (1993). *Road pricing theory and practice*. Thomas Telford.
Lewis-Beck, M., Bryman, A. E., & Liao, T. F. (2003). *The Sage encyclopedia of social science research methods*. Sage.
Li, C. (2012). The end of the CCP's resilient authoritarianism? A tripartite assessment of shifting power in China. *The China Quarterly, 211*, 595–623.
Li, F., Wang, R., Paulussen, J., & Liu, X. (2005). Comprehensive concept planning of urban greening based on ecological principles: A case study in Beijing China. *Landscape and Urban Planning, 72*(4), 325–336.
Li, G. (1995). *A glossary of political terms of the People's Republic of China*. Chinese University Press.
Li, H., Bao, W., Xiu, C., Zhang, Y., & Xu, H. (2010). Energy conservation and circular economy in China's process industries. *Energy, 35*(11), 4273–4281.
Li, J. (2000). *Power, money, and media: Communication patterns and bureaucratic control in cultural China*. Northwestern University Press.
Li, J. (2016). *North China's choking, persistent smog 'a political problem', says outspoken sociologist: Chinese authorities should seek solutions instead of going after critics, says Renmin University sociology professor Zhou Xiaozheng*. http://www.scmp.com/news/china/policies-politics/article/1904753/north-chinas-choking-persistent-smog-political-problem. Accessed 27 July 2019.
Li, L. (2004). Political trust in rural China. *Modern China, 30*(2), 228–258.
Li, L. (2008). Political trust and petitioning in the Chinese countryside. *Comparative Politics, 40*(2), 209–226.
Li, L., Liu, M., & O'Brien, K. J. (2012). Petitioning Beijing: The high tide of 2003–2006. *The China Quarterly, 210*, 313–334.
Li, L., & O'brien, K. J. (2008). Protest leadership in rural China. *The China Quarterly, 193*, 1–23.
Li, P., Zhong, M., Lin, B., & Zhang, H. (2004). Deyu as moral education in modern China: Ideological functions and transformations. *Journal of Moral Education, 33*(4), 449–464.

Li, T., Yang, W., Zhang, H., & Cao, X. (2016). Evaluating the impact of transport investment on the efficiency of regional integrated transport systems in China. *Transport Policy, 45*, 66–76.

Li, W. (2013). "Hukou" status, place affiliation and identity formation: The case of migrant workers in Metropolitan Beijing. *Procedia Environmental Sciences, 17*, 842–851.

Li, W. Y. (1995). The Representation of History in the Peach Blossom Fan. *Journal of the American Oriental Society*, 421–433.

Li, W., & Li, Y. (2010). An analysis on social and cultural background of the resistance for China's education reform and academic pressure. *International Education Studies, 3*(3), 211–215.

Li, X. (2011). Thoughts on Urban Transportation Policy. *Urban Transport of China, 1*, 7–11.

Li, X., Shaw, J. W., Liu, D., & Yuan, Y. (2019). Acceptability of Beijing congestion charging from a business perspective. *Transportation, 46*(3), 753–776.

Li, X., Stanton, B., Fang, X., & Lin, D. (2006). Social stigma and mental health among rural-to-urban migrants in China: A conceptual framework and future research needs. *World Health & Population, 8*(3), 14–31.

Li, X., Zhou, W., & Ouyang, Z. (2013). Forty years of urban expansion in Beijing: What is the relative importance of physical, socioeconomic, and neighborhood factors? *Applied Geography, 38*, 1–10.

Li, Y., Koppenjan, J., & Verweij, S. (2016). Governing environmental conflicts in China: Under what conditions do local governments compromise? *Public Administration, 94*(3), 806–822.

Lian, H., Glendinning, A., & Yin, B. (2016). The issue of 'land-lost' farmers in the People's Republic of China: Reasons for discontent, actions and claims to legitimacy. *Journal of Contemporary China, 25*(101), 718–730.

Liang, K. (2003). The Rise of Mao and his cultural legacy: The Yan'an rectification movement. *Journal of Contemporary China, 12*(34), 225–228.

Liang, W., Lu, M., & Zhang, H. (2016). Housing prices raise wages: Estimating the unexpected effects of land supply regulation in China. *Journal of Housing Economics, 33*, 70–81.

Liao, T. F., & Wang, C. (2018). Permanent emergency: Inequality in access to hospitalisation among urban elderly Chinese. *Global Public Health, 13*(8), 1098–1113.

Lieberthal, K. (1995). *Governing China: From revolution through reform*. WW Norton.

Lieberthal, K., & Oksenberg, M. (1990). *Policy making in China: Leaders, structures, and processes*. Princeton University Press.

Likert, R. (1932). A technique for the measurement of attitudes. *Archives of Psychology, 140*, 44–53.

Lin, C. L. (2008). Sexual issues: The analysis of female role portrayal preferences in Taiwanese print ads. *Journal of Business Ethics, 83*(3), 409–418.

Lin, H., Liu, T., Fang, F., Xiao, J., Zeng, W., Li, X., Guo, L., Tian, L., Schootman, M., Stamatakis, K. A., Qian, Z., & Ma, W. (2017). Mortality benefits of vigorous air quality improvement interventions during the periods of APEC Blue and Parade Blue in Beijing, China. *Environmental Pollution, 220*, 222–227.

Lin, J. Y. (1990). Collectivization and China's agricultural crisis in 1959–1961. *Journal of Political Economy, 98*(6), 1228–1252.

Lin, X. (2014). The differential mode of criminalization in traditional China. *Fudan Journal of the Humanities and Social Sciences, 7*(2), 247–263.

Lin, Y. (2013). *My country and my people*. Read Books Ltd.

Lindley, A. F. (1866). *Ti-ping Tien-kwoh: The History of the Ti-ping Revolution* (Vol. 1). Day & son (limited).

Link, H., & Polak, J. (2003). Acceptability of transport pricing measures among public and professionals in Europe. *Transportation Research Record: Journal of the Transportation Research Board, 1839*, 34–44.

Link, P. (1992). *Evening chats in Beijing: Probing China's predicament*. W.W. Norton.

Lipscomb, M. (2012). Abductive reasoning and qualitative research. *Nursing Philosophy, 13*(4), 244–256.

Lipstein, B. (1975). In defense of small samples. *Journal of Advertising Research, 15*(1), 33–40.

Litman, T. (1996). Using road pricing revenue: Economic efficiency and equity considerations. *Transportation Research Record: Journal of the Transportation Research Board, 1558*, 24–28.

Litman, T. (1999). *The costs of automobile dependency*. Victoria Transportation Policy Institute.

Litman, T. (2002). Evaluating transportation equity. *World Transport Policy & Practice, 8*(2), 50–65.

Litman, T. (2004). *London congestion pricing. Implications for other cities*. Victoria Transport Policy Institute.

Litman, T. (2012). *London congestion pricing: Implications for other cities*. Victoria Transport Policy Institute.

Little, D. (1989). *Understanding peasant China: Case studies in the philosophy of social science*. Yale University Press.

Litwin, M. S., & Fink, A. (1995). *How to measure survey reliability and validity* (Vol. 7). Sage.

Liu, A. A., Linn, J., Qin, P., & Yang, J. (2018). Vehicle ownership restrictions and fertility in Beijing. *Journal of Development Economics, 135*, 85–96.

Liu, J.-F. (2009). The May 4th movement of 1919 and Marxism's spreading in China. *Collected Papers of History Studies, 2*, 003.

Liu, L., Wang, P., & Wu, T. (2017). The role of nongovernmental organizations in China's climate change governance. *Wiley Interdisciplinary Reviews: Climate Change, 8*(6), e483.

Liu, M. W. (1982). The Doctrine of the Buddha-Nature in the Mahāyāna Mahāparinirvāṇa Sūtra. *Journal of the International Association of Buddhist Studies, 5*(2), 63–94.

Liu, Q. (2021). Immobility: Surviving the COVID-19 outbreak. In C. Zhang (Eds.), *Human Security in China—A Post-Pandemic State* (pp. 150–171). Palgrave.

Liu, Q. (2022). Immobility: Surviving the COVID-19 outbreak. In *Human security in China* (pp. 133–154). Palgrave Macmillan.

Liu, Q., An, Z., Liu, Y., Ying, W., & Zhao, P. (2021a). Smartphone-based services, perceived accessibility, and transport inequity during the COVID-19 pandemic: A cross-lagged panel study. *Transportation Research Part D: Transport and Environment, 97*, 102941.

Liu, Q., Liu, Y., Zhang, C., An, Z., & Zhao, P. (2021b). Elderly mobility during the COVID-19 pandemic: A qualitative exploration in Kunming, China. *Journal of Transport Geography*, 103176.

Liu, Q., Lucas, K., & Marsden, G. (2019). Public acceptability of congestion charging in Beijing, China: How transferrable are Western ideas of public acceptability? *International Journal of Sustainable Transportation*, 1–14.

Liu, Q., Lucas, K., & Marsden, G. (2020). Public acceptability of congestion charging in Beijing, China: How transferrable are Western ideas of public acceptability? *International Journal of Sustainable Transportation, 15*(2), 97–110.

Liu, Q., Lucas, K., Marsden, G., & Liu, Y. (2019). Egalitarianism and public perception of social inequities: A case study of Beijing congestion charge. *Transport Policy, 74*, 47–62.

Liu, S. (1991). *Selected Works of Liu Shaoqi*. Foreign Languages Press.

Liu, Shao-chi. (1939/1972). How to be a good communist. In *Essential works of Chinese communism* (2nd ed., W. Chai, Ed., pp. 133–151). Bantam Books.

Liu, T., & Ceder, A. A. (2015). Analysis of a new public-transport-service concept: Customized bus in China. *Transport Policy, 39*, 63–76.

Liu, T., Qi, Y., Cao, G., & Liu, H. (2015). Spatial patterns, driving forces, and urbanization effects of China's internal migration: County-level analysis based on the 2000 and 2010 censuses. *Journal of Geographical Sciences, 25*(2), 236–256.

Liu, Y. (1998). *Origins of Chinese law: Penal and administrative law in its early development*. Oxford University Press.

Liu, Y., Martinez-Vazquez, J., & Qiao, B. (2014). *Falling short: Intergovernmental transfers in China.*

Liu, Z., Li, R., Wang, X. C., & Shang, P. (2018). Effects of vehicle restriction policies: Analysis using license plate recognition data in Langfang, China. *Transportation Research Part A: Policy and Practice, 118*, 89–103.

Locke, J. (1690 [1978]). *Two Treatises of Government*. E. P. Dutton.

Loewe, M. (Ed.). (1993). *Early Chinese texts: A bibliographical guide* (No. 2). University of California Inst of East.

Loewe, M. (1994). Huang Lao thought and the Huainanzi. *Journal of the Royal Asiatic Society (Third Series), 4*(3), 377–395.

Loewe, M., & Shaughnessy, E. L. (1999). *The Cambridge history of ancient China: From the origins of civilization to 221 BC*. Cambridge University Press.

Long, J. S., & Freese, J. (2006). *Regression models for categorical dependent variables using Stata*. Stata Press.

Loo, B. P. (1999). Development of a regional transport infrastructure: Some lessons from the Zhujiang Delta, Guangdong China. *Journal of Transport Geography, 7*(1), 43–63.

Lorenzoni, I., Nicholson-Cole, S., & Whitmarsh, L. (2007). Barriers perceived to engaging with climate change among the UK public and their policy implications. *Global Environmental Change, 17*(3–4), 445–459.

Lorge, P. (2006). *War, politics and society in early modern China, 900–1795*. Routledge.

Low, K. C. P. (2011). Confucianism versus Taoism. *Conflict Resolution & Negotiation Journal, 2011*(4), 111–127.

Lu, C. S., Lai, K. H., & Cheng, T. E. (2007). Application of structural equation modeling to evaluate the intention of shippers to use Internet services in liner shipping. *European Journal of Operational Research, 180*(2), 845–867.

Lu, N. (2018). *The dynamics of foreign-policy decisionmaking in China*. Routledge.

Lu, T. (2001). *Persons, roles, and minds: Identity in Peony Pavilion and Peach Blossom Fan*. Stanford University Press.

Lu, W. M., & Lo, S. F. (2007). A closer look at the economic-environmental disparities for regional development in China. *European Journal of Operational Research, 183*(2), 882–894.

Lu, X. (1990). *Diary of a madman and other stories*. University of Hawaii Press.

Lu, X. (2004). *Rhetoric of the Chinese cultural revolution: The impact on Chinese thought, culture, and communication*. University of South Carolina Press.

Lu, X. (2017). *Jottings under Lamplight*. Harvard University Press.

Lü, X., & Perry, E. J. (Eds.). (1997). *Danwei: The changing Chinese workplace in historical and comparative perspective*. ME Sharpe.

Luo, C. (2004). Uncertainty during economic transition and household consumption behavior in Urban China. *Economic Research Journal, 4*, 010.

Luo, S. (1974). Class Conflict in Qin-Han Dynasty. *Red Flag*, 8. [Online]. https://ccradb.appspot.com/post/3749. Accessed 15 December 2018 (in Chinese).

Lyon, A. (2008). Rhetorical authority in Athenian democracy and the Chinese legalism of Han Fei. *Philosophy and Rhetoric, 41*(1), 51–71.

Lyons, G., & Davidson, C. (2016). Guidance for transport planning and policymaking in the face of an uncertain future. *Transportation Research Part A: Policy and Practice, 88*, 104–116.

Ma, L. (2015). The Beijing Smog: Between media frames and public perceptions. *China Media Research, 11*(4), 6–15.

Ma, S. Y. (1994). The Chinese discourse on civil society. *The China Quarterly, 137*, 180–193.

MacCallum, R. C., & Austin, J. T. (2000). Applications of structural equation modeling in psychological research. *Annual Review of Psychology, 51*(1), 201–226.

MacCallum, R. C., Browne, M. W., & Sugawara, H. M. (1996). Power analysis and determination of sample size for covariance structure modeling. *Psychological Methods, 1*(2), 130.

MacCallum, R. C., & Hong, S. (1997). Power analysis in covariance structure modeling using GFI and AGFI. *Multivariate Behavioral Research, 32*(2), 193–210.

MacCallum, R. C., Widaman, K. F., Zhang, S., & Hong, S. (1999). Sample size in factor analysis. *Psychological Methods, 4*(1), 84.

MacFarquhar, R. (1997). *The origins of the cultural revolution* (Vol. 3). Oxford University Press.

MacFarquhar, R., & Mao, Z. (1989). *The Secret Speeches of Chairman Mao: From the Hundred Flowers to the Great Leap Forward*. Harvard University Press.

Mackett, R. (1999). Towards the solution of urban transport problems in China. *Journal of Environmental Sciences, 11*(3), 334–338.

MacKinnon, R. (2008). Flatter world and thicker walls? Blogs, censorship and civic discourse in China. *Public Choice, 134*(1–2), 31–46.

Mahendra, A. (2008). Vehicle restrictions in four Latin American cities: Is congestion pricing possible? *Transport Reviews, 28*(1), 105–133.

Major, J. S. (1993). *Heaven and earth in early Han thought: Chapters three, four, and five of the Huainanzi*. SUNY Press.

Maness, M., Cirillo, C., & Dugundji, E. R. (2015). Generalized behavioral framework for choice models of social influence: Behavioral and data concerns in travel behavior. *Journal of Transport Geography, 46*, 137–150.

Manin, B. (1997). *The principles of representative government*. Cambridge University Press.

Mann, H. B., & Whitney, D. R. (1947). On a test of whether one of two random variables is stochastically larger than the other. *The Annals of Mathematical Statistics*, 50–60.

Mao, T. (1965). *On contradiction*. Foreign Languages Press.

Mao, T. (2014). *Selected works of Mao Tse-tung*. Elsevier.

Marsden, G., & Stead, D. (2011). Policy transfer and learning in the field of transport: A review of concepts and evidence. *Transport Policy, 18*(3), 492–500.

Marsh, H. W., & Balla, J. (1994). Goodness of fit in confirmatory factor analysis: The effects of sample size and model parsimony. *Quality and Quantity, 28*(2), 185–217.

Marsh, H. W., Lüdtke, O., Muthén, B., Asparouhov, T., Morin, A. J., Trautwein, U., & Nagengast, B. (2010). A new look at the big five factor structure through exploratory structural equation modeling. *Psychological Assessment, 22*(3), 471–491.

Marsh, H. W., Morin, A. J., Parker, P. D., & Kaur, G. (2014). Exploratory structural equation modeling: An integration of the best features of exploratory and confirmatory factor analysis. *Annual Review of Clinical Psychology, 10*, 85–110.

Maruyama, G. (1997). *Basics of structural equation modeling*. Sage.

Maruyama, T., & Harata, N. (2006). Difference between area-based and cordon-based congestion pricing: Investigation by trip-chain-based network equilibrium model with nonadditive path costs. *Transportation Research Record: Journal of the Transportation Research Board, 1964*, 1–8.

Maruyama, T., & Sumalee, A. (2007). Efficiency and equity comparison of cordon-and area-based road pricing schemes using a trip-chain equilibrium model. *Transportation Research Part A: Policy and Practice, 41*(7), 655–671.

Marx, K. (1843 [1977]). *Critique of Hegel's "Philosophy of Right"* (J. O'Malley, Ed.). Cambridge University Press.

Marx, K. (1859 [1979]). *A Contribution to the Critique of Political Economy*. International Publishers.

Marx, K. (1891 [2008]). *Critique of the Gotha program*. Wildside Press LLC.

Marx, K. (1976). *Capital volume I*. Penguin Books.

Mason, J. (2017). *Qualitative researching*. Sage.

Mastny, V. (1998). *The Cold War and Soviet Insecurity: The Stalin Years*. Oxford University Press.

Matell, M. S., & Jacoby, J. (1972). Is there an optimal number of alternatives for Likert-scale items? Effects of testing time and scale properties. *Journal of Applied Psychology, 56*(6), 506.

Mattick, R. P., & Clarke, J. C. (1998). Development and validation of measures of social phobia scrutiny fear and social interaction anxiety. *Behaviour Research and Therapy, 36*(4), 455–470.

Maurer, T. J., & Pierce, H. R. (1998). A comparison of Likert scale and traditional measures of self-efficacy. *Journal of Applied Psychology, 83*(2), 324.

Maxwell, J. A. (2012). *Qualitative research design: An interactive approach*. Sage.

May, A. D., Liu, R., Shepherd, S. P., & Sumalee, A. (2002). The impact of cordon design on the performance of road pricing schemes. *Transport Policy, 9*(3), 209–220.

Maynard, M. L., & Taylor, C. R. (1996). A comparative analysis of Japanese and US attitudes toward direct marketing. *Journal of Direct Marketing, 10*(1), 34–44.

McCoy, J., Rahman, T., & Somer, M. (2018). Polarization and the global crisis of democracy: Common patterns, dynamics, and pernicious consequences for democratic polities. *American Behavioral Scientist, 62*(1), 16–42.

McCullagh, P. (1980). Regression models for ordinal data. *Journal of the Royal Statistical Society. Series B (Methodological), 42*(2), 109–142.

McDermott, J. P. (2006). *A social history of the Chinese book: Books and literati culture in late imperial China*. Hong Kong University Press.

McDonald, R. P. (1996). Path analysis with composite variables. *Multivariate Behavioral Research, 31*(2), 239–270.

McDonald, R. P., & Ho, M. H. R. (2002). Principles and practice in reporting structural equation analyses. *Psychological Methods, 7*(1), 64–82.

McQuaid, R., & Grieco, M. (2005). Edinburgh and the politics of congestion charging: Negotiating road user charging with affected publics. *Transport Policy, 12*(5), 475–476.

McQuitty, S. (2004). Statistical power and structural equation models in business research. *Journal of Business Research, 57*(2), 175–183.

Meisner, M. (1999). *Mao's China and after: A history of the People's Republic*. Simon and Schuster.

Merriam-Webster. (2004). *Merriam-Webster's collegiate dictionary*. Merriam-Webster.

Merry, S. E. (1990). *Getting justice and getting even: Legal consciousness among working-class Americans*. University of Chicago Press.

Mertha, A. (2009). "Fragmented authoritarianism 2.0": Political pluralization in the Chinese policy process. *The China Quarterly, 200*, 995–1012.

Mertha, A. C. (2005). China's "soft" centralization: Shifting tiao/kuai authority relations. *The China Quarterly, 184*, 791–810.

Miao, P. (2003). Deserted streets in a jammed town: The gated community in Chinese cities and its solution. *Journal of Urban Design, 8*(1), 45–66.

Michels, R. (1962). *Political parties: A study of the oligarchical tendencies of modern democracy*. Collier Books.

Michelson, E. (2007). Climbing the dispute pagoda: Grievances and appeals to the official justice system in rural China. *American Sociological Review, 72*(3), 459–485.

Michelson, E. (2008). Justice from above or below? Popular strategies for resolving grievances in rural China. *The China Quarterly, 193*, 43–64.

Miltgen, C. L., & Peyrat-Guillard, D. (2014). Cultural and generational influences on privacy concerns: A qualitative study in seven European countries. *European Journal of Information Systems, 23*(2), 103–125.

Minzner, C. F. (2006). Xinfang: An alternative to formal Chinese legal institutions. *Stanford Journal of International Law., 42*, 103–180.

Miola, A. (2008). *Backcasting approach for sustainable mobility*. EUR—Scientific and Technical Research series—ISSN 1018-5593—ISBN 978-92-79-09189-6. Office for Official Publications of the European Communities Luxembourg.

Misra, K. (1998). *From post-Maoism to post-Marxism: The erosion of official ideology in Deng's China*. Psychology Press.

Moise, E. E. (2017). *Land reform in China and North Vietnam: Consolidating the revolution at the village level*. UNC Press Books.

Mok, K. H. (1998). *Intellectuals and the State in Post-Mao China*. Springer.

Mok, L. W., & Wong, D. S. (2013). Restorative justice and mediation: Diverged or converged? *Asian Journal of Criminology, 8*(4), 335–347.

Moore, C. A. (1967). *The Chinese mind: Essentials of Chinese philosophy and culture*. University of Hawaii Press.

Morton, C., Schuitema, G., & Anable, J. (2011, January). Electric vehicles: Will consumers get charged up. In *Universities's Transport Study Group Conference*.

Mu, R., De Jong, M., & Koppenjan, J. (2011). The rise and fall of Public-Private Partnerships in China: A path-dependent approach. *Journal of Transport Geography, 19*(4), 794–806.

Mu, X. D., Liu, H. P., & Xue, X. J. (2012). Urban growth in Beijing from 1984–2007 as gauged by remote sensing. *Journal of Beijing Normal University, 48*, 81–85.

Muis, J., & Immerzeel, T. (2017). Causes and consequences of the rise of populist radical right parties and movements in Europe. *Current Sociology, 65*(6), 909–930.

Mulaik, S. A., James, L. R., Van Alstine, J., Bennett, N., Lind, S., & Stilwell, C. D. (1989). Evaluation of goodness-of-fit indices for structural equation models. *Psychological Bulletin, 105*(3), 430.

Muldavin, J. S. S. (1996). The political ecology of agrarian reform in China. *Liberation ecologies: Environment, development, and social movements*.

Muller, E. N., Seligson, M. A., & Midlarsky, M. I. (1989). Land inequality and political violence. *American Political Science Review, 83*(2), 577–596.

Nachar, N. (2008). The Mann-Whitney U: A test for assessing whether two independent samples come from the same distribution. *Tutorials in Quantitative Methods for Psychology, 4*(1), 13–20.

Naughton, B. (2007). *The Chinese economy: Transitions and growth*. MIT Press.

Navarria, G. (2016). To censor or not to censor: Roots, current trends and the long-term consequences of the Chinese Communist Party's fear of the internet. *Communication, Politics & Culture, 49*(2), 82–110.

Needham, J. (1981). *Science in traditional China: A comparative perspective*. Chinese University Press.

Needham, J., Wang, L., & Lu, G. D. (1963). *Science and civilisation in China*. Cambridge University Press.

Newbery, D. M., & Santos, G. (1999). Road taxes, road user charges and earmarking. *Fiscal Studies, 20*(2), 103–132.

Newman, P., & Kenworthy, J. (1999). Costs of automobile dependence: Global survey of cities. *Transportation Research Record: Journal of the Transportation Research Board, 1670*, 17–26.

Ng, O. C., & Wang, Q. E. (2005). *Mirroring the past: The writing and use of history in Imperial China*. University of Hawaii Press.

Ngai, P. (2005). Global production, company codes of conduct, and labor conditions in China: A case study of two factories. *The China Journal*, (54), 101–113.

Ngok, K. L., & Huang, G. (2014). Policy paradigm shift and the changing role of the state: The development of social policy in China since 2003. *Social Policy and Society, 13*(2), 251–261.

Nie, Y. (2017). Why is license plate rationing not a good transport policy? *Transportmetrica A: Transport Science, 13*(1), 1–23.

Nietzsche, F. (1996). *Nietzsche: Human, all too human: A book for free spirits*. Cambridge University Press.

Nietzsche, F. (2002). *Nietzsche: Beyond Good and Evil: Prelude to a Philosophy of the Future*. Cambridge University Press.

Nilsson, M., & Küller, R. (2000). Travel behaviour and environmental concern. *Transportation Research Part D: Transport and Environment, 5*(3), 211–234.

Nordin, A., & Richaud, L. (2014). Subverting official language and discourse in China? Type river crab for harmony. *China Information, 28*(1), 47–67.

Norris, M., & Lecavalier, L. (2010). Evaluating the use of exploratory factor analysis in developmental disability psychological research. *Journal of Autism and Developmental Disorders, 40*(1), 8–20.

Novick, G. (2008). Is there a bias against telephone interviews in qualitative research? *Research in Nursing & Health, 31*(4), 391–398.

Nunnally, J. C. (1967). *Psychometric theory*. McGraw-Hill.

O'Brien, K. J., & Li, L. (2004). Suing the local state: Administrative litigation in rural China. *The China Journal, 51*, 75–96.

Oehry, B. (2010). *Critical success factors for implementing road charging systems*. OECD Publishing.

Ó Gráda, C. (2011). *Great Leap into Famine*. http://irserver.ucd.ie/bitstream/handle/10197/6378/WP11_03.pdf?sequence=1. Accessed 27 July 2019.

Ohashi, H. (2009). Effects of transparency in procurement practices on government expenditure: A case study of municipal public works. *Review of Industrial Organization, 34*(3), 267–285.

Ong, B. K. (2012). Grounded Theory Method (GTM) and the Abductive Research Strategy (ARS): A critical analysis of their differences. *International Journal of Social Research Methodology, 15*(5), 417–432.

Organization for Economic Co-operation and Development—OECD. (2000). *Environmentally Sustainable Transport: futures, strategies and best practices.* Synthesis Report of the OECD Project on Environmentally Sustainable Transport (EST)—International EST Conference 4th to 6th October 2000, Vienna, Austria.

Oxford Learner's Dictionaries. (2019). *Accept*. https://www.oxfordlearnersdictionaries.com/definition/english/accept

Pan, H. (2011). *Implementing sustainable urban travel policies in China*. International Transport Forum. [Online]. http://www.internationaltransportforum.org/jtrc/DiscussionPapers/DP201112.pdf. Accessed 27 July 2019.

Pang, Q. (2014). The "two lines control model" in China's state and society relations: Central State's management of Confucian Revival in the new century. *International Journal of China Studies, 5*(3), 627–655.

Park, H., Rehg, M. T., & Lee, D. (2005). The influence of Confucian ethics and collectivism on whistle blowing intentions: A study of South Korean public employees. *Journal of Business Ethics, 58*(4), 387–403.

Park, M., & Chesla, C. (2007). Revisiting Confucianism as a conceptual framework for Asian family study. *Journal of Family Nursing, 13*(3), 293–311.

Parmar, I. (2017). The legitimacy crisis of the US elite and the rise of Donald Trump. *Insight Turkey, 19*(3), 9–22.

Pei, M. (2012). Is CCP rule fragile or resilient? *Journal of Democracy, 23*(1), 27–41.

People's Daily. (2000). *Chinese government supports smooth traffic project*. [Online]. http://en.people.cn/english/200003/11/eng20000311C106.html. Accessed 27 July 2019 (in Chinese)

People.'s Daily. (2010). *Interpretation of current events: Beijing License Plate Lottery from the next year*. [Online]. http://cpc.people.com.cn/GB/64093/82429/83083/13568812.html. Accessed 27 July 2019 (in Chinese).

People's Daily. (2010). *Interpretation of current events: Beijing License Plate Lottery from the next year*. [Online]. Available from: http://cpc.people.com.cn/GB/64093/82429/83083/13568812.html. Accessed 22 November 2018 (in Chinese).

People's Daily. (2015). *Beijing authority reveal the population distribution of Beijing for the first time*. [Online]. http://politics.people.com.cn/n/2015/0522/c1001-27039783.html. Accessed 27 July 2019 (in Chinese).

Perry, E. J. (2001). Challenging the mandate of heaven: Popular protest in modern China. *Critical Asian Studies, 33*(2), 163–180.

Perry, E. J. (2015). *Challenging the Mandate of Heaven: Social Protest and State Power in China: Social Protest and State Power in China*. Routledge.

Perry, E. J., & Goldman, M. (2009). *Grassroots political reform in contemporary China*. Harvard University Press.

Peters, B. G., & Zhao, Y. (2017). Local policy-making process in China: A case study. *Journal of Chinese Governance, 2*(2), 127–148.

Peterson, B., & Harrell, F. E., Jr. (1990). Partial proportional odds models for ordinal response variables. *Applied Statistics, 39*(2), 205–217.

Pines, Y. (2012). *The everlasting empire: The political culture of ancient China and its imperial legacy*. Princeton University Press.

Pines, Y. (2014). *Legalism in Chinese Philosophy* (Winter 2014 Edition, E. N. Zalta, Eds.). The Stanford Encyclopedia of Philosophy. http://plato.stanford.edu/archives/win2014/entries/chinese-legalism/. Accessed 27 July 2019.

Ping, L. (2001). The Influence of "Three Religions in One" on the Peasants' Spirit of Revolt—An Exploration in the Perspective of the Secret Societies in China. *Journal of Jiangsu Institute of Education, 2*, 019.

Podoshen, J. S., Li, L., & Zhang, J. (2011). Materialism and conspicuous consumption in China: A cross-cultural examination. *International Journal of Consumer Studies, 35*(1), 17–25.

Podsakoff, P. M., Ahearne, M., & MacKenzie, S. B. (1997). Organizational citizenship behavior and the quantity and quality of work group performance. *Journal of Applied Psychology, 82*(2), 262–270.

Poell, T., De Kloet, J., & Zeng, G. (2014). Will the real Weibo please stand up? Chinese online contention and actor-network theory. *Chinese Journal of Communication, 7*(1), 1–18.

Popper, K. (2012). *The open society and its enemies*. Routledge.

Posner, E. A. (2009). *Law and social norms*. Harvard University Press.

Postiglione, G. A. (2015). *Education and social change in China: Inequality in a market economy*. Routledge.

Potter, S. H., & Potter, J. M. (1990). *China's Peasants: The Anthropology of a Revolution*. Cambridge University Press.

Pow, C. P. (2009). *Gated communities in China: Class, privilege and the moral politics of the good life*. Routledge.

Powers, D. S. (2016). 'Under the Dome' on Chinese air pollution, a documentary by Chai Jing. *Journal of Public Health Policy, 37*(1), 98–106.

Pucher, J., Peng, Z., Mittal, N., Zhu, Y., & Korattyswaroopam, N. (2007). Urban transport trends and policies in China and India: Impacts of rapid economic growth. *Transport Reviews, 27*(4), 379–410.

Punch, K. F. (2013). *Introduction to social research: Quantitative and qualitative approaches*. Sage.

Pye, L. W. (1990). China: Erratic state, frustrated society. *Foreign Affairs, 69*(4), 56–74.

Pye, M. W., & Pye, L. W. (2009). *Asian power and politics: The cultural dimensions of authority*. Harvard University Press.

Qiu, J. L. (1999). Virtual censorship in China: Keeping the gate between the cyberspaces. *International Journal of Communications Law and Policy, 4*(1), 25.

Quartz. (2016). *Chinese state media is blaming its apocalyptic smog problem on kitchen fumes*. [Online]. https://qz.com/872685/chinese-state-media-is-blaming-its-apocalyptic-smog-problem-on-kitchen-fumes/. Accessed 27 July 2019.

Raaijmakers, Q. A., Van Hoof, J. T. C., t Hart, H., Verbogt, T. F., & Vollebergh, W. A. (2000). Adolescents' midpoint responses on Likert-type scale items: Neutral or missing values? *International Journal of Public Opinion Research, 12*, 208–216.

Rajé, F. (2003). The impact of transport on social exclusion processes with specific emphasis on road user charging. *Transport Policy, 10*(4), 321–338.

Ramalho, R., Adams, P., Huggard, P., & Hoare, K. (2015, August). Literature review and constructivist grounded theory methodology. In *Forum: Qualitative social research* (Vol. 16, No. 3, pp. 1–13). Freie Universität Berlin.

Randall, D. M., & Fernandes, M. F. (1991). The social desirability response bias in ethics research. *Journal of Business Ethics, 10*(11), 805–817.

Raux, C., & Souche, S. (2004). The acceptability of urban road pricing: A theoretical analysis applied to experience in Lyon. *Journal of Transport Economics and Policy, 38*(2), 191–215.

Rawski, T. G., & Li, L. M. (1992). *Chinese history in economic perspective*. University of California Press.

Reed, G. G. (1995). Moral/political education in the People's Republic of China: Learning through role models. *Journal of Moral Education, 24*(2), 99–111.

Reilly, T. H. (2004). *The Taiping Heavenly Kingdom: Rebellion and the Blasphemy of Empire*. University of Washington Press.

Ren, K. (2012). Fighting against academic corruption: A critique of recent policy developments in China. *Higher Education Policy, 25*(1), 19–38.

Rene, H. K. (2013). *China's Sent-down Generation: Public Administration and the Legacies of Mao's Rustication Program*. Georgetown University Press.

Repnikova, M. (2017). Media openings and political transitions: Glasnost versus Yulun Jiandu. *Problems of Post-Communism, 64*(3–4), 141–151.

Rich, A. (2005). *Think tanks, public policy, and the politics of expertise*. Cambridge University Press.

Rickett, W. A., & Guan, Z. (2001). *Guanzi: Political, economic, and philosophical essays from early China, a study and translation*. Cheng & Tsui.

Rienstra, S. A., Rietveld, P., & Verhoef, E. T. (1999). The social support for policy measures in passenger transport: A statistical analysis for the Netherlands. *Transportation Research Part D: Transport and Environment, 4*(3), 181–200.

Riskin, C., Zhao, R., & Li, S. (2001). *China's retreat from equality: Income distribution and economic transition*. ME Sharpe.

Ritchie, J., Lewis, J., Nicholls, C. M., & Ormston, R. (Eds.). (2013). *Qualitative research practice: A guide for social science students and researchers*. Sage.

Robinet, I. (1997). *Taoism: Growth of a religion*. Stanford University Press.

Robson, C., & McCartan, K. (2016). *Real world research*. Wiley.

Roddy, S. (1998). *Literati identity and its fictional representations in late imperial China*. Stanford University Press.

Rößger, L., Schade, J., Obst, D., Gehlert, T., Schlag, B., Bonsall, P., & Lythgoe, B. (2008). *Psychological constraints of user reactions towards differentiated charging*. Deliverable 4. 2. EU-Project DIFFERENT, Dresden, Leeds.

Rouwendal, J., & Verhoef, E. T. (2006). Basic economic principles of road pricing: From theory to applications. *Transport Policy, 13*(2), 106–114.

Russell, B. (2013). *History of western philosophy* (Collectors). Routledge.

Rye, T., Gaunt, M., & Ison, S. (2008). Edinburgh's congestion charging plans: An analysis of reasons for non-implementation. *Transportation Planning and Technology, 31*(6), 641–661.

Sabatier, C., & Lannegrand-Willems, L. (2005). Transmission of family values and attachment: A French three-generation study. *Applied Psychology, 54*(3), 378–395.

Saich, T. (2010). *Governance and politics of China*. Macmillan International Higher Education.

Sailey, J. (1978). *The master who embraces simplicity: A study of the philosopher Ko Hung, AD 283–343*. Chinese Materials Center Inc.

Sale, J. E., Lohfeld, L. H., & Brazil, K. (2002). Revisiting the quantitative-qualitative debate: Implications for mixed-methods research. *Quality and Quantity, 36*(1), 43–53.

Santos, G. (2004). Urban congestion charging: A second-best alternative. *Journal of Transport Economics and Policy, 38*(3), 345–369.

Santos, G., & Bhakar, J. (2006). The impact of the London congestion charging scheme on the generalised cost of car commuters to the city of London from a value of travel time savings perspective. *Transport Policy, 13*(1), 22–33.

Santos, G., & Harrell, S. (Eds.). (2017). *Transforming patriarchy: Chinese families in the twenty-first century*. University of Washington Press.

Santos, G., & Rojey, L. (2004). Distributional impacts of road pricing: The truth behind the myth. *Transportation, 31*(1), 21–42.

Santos, G., & Shaffer, B. (2004). Preliminary results of the London congestion charging scheme. *Public Works Management & Policy, 9*(2), 164–181.

Santos, M., & Slaner, S. (1977). Society and space: Social formation as theory and method. *Antipode, 9*(1), 3–13.

Sarantakos, S. (2012). *Social research*. Palgrave Macmillan.

Saunders, J. P. (2005). The rise and fall of Edinburgh's congestion charging plans. *Proceedings of the Institution of Civil Engineers-Transport, 158*(4), 193–220.

Savvanidou, E., Zervas, E., & Tsagarakis, K. P. (2010). Public acceptance of biofuels. *Energy Policy, 38*(7), 3482–3488.

Saxe, R., & Weitz, B. A. (1982). The SOCO scale: A measure of the customer orientation of salespeople. *Journal of Marketing Research, 19*(3), 343–351.

Schade, J., & Baum, M. (2007). Reactance or acceptance? Reactions towards the introduction of road pricing. *Transportation Research Part A: Policy and Practice, 41*(1), 41–48.

Schade, J., & Schlag, B. (2000a). Public acceptability of traffic demand management in Europe. *Traffic Engineering and Control, 41*(8), 314–318.

Schade, J., & Schlag, B. (2000b). *Acceptability of urban transport pricing* (VATT Research Reports 72). Helsinki.

Schade, J., & Schlag, B. (2003). Acceptability of urban transport pricing strategies. *Transportation Research Part F: Traffic Psychology and Behaviour, 6*(1), 45–61.

Schermelleh-Engel, K., Moosbrugger, H., & Müller, H. (2003). Evaluating the fit of structural equation models: Tests of significance and descriptive goodness-of-fit measures. *Methods of Psychological Research Online, 8*(2), 23–74.

Schlag, B., & Teubel, U. (1997). Public acceptability of transport pricing. *IATSS Research, 21*, 134–142.

Schlegel, K., Grandjean, D., & Scherer, K. R. (2012). Emotion recognition: Unidimensional ability or a set of modality-and emotion-specific skills? *Personality and Individual Differences, 53*(1), 16–21.

Schmöcker, J. D., Pettersson, P., & Fujii, S. (2012). Comparative analysis of proximal and distal determinants for the acceptance of coercive charging policies in the UK and Japan. *International Journal of Sustainable Transportation, 6*(3), 156–173.

Schneider, A. (2003). Reconciling history with the nation? Historicity, national particularity, and the question of universals. *Historiography East and West, 1*(1), 117–136.

Schopenhauer, A. (1998). *On the basis of morality*. Hackett Publishing.

Schrift, M. (2001). *Biography of a Chairman Mao badge: The creation and mass consumption of a personality cult*. Rutgers University Press.

Schuitema, G., & Steg, L. (2008). The role of revenue use in the acceptability of transport pricing policies. *Transportation Research Part F: Traffic Psychology and Behaviour, 11*(3), 221–231.

Schuitema, G., Steg, L., & Forward, S. (2010). Explaining differences in acceptability before and acceptance after the implementation of a congestion charge in Stockholm. *Transportation Research Part A: Policy and Practice, 44*(2), 99–109.

Schurmann, F. (1971). *Ideology and organization in communist China*. University of California Press.

Schwarcz, V. (1986). *The Chinese enlightenment: Intellectuals and the legacy of the May Fourth Movement of 1919*. University of California Press.

Seidel, A. K. (1969). The image of the perfect ruler in early Taoist Messianism: Lao-tzu and Li Hung. *History of Religions, 9*(2/3), 216–247.

Sellmann, J. D. (2012). *Timing and Rulership in Master Lu's Spring and Autumn Annals (Lushichunqiu)*. SUNY Press.

Settle, J. E., Dawes, C. T., & Fowler, J. H. (2009). The heritability of partisan attachment. *Political Research Quarterly, 62*(3), 601–613.

Shafer, W. E., & Simmons, R. S. (2011). Effects of organizational ethical culture on the ethical decisions of tax practitioners in mainland China. *Accounting, Auditing & Accountability Journal, 24*(5), 647–668.

Shah, R., & Goldstein, S. M. (2006). Use of structural equation modeling in operations management research: Looking back and forward. *Journal of Operations Management, 24*(2), 148–169.

Shambaugh, D. (2007). China's propaganda system: Institutions, processes and efficacy. *The China Journal, 57*, 25–58.

Shang Yang. (1928). *The book of Lord Shang. A classic of the Chinese School of Law* (Duyvendak, Trans.). Arthur Probsthain.

Shang, Y. (2017). *The book of Lord Shang: Apologetics of state power in early China*. Columbia University Press.

Shei, C. (2014). *Understanding the Chinese Language: A Comprehensive Linguistic Introduction*. Routledge.

Shen, J. (2013). Increasing internal migration in China from 1985 to 2005: Institutional versus economic drivers. *Habitat International, 39*, 1–7.

Shen, Z. (2012). *Mao, Stalin and the Korean War: Trilateral communist relations in the 1950s*. Routledge.

Shirk, S. L. (1993). *The political logic of economic reform in China* (Vol. 24). University of California Press.

Shook, N. J., & Fazio, R. H. (2009). Political ideology, exploration of novel stimuli, and attitude formation. *Journal of Experimental Social Psychology, 45*(4), 995–998.

Shorten, R. (2012). *Modernism and totalitarianism: Rethinking the intellectual sources of Nazism and Stalinism, 1945 to the present*. Springer.

Silbey, S. S. (1998). *The common place of law: Stories from everyday life*. University of Chicago Press.

Silverman, D. (2015). *Interpreting qualitative data*. Sage.

Sima, Q. (2011). *Records of the grand historian*. Columbia University Press.

Simmons, B. A., & Elkins, Z. (2004). The globalization of liberalization: Policy diffusion in the international political economy. *American Political Science Review, 98*(1), 171–189.

Sina. (2009). *A Peking University professor: 99% of petitioners suffer from mental illnesses*. [Online]. http://news.sina.com.cn/c/2009-04-04/040815416940s.shtml. Accessed 27 July 2019 (in Chinese).

Small, K. A. (1992). Using the revenues from congestion pricing. *Transportation, 19*(4), 359–381.

Small, K. A., & Gómez-Ibáñez, J. A. (1998). Road pricing for congestion management: The transition from theory to policy. In K. J. Button & E. T. Verhoef (Eds.), *Road pricing, traffic congestion and the environment: Issues of efficiency and social feasibility* (pp. 213–246). Edward Elgar.

Smyth, R. (2000). Asset stripping in Chinese state-owned enterprises. *Journal of Contemporary Asia, 30*(1), 3–16.

Snell, R. S. (1999). Obedience to authority and ethical dilemmas in Hong Kong companies. *Business Ethics Quarterly, 9*(3), 507–526.

Sohu. *A Chinese-style trouble: Difficult to get a license plate, more difficult than giving birth to a child*. [Online]. https://news.sohu.com/s2013/5599/s367867944/. Accessed 27 July, 2019 (in Chinese).

Song, S. (2015). Should China implement congestion pricing? *Chinese Economy, 48*(1), 57–67.

Speckens, A. E., Spinhoven, P., Sloekers, P. P., Bolk, J. H., & van Hemert, A. M. (1996). A validation study of the Whitely Index, the Illness Attitude Scales, and the Somatosensory Amplification Scale in general medical and general practice patients. *Journal of Psychosomatic Research, 40*(1), 95–104.

Spector, P. E. (1992). *Summated rating scale construction: An introduction* (No. 82). Sage.

Spence, J. D. (1996). *God's Chinese Son: The Taiping Heavenly Kingdom of Hong Xiuquan*. WW Norton & Company.

Steffek, J., Kissling, C., & Nanz, P. (Eds.). (2007). *Civil society participation in European and global governance: A cure for the democratic deficit?* Springer.

Steg, L. (2005). Car use: lust and must. Instrumental, symbolic and affective motives for car use. *Transportation Research Part A: Policy and Practice, 39*(2), 147–162.

Steg, L., Dreijerink, L., & Abrahamse, W. (2006). Why are energy policies acceptable and effective? *Environment and Behavior, 38*(1), 92–111.

Steidlmeier, P. (1999). Gift giving, bribery and corruption: Ethical management of business relationships in China. *Journal of Business Ethics, 20*(2), 121–132.

Steiner, H. A. (1950). The people's democratic dictatorship in China. *Western Political Quarterly, 3*(1), 38–51.

Steiger, J. H. (1990). Structural model evaluation and modification: An interval estimation approach. *Multivariate Behavioral Research, 25*(2), 173–180.

Steiger, J. H. (2007). Understanding the limitations of global fit assessment in structural equation modeling. *Personality and Individual Differences, 42*(5), 893–898.

Steinfeld, E. S. (1999). *Forging reform in China: The fate of state-owned industry*. Cambridge University Press.

Steinhardt, H. C. (2015). From blind spot to media spotlight: Propaganda policy, media activism and the emergence of protest events in the Chinese public sphere. *Asian Studies Review, 39*(1), 119–137.

Stockmann, D., & Gallagher, M. E. (2011). Remote control: How the media sustain authoritarian rule in China. *Comparative Political Studies, 44*(4), 436–467.

Stokes, G., & Taylor, B. (1995). The public acceptability of sustainable transport policies: Findings from the British Social Attitudes survey. *PTRC-PUBLICATIONS-P*, 121–136.

Stout, W. (2002). Psychometrics: From practice to theory and back. *Psychometrika, 67*(4), 485–518.

Strauss, A. L. (1987). *Qualitative analysis for social scientists*. Cambridge University Press.

Struve, L. A. (1980). History and the Peach Blossom Fan. *Chinese Literature: Essays, Articles, Reviews, 2*(1), 55–72.

Struve, L. A. (1988). Huang Zongxi in context: A reappraisal of his major writings. *The Journal of Asian Studies, 47*(3), 474–502.

Su, C., & Littlefield, J. E. (2001). Entering guanxi: A business ethical dilemma in mainland China? *Journal of Business Ethics, 33*(3), 199–210.

Su, C., Sirgy, M. J., & Littlefield, J. E. (2003). Is guanxi orientation bad, ethically speaking? A study of Chinese enterprises. *Journal of Business Ethics, 44*(4), 303–312.

Su, D., & Fleisher, B. M. (1999). An empirical investigation of underpricing in Chinese IPOs. *Pacific-Basin Finance Journal, 7*(2), 173–202.

Suen, H., Cheung, S. O., & Mondejar, R. (2007). Managing ethical behaviour in construction organizations in Asia: How do the teachings of Confucianism, Taoism and Buddhism and Globalization influence ethics management? *International Journal of Project Management, 25*(3), 257–265.

Sugawara, H. M., & MacCallum, R. C. (1993). Effect of estimation method on incremental fit indexes for covariance structure models. *Applied Psychological Measurement, 17*(4), 365–377.

Suhr, D. D. (2005). Principal component analysis vs. exploratory factor analysis. *SUGI 30 Proceedings, 203*, 230.

Sun, C., Yuan, X., & Xu, M. (2016). The public perceptions and willingness to pay: From the perspective of the smog crisis in China. *Journal of Cleaner Production, 112*, 1635–1644.

Sun, J., Buys, N., & Wang, X. (2012). Association between low income, depression, self-efficacy and mass-incident-related strains: An understanding of mass incidents in China. *Journal of Public Health, 34*(3), 340–347.

Sun Tzu. (2011). *The art of war*. Shambhala Publications.

Sun, X., Feng, S., & Lu, J. (2016). Psychological factors influencing the public acceptability of congestion pricing in China. *Transportation Research Part F: Traffic Psychology and Behaviour, 41*, 104–112.

Sun, Y. (1995). *The Chinese Reassessment of Socialism, 1976–1992*. Princeton University Press.

Sun, Y. (1999). Reform, state, and corruption: Is corruption less destructive in China than in Russia? *Comparative Politics, 32*(1), 1–20.

Sun, Y. (2004). *Corruption and market in contemporary China*. Cornell University Press.

Sun, Y. (2017). The rise of Protestantism in post-Mao China: State and religion in historical perspective. *American Journal of Sociology, 122*(6), 1664–1725.

Sun, Y., & Cui, Y. (2018). Evaluating the coordinated development of economic, social and environmental benefits of urban public transportation infrastructure: Case study of four Chinese autonomous municipalities. *Transport Policy, 66*, 116–126.

Sun, Y., Zhuang, G., Tang, A., Wang, Y., & An, Z. (2006). Chemical characteristics of PM2. 5 and PM10 in haze-fog episodes in Beijing. *Environmental Science & Technology, 40*(10), 3148–3155.

Sutter, R. G. (2012). *Chinese foreign relations: Power and policy since the Cold War*. Rowman & Littlefield Publishers.

Tabachnick, B. G., & Fidell, L. S. (2007). *Using multivariate statistics*. Allyn & Bacon/Pearson Education.

Takano, Y., & Sogon, S. (2008). Are Japanese more collectivistic than Americans? Examining conformity in in-groups and the reference-group effect. *Journal of Cross-Cultural Psychology, 39*(3), 237–250.

Tanaka, J. S. (1987). "How big is big enough?": Sample size and goodness of fit in structural equation models with latent variables. *Child Development, 58*(1), 134–146.

Tanaka, J. S. (1993). Multifaceted conceptions of fit in structure equation models. In K. A. Bollen & J. S. Long (Eds.), *Testing structural equation models* (pp. 136–162). Sage.

Tang, J., Folmer, H., & Xue, J. (2013). Estimation of awareness and perception of water scarcity among farmers in the Guanzhong Plain, China, by means of a structural equation model. *Journal of Environmental Management, 126*, 55–62.

Tang, S., & Lo, H. K. (2008). The impact of public transport policy on the viability and sustainability of mass railway transit—The Hong Kong experience. *Transportation Research Part A: Policy and Practice, 42*(4), 563–576.

Tang, W., & Iyengar, S. (2011). The emerging media system in China: Implications for regime change. *Political Communication, 28*(3), 263–267.

Tao, J., Zhang, L., Zhang, Z., Huang, R., Wu, Y., Zhang, R., Cao, J., & Zhang, Y. (2015). Control of $PM_{2.5}$ in Guangzhou during the 16th Asian Games period: Implication for hazy weather prevention. *Science of the Total Environment, 508*, 57–66.

Tao, R., & Xu, Z. (2007). Urbanization, rural land system and social security for migrants in China. *The Journal of Development Studies, 43*(7), 1301–1320.

Tavakol, M., & Dennick, R. (2011). Making sense of Cronbach's alpha. *International Journal of Medical Education, 2*, 53–55.

Taylor, B., & Brook, L. (1998). Public Attitudes to transport issues: Findings from the British social attitudes surveys. *Transport Policy and the Environment*.

Taylor, B., & Kalauskas, R. (2010). Addressing equity in political debates over road pricing: Lessons from recent projects. *Transportation Research Record: Journal of the Transportation Research Board, 2187*, 44–52.

Teets, J. C. (2013). Let many civil societies bloom: The rise of consultative authoritarianism in China. *The China Quarterly, 213*, 19–38.

Teets, J. C. (2014). *Civil society under authoritarianism: The China model*. Cambridge University Press.

Tertoolen, G., Van Kreveld, D., & Verstraten, B. (1998). Psychological resistance against attempts to reduce private car use. *Transportation Research Part A: Policy and Practice, 32*(3), 171–181.

The Beijing News. (2011). *Polls show that almost eighty percent of people think congestion alleviation measures are ineffective*. http://auto.people.com.cn/GB/1049/15213780.html. Accessed 27 July 2019 (in Chinese).

The Chinese Culture Connection. (1987). Chinese Values and the Search for Culture-Free Dimensions of Culture: The Chinese Culture Connection. *Journal of Cross-Cultural Psychology, 18*(2), 143–64.

The Guardian. (2013). *Chinese struggle through 'airpocalypse' smog*. [Online]. http://www.theguardian.com/world/2013/feb/16/chinese-struggle-through-airpocalypse-smog. Accessed 27 July 2019.

The Guardian. (2015). *Beijing issues first pollution red alert as smog engulfs capital*. [Online]. http://www.theguardian.com/environment/2015/dec/07/beijing-pollution-red-alert-smog-engulfs-capital. Accessed 27 July 2019.

Thomas, D. R. (2006). A general inductive approach for analyzing qualitative evaluation data. *American Journal of Evaluation, 27*(2), 237–246.

Thorkildsen, K. M., Eriksson, K., & Råholm, M. B. (2013). The substance of love when encountering suffering: An interpretative research synthesis with an abductive approach. *Scandinavian Journal of Caring Sciences, 27*(2), 449–459.

Thorpe, N., Hills, P., & Jaensirisak, S. (2000). Public attitudes to TDM measures: A comparative study. *Transport Policy, 7*(4), 243–257.

Thurston, A. F. (1988). *Enemies of the people: The ordeal of the intellectuals in China's great Cultural Revolution*. Harvard University Press.

Thurstone, L. L. (1947). *Multiple-factor analysis: A development and expansion of the vectors of mind*. University of Chicago Press.

Tilt, B. (2007). The political ecology of pollution enforcement in China: A case from Sichuan's rural industrial sector. *The China Quarterly, 192*, 915–932.

Tong, J. (2009). Press self-censorship in China: A case study in the transformation of discourse. *Discourse & Society, 20*(5), 593–612.

Tong, J. (2010). The crisis of the centralized media control theory: How local power controls media in China. *Media, Culture & Society, 32*(6), 925–942.

Tong, J., & Zuo, L. (2014). Weibo communication and government legitimacy in China: A computer-assisted analysis of Weibo messages on two 'mass incidents.' *Information, Communication & Society, 17*(1), 66–85.

Tong, Y., & Lei, S. (2010). Large-scale mass incidents and government responses in China. *International Journal of China Studies, 1*(2), 487–508.

Tong, Y., & Lei, S. (2013a). *Social protest in contemporary China, 2003–2010: Transitional pains and regime legitimacy*. Routledge.

Tong, Y., & Lei, S. (2013b). War of position and microblogging in China. *Journal of Contemporary China, 22*(80), 292–311.

Torres, M. S., & Qin, L. (2017). Chinese high school students' perceptions of freedom of expression: Implications for researching emerging civil liberties in global educational contexts. *Asia Pacific Education Review, 18*(1), 53–64.

Triandis, H. (1988). Collectivism v. individualism: A reconceptualisation of a basic concept in cross-cultural social psychology. In *Cross-cultural studies of personality, attitudes and cognition* (pp. 60–95). Palgrave Macmillan.

Triandis, H. C. (1994). *Culture and social behavior*. Mcgraw-Hill Book Company.

Trier-Bieniek, A. (2012). Framing the telephone interview as a participant-centred tool for qualitative research: A methodological discussion. *Qualitative Research, 12*(6), 630–644.

Tsui, A. S., & Farh, J. L. L. (1997). Where guanxi matters relational demography and guanxi in the Chinese context. *Work and Occupations, 24*(1), 56–79.

Tu, F. (2016). WeChat and civil society in China. *Communication and the Public, 1*(3), 343–350.

Turner, D. W., III. (2010). Qualitative interview design: A practical guide for novice investigators. *The Qualitative Report, 15*(3), 754–760.

Twitchett, D. C. & Fairbank, J. K. (Eds.). (1978). *The Cambridge History of China*. Cambridge University Press.

Tylor, E. B. (2010). *Primitive culture: Researches into the development of mythology, philosophy, religion, art, and custom*. Cambridge University Press.

van Ess, H., Elman, B. A., Duncan, J. B., & Ooms, H. (2005). Rethinking confucianism, past and present in China, Japan, Korea, and Vietnam. *Monumenta Serica, 53*, 500–504.

Vandenberg, R. J. (2006). Statistical and methodological myths and urban legends: Where, pray tell, did they get this idea? *Organizational Research Methods, 9*, 194–201.

Van Vuuren, D., Fengqi, Z., De Vries, B., Kejun, J., Graveland, C., & Yun, L. (2003). Energy and emission scenarios for China in the 21st century—Exploration of baseline development and mitigation options. *Energy Policy, 31*(4), 369–387.

Verhoef, E. T., Nijkamp, P., & Rietveld, P. (1997). The social feasibility of road pricing: A case study for the Randstad area. *Journal of Transport Economics and Policy, 31*, 255–276.

Vermeer, E. B. (2004). Egalitarianism and the land question in China a survey of three thousand households in industrializing Wuxi and Agricultural Baoding. *China Information, 18*(1), 107–140.

Verplanken, B., Aarts, H., & Van Knippenberg, A. (1997). Habit, information acquisition, and the process of making travel mode choices. *European Journal of Social Psychology, 27*, 539–560.

Viegas, J. M. (2001). Making urban road pricing acceptable and effective: Searching for quality and equity in urban mobility. *Transport Policy, 8*(4), 289–294.

Visser, R. (2004). Spaces of disappearance: Aesthetic responses to contemporary Beijing city planning. *Journal of Contemporary China, 13*(39), 277–310.

Vladimirov, P. P. (1975). *The Vladimirov Diaries: Yenan, China, 1942–1945*. Doubleday.

Vogel, E. F. (2011). *Deng Xiaoping and the transformation of China*. Belknap Press of Harvard University Press.

Waldron, A. (1995). Scholarship and patriotic education: The Great Wall Conference, 1994. *The China Quarterly, 143*, 844–850.

Waley, P. (2007). Tokyo-as-world-city: Reassessing the role of capital and the state in urban restructuring. *Urban Studies, 44*(8), 1465–1490.

Wallace, J. L., & Weiss, J. C. (2015). The political geography of nationalist protest in China: Cities and the 2012 anti-Japanese protests. *The China Quarterly, 222*, 403–429.

Walton, D. (2001). Abductive, presumptive and plausible arguments. *Informal Logic, 21*(2), 141–169.

Wang, D., & Chai, Y. (2009). The jobs–housing relationship and commuting in Beijing, China: The legacy of Danwei. *Journal of Transport Geography, 17*(1), 30–38.

Wang, F. L. (2017). *The China Order: Centralia, World Empire, and the Nature of Chinese Power*. SUNY Press.

Wang, L., Xu, J., & Qin, P. (2014). Will a driving restriction policy reduce car trips?—The case study of Beijing, China. *Transportation Research Part A: Policy and Practice, 67*, 279–290.

Wang, M. (2004). *50 Years of the CCP*, Orient Press (in Chinese).

Wang, M. W., Chen, J., & Cai, R. (2018). Air quality and acute myocardial infarction in adults during the 2016 Hangzhou G20 summit. *Environmental Science and Pollution Research, 25*(10), 9949–9956.

Wang, P. (2016). Military corruption in China: The role of *guanxi* in the buying and selling of military positions. *The China Quarterly, 228*, 970–991.

Wang, Q., & Guo, G. (2015). Yu Keping and Chinese intellectual discourse on good governance. *The China Quarterly, 224*, 985–1005.

Wang, R. (2010). Shaping urban transport policies in China: Will copying foreign policies work? *Transport Policy, 17*(3), 147–152.

Wang, S., Paul, M. J., & Dredze, M. (2015). Social media as a sensor of air quality and public response in China. *Journal of Medical Internet Research, 17*(3), e22.

Wang, W., Zheng, X., & Zhao, Z. J. (2011). *Province-Managing-County reform and public education spending: A quasi-natural experiment of fiscal decentralization in China* (Doctoral dissertation). University of Minnesota.

Wang, Y. (2015). Politically connected polluters under smog. *Business and Politics, 17*(1), 97–123.

Wang, Y. P., Wang, Y., & Bramley, G. (2005). Chinese housing reform in state-owned enterprises and its impacts on different social groups. *Urban Studies, 42*(10), 1859–1878.

Wang, Y., Sun, M., Yang, X., & Yuan, X. (2016). Public awareness and willingness to pay for tackling smog pollution in China: A case study. *Journal of Cleaner Production, 112*, 1627–1634.

Wang, Y., Wang, Y., Xie, L., & Zhou, H. (2019). Impact of perceived uncertainty on public acceptability of congestion charging: An empirical study in China. *Sustainability, 11*(1), 129.

Wang, Y., Zhang, Y., Schauer, J. J., de Foy, B., Guo, B., & Zhang, Y. (2016). Relative impact of emissions controls and meteorology on air pollution mitigation associated with the Asia-Pacific Economic Cooperation (APEC) conference in Beijing, China. *Science of the Total Environment, 571*, 1467–1476.

Wang, Z. (2008). National humiliation, history education, and the politics of historical memory: Patriotic education campaign in China. *International Studies Quarterly, 52*(4), 783–806.

Warner, M. (2012). *The Dragon Empress: Life and Times of Tz'u-hsi 1835–1908 Empress Dowager of China*. Random House.

Wasserstrom, J. N. (2018). *Popular protest and political culture in modern China*. Routledge.

Weaver, R. (2017). *Think tanks and civil societies: Catalysts for ideas and action*. Routledge.

Weber, I., & Jia, L. (2007). Internet and self-regulation in China: The cultural logic of controlled commodification. *Media, Culture & Society, 29*(5), 772–789.

Weber, M., & Gerth, H. H. (1953). *The religion of China, Confucianism and Taoism*. Routledge and Kegan Paul.

Wei, C. G. (2011). Mao's Legacy Revisited: Its lasting impact on China and Post-Mao Era Reform. *Asian Politics & Policy, 3*(1), 3–27.

Wei, J., Zhou, L., Wei, Y., & Zhao, D. (2014). Collective Behavior in Mass Incidents: A study of contemporary China. *Journal of Contemporary China, 23*(88), 715–735.

Wei, Z., Wang, B., Chen, T., & Lin, Y. (2016). Community development in urban Guangzhou since 1980: A social sustainability perspective. *International Review for Spatial Planning and Sustainable Development, 4*(4), 58–68.

Weingast, B. R. (1997). The political foundations of democracy and the rule of the law. *American Political Science Review, 91*(2), 245–263.

Weinstein, A., & Sciara, G. C. (2006). Unraveling equity in HOT lane planning: A view from practice. *Journal of Planning Education and Research, 26*(2), 174–184.

Weiss, R. S. (1995). *Learning from strangers: The art and method of qualitative interview studies*. Simon and Schuster.

Wettig, G. (2008). *Stalin and the Cold War in Europe: The emergence and development of East-West conflict, 1939–1953*. Rowman & Littlefield.

Wheaton, B., Muthen, B., Alwin, D. F., & Summers, G. F. (1977). Assessing reliability and stability in panel models. *Sociological Methodology, 8*, 84–136.

Wheeland, M. (2015). *China tackles pollution, but has long way to go on labor*. [Online]. https://www.theguardian.com/sustainable-business/2015/may/04/china-labor-pollution-smog-labor-under-the-dome. Accessed 27 July 2019.

White, G. (1996). Corruption and market reform in China. *IDS Bulletin, 27*(2), 40–47.

White, L. (1967). The historical roots of our ecological crisis. *This sacred earth: religion, nature, environment*, 184–193.

Whitfield, S. J. (1996). *The culture of the Cold War*. JHU Press.

Widaman, K. F. (1993). Common factor analysis versus principal component analysis: Differential bias in representing model parameters? *Multivariate Behavioral Research, 28*(3), 263–311.

Wilkinson, E. P. (2000). *Chinese history: A manual* (Vol. 52). Harvard University Asia Center.

Williams, L. J., & Holahan, P. J. (1994). Parsimony-based fit indices for multiple-indicator models: Do they work? *Structural Equation Modeling: A Multidisciplinary Journal, 1*(2), 161–189.

Williams, R. (1983). *Culture and society, 1780–1950*. Columbia University Press.

Williams, R. (2006). Generalized ordered logit/partial proportional odds models for ordinal dependent variables. *Stata Journal, 6*(1), 58–62.

Williams, R. (2016). Understanding and interpreting generalized ordered logit models. *The Journal of Mathematical Sociology, 40*(1), 7–20.

Winslott-Hiselius, L., Brundell-Freij, K., Vagland, Å., & Byström, C. (2009). The development of public attitudes towards the Stockholm congestion trial. *Transportation Research Part a: Policy and Practice, 43*(3), 269–282.

Wolf, E. J., Harrington, K. M., Clark, S. L., & Miller, M. W. (2013). Sample size requirements for structural equation models: An evaluation of power, bias, and solution propriety. *Educational and Psychological Measurement, 73*(6), 913–934.

Wong, K., Fu, D., Li, C. Y., & Song, H. X. (2007). Rural migrant workers in urban China: Living a marginalised life. *International Journal of Social Welfare, 16*(1), 32–40.

Wong, C. P. (1991). Central–local relations in an era of fiscal decline: The paradox of fiscal decentralization in post-Mao China. *The China Quarterly, 128*, 691–715.

Wong, H. (2013). *2013 will be remembered as the year that deadly, suffocating smog consumed China*. [Online]. http://qz.com/159105/2013-will-be-remembered-as-the-year-that-deadly-suffocating-smog-consumed-china/. Accessed 27 July 2019.

Wong, K. K. (2003). The environmental awareness of university students in Beijing China. *Journal of Contemporary China, 12*(36), 519–536.

Wong, Y., & Tsai, J. (2007). Cultural models of shame and guilt. *The self-conscious emotions: Theory and research*, 209–223.

Woo, W. T. (1999). The real reasons for China's growth. *The China Journal, 41*, 115–137.

Worthington, R. L., & Whittaker, T. A. (2006). Scale development research: A content analysis and recommendations for best practices. *The Counseling Psychologist, 34*(6), 806–838.

Wright, A. F. (1960). *The Confucian Persuasion*. Stanford University Press.

Wright, E. O., Levine, A., & Sober, E. (1992). *Reconstructing Marxism: Essays on explanation and the theory of history*. Verso.

Wu, F., & Webber, K. (2004). The rise of "foreign gated communities" in Beijing: Between economic globalization and local institutions. *Cities, 21*(3), 203–213.

Wu, G. (2015a). *China's Party Congress: Power, legitimacy, and institutional manipulation*. Cambridge University Press.

Wu, G. (2015b). *Paradoxes of China's Prosperity: Political Dilemmas and Global Implications*. World Scientific.

Wu, G., & Lansdowne, H. (2009). *Socialist China, capitalist China: Social tension and political adaptation under economic globalization*. Routledge.

Wu, J., Xu, M., & Zhang, P. (2018). The impacts of governmental performance assessment policy and citizen participation on improving environmental performance across Chinese provinces. *Journal of Cleaner Production, 184*, 227–238.

Wu, J. Y., & Xiao, Y. (2001). Seeing the Chinese gardens through the idea of the Chinese traditional culture. *Journal of Chinese Landscape Architecture, 3*, 037.

Wu, K., Chen, Y., Ma, J., Bai, S., & Tang, X. (2017). Traffic and emissions impact of congestion charging in the central Beijing urban area: A simulation analysis. *Transportation Research Part d: Transport and Environment, 51*, 203–215.

Wu, S. (2014). The Revival of Confucianism and the CCP's Struggle for Cultural Leadership: A content analysis of the People's Daily, 2000–2009. *Journal of Contemporary China, 23*(89), 971–991.

Wu, X. (2009). Income inequality and distributive justice: A comparative analysis of mainland China and Hong Kong. *The China Quarterly, 200*, 1033–1052.

Wu, X. (2010). Economic transition, school expansion and educational inequality in China, 1990–2000. *Research in Social Stratification and Mobility, 28*(1), 91–108.

Xi, J. (2017, October 18). *Secure a Decisive Victory in Building a Moderately Prosperous Society in All Respects and Strive for the Great Success of Socialism with Chinese Characteristics for a New Era*, delivered at the 19th National Congress of the Communist Party of China. [Online]. http://language.chinadaily.com.cn/19thcpcnationalcongress/2017-11/06/content_34188086_6.htm. Accessed 27 July 2019.

Xiao, J., Zhou, X., & Hu, W. M. (2017). Welfare analysis of the vehicle quota system in China. *International Economic Review, 58*(2), 617–650.

Xie, Y., & Costa, F. J. (1993). Urban planning in socialist China: Theory and practice. *Cities, 10*(2), 103–114.

Xinhua. (2008). *Beijing will implement the road space rationing policy during the Olympic Games*. [Online]. http://www.gov.cn/jrzg/2008-06/20/content_1022742.htm. Accessed 27 July 2019 (in Chinese).

Xinhua. (2014). *Xi promises harsher anti-corruption drive*. [Online]. http://www.globaltimes.cn/content/837556.shtml. Accessed 27 July 2019.

Xinhua. (2015). *Xi calls for more anti-corruption efforts despite achievements*. [Online]. http://www.china.org.cn/china/2015-01/14/content_34552119.htm. Accessed 27 July 2019.

Xu, X. (2003). *The Jews of Kaifeng, China: History, culture, and religion*. KTAV Publishing House Inc.

Yamamoto, K. (1974). *The Mahayana Mahaparinirvana-sutra: A Complete Translation from the Classical Chinese Language* (3 vols). Karinbunko 1973–1975. PDF version online (ed. and rev. Tony Page). http://info.stiltij.nl/publiek/meditatie/soetras/mahaparinirvana.pdf

Yan, J., & Sorenson, R. (2006). The effect of Confucian values on succession in family business. *Family Business Review, 19*(3), 235–250.

Yan, Y. (2009). The Good Samaritan's new trouble: A study of the changing moral landscape in contemporary China 1. *Social Anthropology, 17*(1), 9–24.

Yan, Y. (2012). Moral Hierarchy and Social Egoism in a Networked Society: The Chaxugeju Thesis Revisited. *Understanding China and Engaging with Chinese People: The 100th Anniversary of the birth of Professor Fei Xiaotong*, forthcoming by Airiti Press.

Yang, D. T. (2008). China's agricultural crisis and famine of 1959–1961: A survey and comparison to soviet famines. *Comparative Economic Studies, 50*(1), 1–29.

Yang, G. (2009). *The power of the internet in China: Citizen activism online*. Columbia University Press.

Yang, G. (2014). The return of ideology and the future of Chinese Internet policy. *Critical Studies in Media Communication, 31*(2), 109–113.

Yang, G., & Jiang, M. (2015). The networked practice of online political satire in China: Between ritual and resistance. *International Communication Gazette, 77*(3), 215–231.

Yang, J. (2012). *Tombstone: The great Chinese famine, 1958–1962*. Macmillan.

Yang, J., & Gakenheimer, R. (2007). Assessing the transportation consequences of land use transformation in urban China. *Habitat International, 31*(3), 345–353.

Yang, J., Liu, Y., Qin, P., & Liu, A. A. (2014). A review of Beijing's vehicle registration lottery: Short-term effects on vehicle growth and fuel consumption. *Energy Policy, 75*, 157–166.

Yang, J. Z., & Huang, J. (2017). Seeking for your own sake: Chinese citizens' motivations for information seeking about air pollution. *Environmental Communication*, 1–14.

Yang, P., Ren, G., & Liu, W. (2013). Spatial and temporal characteristics of Beijing urban heat island intensity. *Journal of Applied Meteorology and Climatology, 52*(8), 1803–1816.

Yang, R. (2005). Corruption in china's higher education: A malignant tumor. *International Higher Education, 39*, 18–20.

Yang, X., Jin, W., Jiang, H., Xie, Q., Shen, W., & Han, W. (2017). Car ownership policies in China: Preferences of residents and influence on the choice of electric cars. *Transport Policy, 58*, 62–71.

Yang, Z., Cai, J., Ottens, H. F. L., & Sliuzas, R. (2013). Beijing. *Cities, 31*, 491–506.

Yao, X. (2000). *An introduction to Confucianism*. Cambridge University Press.

Yardley, J. (2006). *First comes the car, then the $10,000 license plate*. [Online]. http://www.nytimes.com/2006/07/05/world/asia/05china.html?_r=1&. Accessed 27 July 2019.

Yates, R. D. (1995). State Control of Bureaucrats under the Qin: Techniques and Procedures. *Early China, 20*, 331–365.

Ye, G., Jin, Z., Xia, B., & Skitmore, M. (2014). Analyzing causes for reworks in construction projects in China. *Journal of Management in Engineering, 31*(6), 04014097.

Yeh, A. G. O., & Wu, F. (1999). The transformation of the urban planning system in China from a centrally-planned to transitional economy. *Progress in Planning, 51*(3), 167–252.

Yin, K., Wang, R., An, Q., Yao, L., & Liang, J. (2014). Using eco-efficiency as an indicator for sustainable urban development: A case study of Chinese provincial capital cities. *Ecological Indicators, 36*, 665–671.

Yip, K. S. (2004). Taoism and its impact on mental health of the Chinese communities. *International Journal of Social Psychiatry, 50*(1), 25–42.

Yong, A. G., & Pearce, S. (2013). A beginner's guide to factor analysis: Focusing on exploratory factor analysis. *Tutorials in Quantitative Methods for Psychology, 9*(2), 79–94.

Yoo, B., & Donthu, N. (2001). Developing a scale to measure the perceived quality of an Internet shopping site (SITEQUAL). *Quarterly Journal of Electronic Commerce, 2*(1), 31–45.

Yu, K. (2006). Civil Society in China: Concepts, Classification and Institutional Environment. *Social Sciences in China, 1*, 109–122.

Yu, K. (2016). Learning, training, and governing: The CCP's cadre education since the reform. *Journal of Chinese Governance, 1*(1), 41–54.

Yu, N., De Jong, M., Storm, S., & Mi, J. (2012a). The growth impact of transport infrastructure investment: A regional analysis for China (1978–2008). *Policy and Society, 31*(1), 25–38.

Yu, N., De Jong, M., Storm, S., & Mi, J. (2012b). Transport infrastructure, spatial clusters and regional economic growth in China. *Transport Reviews, 32*(1), 3–28.

Yu, N., de Roo, G., De Jong, M., & Storm, S. (2016). Does the expansion of a motorway network lead to economic agglomeration? Evidence from China. *Transport Policy, 45*, 218–227.

Yu, T. (2008). The revival of Confucianism in Chinese schools: A historical-political review. *Asia Pacific Journal of Education, 28*(2), 113–129.

Zeng, H. (2012). *China transportation briefing: Booming public bikes.* [Online]. http://thecityfix.com/blog/china-transportation-briefing-booming-public-bikes/. Accessed 27 July 2019.

Zhai, Y. (2017). Values of deference to authority in Japan and China. *International Journal of Comparative Sociology, 58*(2), 120–139.

Zhang, D., Schmöcker, J. D., Fujii, S., & Yang, X. (2016). Social norms and public transport usage: Empirical study from Shanghai. *Transportation, 43*(5), 869–888.

Zhang, H., & Chen, F. (2004). Studies In science of science. Public participation in technological decisionmaking process. *Studies in Science of Science, 22*, 476–481.

Zhang, H., Wang, S., Hao, J., Wang, X., Wang, S., Chai, F., & Li, M. (2016). Air pollution and control action in Beijing. *Journal of Cleaner Production, 112*, 1519–1527.

Zhang, J. (2001). *Beijing urban plan and constructions 50 years.* China's Bookstore. (in Chinese).

Zhang, J., Wieczorek, W. F., Conwell, Y., & Tu, X. M. (2011). Psychological strains and youth suicide in rural China. *Social Science & Medicine, 72*(12), 2003–2010.

Zhang, J., Yan, X., An, M., & Sun, L. (2017). The impact of Beijing subway's new fare policy on riders' attitude, travel pattern and demand. *Sustainability, 9*(5), 689.

Zhang, L. L. (2006). Behind the 'Great Firewall' decoding China's internet media policies from the inside. *Convergence, 12*(3), 271–291.

Zhang, L., Zhang, J., Duan, Z. Y., & Bryde, D. (2015). Sustainable bike-sharing systems: Characteristics and commonalities across cases in urban China. *Journal of Cleaner Production, 97*, 124–133.

Zhang, Q., & Chan, J. L. (2013). New development: Fiscal transparency in China—Government policy and the role of social media. *Public Money & Management, 33*(1), 71–75.

Zhang, T., & Schwartz, B. (1997). Confucius and the cultural revolution: A study in collective memory. *International Journal of Politics, Culture, and Society, 11*(2), 189–212.

Zhang, T., & Zou, H. F. (1998). Fiscal decentralization, public spending, and economic growth in China. *Journal of Public Economics, 67*(2), 221–240.

Zhang, X. (2006). Fiscal decentralization and political centralization in China: Implications for growth and inequality. *Journal of Comparative Economics, 34*(4), 713–726.

Zhang, X. (2011). *The transformation of political communication in China: From propaganda to hegemony*. World Scientific.

Zhang, X., Bai, X., & Zhong, H. (2018). Electric vehicle adoption in license plate-controlled big cities: Evidence from Beijing. *Journal of Cleaner Production, 202*, 191–196.

Zhang, X., Fan, S., Zhang, L., & Huang, J. (2004). Local governance and public goods provision in rural China. *Journal of Public Economics, 88*(12), 2857–2871.

Zhang, Y. (2008). Steering towards growth: Symbolic urban preservation in Beijing, 1990–2005. *Town Planning Review, 79*(2–3), 187–208.

Zhang, Y. B., Lin, M. C., Nonaka, A., & Beom, K. (2005). Harmony, hierarchy and conservatism: A cross-cultural comparison of Confucian values in China, Korea, Japan, and Taiwan. *Communication Research Reports, 22*(2), 107–115.

Zhang, Y., Yang, J. Q., & Zhang, J. H. (2009). Equity Evaluation of Road Congestion Charging. *Technology & Economy in Areas of Communications., 6*, 16.

Zhang, Z. Q., Zhou, Y., Lu, S. X., & Chen, Y. H. (2007). Return migration of rural laborer from western China: Causes and strategies. *Stat Res, 24*, 9–15.

Zhao, D. (2015). *The Confucian-Legalist State: A new theory of Chinese history*. Oxford University Press.

Zhao, J. (2005). Defects and improvement of public participation principle in Chinese environment law. *Environmental Science and Technology, 28*(2), 54–55.

Zhao, G. (1986). *Man and land in Chinese history: An economic analysis*. Stanford University Press.

Zhao, S. (1993). Deng Xiaoping's southern tour: Elite politics in post-Tiananmen China. *Asian Survey, 33*(8), 739–756.

Zhao, S. (1998). A state-led nationalism: The patriotic education campaign in post-Tiananmen China. *Communist and Post-Communist Studies, 31*(3), 287–302.

Zhao, S. (2000). Chinese nationalism and its international orientations. *Political Science Quarterly, 115*(1), 1–33.

Zhao, S. (2004). *A nation-state by construction: Dynamics of modern Chinese nationalism*. Stanford University Press.

Zhao, X., & Belk, R. W. (2008). Politicizing consumer culture: Advertising's appropriation of political ideology in China's social transition. *Journal of Consumer Research, 35*(2), 231–244.

Zhao, Y. (1999). Leaving the countryside: Rural-to-urban migration decisions in China. *American Economic Review, 89*(2), 281–286.

Zhao, Z. (2009). *Prisoner of the State: The Secret Journal of Premier Zhao Ziyang*. Simon and Schuster.

Zheng, D., & Shi, M. (2017). Multiple environmental policies and pollution haven hypothesis: Evidence from China's polluting industries. *Journal of Cleaner Production, 141*, 295–304.

Zheng, S., Long, F., Fan, C. C., & Gu, Y. (2009). Urban villages in China: A 2008 survey of migrant settlements in Beijing. *Eurasian Geography and Economics, 50*(4), 425–446.

Zheng, X. (2009). *The making of modern Chinese politics: Political culture, protest repertoires, and nationalism in the Sichuan Railway Protection Movement* (Doctoral dissertation). UC San Diego.

Zheng, Y. (1999). *Discovering Chinese nationalism in China: Modernization, identity, and international relations*. Cambridge University Press.

Zhong, X., Wang, Z., & Di, B. (Eds.). (2001). *Some of us: Chinese women growing up in the Mao era*. Rutgers University Press.

Zhou, H. (2000). Working with a dying ideology: Dissonance and its reduction in Chinese journalism. *Journalism Studies, 1*(4), 599–616.

Zhou, N., Levine, M. D., & Price, L. (2010). Overview of current energy-efficiency policies in China. *Energy Policy, 38*(11), 6439–6452.

Zhou, R., Horrey, W. J., & Yu, R. (2009). The effect of conformity tendency on pedestrians' road-crossing intentions in China: An application of the theory of planned behavior. *Accident Analysis & Prevention., 41*(3), 491–497.

Zhou, X. (2010). The institutional logic of collusion among local governments in China. *Modern China, 36*(1), 47–78.

Zhou, Y., & Ap, J. (2009). Residents' perceptions towards the impacts of the Beijing 2008 Olympic Games. *Journal of Travel Research, 48*(1), 78–91.

Zhu, J. (2008). Why are offices for sale in China? A case study of the office-selling chain in Heilongjiang Province. *Asian Survey, 48*(4), 558–579.

Zhu, J., Zhang, Q., & Liu, Z. (2017). Eating, drinking, and power signaling in institutionalized authoritarianism: China's antiwaste campaign since 2012. *Journal of Contemporary China, 26*(105), 337–352.

Zhu, J., Zhao, X., & Li, H. (1990). Public political consciousness in China: An empirical profile. *Asian Survey*, 992–1006.

Zhu, N. (2002). The impacts of income gaps on migration decisions in China. *China Economic Review, 13*(2–3), 213–230.

Zhu, Q. (2008). Reorientation and prospect of China's combat against corruption. *Crime, Law and Social Change, 49*(2), 81–95.

Zhu, Z. (2017). Backfired government action and the spillover effect of contention: A case study of the anti-PX protests in Maoming China. *Journal of Contemporary China, 26*(106), 521–535.

Zi, Z. (1987). The relationship of Chinese traditional culture to the modernization of China: An introduction to the current discussion. *Asian Survey, 1987*, 442–458.

Ziegler, M., & Hagemann, D. (2015). Testing the unidimensionality of items: Pitfalls and Loopholes. *European Journal of Psychological Assessment, 31*, 231–237.

Zittel, T., & Fuchs, D. (Eds.). (2007). *Participatory democracy and political participation: Can participatory engineering bring citizens back in?* Routledge.

Zweig, D. (1983). Opposition to change in rural China: The system of responsibility and people's communes. *Asian Survey, 23*(7), 879–900.

余英时. (2003). *中国思想传统的现代诠释*. 南京: 江苏人民出版社. (in Chinese. Yu, Y. S. (2003). *Zhong Guo Si Xiang Chuan Tong De Xian Dai Quan Shi*. Jiangsu People Publishing, LTD.

司马谈, & 司马迁. (1959). 论六家之要指. 北京: 中华书局. (in Chinese. Sima, T. & Sima, Q. (1959). *Lun Liu Jia Zhi Yao Zhi*. Chung Hwa Book Co.)

熊伟. (1938). 从先秦学术思想变迁大势观测〈老子〉的年代. *古史辨, 6*, 566–597. (in Chinese. Xiong, W. (1938). Cong Xian Qin Xue Shu Si Xiang Bian Qian Da Shi Guan Ce 'Laozi' De Nian Dai. *Gu Shi Bian, 6*, 566–597).

Index

Q. Liu, *Public Acceptability of Congestion Charging in China*,
https://doi.org/10.1007/978-981-19-0236-9

Printed in the United States
by Baker & Taylor Publisher Services